Creating SQL Queries Using PostgreSQL Made Easy

By Indera E. Murphy

Creating SQL Queries Using PostgreSQL Made Easy

Tolana Publishing
PO Box 719
Teaneck, NJ 07666 USA

Find us online at www.tolanapublishing.com

ISBN-13: 978-1-935208-47-1
ISBN-10: 1-935208-47-0

Library of Congress Control Number: 2020900141

Printed and bound in the United States Of America

V2.0

About The SQL Series

Creating SQL Queries Using PostgreSQL Made Easy, is part of a series of computer software books that cover creating queries with the SQL programming language. This book has been designed to be used as a self-paced learning tool, in a classroom setting or in an online class. All of the books contain an abundance of step-by-step instructions and screen shots to help reduce the "stress" often associated with learning new software. Some of the titles from all of the series are shown below.

ISBN: 978-1-935208-42-6

ISBN: 978-1-935208-37-2

ISBN: 978-1-935208-44-0

ISBN: 978-1-935208-45-7

ISBN: 978-1-935208-43-3

ISBN: 978-1-935208-36-5

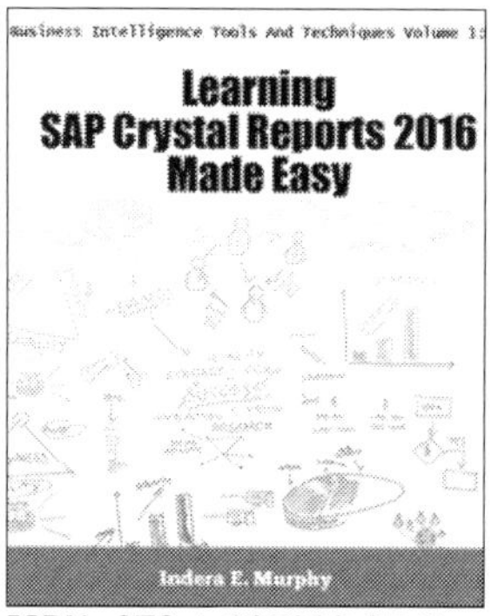

ISBN: 978-1-935208-35-8

ISBN: 978-1-935208-47-1

ISBN: 978-1-935208-19-8

ISBN: 978-1-935208-38-9

ISBN: 978-1-935208-39-6

ISBN: 978-1-935208-18-1

Visit us online at www.tolanapublishing.com for more titles and information

Why A Book On PostgreSQL?

I felt that readers, especially people new to learning PostgreSQL, would prefer to have more assistance in learning how to create queries. I do not feel that flipping between web sites is the most ideal way to initially learn how to create queries.

In general, there are very few books that provide hands-on exercises for learning software or a programming language. I know that many books claim to have "step-by-step instructions". If you have tried to follow books that make this claim and you got lost or could not complete a task as instructed, it may not have been your fault. When I decided to write computer books, I vowed to really have step-by-step instructions that actually included every step. This includes steps like which file to open, which menu option to select and more. In my opinion, it is this level of detail that makes a computer book easy to follow. I hope that you feel the same way.

Over the years, I have come to realize that many people only use a small percent of the features that software or a programming language has to offer. One of my goals in all of the books that I write, is to point out as many features as possible. My theory is that if more people knew about more than 10% of the features that are available, at the very least, they would try a few of them.

About The Author

Dr. Indera E. Murphy is an author, educator and IT professional that has over 25 years of experience in the Information Technology field and has written over 50 books. She has held a variety of positions including technical writer, programmer, consultant, web designer, course developer and project leader. Indera has designed and developed software applications and web sites, as well as, manage technology driven projects in several industries. In addition to being an Executive Director and consultant, as an online adjunct professor, she has taught courses in a variety of areas including project management, technical writing, information processing, Access, HTML, Windows, Excel, Dreamweaver and critical thinking.

Thank you for purchasing this book!

CONTENTS

GETTING STARTED WITH POSTGRESQL.................... 1-1
Welcome To PostgreSQL! 1-2
Why Learn PostgreSQL? 1-2
How Do I Get Started? 1-3
How This Book Is Organized 1-5
What Is SQL?.................... 1-8
What Is PostgreSQL?.................... 1-9
What Is pgAdmin?.................... 1-9
pgAdmin Alternatives 1-9
Exercise 1.1: Create A Folder For Your Files.................... 1-10
Exercise 1.2: Download And Install PostgreSQL And pgAdmin.................... 1-10
Download PostgreSQL For Windows.................... 1-10
Install PostgreSQL And pgAdmin.................... 1-11
Database Concepts And Terminology.................... 1-14
Why Store Data In Multiple Tables?.................... 1-15
What Is A Schema?.................... 1-16
What Is A Relationship?.................... 1-16
Relational Databases.................... 1-17
Types Of Relationships 1-18
PostgreSQL vs MySQL 1-21

USING pgAdmin.................... 2-1
Getting Started With pgAdmin.................... 2-2
Exercise 2.1: Connect To The PostgreSQL Server Using pgAdmin.................... 2-2
Quick Tour Of pgAdmin 2-2
pgAdmin Home Page.................... 2-2
Section 1: Browser Tree Control 2-2
Section 2: Tabbed Browser.................... 2-4
Section 3: Menu Bar.................... 2-4
pgAdmin Workspace.................... 2-6
Query Editor 2-6
Section 1: Query Editor Panel 2-6
Query Editor Tab 2-6
Query History Tab.................... 2-7
Section 2: Data Output Panel 2-7
Data Output Tab.................... 2-7
Explain Tab 2-7
Messages Tab.................... 2-8
Notifications Tab.................... 2-8
Scratch Pad 2-8
Query Editor Toolbar.................... 2-9
Customizing pgAdmin.................... 2-10
Preferences Dialog Box.................... 2-11
Browser Nodes Options.................... 2-11
Debugger Display Option.................... 2-11
Themes.................... 2-11
Query Tool Preferences 2-11
Auto Completion.................... 2-11
CSV Output 2-12
Display.................... 2-12
Editor.................... 2-12
Explain.................... 2-13
Keyboard Shortcuts.................... 2-13
Options 2-13
Results Grid.................... 2-14

Exercise 2.2: Create A Database 2-14
Exercise 2.3: Restore A Database 2-14
Exercise 2.4: Create A Query 2-16
Handling Syntax Errors 2-17
Exercise 2.5: Viewing Data In The Database 2-18
Understanding Nulls 2-19
Tables In The Practice Database 2-19
Script Files 2-21
Exercise 2.6: Run A Query Using A Script File 2-21

CREATING SINGLE TABLE QUERIES 3-1
What Is A Query? 3-2
PostgreSQL Data Types 3-2
String Data Types 3-2
Numeric Data Types 3-3
Date And Time Data Types 3-4
Boolean Data Type 3-4
SQL Statements 3-5
SELECT Statements 3-6
Keywords 3-7
SQL Query Syntax 3-7
Exercise 3.1: Display Sales Rep Data 3-10
Exercise 3.2: Return Multiple Columns 3-11
What Is A Column Alias? 3-12
Exercise 3.3: Create A Column Alias 3-12
Selecting Distinct Values 3-13
Exercise 3.4: Find Distinct Values In A Column 3-13
What Is An Expression? 3-14
Creating Calculations 3-14
What Is A Calculated Field? 3-15
Handling NULL Values 3-15
Combining Columns Of Data 3-16
Exercise 3.5: Create A Query That Uses A Field With Null Values 3-16
Exercise 3.6: One NULL Values Solution 3-17
Exercise 3.7: Use The LIMIT Clause 3-18
Mathematical Operators 3-19
Exercise 3.8: Create An Expression That Creates A New Column Of Data 3-20
Exercise 3.9: Create An Expression To Calculate The Line Item Total 3-20
Adding Comments To A Query 3-20

FILTER DATA 4-1
WHERE Clause 4-2
Comparison Operators 4-5
Using The Equal To Operator 4-5
Exercise 4.1: Find The Orders For A Sales Rep 4-5
Exercise 4.2: Find Orders Over $15,000 4-7
Exercise 4.3: Use The Greater Than Or Equal To Operator 4-8
IS NULL Operator 4-9
Exercise 4.4: Use The IS NULL Operator With A String Field 4-9
Creating Filter Criteria That Has More Than One Condition 4-10
Exercise 4.5: Find All Products That Are Missing A Size And Color Value 4-11
Exercise 4.6: Find Orders With A Missing Payment Type 4-11
Using The OR Operator 4-12
Exercise 4.7: OR Operator Used More Than Once With Different Fields 4-12
Exercise 4.8: Use The AND And OR Operators 4-13
Order Of Evaluation 4-14
How Parentheses On The WHERE Clause Are Processed 4-15
Using The BETWEEN Operator 4-17
Exercise 4.9: Find Orders In A Specific Order Amount Range 4-18
Exercise 4.10: Emulating The BETWEEN Operator 4-18
Exercise 4.11: Use The BETWEEN Operator To Create A Date Range Filter 4-19

Using The IN Operator 4-19
Exercise 4.12: Find Products In Specific Categories 4-20
Exercise 4.13: Create Multiple Sets Of Filter Criteria 4-21
Using The NOT Operator 4-21
Exercise 4.14: Find Products That Are Not In Specific Sub Categories..4-22
Using The WHERE Clause To Compare Columns..4-22
Exercise 4.15: Compare The Values In Numeric Columns..4-22
Using The LIKE Operator 4-23
Wildcard Characters 4-23
Exercise 4.16: Find Job Titles That Start With The Word "Sales" 4-24
Exercise 4.17: Use The Underscore Wildcard Character To Filter Data 4-25
Creating Filter Criteria For Boolean Fields 4-26
Exercise 4.18: Find Products That Have Been Retired..4-27
Using Dates To Filter Data..4-27
Exercise 4.19: Find Orders On A Specific Date 4-27
Exercise 4.20: Find Orders Shipped After A Specific Date..4-28
Exercise 4.21: Find Orders In A Date Range 4-28
Exercise 4.22: Find Orders That Are Not In The Date Range..4-29
Exercise 4.23: Find Orders That Meet Date And Non Date Filter Criteria 4-29
Exercise 4.24: Find Orders In Specific Years 4-30
Exercise 4.25: Compare Values In Date Columns 4-30
Exercise 4.26: Filter Data Using A Calculation 4-30
CASE Function 4-31
How The Simple CASE Function Works..4-32
How The Searched CASE Function Works..4-32
Exercise 4.27: Create Product Categories Using The CASE Function 4-33
Exercise 4.28: Use The CASE Function With Numeric Values..4-33

CREATING ADVANCED SINGLE TABLE QUERIES 5-1
SELECT Statement Clauses.. 5-2
Sorting The Data In A Query.. 5-2
ORDER BY Clause 5-2
Exercise 5.1: Sort The Data In The Products Table.. 5-4
Exercise 5.2: Sort On Two Columns.. 5-5
Exercise 5.3: Sort On Three Columns 5-5
Exercise 5.4: Sort On Numeric And String Data.. 5-5
Exercise 5.5: Sort On Two Numeric Fields.. 5-6
Sort Values By Using The LIMIT Clause 5-6
Use The ORDER BY Clause With The WHERE Clause To Sort Data 5-8
Exercise 5.6: Sort The Orders For A Specific Sales Rep.. 5-8
Exercise 5.7: Sort The Filtered Data On Two Columns 5-9
Exercise 5.8: Filter The Top 10 Rows.. 5-9
Exercise 5.9: Sort Data That Is In A Date Range..5-10
Exercise 5.10: Find The Top 10 Orders In 2018 5-10
Exercise 5.11: Sort Using An Expression..5-11
Exercise 5.12: Modify The NULL Values Calculation 5-11
Grouping Data 5-13
Sorting vs Grouping Data..5-13
GROUP BY Clause 5-13
Exercise 5.13: Group The Count Of Customer Orders By Year..5-15
Exercise 5.14: Group Last Years Sales By Country And Region 5-15
Exercise 5.15: Create A Count Of Products For Each Vendor..5-17
Creating Group Filters..5-17
HAVING Clause..5-17
Exercise 5.16: Create A Valid Expression For The HAVING Clause 5-19
Exercise 5.17: Use The HAVING Clause To Filter The Groups..5-19
Exercise 5.18: Filter The Detail Rows Before The Groups Are Created..5-20
Exercise 5.19: Group Orders By Sales Rep..5-20
Exercise 5.20: Count, Sum And Group Sales Reps Orders 5-21
Exercise 5.21: Total And Group Last Years Sales By State..5-21
Exercise 5.22: Group And Count Products In Specific Categories..5-22

Sorting And Grouping 5-22
Exercise 5.23: Group Sales By Category And Year 5-23
Exercise 5.24: Group And Sort Sales By Category And Sub Category 5-23
Exercise 5.25: Group And Sort Orders By Date 5-24
Exercise 5.26: Find The Top 3 Sales Reps 5-24
Exercise 5.27: Find The Top 3 Sales Reps In A Date Range 5-25
Exercise 5.28: Group Customers By Region 5-25
Using The GROUP BY Clause With An Expression 5-25
Exercise 5.29: Create A Valid Expression On The GROUP BY Clause 5-25
Exercise 5.30: Find The Top 10 Regions By Sales 5-26
Exercise 5.31: Calculate The Number Of Orders By Year 5-26
Exercise 5.32: Group Orders By Sales Rep And Order Year 5-27
Exercise 5.33: Calculate The Sales To Cost Ratio 5-28

CREATING QUERIES THAT USE MULTIPLE TABLES 6-1
Joining Tables 6-2
Exercise 6.1: Create A Cross Join Query 6-6
What Is A Star Schema? 6-6
Creating Joins 6-7
INNER JOINS 6-8
The WHERE Clause Isn't Just For Creating Filter Criteria Anymore 6-10
Exercise 6.2: Retrieve Each Customers Region And Division 6-10
Exercise 6.3: Retrieve Each Sales Reps Name 6-11
Exercise 6.4: Retrieve The Products Category Name 6-12
Exercise 6.5: Find Customers That Placed An Order In June 2018 6-12
Exercise 6.6: Count Products In Each Category 6-14
Exercise 6.7: Use The WHERE Clause To Join Tables And Filter Data 6-14
Exercise 6.8: Find Orders In A Date Range 6-15
Exercise 6.9: Filter Sub Categories 6-15
Exercise 6.10: Count Customers In Each Region 6-15
Exercise 6.11: Create Two Groups 6-16
Exercise 6.12: Add The Vendor Name To An Existing Query 6-16
Joining Three Or More Tables 6-17
Exercise 6.13: Add A Third Table To The Query 6-17
Exercise 6.14: Find Customer Orders In 2017 Or 2018 6-18
Exercise 6.15: Create An Intermediate Table Join 6-18
Exercise 6.16: Count The Number Of Sub Categories 6-19
Exercise 6.17: Creating Joins That Use Multiple Fields 6-20
Exercise 6.18: Use Joins To Filter Data 6-21

USING OUTER JOINS TO LINK TABLES 7-1
OUTER JOINS 7-2
Exercise 7.1: Modify The E6.2 Query To Return All Rows 7-3
Understanding OUTER JOIN Filters 7-4
Exercise 7.2: Find NULL Values In A Join 7-4
Exercise 7.3: Lookup The Category Name For Each Sub Category 7-5
Other Ways To Join Tables 7-5
Exercise 7.4: Lookup Order Detail Records 7-5
Exercise 7.5: Find Products That Have Not Been Ordered 7-6
Exercise 7.6: Use LEFT OUTER JOINS To Return Data From Multiple Tables 7-6
Using Aggregate Functions With Joins 7-7
Using The COUNT Function With An OUTER JOIN 7-8
Self Joins 7-9
Exercise 7.7: Create A Query Using A Self Join 7-9
Exercise 7.8: Group Orders By Region Name And Year 7-10
Exercise 7.9: Combine Queries Using The UNION Operator 7-11
Exercise 7.10: Learn The Difference Between The UNION And UNION ALL Operators 7-12

FORMATTING TEXT AND NUMERIC DATA 8-1
What Is A Function? 8-2
Built-In Functions 8-2
String Formatting Functions 8-2
Concatenation Expressions 8-3
Converting Data 8-3
Exercise 8.1: Use The CONCAT Function To Combine Fields 8-4
Exercise 8.2: Use The CONCAT Function To Combine Data In String And Numeric Fields 8-5
Exercise 8.3: Use The CONCAT_WS Function To Combine Three Fields 8-5
Exercise 8.4: Use The LEFT Function 8-6
Exercise 8.5: Reformat The Phone Number Field 8-7
Exercise 8.6: Use The SUBSTRING Function 8-8
Exercise 8.7: Filter Data Using A Function 8-9
Exercise 8.8: Use The UPPER Function 8-9
Exercise 8.9: Combine Text With A String Field 8-9
Math Expressions 8-11
Exercise 8.10: Calculate The Inventory Value 8-11
Mathematical Formatting Functions 8-11
Exercise 8.11: Use The CEILING And FLOOR Functions 8-12
Exercise 8.12: Use The ROUND Function 8-12
Conditional Functions 8-13
Exercise 8.13: How To Emulate The IF Function 8-13
Exercise 8.14: Emulate The IFNULL Function 8-13
Exercise 8.15: Use The COALESCE Function 8-14

FORMATTING AND USING DATE FIELDS 9-1
What Is Time Intelligence? 9-2
Date Functions 9-2
DATE_PART Function Identifiers 9-3
Date Formatting Options 9-4
Exercise 9.1: Format A Date Field Without The Time 9-4
Exercise 9.2: Calculate Weekly Totals 9-5
Exercise 9.3: Create Monthly Order Totals By Year 9-6
Exercise 9.4: Group Orders By Month 9-6
Exercise 9.5: Filter Data For Specific Months 9-7
Exercise 9.6: Count And Sum Orders By Quarter 9-7
Exercise 9.7: Create Quarterly Order Totals By Year 9-8
Exercise 9.8: Filter, Group And Sort Data 9-8
Exercise 9.9: Filter Data For A Specific Quarter 9-9
Exercise 9.10: Calculate The Expected Order Ship Date 9-10
Exercise 9.11: Use The INTERVAL Function To Create A Date Range 9-10
Exercise 9.12: Calculate The Order Processing Time 9-11
Exercise 9.13: Find Out If Orders Were Shipped On Time 9-11
Exercise 9.14: Find Past, Current And Future End Of Month Dates 9-13
Exercise 9.15: Calculate Daily Sales Totals 9-14
Exercise 9.16: Calculate A Persons Age 9-15
Displaying Month Names 9-16
Exercise 9.17: Format A Date Field To Display The Month Name 9-16
Exercise 9.18: Group Orders By The Week Day 9-17

USING AGGREGATE FUNCTIONS AND CREATING SUMMARY QUERIES 10-1
Introduction To Aggregating Data 10-2
What Is A Summary Query? 10-3
Aggregate Functions 10-3
AVG Function 10-4
Exercise 10.1: Calculate The Average Retail Price Of All Products 10-5
Exercise 10.2: Calculate The Average List Price For Each Product Category 10-5
Exercise 10.3: Filter The Product Categories Average Retail Price 10-6
MAX Function 10-7
Exercise 10.4: Find The Highest Retail Price In Each Product Category 10-7
Exercise 10.5: Categories With A Product That Has A Retail Price Over $300 10-9

MIN Function 10-9
Exercise 10.6: Use The AVG, MAX And MIN Functions 10-9
Exercise 10.7: Calculate The AVG, MIN And MAX Product Selling Price By Category 10-9
Exercise 10.8: Calculate The Standard Deviation 10-10
COUNT Function 10-10
Exercise 10.9: Count The Number Of Orders With An Order Amount >= 5000 10-11
Exercise 10.10: Count The Number Of Customers With Each Job Title 10-12
Exercise 10.11: Count The Number Of Products In Each Category 10-12
SUM Function 10-13
Exercise 10.12: Calculate The Store Inventory 10-13
Exercise 10.13: Calculate The Gross Profit 10-13
Exercise 10.14: Use The DISTINCT Keyword With The COUNT Function 10-14
Exercise 10.15: Fix The Query In Example #14 10-15
Exercise 10.16: Use An Aggregate Function On The HAVING Clause 10-16
Exercise 10.17: Group Orders By Region And Order Year 10-16
Exercise 10.18: Create A Grouped Aggregation 10-17
Exercise 10.19: Count The Quantity Of Products Sold 10-17
Exercise 10.20: Count Orders By Status 10-18
Exercise 10.21: Create Yearly Order Totals 10-19
Exercise 10.22: Count Customer Totals By Year 10-19
Exercise 10.23: Find The Top 10 Selling Products 10-20
Exercise 10.24: Group Customers By Region, State And Customer Type 10-20
GROUP BY Subclauses 10-21
ROLLUP Subclause 10-21
Exercise 10.25: Use The ROLLUP Subclause To Only Generate A Grand Total 10-21
Exercise 10.26: Use The ROLLUP Subclause To Calculate Grand Totals 10-22
Exercise 10.27: Use The ROLLUP Subclause To Calculate Subtotals And A Grand Total 10-23
Replacing NULL Values In Queries That Use The ROLLUP Subclause 10-23
Exercise 10.28: Displaying Text Instead Of NULL Values 10-23
Exercise 10.29: Create A Grand Total For Each Group 10-24
CUBE Subclause 10-25
Exercise 10.30: Use The CUBE Subclause 10-26
Exercise 10.31: Create Specific Grouping Sets With The CUBE Subclause 10-27
Exercise 10.32: Replace The ROLLUP Subclause With The CUBE Subclause 10-27
GROUPING SETS Subclause 10-28
Exercise 10.33: Use The GROUPING SETS, CUBE And ROLLUP Subclauses 10-28
Exercise 10.34: Create The Sub Category Grouping Set 10-29
Exercise 10.35: Create A Query That Uses The GROUPING SETS Subclause 10-31
Exercise 10.36: Use The GROUPING Function 10-32
Exercise 10.37: Group On Four Fields 10-32
Exercise 10.38: Use The GROUPING SETS Subclause Instead Of The ROLLUP Subclause 10-33

CREATING SUBQUERIES 11-1
What Is A SubQuery? 11-2
Self Contained Scalar Subqueries 11-3
Exercise 11.1: Find Orders Shipped In September 2018 11-4
Using Aggregate Functions In A Subquery 11-5
Creating Subqueries On The SELECT Clause 11-5
Exercise 11.2: Find The Most Recent Order Date For Each Customer 11-5
Exercise 11.3: Calculate The Number Of Orders Each Customer Has Placed 11-6
Exercise 11.4: Display All Customers And Their Largest Order Total 11-6
Create Filters Using Aggregate Functions In Subqueries 11-6
Exercise 11.5: Find Orders With An Order Amount >= The Average Order Amount 11-6
Exercise 11.6: Use The ANY Keyword In A Subquery 11-7
Exercise 11.7: Find Products With A Quantity Of Four Or More On One Order 11-8
Exercise 11.8: Find Products With A Retail Price Greater Than The Average Retail Price 11-8
Exercise 11.9: Use The ALL Keyword In A Subquery 11-9
Exercise 11.10: Use The IN Operator In A Subquery 11-9
Exercise 11.11: Use A Subquery To Find Customer Orders 11-10
How To Run The Subquery By Itself 11-11
Creating A Calculated Field In A Subquery 11-11

Exercise 11.12: Find The Largest Product Total In Each Order 11-11
Exercise 11.13: Count The Number Of Orders For Each Sales Rep........ 11-12
Exercise 11.14: Calculate The Percent Of The Total........ 11-12
Exercise 11.15: Find The Top 5 Selling Products 11-13
Nesting Subqueries 11-14
Exercise 11.16: Create A Query That Uses Two Subqueries 11-14
Correlated Subqueries 11-14
Exercise 11.17: Find Each Customers First Order........ 11-15
Exercise 11.18: Use A Correlated Subquery To Find Products With A Maximum List Price 11-15
Exercise 11.19: Find Sales Reps That Sold A Specific Product........ 11-16
Exercise 11.20: Use The EXISTS Keyword In A Subquery 11-17
Exercise 11.21: Find Customers That Placed An Order In June 2018 11-17
Using The HAVING Clause In A Subquery 11-18
Exercise 11.22: Find The Customers That Have Placed 10 Or More Orders 11-18
Exercise 11.23: Find The Sales Reps That Have An Average Order Amount >= The Overall Average Order Amount........ 11-19

CREATING AND USING VIEWS 12-1
What Is A View?........ 12-2
Advantages Of Creating Views........ 12-2
View Requirements........ 12-3
Exercise 12.1: Create A Sales Reps View 12-4
Exercise 12.2: Create A View Using Two Tables 12-5
Exercise 12.3: Use Multiple Tables To Create A View........ 12-5
Exercise 12.4: Create An Order Details View 12-6
Exercise 12.5: Filter The Orders Data 12-7
Exercise 12.6: Filter The Customers Table 12-7
Exercise 12.7: Check For NULL Values........ 12-7
Exercise 12.8: Display The Top 10 Most Profitable Products Based On Production Costs 12-8
Exercise 12.9: Create A View That Displays The Top 10 Orders........ 12-8
Exercise 12.10: Calculate The Sales Reps Total Sales By Year........ 12-9
Exercise 12.11: Use A View In A Query........ 12-9
Exercise 12.12: Query The Data In A View........ 12-9
Exercise 12.13: Join A View And A Table 12-10
Modifying Views........ 12-10
Exercise 12.14: Add A Field To An Existing View 12-10

GETTING STARTED WITH POSTGRESQL

After reading this chapter and completing the exercises you will:

- ☑ Have an understanding of PostgreSQL
- ☑ Have installed PostgreSQL and pgAdmin, if necessary
- ☑ Have a better understanding of database concepts and terminology
- ☑ Have an understanding of relational databases and relationships

CHAPTER 1

Welcome To PostgreSQL!

PostgreSQL is a popular open source (free), relational database management system. In addition to being able to meet a variety of storage needs, it is fast and reliable. That is because it is scalable and can be used for small projects to projects that have to store millions of rows of data. This book is based on the Windows version of PostgreSQL. This book uses pgAdmin, which is also free, to connect to PostgreSQL databases and create queries.

SQL is one of the most popular and most used query languages on the market today. PostgreSQL is a relational database that supports the SQL language. This book is for people that are new to PostgreSQL, and want to learn how to create queries, in a relatively short amount of time, without having to read about it's history and advances through the years. Equally important, this book is for people that have a project starting soon, that requires using a PostgreSQL database to create queries.

It is no secret that many companies are spending obscene amounts of money to gather and warehouse (store) data. That's great, as long as they keep my name out of their databases. <smile> What these companies are finding out, is that they do not have enough staff that knows what to do with the data, once they get it, how to retrieve the data from a database or how to analyze the data. Those that know SQL are at least able to retrieve the data and manipulate it. This makes SQL, a good skill to have. SQL is no longer only used by people in the IT department.

Most businesses store their data in a relational database. A relational database management system (RDBMS) is software that is used to create and maintain one or more databases. The basic concepts and principles are covered in this chapter. Not surprising is the fact that the bulk of these relational databases use SQL or a close cousin (PostgreSQL is a close cousin), to query the data. This means that SQL is key for data analysis. To me, that is good news because it means that SQL is a skill that will be needed for a very long time. Keep in mind that queries are usually created to be used as the data source for creating reports, be they paper based reports or visualizations (charts, for example).

PostgreSQL has the ability to create a variety of queries, from a basic query that displays a list of customers, to a complex query that returns financial data, for analysis. This book is for everyone that has little to no experience with SQL or databases, but wants to become proficient in creating queries. This book is also for people that have created queries using a different SQL database. This book introduces you to the core concepts and techniques that are used to create a variety of queries.

Why Learn PostgreSQL?

As time goes on, for a variety of reasons, more and more people outside of the IT department are being tasked with retrieving data from a database to gain insight about the data that is collected. Currently, SQL is the primary language that is used to communicate, if you will, with relational databases. Having a good working knowledge of SQL is a good skill to have.

Fortunately, SQL is a query language that is used to make requests to retrieve data by typing in statements that resemble sentences in the English language. For example, the following statement will retrieve all customer data from the Customers table.

```
SELECT * FROM Customers;
```

Knowing SQL means that you do not have to wait for IT to retrieve the data for you. As a business person, knowing SQL can often make it easier to explain to an IT person what you are trying to accomplish. Knowing SQL is the beginning of learning **DATA MINING**.

Because SQL is governed by an International Standard (ISO), the core function of the language and commands are the same, regardless of which database (SQL Server, MySQL, PostgreSQL, et al) that you are using. There will be some differences from one database to another and all databases do not implement all of the features and functionality, in the standard. The biggest difference is that some of the syntax is different.

However, the functions that most people need, the standard syntax will work, regardless of the database that you use. This means that once you learn the basics of SQL for one database, you will be better able to create queries for any database that supports SQL.

This is a good time to learn any version of SQL, including PostgreSQL. I have seen many front-end (aka end-user) tools that allow SQL queries to be created to retrieve the data that they need. I don't know how many end-users know SQL. My guess is not many, so they use other features of the tool to try and get the data that they need. The good news is that even though you will learn PostgreSQL in this book, it is not an uphill battle to transfer the skills covered in this book to another version of SQL, like Oracle, or to report writing software, down the road, if necessary. This book provides the tools, examples and exercises needed to create and modify queries using a PostgreSQL database.

Knowing any version of SQL will make you more $valuable$ in the workplace, especially if you are **NOT** in the IT department. Having said that, you have to keep in mind that each version of SQL has differences, including PostgreSQL. Sometimes, these differences are enough to slow you down for a while, until you get up to speed again, when going from one version of SQL to another.

How Do I Get Started?

Once you have installed the software and have restored the database used in this book, you can start learning how to use PostgreSQL to create queries that retrieve data from a single table. Each chapter builds on previous chapters, by adding more code to the query. This allows you time to understand the basics before taking on more complex topics, like including calculations in queries. The exercises and example queries in this book are designed to teach a novice how to create queries using SQL and how to solve business problems.

A goal of this book is to discuss potential problems and solutions on how to resolve them. The good thing is that you have taken a great first step towards learning PostgreSQL, by purchasing this book. Now, all you have to do, is use this book to learn how to overcome the hurdles. From time to time, I will point out functionality that may not work as expected. When I do this, I am not complaining, merely pointing out things that I think you should be aware of.

In many respects, because this book is for people new to creating queries, it levels the playing field for people that do not have an IT background. That means that a business or data analyst, a student or financial planner, are starting at the same place, when it comes to learning PostgreSQL. To achieve the expected goal of being able to create queries in PostgreSQL, all I ask is that you take your time and reread or redo exercises that you are not sure that you understand.

In the beginning, queries were created by programmers in the IT department. These programmers, of which I was one of, had some type of formal training. Today, people outside of the IT department are creating queries and reports, with and without having "formal" training. If you fall into the latter category, don't worry, I purposely keep the technical jargon to a minimum. My goal for writing this book, and all of the books that I write, for that matter, is to help people, that have various backgrounds, learn how to create SQL queries, and more importantly, learn some of the logic skills that are required to create queries that retrieve the correct data.

Learning any version of SQL is important if you need to analyze data or if you need to retrieve the data that will be handed off to someone else, that will analyze it. Learning new tips and shortcuts will let you work faster and smarter. The more you know about PostgreSQL, the easier your day to day query design experiences will be.

I am sure that you looked at a few other books that cover using PostgreSQL to create queries, before purchasing this one. You may have gotten the feeling that there was more "reading" about such and such topic, opposed to "these are the steps to do such and such topic". People usually learn more by doing, especially in the beginning, then just reading about what can be done.

A hands-on approach is usually the best way to learn most things in life. This book is a visual guide that has over 345 ready to use queries, in the examples and exercises, that you can use on your own, to create queries. There are over 395 illustrations that practically eliminate the guess work and let you know that you are creating the queries correctly. As you read the examples and work through the exercises in this book, my hope is that you start to visualize how you can take some of the topics covered and apply them to the queries that you need to create on your own. I wrote this book to help people learn how to create queries using a PostgreSQL database and become efficient and proficient at it.

Like all of the computer books that I write, this book is also for people that want to learn a new software tool or programming language from a book, that has step by step instructions that can be followed. Then, take that knowledge and apply it to their own projects and tasks.

One goal and hope that I have for this book is to help bridge the SQL query knowledge gap between IT programmers and business users. I am cognizant of the fact that more and more business users are being tasked (whether they want to or not) with more data analysis responsibilities. The foundation of data analysis has three main components, as explained below.

① To learn more about the data that needs to be analyzed.

② To know how to query databases to return the data needed to answer business questions.

③ Create reports and visualizations that clearly represent the data that was retrieved, so that decisions can be made.

It should not come as a surprise, but this book does not cover all of these components. This book cannot teach you about the specific data that you need to analyze, but I do point out some things that you should be aware of and look out for about data in general. This book does not cover creating reports and visualizations. I have already written a few books on report creation and as of the date this book went to print, I have three new report titles that I will write. What this book does cover is learning how to use pgAdmin to create queries, using data stored in a PostgreSQL database, which includes learning how to determine what columns of data are needed.

It is my sincere hope that whatever your current skill level is with creating queries, that you will learn more about topics that you are already familiar with as you go through this book, and that you learn about functionality that you did not know existed. I also hope that you find that this book gets you up to speed quickly, as time is money!

So sit back and lets get started!

Why A Book Specifically For PostgreSQL, When There Are Already Books On SQL?

Many books on SQL cover several database management systems that can use SQL, in one book. This means that topics, like functions or syntax, that are specific to a particular database, like SQLite or PostgreSQL aren't covered and if they are covered, it may not be covered enough detail. This means that a number of topics have to be reduced to what works with "most relational database management systems that support SQL". What I write in this book about PostgreSQL, does not have to take into consideration whether or not a concept, keyword or function is available or works in any other database that supports any other version of SQL.

For example, SQL Server supports the TOP keyword to create what is known as "TOP N" functionality. PostgreSQL does not support the TOP keyword. PostgreSQL supports the LIMIT clause, which provides some of the functionality that the TOP keyword has. If this was a generic SQL book, at best, only one of these options would be covered. With this book being specifically for PostgreSQL, I can cover the LIMIT clause and its functionality and not have to consider the TOP keyword.

Each version of SQL has it's own unique features. I can't speak for everyone, but if I want to learn about one version of SQL, I want the book that I purchase to only be about that version, not a combination of several versions of SQL, that only covers functionality that all versions of SQL have in common. If that is how you feel, this is the book for you.

This book is PostgreSQL all day. Also keep in mind that "SQL" is a set of standards if you will, and each SQL supported database is built from these standards. To be more specific, other then installing pgAdmin, this book is all about creating queries in PostgreSQL. Why? Because that is what most people initially need to do. You do not even need to learn how to create tables, to use this book successfully. That is because I provide a database that has the tables and data for you. While I haven't checked every book on PostgreSQL, this book may be the only one on the market that does not cover creating and designing a database, setting security rights, etc. Similar to how I started this paragraph, I'll say it again, **THIS BOOK IS ALL ABOUT CREATING QUERIES USING A POSTGRESQL DATABASE**, all day.

Keep in mind that each SQL database, like PostgreSQL and Oracle SQL, have their own client software to create queries, and there are a few third-party software packages that support using one or more SQL databases. Do you really want to learn PostgreSQL and see screen shots of SQL Server Management Studio, which is the client software most used to work with SQL Server databases, while learning PostgreSQL? Probably not. That would be like trying to learn Spanish from a book written in French. While possible, it is probably not the best solution, if you don't already know French.

Having said that, I know some readers already know another version of SQL, so I point out some differences between PostgreSQL and other SQL databases. If you look in the index, the other versions of SQL databases, like those mentioned above, are listed. The page numbers are where I briefly point something out about another SQL database.

I was motivated to write books on a variety of computer software, including a series of books on SQL, because way back when, I went to a book store because I needed to learn Microsoft Access to develop a few applications. I looked at every Access book, they had. They were either too short and didn't have enough examples or they were at least 500 pages of mostly text that explained probably 95% of the features, but did not have a lot of examples or screen shots of what they were talking about. The book that came with the software was just a lot of pages of basically nothing useful. Yes, there was a time when software came with a paperback book. Maybe its just me, but I do not find reference books helpful when first trying to learn a new software package.

If this is not the first SQL database that you have used to create queries, you know that each SQL database has their own version of the "standard SQL". The books that I write are for a specific software package. They are not 500 plus pages of mostly text. They have a lot of screen shots, examples that you can be use out in the real world, as they say, and the code when needed. Hopefully, this is the type of book that you want to learn PostgreSQL from, because that is how I wrote this book.

Not to be funny, but did you notice that there were two different SQL names used in the heading for this section? That is because each flavor, if you will, of SQL has slightly different features, functions and syntax. Yes, there are a lot of books available that have "SQL" in the title, but after you read the description of what the book covers, you find out one of two things:

① The book says it covers several flavors (PostgreSQL, MySQL etc.) of SQL by only covering features that they all have in common. As each flavor has its own front end software that is used to create queries, the chances of seeing software for three or four versions of the software used to create the queries is slim to none.
② The book really only covers standard SQL. Helpful? Yes, if you do not need to learn the specifics about a particular SQL database. Not so much, if you want to learn a specific flavor of SQL.

No, I am not bashing these books. I just want you to know why I selected a different route for writing a book specifically for PostgreSQL. I feel that transparency in this situation, is a good thing. Take from this what you will.

How This Book Is Organized

The order that the topics are covered in this book, is not an accident on my part. They are in the order that I think makes the most sense, from a data flow perspective, to learn them in. This book is aimed at users that probably have a wide range of experience, from beginner to intermediate level skills. The first two chapters cover terms that you need to understand that will make it easier to understand databases and relationships. The options for pgAdmin that are used to create queries are covered, as well as creating your first query. Those chapters are followed by the first chapter that shows you how to create a variety of queries.

I do not recommend laying in a hammock in your backyard and reading this book. The problem with doing that is that this book is designed to be a **HANDS-ON**, **SITTING IN FRONT OF YOUR COMPUTER**, **CREATING THE QUERIES IN THE EXERCISES**, type of book. Reading this book, without following along using your computer will not give you the level of learning that you want or need. And then, when you are creating queries on your own, the chance of you getting lost and not knowing what to do is high. I am almost 100% sure that you aren't trying to learn SQL because you have nothing better to do. <smile> More than likely, you want to learn SQL to further your career and increase your income. If so, you owe it to yourself to take the time to complete the step-by-step exercises in this book.

To get the most out of this book, it is not advised that you skip around. The first reason is because some of the queries used in later chapters are created in earlier exercises. Additionally, working through the exercises in the order that they are presented, provides a better understanding of the concepts, because you can see first hand what SQL is capable of. The topics are presented in a way that you will understand what it offers and more importantly, when to use it.

The other reason skipping around in this book is not a good idea, is that a feature or option may have been covered in more detail earlier in the book. If you decide to skip around and cannot complete an exercise because there is something that you do not understand, you will have to go back and find the section that covers the topic that you have a question about. While this book is designed for people that are new to PostgreSQL, some topics may be considered advanced. I included them because regardless of how the topic may be categorized, I felt that you may have a need to use it and probably would, if you know that it exists. Below is an overview of what is covered in each chapter.

Chapter 1, Getting Started With PostgreSQL provides an overview of SQL, PostgreSQL and pgAdmin. This chapter also walks you through installing the software that is needed. The concepts of relationships and relational databases are introduced.

Chapter 2, Using pgAdmin shows you how to restore to a database, learn how to use pgAdmin, view data in tables in a PostgreSQL database and more.

Chapter 3, Creating Single Table Queries introduces you to basic SQL concepts. You will learn about the SELECT statement and how to create basic queries that return rows and columns of data from a table. Creating queries with math calculations is introduced in this chapter. PostgreSQL data types are also covered. A variety of techniques are covered, including finding distinct values, combining data from two or more columns, handling NULL values and creating what is commonly known as TOP N queries. The techniques that are covered are fundamental and will give you a foundation to build on, in future chapters.

Chapter 4, Filter Data introduces the concept of creating criteria to select specific rows of data to retrieve. Then the chapter advances to showing you how to combine filter criteria to create more complex queries.

Chapter 5, Creating Advanced Single Table Queries picks up where Chapter 3 left off. This chapter covers the following clauses: GROUP BY, HAVING and ORDER BY. They are used with the SELECT statement and provide more query functionality. These clauses are used to sort and group the rows of data, returned from the query.

Chapter 6, Creating Queries That Use Multiple Tables introduces you to join types and shows you how to use them to create queries that return data from more than one table, at the same time, in the same query.

Chapter 7, Using Outer Joins To Link Tables picks up where Chapter 6 left off. The focus of this chapter is creating table joins, using the OUTER JOIN options.

Chapter 8, Formatting Text And Numeric Data covers the functions that are used to format text and numeric data. These functions are used to change how text and numeric values are displayed. This chapter also covers creating math calculations in a query.

Chapter 9, Formatting And Using Date Fields continues with more formatting options. In this chapter, you will learn about the functions used to format date fields. In addition to formatting functions, other date functions are covered that are used to extract a portion of a date, calculate the difference between two dates and more.

Chapter 10, Using Aggregate Functions And Creating Summary Queries covers creating queries that summarize data and the functions that are used to aggregate the data that summary queries need. Some aggregate functions are used to create subtotals and grand totals. The GROUP BY subclauses ROLLUP, CUBE and GROUPING SETS are covered.

Chapter 11, Creating Subqueries covers how to create a query within a query. Like many other query topics, there are several ways to create subqueries, including using derived tables and the more popular use of creating a subquery as part of the WHERE clause. This is the subquery option covered in this chapter.

Chapter 12, Creating And Using Views covers creating queries that create views. Creating views is helpful because they keep you from having to create the same code over and over. Views are also used to restrict users from having access to some columns of data. You can create one view and several reports can be created from the data that the view retrieves.

Objectives Of This Book

This book is written to accommodate self-paced, classroom and online training. While there are no required prerequisites to successfully complete the exercises in this book, having a general knowledge of any or all of the following would be helpful.

- ☑ Creating basic SQL queries
- ☑ Relational database management systems
- ☑ Report writing software like SQL Server Reporting Services (SSRS) or Crystal Reports.
- ☑ VLOOKUP or filtering data in Excel.
- ☑ Creating formulas (expressions) and using aggregate functions, like COUNT and SUM that are available in Excel.

Don't panic if you do not have knowledge or experience with any of the topics listed above. It just means that it will take you a little longer to work through and understand the topics and exercises in this book, because everything will be new. All of the SQL equivalents of the concepts and topics listed above are covered in this book, except report writing.

Step-by-step instructions are included throughout this book, in the exercises. This book takes a hands-on approach to teaching you how query data using SQL. After completing the exercises in this book, you will be able to perform the following tasks and more:

- ☑ Connect to a PostgreSQL database

☑ Understand database concepts and relationships
☑ Write SQL SELECT statements
☑ Use the WHERE, GROUP BY and ORDER BY clauses
☑ Create queries that return data from more than one table
☑ Format text, numbers and dates
☑ Sort and group data
☑ Create queries that use functions
☑ Create summary queries

If you have not written a line of code before, don't worry. Topics are broken down into easy to follow steps. Examples with code are all throughout this book. The result (output) that the queries create, is also shown.

This Book May Not Be For You

The previous two sections provided an overview of the topics covered in this book. Most technical books are for a specific audience, usually either beginner/intermediate or advanced. This book is no exception. It is for the beginner, that wants to learn how to create SQL queries. This book does not cover advanced topics like stored procedures, triggers, transactions, database security, Window functions, common table expressions (CTE's), using SQL as a programming tool (which is different then creating queries), creating and using variables, temporary tables and derived tables.

Conventions Used In This Book

I designed the following conventions to make it easier for you to follow the instructions in this book.

☑ The `Courier` font is used to indicate what you should type.
☑ **SMALL CAPS** are used to indicate an option to click on or to bring something to your attention.
☑ This icon indicates a shortcut or another way to complete the task that is being discussed. It can also indicate a tip or additional information about the topic that is being discussed.
☑ This icon indicates a warning, like a feature that has been removed or information that you need to be aware of. This icon can also represent what I call a quirk, meaning a feature that did not work, as I expected it to.
☑ This icon indicates one of two things: That some of the data returned by the query is not displayed in the figure. The majority of queries created in this book return a lot of data. Most of the time, only the first few rows are displayed in the figures, as that is enough to let you know that the query is working as intended. This icon also indicates that some of the dialog box or workspace is not shown. In both cases, that is because the content that is not displayed, does not provide any value.
☑ The column names in the database used in this book are one word, like CompanyName. To make it easer to read, I put a space between "Company" and "Name", when discussing a topic. In the actual query, it is shown as one word.
☑ [Text in brackets] references a section, table or figure, that has more information about the topic being discussed. If the reference is in a different chapter, the chapter number is included in the reference, like this: [See Chapter 2, Update Options].
☑ When you see "**FIGURE X-X SHOWS THE RESULT**" or "**YOU SHOULD HAVE THE OPTIONS SHOWN IN FIGURE X-X**" or something similar in the exercises, check to make sure that your screen does look like the figure. If it does, continue with the next set of instructions. If your screen does not look like the figure, redo the steps that you just completed, so that your screen does match the figure. Not doing so may cause you problems when trying to complete exercises later in the book.
☑ The heading **EXERCISE X.Y:** (X equals the chapter number and Y equals the exercise number, in the chapter) represents exercises that have step-by-step instructions that you should complete. You will also see sections that have step-by-step instructions that are not an exercise. Completing them as you go through the book is optional.
☑ The heading **EXAMPLE #** contains at least one query that demonstrates a function, topic or alternate query that accomplishes what another query does.
☑ "E2.1 Query Name" is the naming convention for the queries that you will create. E2.1 stands for Chapter 2, Exercise 1. You may consider some of the query file names to be long. I did this on purpose, so that it is easier to know what topic the query covers. If you do not like to type or do not want to type the full query files name, you can just type the first part as the file name. That way, when you have to find a query file to complete another exercise, you will be able to find the correct file. For example, if the query file name is E5.5 Orders shipped between 4-1-2016 and 6-30-2016, you can type E5.5, as the query file name.

☑ "Save the Ex.y query as" means to open the Ex.y query and save it with the new file name specified in the step. The reason that I have you do this is to keep the queries that you create intact, as some queries are used more than once, as the starting point for other queries.

☑ Some queries have blank lines in the code. I did that to make the query easier to read. You do not have to include blank lines, when you type the query.

Assumptions

Yes, I know one should never assume anything, but the following assumptions have been made. It is assumed that . . .

☑ You know that this book is based on the Windows version of PostgreSQL and pgAdmin. If a newer version (then the one used in this book) of this software is available, you can download and use the newer version.

☑ You know that the operating system used to write this book is Windows 8.1. If you are using a different version of Windows, any or all of the following can apply:

① Some of the screen shots may have a slightly different look.

② Some of the instructions for Windows tasks may be different.

③ The path to folders and files (for the software) on your computer may be different then the paths listed in this book.

☑ You know that I am not perfect and sadly, you may find minor mistakes in this book. It is not intentional and I apologize for any inconvenience.

☑ You know that when you see <smile>, that signifies my attempt of adding humor to the learning process.

☑ You know that I use the words "field" and "column" interchangeably. They are one in the same.

☑ You know that I use the words "retrieve" and "return" interchangeably. They are one in the same and both refer to getting data from one or more tables, in the database.

☑ You know that the end of each chapter in this book has a summary section. In addition to providing a recap of the topics covered, some chapter summaries contain new information, like explaining another way to accomplish a task that was already covered or related content that did not fit in the main part of the chapter. I did this to not interrupt the flow of the chapter.

☑ You know that the links (to other web sites) in this book worked when this book went to print and that I have no control over when or if the web site owner changes or removes web pages. In other words, please do not contact me, if a link listed in this book no longer works. Most of the time, if you start on the home page of the web site, you will be able to find the page that you need.

Software Updates
Many software companies have changed to a faster update release schedule for some of their software titles. PostgreSQL and pgAdmin fall into this category. The core functionality of the software does not change frequently. A large portion of the updates are modifications to existing functionality or name changes of existing options. What many people like is that there is a major software release/upgrade every year, usually in September or October. In addition to this yearly release, there are also incremental releases to both software packages, throughout the year.

For users, the frequent software updates are great. For authors that write books about the software, the frequent updating presents a problem. By the time you read this book, or any book on PostgreSQL for that matter, some parts of the book may be slightly out of date. Sadly, there isn't anything that I can do about this, other then what I am doing right now, and that is to be up front about a situation that I cannot control.

What Is SQL?

SQL is the abbreviation for **STRUCTURED QUERY LANGUAGE**. (To pronounce it, just say the letters.) SQL was developed by IBM in the 1970's, for its own relational database management system (RDBMS), named DB2. It is the programming language that was designed to query and manage data in a relational database. SQL is the language that is used to interact with relational databases. Even though SQL is not a proprietary language, no two database management systems implement SQL exactly the same.

As covered earlier, SQL is supported by several database vendors. This may be hard to believe, but all SQL databases are not owned by Microsoft. <smile> I think many people think that they are, because many Microsoft products have "SQL" in the name. **MYSQL** and **ORACLE SQL** are examples of SQL databases that are owned by other companies.

SQL is the language that is used to communicate with most relational database management systems. SQL is relatively easy to learn. That is because SQL does not have a lot of words, by design. SQL was designed to read and write data to a database. Without knowing SQL, just by looking at many of the keywords, you will have a pretty good idea of what they do. Examples are **INSERT**, **DELETE**, **GROUP BY** and **CONTAINS**.

SQL is the original language used to query relational databases. Over time, databases like those listed above, adopted SQL and tweaked it to work with their database. The good thing about learning a database specific version of SQL, like PostgreSQL, is that once you learn one, it is relatively easy to learn a version that is for another relational database management system, even though there are some differences. Usually, the biggest difference between the versions, is the syntax.

Introduction To The PostgreSQL Environment

The next few sections introduce you to the PostgreSQL environment. There is much more that can and has been written about the PostgreSQL environment. But the "environment" is not the focus of this book. The focus is to teach you how to create queries.

Like all software, PostgreSQL and pgAdmin are updated on a regular basis. Each version has new and updated features. But don't worry, the core query functionality basically stays the same. **TIP**: This is why you rarely see the software version number in the title of computer books anymore. Some authors, including yours truly, update a book periodically, to include new features or functionality. For example, within two or three years from the date that this book went to print, there will be new functions. Some will be for queries and some will be system functions. I will update this book to include at least some of the new query related functions.

What Is PostgreSQL?

PostgreSQL is a free, open source, object relational database management system. It was initially created in the 1980's to only run on UNIX platforms, but later PostgreSQL was modified to be portable and run on Windows, Mac OS and Linux platforms. What many people like is that PostgreSQL requires very little effort to maintain.

PostgreSQL was designed to be customized. While many SQL databases force you to use data types from a predefined list, PostgreSQL allows you to create/define additional data types, custom functions, functional language and custom plug-ins. While this book only covers creating queries using a PostgreSQL database, I wanted to let you know that this software can also be used as an application platform.

What Is pgAdmin?

pgAdmin is the free management tool for PostgreSQL. It has a graphical interface that is used to configure and manage your PostgreSQL server and databases. It is also has an SQL query tool that is used to create, save and run queries. This is the part of pgAdmin that will be used in this book. Chapter 2 covers pgAdmin in more detail. There are other tools that can be used to create and manage a PostgreSQL server and create queries. Some are listed in the next section.

pgAdmin Alternatives

These tools are not covered or used in this book, but I wanted to let you know that you have options, when it comes to selecting a tool to use with PostgreSQL databases.

☑ The **POSTGRESQL COMMAND LINE TOOL**, named psql. This utility does not have a graphical interface. Instead, you use a command prompt dialog box, also known as a terminal window. This software can be installed when you install PostgreSQL.

☑ **PGMANAGE** This is a free tool (for Windows, Linux and Mac OS) that has a graphical interface. [See https://github.com/pgManage/pgManage/]

How pgAdmin Can Be Used

There are two ways that pgAdmin can be used, as explained below.

① **AS A QUERY TOOL**. This option is used to retrieve data from one or more tables in a database. The goal of creating a query is to answer questions like "Which customers purchased products last September?", "How many orders were shipped late in 2018?" or "Which products had sales of more than $100,000 in 2018?". This is the way that pgAdmin is covered in this book. Most of the time, the dataset returned from these queries are used to create reports in another tool.

② **AS A PROGRAMMING TOOL.** By this I mean that pgAdmin is used to create temporary tables, stored procedures, triggers, write error handling routines, use Window functions and much more. These topics are not covered in this book.

In addition to the two uses discussed above, pgAdmin can also be used to create and populate tables with data and modify existing data in a database. Before you start to frown, the answer is no. For the most part, you do not have to type a lot of code to retrieve the data that you need, for the queries that you will create in this book.

Getting Help With PostgreSQL And pgAdmin

Below are ways to get help if you have a question on how to use a feature or option in PostgreSQL or pgAdmin.

① **Read this book** from cover to cover and complete the exercises. Many of the basic questions that you may have are probably covered in this book.

② **PostgreSQL Mailing Lists** The mailing lists and forum can be invaluable resources.

You can post questions and learn how other people are using the software. The mailing list is also a great way to keep current on the latest trends and for getting ideas on how to enhance the queries that you create.

From time to time, you may find it helpful to just read some questions and solutions that are posted on a mailing list or forum. This is another way to learn more about SQL. While some of the questions are advanced and you may not fully understand the solution, you will gain a better understanding of what is possible. The link for the PostgreSQL mailing lists is https://www.postgresql.org/list/.

③ **pgAdmin Mailing List** The link for the pgAdmin mailing list is https://www.pgadmin.org/support/list/.

④ **PostgreSQL Online Documentation** It is available in PDF and HTML format. The link is www.postgresql.org/docs. There is also a shortcut to the documentation on the home page of the pgAdmin software.

Exercise 1.1: Create A Folder For Your Files

You will create and modify several queries in this book. It is a good idea to store all of the queries in the same folder on your computers hard drive, so that you can find them easily. I will refer to this folder as "your folder" throughout the book. The instructions below show you how to create the folder at the root of the C drive.

1. Open Windows Explorer ⇒ Right-click on the C drive icon ⇒ New ⇒ Folder.

2. Type `PostgreSQL Book` as the folder name, then press Enter.

3. To get the most out of this book, you should download the copy of the database that is used in this book. The database is in a zip file. To have the link for the zip file sent to you, send an email to postgresql@tolanapublishing.com.

   If you do not receive an email in a few minutes with the subject line PostgreSQL Book Files, check the spam folder in your email software.

4. When you receive the email, click on the link for the web page that has the zip file ⇒ On the web page, download the zip file to the folder that you created in step 2.

5. In Windows Explorer, right-click on the zip file and select the option to extract the file. Use the zip software that you currently have or you can use the compression tool in Windows Explorer.

Exercise 1.2: Download And Install PostgreSQL And pgAdmin

If you already have PostgreSQL version 12 and pgAdmin version 4.15 or higher installed, you can skip this exercise.

Download PostgreSQL For Windows

Believe it or not, the best installer for PostgreSQL is by a company named EnterpriseDB. They bundle PostgreSQL and pgAdmin into one installation.

1. Go to www.postgresql.org/download/windows/ ⇒ Click on the **DOWNLOAD THE INSTALLER** link. You should see a page similar to the one shown in Figure 1-1.

PostgreSQL Version	Linux x86-64	Linux x86-32	Mac OS X	Windows x86-64	Windows x86-32
12.1	N/A	N/A	Download	Download	N/A
11.6	N/A	N/A	Download	Download	N/A
10.11	Download	Download	Download	Download	Download
9.6.16	Download	Download	Download	Download	Download
9.5.20	Download	Download	Download	Download	Download
9.4.25	Download	Download	Download	Download	Download
9.3.25 (Not Supported)	Download	Download	Download	Download	Download

Figure 1-1 PostgreSQL download options

2. Click on the **DOWNLOAD** link for the most recent 64-bit Windows version, as illustrated above in Figure 1-1.

3. You can save the file to your desktop or to the folder that you created for this book. Depending on your internet connection speed, this can take a few minutes to download. Once the download is complete, go to the next section.

Install PostgreSQL And pgAdmin

1. Right-click on the postgresql.exe file that you just downloaded and select **RUN AS ADMINISTRATOR**.

2. On the screen shown in Figure 1-2, click Next.

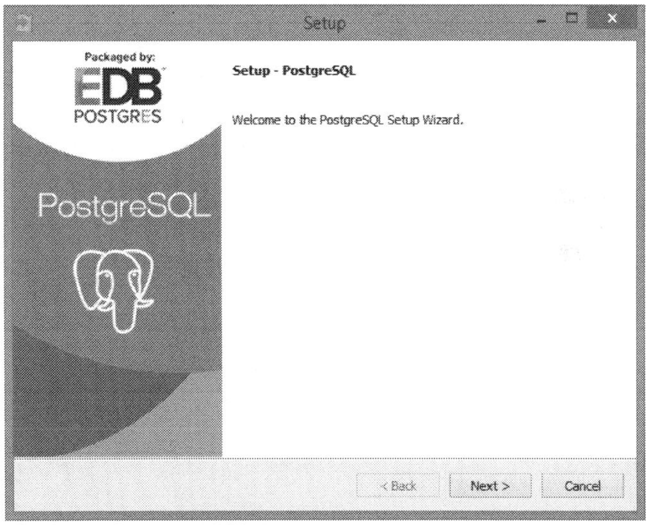

Figure 1-2 PostgreSQL Setup screen

3. On the screen shown in Figure 1-3, you can accept the default option shown, unless you have a really good reason not to ⇒ Click Next.

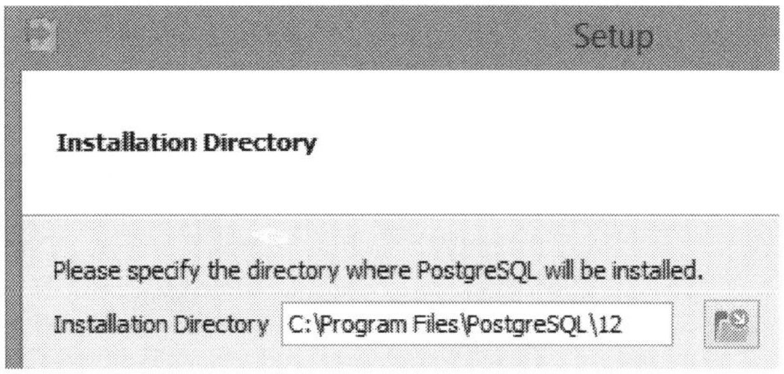

Figure 1-3 Installation Directory options

4. On the screen shown in Figure 1-4, make sure that the first two options are checked.

   For the purposes of this book, Stack Builder and the Command Line Tools components do not have to be installed ⇒ Click Next.

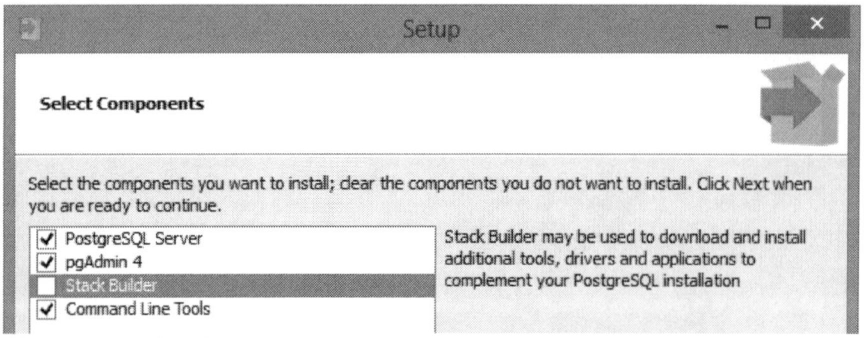

Figure 1-4 Select Components options

5. The path in the **DATA DIRECTORY** is the default location where the data will be stored.

   You can accept the default or click the folder icon button at the end of the field, shown in Figure 1-5 and select a different folder.

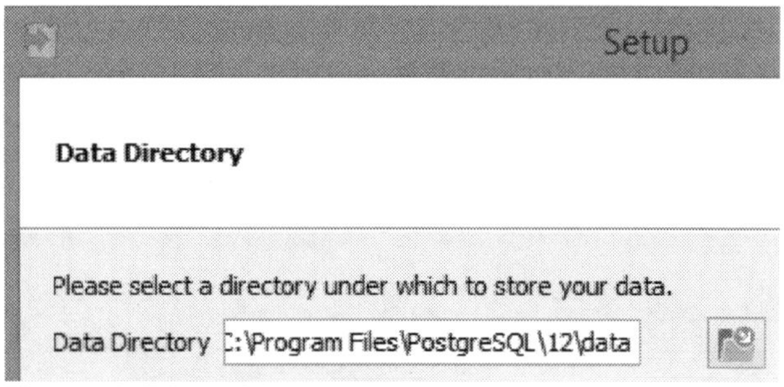

Figure 1-5 Data Directory option

6. The password created on the screen shown in Figure 1-6 is for the postgres supervisor account (aka the login account that has rights to everything). Type in the same password in both fields ⇒ Click Next.

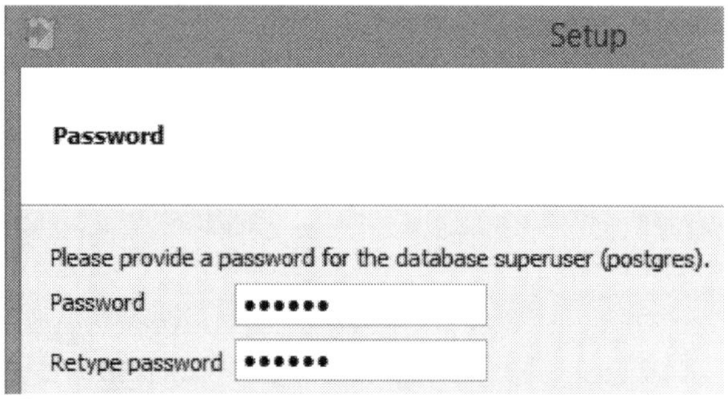

Figure 1-6 Password option

7. The default port 5432, shown in Figure 1-7, is the port number that the PostgreSQL server will listen to and communicate with. Unless you have another software package that is using this port, accept it as the default.

   If you see a different number like 5433, it means that port 5432 is already in use on your computer ⇒ Click Next.

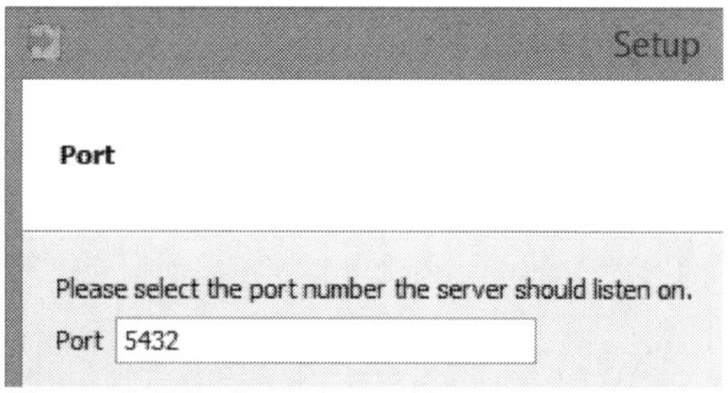

Figure 1-7 Port number option

8. Select your locale. The [Default locale] option shown in Figure 1-8, means to use the same locale that Windows is using. Accept this option ⇒ Click Next.

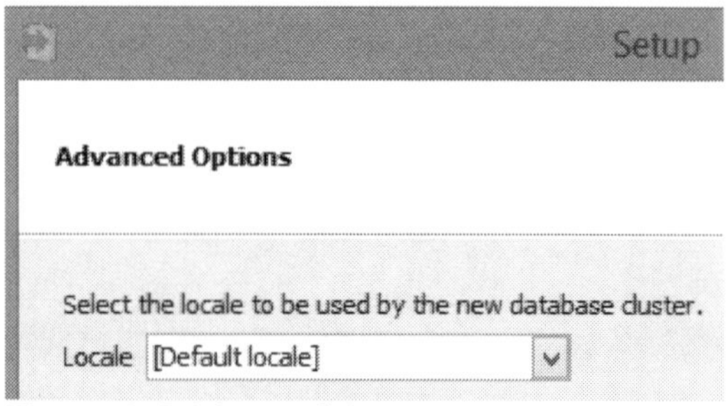

Figure 1-8 Advanced Options

9. The screen shown in Figure 1-9 displays the options that you have selected to be installed.

   If you need to change something, click the Back button, otherwise, click Next.

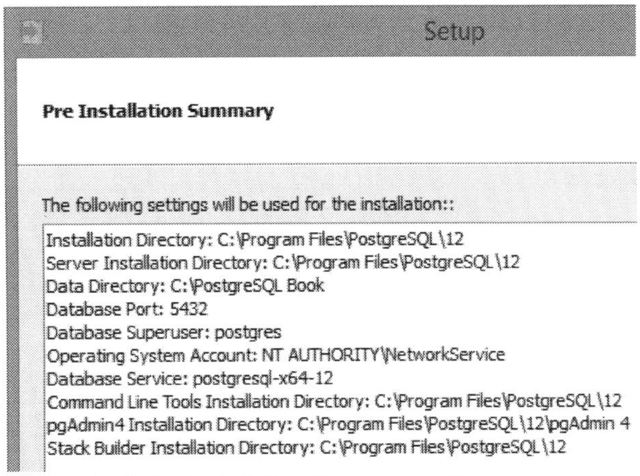

Figure 1-9 Pre-Installation Summary options

10. On the screen shown in Figure 1-10, click Next to start the installation. You will see the screen shown in Figure 1-11. The installation may take a few minutes.

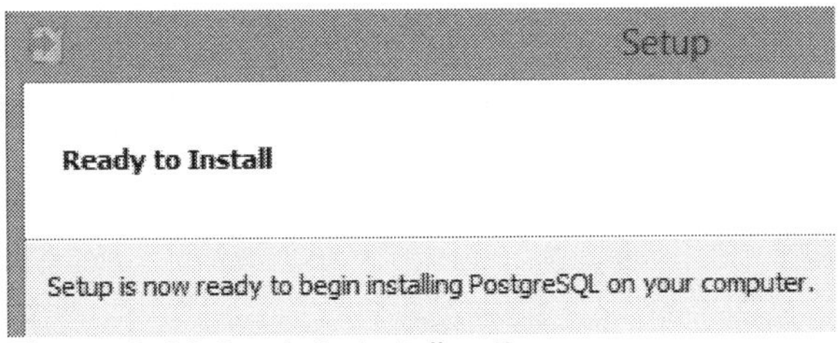

Figure 1-10 Ready to install options

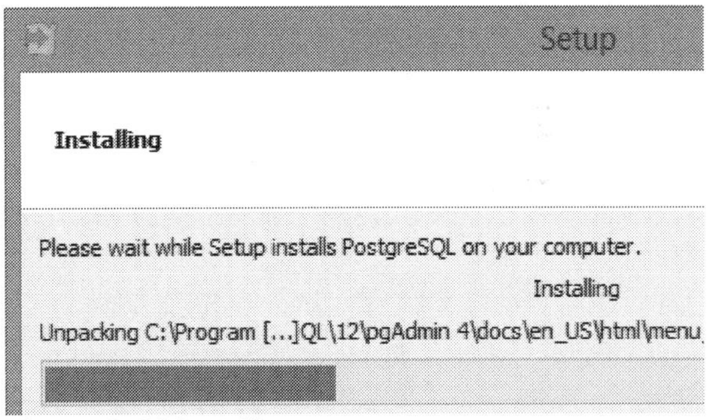

Figure 1-11 Installing screen

11. If you installed Stack Builder, your finish screen will look like the one shown in Figure 1-12.

    For now, you can clear the check mark.

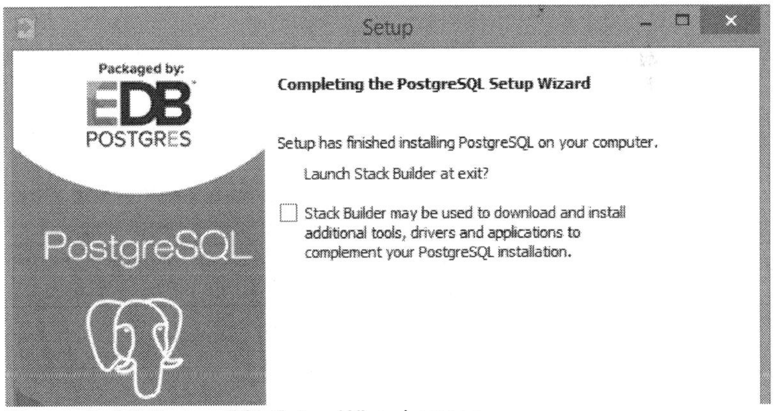

Figure 1-12 PostgreSQL Setup Wizard screen

12. Click Finish.

13. To confirm that your installation is complete, you should see the tiles shown in Figure 1-13 on the Start menu.

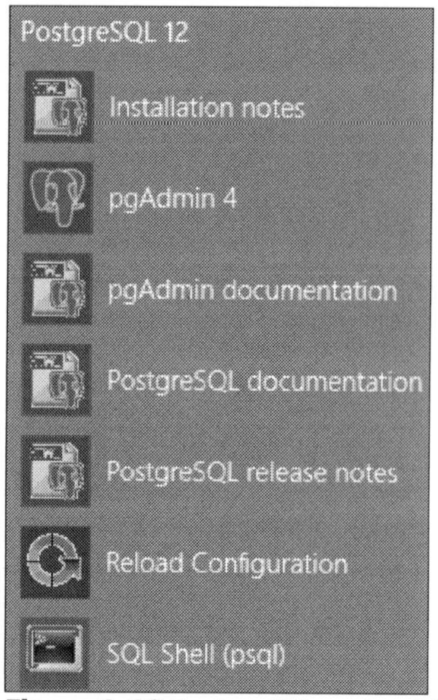

Figure 1-13 PostgreSQL and pgAdmin tiles

Create A Shortcut Icon On Your Desktop For pgAdmin

If you are not using the Windows tiled interface that automatically displays tiles for each software package that is installed on your computer, you may want to create a shortcut icon on your desktop, to be able to easily access pgAdmin. While doing this is optional, for completing the exercises in this book, if will make life a little easier to open pgAdmin.

The path to the pgAdmin executable file is listed below. The path is based on accepting the default installation options and is based on having Windows 8.1 installed. If you do not see the file in the path shown, search your computers hard drive, for the .exe file. The path where it is installed on your computer was also shown earlier in Figure 1-3. If a newer version is available, the numbers in the path will be higher.

Path to pgAdmin C:\Program Files\PostgreSQL\12\pgAdmin 4\bin\pgAdmin4.exe

To create the shortcut, follow the steps below.

1. Navigate to and click on the PostgreSQL folder, shown in the path above.

2. Scroll down the list on the right side of Windows Explorer and right-click on the pgAdmin4.exe file ⇒ **CREATE SHORTCUT** ⇒ Click Yes, when prompted to place the shortcut on the desktop.

Once you create the shortcut icon, you may want to change it to run in administrator mode by default, as some features in pgAdmin require this. To do this, after you create the shortcut icon on your desktop, right-click on the shortcut icon ⇒ Properties ⇒ Shortcut tab ⇒ Advanced button ⇒ Select **RUN AS ADMINISTRATOR** ⇒ Click Apply ⇒ Click OK.

Database Concepts And Terminology

A key component of mastering SQL to create queries, is having an above average understanding of the data that you will use to create queries. This section provides a high level overview of what a database is and what its components are.

Before you start using any software to create queries, there are some database concepts and terminology that you need to understand. While most people use different databases throughout their daily lives and probably are not aware of it (smart phones have a database), as someone that is about to learn SQL, you need to know more than the average person. Below are some terms that you should understand, in order to work with SQL efficiently and effectively.

Database A database is a collection of information (data) that is stored in one or more tables. A database is a container, if you will, to store tables, views, stored procedures and other objects. In many relational database environments, in addition to the databases that store the data that you use to create queries, several system databases are automatically created, when the server software is installed.

Way back in the day, when I was in programming school, the analogy that was used, was to think of a database as a file cabinet, because both are a way to **PHYSICALLY** store data in an organized way. Data is stored in tables in a database. The file cabinet is a physical location that is used to store data. In a file cabinet, it does not matter as much how the data is organized or what the data is. Alphabetically or numerically is nice, but it is not a requirement. Unlike a file cabinet, a database stores data in an organized manner.

Table A table is stored in a database and is a collection of records. Most databases have more than one table. One way to think of a table is that it is the equivalent of a file folder that goes in a file cabinet. In a file folder, all of the paper in it is usually related. In a database, each table is the equivalent of a file folder.

Just like you give each file folder its own unique name, each table in a database, has to have its own unique name. While the table name must be unique in the database, another database can have a table with the same name. Tables may remind you of a spreadsheet, because tables also have rows and columns. Each table is a structured file that stores information about a specific topic. For example, a well designed customers table would only contain information about customers. The customers table would not contain information about products. Tables need to be organized in a way that they do not contain duplicate fields of data.

Record A record has one or more fields. Each of the fields in a record are related. A record looks like a row of data in a spreadsheet. For example, each record in a customers table only contains information for one customer. Records are stored in a table. The SQL standard name for a record is "row".

Field A field contains one piece of information and is stored in a record. Examples of fields include customer name and order amount. By design, each field stores a unique piece of data. For example, the customer name field should not store the order amount. Storing each piece of information (the data) in its own field allows the data to be sorted, filtered and grouped on properly. The SQL standard name for a field is "column".

This is just one of a long list of reasons why programmers do not like to work with data that is stored in a spreadsheet. It is too free form. The customer name and order amount can be entered in the same column, in a spreadsheet, but those fields cannot be in the same column in a table. Each column in a table has a data type. Data types are covered in Chapter 3.

The data type selected, depends on the data that will be stored in the field. A field that will store a customers name would have a string (text) data type. A field that stores an order amount would have a numeric (currency/money) data type. Data types restrict the type of data that can be entered in the field. For example, a field that has a numeric data type, cannot store a date. The exception is the string data type. It allows almost any type of data that you can think of.

Think of a database this way. A database is the equivalent of an Excel file. A table is the equivalent of a sheet (a tab) in an Excel file, with each sheet representing one type of data (customers, products, etc.). A field in a table is the equivalent to a column on a sheet. A record is the equivalent to a row on a sheet. While there is a limit of rows and columns on a sheet in Excel, in a database, there is virtually no limit to the number of rows and columns that a table can have. The limit is usually based on the amount of space that is available on the server, that the database is on.

While SQL has standard names that are used to reference parts of a database, I, like many other people that have developed applications on a variety of platforms, use the names interchangeably.

Why Store Data In Multiple Tables?

Yes, I think I know what you are thinking. "Why save data in multiple tables and then have to create links to join the tables in a query?" As you will see, there are several reasons and advantages for doing this.

The first reason is that the concept and objective of a relational database is to avoid duplication of data. If the same data is stored in more than one table, when that data needs to be modified, it would have to be modified in each table, that it is stored in. Besides being a lot of work, it opens the door for a lot of data errors and incorrect data being in a table that wasn't updated. Then the question becomes, which table has the correct data or the most recent data. Relational databases prevent this, by only storing the same data in one table.

Data that needs to be used frequently with other data, needs to be stored separately. This data is often referred to as "lookup data" or "lookup tables".

When the same data is not stored in multiple tables, there is less data to store. This means that the cost of storing data is less. And with the ever increasing amount of data that is being captured and stored currently, that is a good thing for a companies bottom line. <smile>

Storing data in multiple tables, allows the data to be read from and written to tables faster. The rest of this chapter, covers relational databases and relationships in more detail, because understanding these concepts is needed to be able to use the tables in a database correctly.

What Is A Schema?

In PostgreSQL, a schema is a name space that stores named database objects, like data types, tables, functions, views and more. While a database can have multiple schemas, each schema only belongs to one database. Two schemas can have different objects that have the same name.

Databases and tables have properties that are stored in the schema, like the relationships between tables. Tables have properties that describe what data can be stored, the column name, the data type for each column. Collectively, this information is known as a **SCHEMA**.

There are several reasons why you would want to use schemas. The most useful reason to use schemas is because they can be used to organize the objects (tables and views for example) into groups, which makes them easier to manage.

By default, PostgreSQL creates a schema named **PUBLIC**, for each database that is created. This schema will automatically be applied to new objects that are created, when a schema is not specified. Using schemas is optional. If you create objects without using a schema name, the object is automatically added to the public schema.
The **CREATE SCHEMA STATEMENT** is used to create a new schema. The code CREATE SCHEMA orders; creates a schema named orders.

For example, the orders schema can have a table named customers and the suppliers schema can have a table named customers. To reference an object in a schema, you have to include the schema name, as shown below.

orders.customers or suppliers.customers.

Another reason to use schemas is because they can be used to control the objects that each person that uses the database can have access to.

Schemas can also be created for other objects in the database, like stored procedures. In addition to being able to control permissions at the schema level, schemas can be used to categorize or group objects like tables or views. There is no limit to the number of schemas that a database can have. You can create names to match the tables that you want grouped together. My advice is to not make the schema names very long, because you will have to type them in, in the queries that you create.

When you create queries, it is recommended to include the schema for the table or object in the code. The exception (isn't there always an exception) <smile>, is objects that use the public schema. That is because this is the default schema for all PostgreSQL databases and does not need to be referenced in the code, if there are no other schemas in the database.

What may not be obvious is that you can reference objects in other databases, in a query, by adding the database name as a prefix, which is known as a three part object name.

What Is A Relationship?

A relationship is a connection between two tables. It is how two or more tables are joined (linked). Tables can be joined when they have at least one field in each table, that has the same value. Tables can have more than one relationship. For example, an Invoice table can be joined to a Products table because each invoice will have at least one item from the Products table. The Invoice table can also be linked to the Customers table, because each invoice has a customer. If not, run, don't walk. <smile>

In order to be able to use the tables in a database together, to create a query, there has to be a connection between the tables. The actual connection is called a **LINK**. The lines between the tables are the visual representation of the links that I am referring to. The result of a link between tables is called a **RELATIONSHIP**. The ability to create relationships to join tables and use the data from multiple tables to create a query is probably one of the top reasons that the relational databases exist.

Relationships are created between a column of data that two tables have in common. Relationships between tables allow for a higher level of analysis, because columns of data from different tables can be used together. Data in one table can be filtered by data in another table, which provides even more flexibility and control over the data that is retrieved from a query or displayed on a report. The types of relationships that are available, are covered later in this chapter.

Relational Databases

A relational database is a collection of **RELATED** information that is stored in two or more tables in the database. Relational databases are also known as a **RELATIONAL DATABASE MANAGEMENT SYSTEM**, or RDBMS for short.

What makes for a well designed relational database is that it contains tables that have fields of data that are stored in records. All of which, allows the tables to be used independently or they can be linked (joined) together when needed, to retrieve data from two or more tables, at the same time.

The reason that tables can have relationships created between them is because there is at least one column in each table, that has the same related data, thus the term "Relational Databases". Yes, this is a complicated topic and there are a lot of books on the concepts associated with relational databases and how to create them, so I won't bore you with all of the details, but please hear me out and don't skip this section. Creating relationships is a concept that is necessary to understand. Creating relationships in a data model and creating relationships in a database is the same concept and process.

While databases are not the primary focus of this chapter, it is important that you understand a little more than the fundamentals. My goal is to explain, as painless as possible, how all of the components fit together. <smile>
The reason that you need to understand this database concept is because it is a key component of being able to create more than a basic query. If you have never created a database, or have very little experience creating them, the next few sections in this chapter will be your crash course in databases and relationships. Figures 1-14 and 1-15 illustrate the layout of two tables, in a database.

Orders			
Order ID	Order Date	Order Amount	Cust ID
1000	1/2/2015	$263.99	48
1001	1/2/2015	$322.45	57
1002	1/3/2015	$196.00	3
1003	1/4/2015	$124.99	48

Table Name
Field Names
Records

Figure 1-14 Orders table

Order Details		
Order ID	Product ID	Quantity
1000	43	4
1000	76	2
1001	76	3
1001	10	2
1003	10	1
1004	25	3

Table Name
Field Names
Records

Figure 1-15 Order Details table

Primary Keys

A primary key is a unique identifier for each row of data in the table. Primary keys are usually numeric and system generated, sequentially. Think invoice numbers. They are used to create relationships (links) between tables. "Primary key fields" and "ID fields" are terms that are used interchangeably. I prefer to use the term ID field, because primary key fields in databases often have "ID" as part of the field name. Recently though, I have seen the word "Key" at the end of a field name to signify that the field is a primary key field.

ID is short for identification. It is jargon that the computer programming community has used for decades, to know whether or not a field was created to be used to link one table to another table.

Primary key fields or the field used to reference the row, is usually the first column in a table.

The tables in the database that is used in this book, have at least one ID field. Hopefully, you will find that this is also true out in the real world. The reason that ID fields are used, is because by design, they provide a way for each record in the table to have a unique way to be identified. The primary key field cannot have NULL values. I have not seen it used often, but a primary key can be the combination of the data that is stored in two or more fields.

In addition to not being able to link (join) tables, without a key field in each table, updating or deleting specific rows, is way past difficult because there is no way to ensure that the query is selecting the correct rows to update or delete.

Foreign Keys

A foreign key is a column in a table that contains the primary key values from another table. It is used to point back to a primary key in a related table. A foreign key has to be the same or compatible data type as the primary key that it will be used to join tables on. This key is used to define the relationship between tables. An example of a foreign key is the Cust ID field, that is stored in the Orders table, shown earlier in Figure 1-14. The Cust ID field in Figure 1-14, is the primary field in the Customers table. It is used to create a relationship with the Orders table. If data in the Customers table is updated, like the customers address changes, data in the related tables does not change.

Relationships

I have taught several database classes and almost without fail, this topic causes a lot of confusion. For some reason, people want to create relationships using string (text) fields. Please don't do that. It can cause you problems and should be avoided. It is also a bad table design choice. However, if you have a dataset that uses text fields as primary key fields, creating relationships for tables using text fields is acceptable, in particular, for data that is not imported from a database.

If you needed to create a report that displays all of the orders and what items were on each order, you would need a way to link the Orders and Order Details tables. Think of creating relationships as having the ability to combine two or more tables "virtually" and being able to display the result of this "virtual linking" on a report. The virtual relationship linking discussed in this chapter refers to the process of joining two tables based on data in a column, that the tables have in common.

In Figures 1-14 and 1-15 shown earlier, the common ID field is the Order ID field. If you look at the data in the Order Details table, you will see that some records have the same Order ID number. That's okay because the Order ID field in the Order Details table is a foreign key field. This means that some orders have more than one item. Each record in the Order Details table represents one item that was ordered. Virtually joined tables represent the concept of creating joins between tables, which is covered in Chapter 6. If you were to "virtually" join the two tables shown earlier, the **VIRTUAL TABLE** would look like the one shown in Figure 1-16.

This "virtual" join is what happens when tables are **LINKED** (have a relationship).

If all of this data was stored in one table instead of two, at the very minimum, all of the fields in the Orders table would be repeated for every record that is in the Order Details table.

Orders				Order Details		
Order ID	Order Date	Order Amount	Cust ID	Order ID	Product ID	Quantity
1000	01/02/2015	$263.99	48	1000	43	4
1000	01/02/2015	$263.99	48	1000	76	2
1001	01/02/2015	$322.45	57	1001	76	3
1001	01/02/2015	$322.45	57	1001	10	2
1002	01/03/2015	$196.00	3			
1003	01/04/2015	$124.99	48	1003	10	1
				1004	25	3

Figure 1-16 Virtually joined tables

Repetition of data is why this information is stored in two tables in a database, instead of one. In this example, an additional row would be added to the Orders table for each row in the Order Details table. It is poor table design to have the same information (other than fields that are used to join tables) stored in more than one table.

Usually if you see a record in the Order Details table, like Order ID 1004, shown above in Figure 1-16, or any **CHILD TABLE** that is in a **PARENT-CHILD RELATIONSHIP**, there is a problem (usually with referential integrity not being enabled, or enabled incorrectly) with the data, in at least one of the tables because all of the records in the child table should have at least one matching record in the parent table. Parent tables are used to get data from a **CHILD TABLE**, also known as a **LOOKUP TABLE**. In this scenario, the record for Order ID 1004, in the Order Details table, would not be returned or shown on a report, depending on the join type used to create the parent-child relationship.

In addition to using primary key fields to create a relationship between tables, they are needed to update or delete a specific record in a table.

Types Of Relationships

Relationships are created using the primary and foreign keys discussed earlier in this chapter. Not all tables in a database can be linked to another table. To link tables, they must meet the criteria of one of the following three relationship types discussed below.

One-To-One Relationship

This type of relationship requires that each row in one table only have one matching row in the table that it will be joined to. The relationship is created by using the primary key (in the primary or parent table) and the foreign key (in the secondary or child table) to link the two tables. Most of the time, the foreign key in the child table doubles as the primary key for the table.

An example is the Employee and Employee Addresses tables shown in Figures 1-17 and 1-18.

Each employee, only has one matching row in the address table.

Employee

Employee ID	Supervisor ID	Last Name	First Name	Position
1	5	Davolio	Nancy	Sales Representative
2		Fuller	Andrew	Vice President, Sales
3	5	Leverling	Janet	Sales Representative
4	5	Peacock	Margaret	Sales Representative
5	2	Buchanan	Steven	Sales Manager
6	5	Suyama	Michael	Sales Representative

Figure 1-17 Employee table

Employee Addresses

Employee ID	Address1	Address2	City	Region	Country	Postal Code
1	507 - 20th Ave. E.		Port Moody	BC	Canada	V3D 4F6
2	908 W. Capital Way	Suite 100	Coquitlam	BC	Canada	V3H4J7
3	722 Moss Bay Blvd.		Vancouver	BC	Canada	V6M 8S9
4	4110 Old Redmond Rd.		Richmond	BC	Canada	V5S 6H7
5	14 Garrett Hill		London		UK	SW1 8JR
6	Coventry House		London		UK	EC2 7JR

Figure 1-18 Employee Addresses table

One-To-Many Relationship

In this type of relationship, each row in the primary table can have many matching rows in the child table. Each row in the child table can only have one matching row in the primary table. The primary key in the "one" table is used to create the link to all of the records in the "many" table, that have the same value in the foreign key field.

In Figure 1-16 shown earlier, the Orders table is the "one" table and the Order Details table is the "many" table. Each row in the Orders table has one or more matching rows in the Order Details table. That is because each order can have multiple items that were purchased. And each row in the Order Details table, only has one matching row in the Orders table. This is the most popular relationship type. It is often referred to as a **PARENT-CHILD RELATIONSHIP**.

Many-To-Many Relationship

This type of relationship can be created when each row in the primary table has many matching rows in the child table and each row in the child table has many matching rows in the primary table. This is the least used relationship type. And some databases do not support it.

An example of this type of relationship would be the Customers and Sales Reps tables. Each customer could have placed orders with different sales reps and each sales rep could have taken orders from different customers. The problem with these two tables is that they do not have a common field to link on.

The solution is to join the Customers and Sales Reps tables to a third (**INTERMEDIATE**) table that has a primary key field that each of these tables have. In the database used in this book, the third table is the Orders table because it has a relationship with the other tables (a foreign key for the Customers table and a foreign key for the Sales Reps table), as illustrated in Figure 1-19.

CustomerID	CompanyName	FirstName	LastName
1	City Cyclists	Chris	Christianson
2	Pathfinders	Christine	Manley
3	Bike-A-Holics Anonymous	Gary	Jannis
4	Psycho-Cycle	Alexander	Mast
5	Sporting Wheels Inc.	Patrick	Reyess

OrderID	OrderAmount	CustomerID	SalesRepID	OrderDate
88	$2,939.85	1	1	01/26/2016
107	$659.70	1	4	01/30/2016
130	$931.05	1	1	02/02/2016
135	$27.00	1	1	02/04/2016

SalesRepID	SupervisorID	FirstName	Middle	LastName
1	5	Nancy	A	Davolio
2		Andrew		Fuller
3	5	Janet	E	Leverling
4	5	Margaret	I	Peacock
5	2	Steven		Buchanan

Figure 1-19 Third table needed to link the Customers and Sales Reps tables

The Customers table (at the top of the figure) uses the Customer ID field to link to the Orders table. The Sales Reps table (at the bottom of the figure) uses the Sales Rep ID field to link to the Orders table. Now, you can retrieve any related sales reps for one customer or return all of the customers for a specific sales rep.

Understanding relationships and the rows that each type of relationship will retrieve, is critical to being able to select the correct join type when you need to use more than one table in a query. Chapters 6 and 7 cover using more than one table in a query.

How Relationships Work

Hopefully, you are still with me. Don't worry, the relationship and relational database "lecturette" is almost over. More than likely, the requirements for most queries that you will need to create, will require data from more than one table. For example, reports that display the equivalent of a Product List report will probably only use one table, so there is no linking required. If the Product List report, also needed a count of how many of each product were sold, data from two or more tables would be needed and those tables need to be linked, by creating a relationship between them.

When creating queries, any relationship that is needed, is created using code, instead of using a graphical interface. Even though you cannot see the relationships, like they are shown in Chapter 2, Figure 2-52, when creating a query, it is important to understand what is going on behind the scenes, as they say. The best way to understand the basic concept of creating relationships between tables, especially if you are not familiar with the data, is to take the time to view at least some of the data in the two tables that need to have a relationship created.

Depending on the table structure, tables can have more than one field that they can be linked on. One example was illustrated earlier in Figure 1-19. Another example of this would be the Order Details table. This table has an ID field that would be used to link it to the Orders table. There is also a Product ID field in the Order Details table, that would be used to retrieve the Product Name from another table (the Products table) to display on the report, in addition to displaying the Product ID number. Displaying the product name is more meaningful then only displaying the Product ID field, which contains a number. If you are asking why the Product Name is not stored in the Order Details table, there are three reasons that I can think of, as explained below.

① The ID field takes up less space then the Product Name field, thereby keeping the size of the Order Details table (and any other table that would store the Product Name field instead of the Product ID field) smaller.

② If a product name has to be changed for any reason, it only has to be changed once, in the Products table. Every report that the Product Name field is displayed on, would automatically be updated with the revised product name, the next time the data for the report is refreshed. If the product name was stored in the Order Details table, every record in the Order Details table that had that product name field would have to be changed, as well as, any other table that stored the product name. That would be a lot of extra work (possibly for you) and increase the chance for having inaccurate data, because you may not know about all of the tables that were storing the product name.

③ Without a Products table, there would be no place to add new products and all of the data about each product.

> Keep in mind that if the relationships are incorrect, the data displayed on visualizations or retrieved from a query, that are created from tables that have an incorrect relationship, will not display the correct data or may not display any data.

Relational data is stored efficiently and is easier to use. And more important, relational databases are more **SCALABLE**, then non relational databases. Scalable databases can handle all of a workload and more records without failing. The relationship and relational data lecturette is now over. Hopefully, you found this lecturette helpful. <smile>

Summary

In this chapter, you learned about PostgreSQL and pgAdmin. These tools were explained to provide an overview of the options and more importantly, to let you know that some free things are actually worth while. <smile> Hopefully, your installation of PostgreSQL and pgAdmin went smoothly.

As you will see throughout the rest of this book, there is a need to understand how relationships, relational databases and key fields (primary and foreign) are a big part of being able to create queries. It is to your advantage to learn as much as you can about these topics, because in addition to being familiar with the data that you will use, these topics are the foundation of being able to create queries. While there are a lot of queries that can be created only using one table, the bulk of queries that you will need to create, will require two or more tables.

The reason is because the majority of commercially used databases, and many free ones also, are relational, including databases used on the web and in the cloud. Relational databases have been around for decades and will not be replaced any time soon, if ever. While as a programmer or business user that needs to create queries, you may not have to create the database and populate it with data. In my opinion, the more that you know about databases, the easier it will be for you to create queries and reports, for that matter.

As I mentioned earlier in this chapter, there are several relational database management systems on the market today, that each use their own flavor, if you will, of SQL. Once you learn one relatively well, the next one will be much easier to learn. As companies grow, database needs change. For example, a company that uses Microsoft Access today, which also supports SQL, may find that their Access databases no longer handle the amount of data that needs to be stored and the company decides to move to PostgreSQL.

The relational database and SQL skills that you learn using PostgreSQL can be transferred to SQL Server, thus reducing the learning curve. What you will need to learn are the differences between the flavors of SQL. In other words, the "brand" of relational database may change or go away, but SQL is here to stay!

By the time that you finish reading this book and completing the hands on exercises, you should have enough knowledge to start creating queries, using your own data.

While this book takes you by the hand and explains the concepts, syntax and functions needed to create a variety of queries, I can tell you from decades of experience, that the first few queries that you create on your own, using your own data can be nerve wracking and stressful. I am not saying this to scare you, just the opposite. I want you to know that is normal. Learn as much as you can from this book.

If you know or have an idea of queries that you will need to create on your own, take a few minutes now, to write them down. You can write them in the form of a question or any format that works for you. Keep this list out, as you are reading this book and creating the queries. If you see a query that is exactly what you need or is close to what you need, write down the page number next to the query on your list. Not only will doing this give you a head start, but it will also help you see which SQL keywords, functions and topics that you need to learn the most about.

What I know for sure, is that to become proficient in SQL or anything else in life for that matter, it takes practice, practice and more practice. That is exactly why I include so many query examples and exercises in this book.

Another thing that I know for sure, is that the more you know, the more you are $worth$. In this overly competitive job market, the more the skills that you bring to the table, helps distinguish you from your co-workers or other people that are applying for the same position that you are. It would not be me, if I did not encourage you to also learn at least one other version of SQL and at least two report writing tools. And the good thing is that the most popular SQL databases have a FREE version! What is required are some books, a computer and your time. And I have discovered, that a spirited beverage and really good, just cooked onion rings, allows me to work (aka learn) into the wee hours of the night. <smile>

PostgreSQL vs MySQL

When selecting a relational database management system, usually two or more systems are compared and contrasted. While PostgreSQL has more advanced features then MySQL, MySQL is known for its ease of use and speed. Both are open source and can compete with SQL Server and Oracle's enterprise solution. Table 1-1 is a brief overview of features that will help decide which is best for your current database needs.

Feature	PostgreSQL	MySQL
The software was developed in	C	C and C++
Storage engine	A single storage engine	Multiple storage engines, InnoDB and MYISAM
Free tool included to manage databases and create queries. (1)	Yes, pgAdmin	Yes, MySQL Workbench
Data types	SQL Standard and advanced, like user defined and hstore.	SQL Standard
Boolean data type	Yes	Yes
Unsigned integers supported	No	Yes
Full Outer Join supported	Yes	No
Auto Increment column functionality	Yes	Yes
EXCEPT and INTERSECT operators	Yes	No
Full text search	Yes	Yes
Stored procedure programming languages	SQL, Python, Perl, Java Script and more	SQL
Supported by most shared hosting companies	No	Yes
Triggers	Yes	Limited
Common Table Expressions (CTE)	Yes	Yes
Analytic functions	Yes	No

Table 1-1 PostgreSQL vs MySQL feature comparison

(1) By default, PostgreSQL's pgAdmin software is web based. There is a "Desktop mode", but it cannot be installed as a stand alone software package, like MySQL Workbench can. To enable pgAdmin's desktop mode, a configuration file has to be modified.

USING pgAdmin

After reading this chapter and completing the exercises you will:

- ☑ Know how to create a database and restore a database
- ☑ Know about the features and options in pgAdmin that are used to create queries
- ☑ Be able to view data in a table
- ☑ Know about the customization options that are available for pgAdmin
- ☑ Create a basic query

CHAPTER 2

Getting Started With pgAdmin

In Chapter 1, you installed the pgAdmin software. This chapter will introduce the pgAdmin workspace. pgAdmin is a tool that many people use to work with PostgreSQL databases. I know that you are ready to create queries. In order to do that, you need to learn about the software that you will use to create the queries. You also need to learn how to restore a database, so that you can access the data that is used in this book.

Even though you installed PostgreSQL and pgAdmin on your computer, this is still a **CLIENT-SERVER MODEL**. pgAdmin is the **CLIENT SOFTWARE** that is used to connect to the PostgreSQL server, which is the **SERVER SOFTWARE**, in the client-server model. The "server" portion is software that manages access to the data and how it is manipulated. This software is installed on a computer that functions as a database server. Fortunately, most home computers have the speed and capacity to be a database server, for learning purposes. pgAdmin is the tool that is used to create queries using data in a PostgreSQL server database. Like PostgreSQL, pgAdmin is reliable and efficient.

At some point, you may have the need to learn more about pgAdmin, then what is covered in this chapter. If that is the case, you will be happy to know that this software has it's own web site. [See www.pgadmin.org]

Exercise 2.1: Connect To The PostgreSQL Server Using pgAdmin

The steps below will show you how to connect to the PostgreSQL server.

1. Open pgAdmin. The first time that you open the software, it will take a little longer, then expected. That is because the software is configuring some options.

2. When you see the dialog box shown in Figure 2-1, type in a password.

   For the purposes of this book, you can use the same password that you used during the installation ⇒ Click OK.

   You will see the window shown in Figure 2-2.

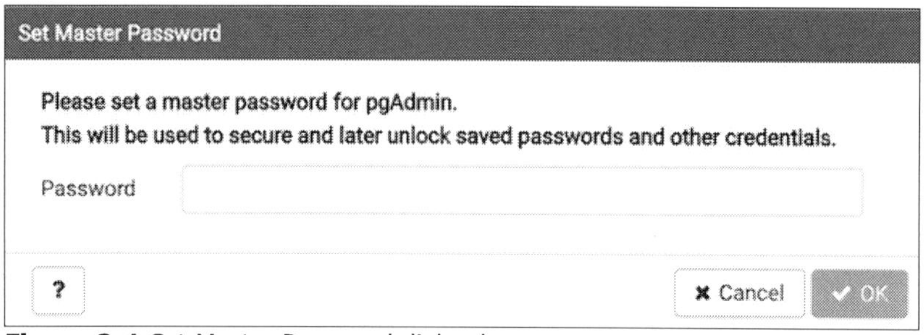

Figure 2-1 Set Master Password dialog box

Quick Tour Of pgAdmin

The reason that I call it a quick tour is because to create queries, you will not use the majority of options that the software has. The goal of this tour is to get you acquainted with the options that you will use to create and edit queries.

pgAdmin Home Page

The pgAdmin home page window has two panels: The Browser Tree Control and Tabbed Browser. The three numbered sections in Figure 2-2, are explained below.

Section 1: Browser Tree Control

The panel on the left is the **BROWSER TREE CONTROL**, but most people call it the Browser panel or Browser pane. It displays a list of available servers, databases, tables, users and other objects.

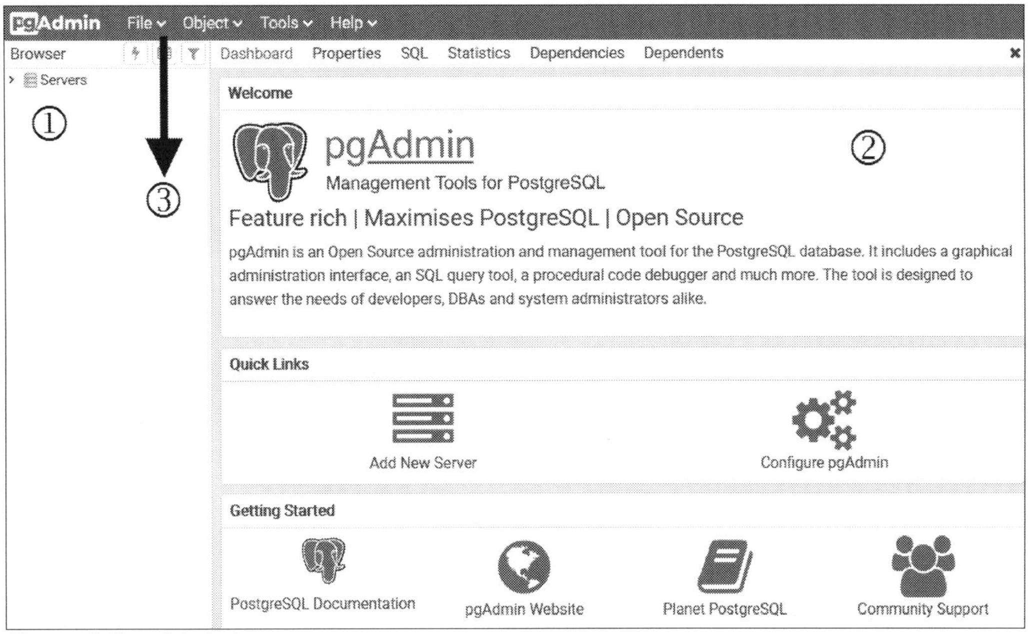

Figure 2-2 pgAdmin home page

1. To expand the Browser panel, click the greater than symbol (>), that is to the left of the Servers node.

   If prompted for a server password, type it in and check the Save Password option, shown in Figure 2-3.

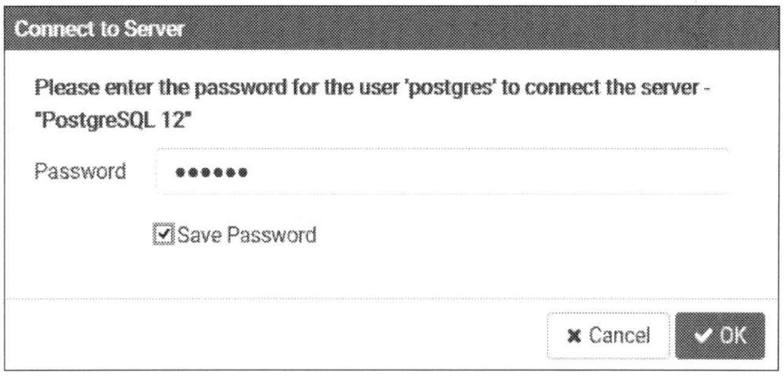

Figure 2-3 Connect to Server password dialog box

2. Expanding a few more nodes, will display the options shown in Figure 2-4.

   Depending on your operating system, you will either see **LOCALHOST** or PostgreSQL X, where X is the version of PostgreSQL that you have installed. This is your default server.

   As you can see, PostgreSQL has a lot of objects. More than most other relational databases. And to think, what you see in the figure is before installing any add-ons. <smile>

   The objects shown in the figure define all of the features of your database server and the **DEFAULT DATABASE NAMED POSTGRES**.

   Notice the following:

   ☑ Next to the **TABLES FOLDER**, is the number of tables in the database.
   ☑ Next to the **COLUMNS FOLDER** for a table, is the number of columns (fields) in the table.

   Yes, it's a lot. The good thing is that, the Tables folder is the object that you will use the most, in a database.

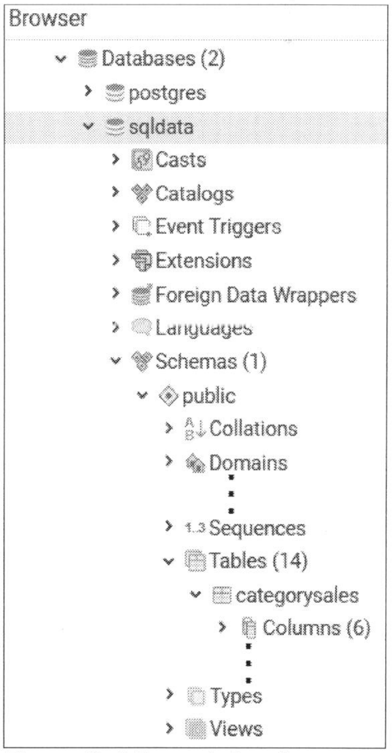

Figure 2-4 Expanded nodes

In addition to the Tables folder, it would be helpful if you are familiar with the following objects/folders.

- ☑ The **DATABASES OBJECT** can store many individual databases.
- ☑ The **EXTENSIONS OBJECT** is used to store data types, tables, variables, functions and more, that are used to create what is known as a **PACKAGE**. Extensions that you install are also stored in this folder. If you are familiar with **ORACLE PACKAGES**, extensions in PostgreSQL are similar.
- ☑ The **SCHEMAS OBJECT** is part of the ANSI SQL standard. If your database only has a few tables, using the default **PUBLIC SCHEMA** is fine. If your database has hundreds or thousands of tables, you should create schemas for the different categories of tables, like finance, marketing or customer service, for example.
- ☑ The **VIEWS OBJECT** stores the views that have been created for the database. While views are usually read-only, PostgreSQL allows you to update the underlying data by updating the view. Views are covered in Chapter 12.

Section 2: Tabbed Browser

This section has links for adding a server and configuring pgAdmin, as shown earlier in Figure 2-2. The links in the Getting Started section open a new tab. They provide information about PostgreSQL.

The window shown in Figure 2-5 is displayed when an object is selected in the Browser Tree Control panel. The dashboard displays information about the selected object. This window is also used to create queries.

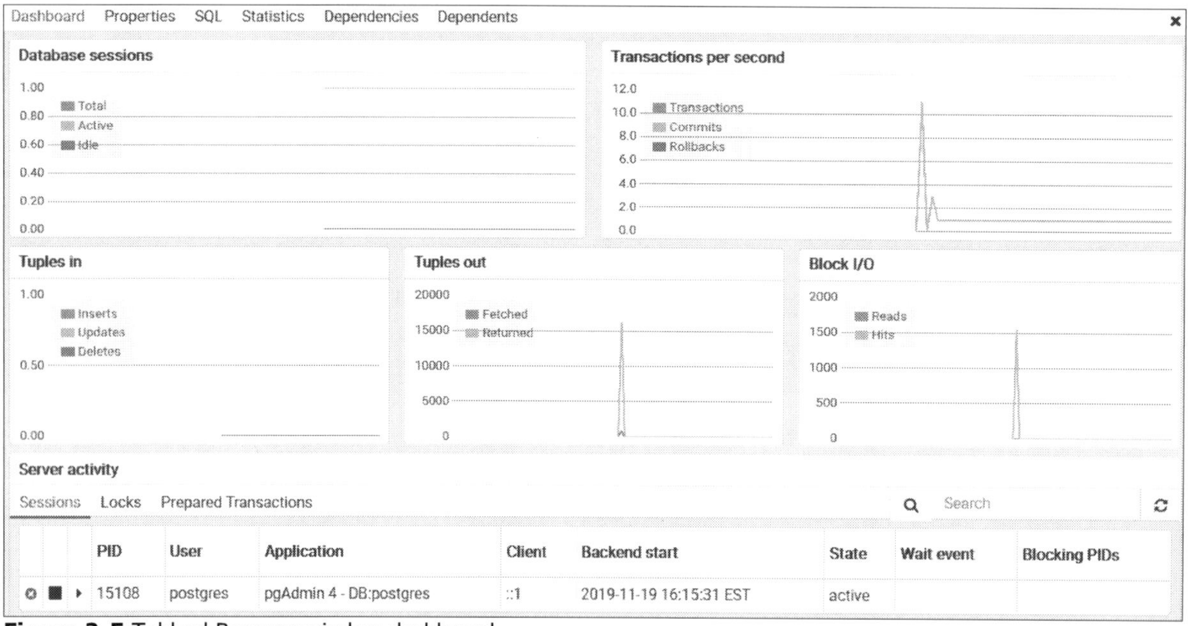

Figure 2-5 Tabbed Browser window dashboard

> The two panels (the Browser and Tabbed) can be resized horizontally, by placing the mouse pointer on the gray line that separates the panels and dragging the line left or right.

Section 3: Menu Bar

The menu bar (File, Object, Tools and Help) has drop-down menus that contain commands, utilities and other options.

File Menu

Figure 2-6 shows the options on the **FILE MENU**. The **PREFERENCES** option is used to customize pgAdmin. It is covered later in this chapter.

If you manage to mess up the layout of the Query Editor window, the **RESET LAYOUT** option will restore the layout. If you have not saved the changes to a query when this happens, save the query first, then select this option.

The **LOCK LAYOUT** option has the three options shown in the figure. The **FULL LOCK** option will keep you from messing up the default layout. The downside to selecting this option, is that if you need to resize a section of the Query Editor window, you can't. My advice is to use the **RESET LAYOUT** option, when needed.

Object Menu

Figure 2-7 shows the options on the **OBJECT MENU**. The options displayed, depend on the object that is selected. As shown on the left side of the figure, the Databases object is selected. Other options that are available are for changing passwords, connecting to a server and creating a schema.

Tools Menu

Figure 2-8 shows the options on the **TOOLS MENU**, when a database is selected. The option that you will use the most is the **QUERY TOOL** option. It displays the window shown later in Figure 2-10. This is where you create, run and debug queries. It is covered in more detail, later in this chapter.

The **IMPORT/EXPORT OPTION** is used to import (add) data into a table, from a CSV, text (.txt) or binary file and save (export) data to a CSV, text (.txt) or binary file.

While PostgreSQL supports the **COPY FUNCTION** to copy tables, there are times with it cannot handle some imports or exports. For example, if you are connected to a PostgreSQL instance that is not the one that the database and/or tables were created on, meaning not your computer, you may not be able to access your computers file system, from a different computer. This makes setting the path on the FROM or TO clause difficult. This is why I do not use the Copy function and do not cover or demonstrate how to use it in this book. Instead, I use the import/export option.

The **BACKUP OPTION** is used to create a backup copy of the database.

Help Menu

Figure 2-9 shows the options on the **HELP MENU**. The options are similar to the options in the Getting Started section of the Home page. [See Figure 2-2] They are used to access online help documents.

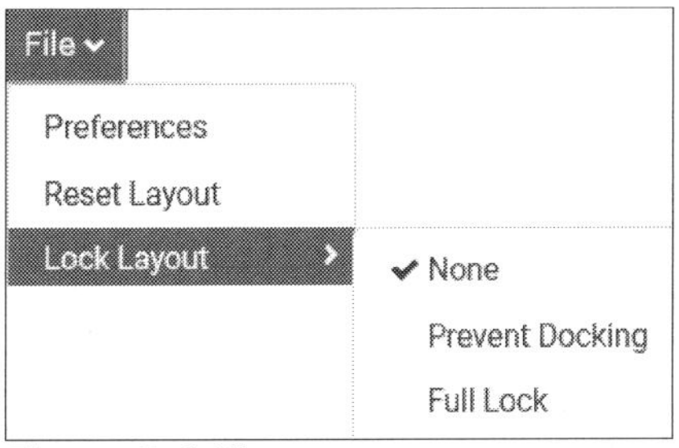

Figure 2-6 File menu

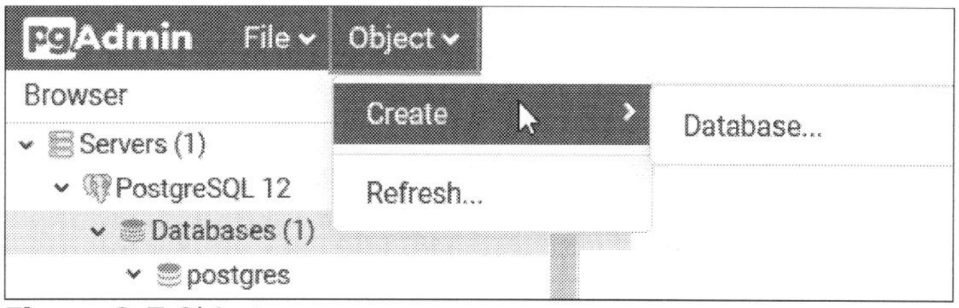

Figure 2-7 Object menu

Figure 2-8 Tools menu

Figure 2-9 Help menu

pgAdmin Workspace

Yes, pgAdmin has a lot of options, but fortunately, to create and run queries, you only need to use a few of the options. <smile> The most important one is discussed next.

Query Editor

As you may have figured out, this is where the query magic happens! <smile>

Figure 2-10 shows the Query Editor window. There are multiple ways to open the Query Editor, as listed below. A database has to be selected in the Browser Tree Control panel to enable these options.

① Tools ⇒ Query Tool, as shown above in Figure 2-8.
② Click the Query Tool button, illustrated in Figure 2-11.
③ In the Browser panel, right-click on a database, table or field in a table ⇒ Query Tool, as shown in Figure 2-12.

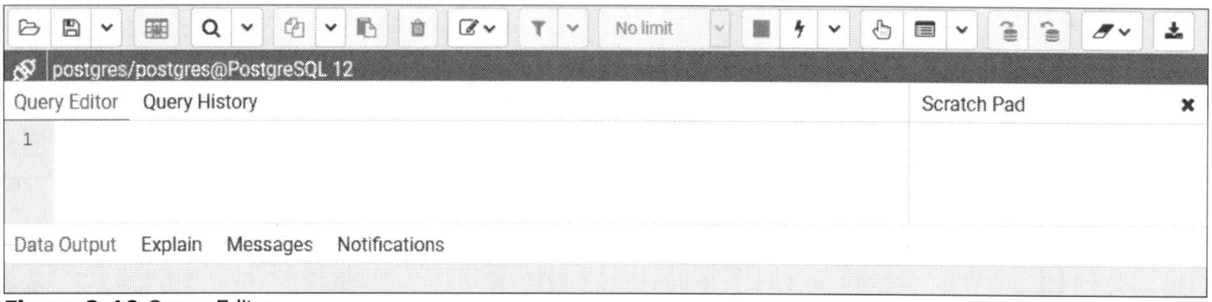

Figure 2-10 Query Editor

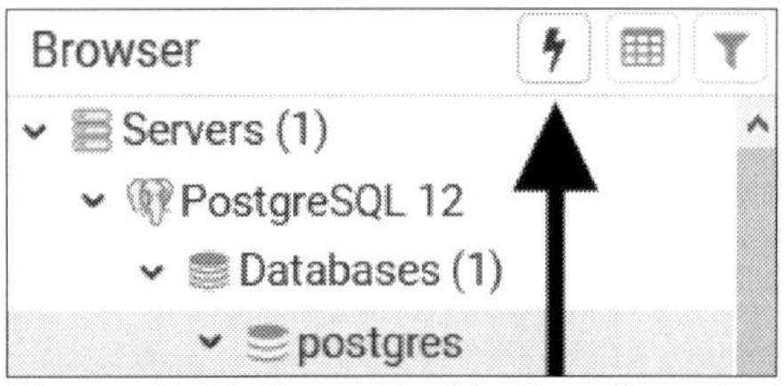

Figure 2-11 Query Tool button illustrated in the Browser panel

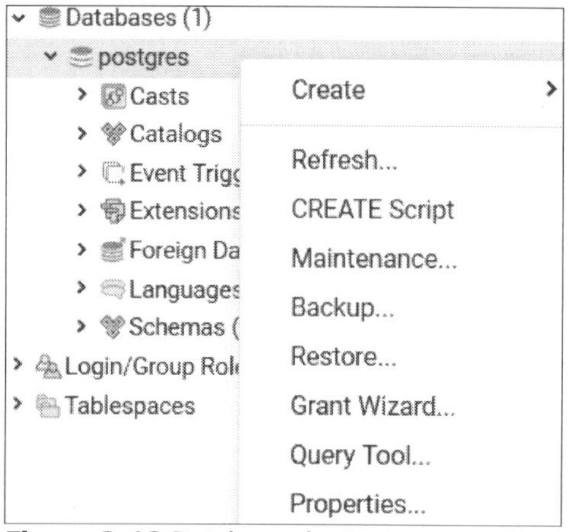

Figure 2-12 Database shortcut menu options

The Query Tool has two panels, and each panel has its own set of tabs, as explained below.

① The top panel is formally know as the **SQL EDITOR**, but many, including yours truly, call it the Query Editor. It is used for creating and editing queries.
② The bottom panel is formally known as the **DATA OUTPUT PANEL**. It is used for viewing the data retrieved from running the query (also known as the **RESULT** of the query).

Section 1: Query Editor Panel

As shown earlier in Figure 2-10, this panel has two tabs. They are explained below.

Query Editor Tab

This is the tab that you type the query in or open what is known as a **SCRIPT FILE** and run it.

> **Query Editor Tips**
> ① In addition to typing the code for the query, you can also copy and paste code from another source.
> ② You can have more than one query editor window open at the same time. Just click the Query Tool button again. [See Figure 2-11]

Query History Tab

The Query History tab, shown in Figure 2-13, displays a list of all queries that you have run, on the left. If you click on a query in this list, the code for the query will be displayed in the section shown on the right side of the figure. Once a query is selected, you can run the query. You can also copy the code in the query to a new query window, by clicking the **COPY TO QUERY EDITOR BUTTON**, illustrated in the figure.

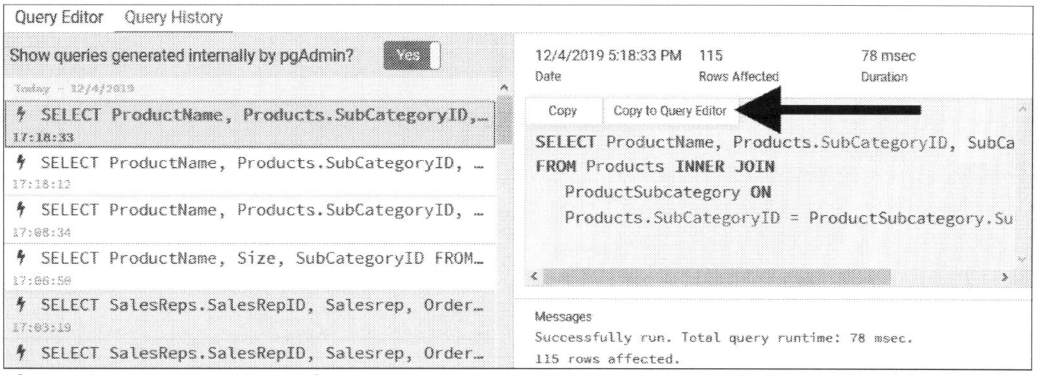

Figure 2-13 Query History tab

The panel on the right displays information about recent queries, including the following:

- ☑ The date and time that the query was run.
- ☑ The code for the query.
- ☑ The number of rows that the query returned, in the Messages window, in the lower right corner of the figure.

By default, this tab stores the last 20 queries that you have run for the database. When the 21st query is run, the oldest query is automatically deleted. The MAX_QUERY_HIST_STORED value in the **CONFIG_LOCAL.PY FILE** can be changed, to increase the number of queries that will be retained, on this tab.

Section 2: Data Output Panel

As shown earlier in Figure 2-10, this panel has four tabs. They are explained below.

Data Output Tab

As you may have guessed, this tab displays the data that the query retrieves, as shown in Figure 2-14. The first column in the figure displays the row number.

In addition to viewing the data, the following functionality is available for the data displayed on this tab.

- ☑ Export the data to a comma delimited CSV, .txt or binary file.
- ☑ Edit the data in fields that are updateable.

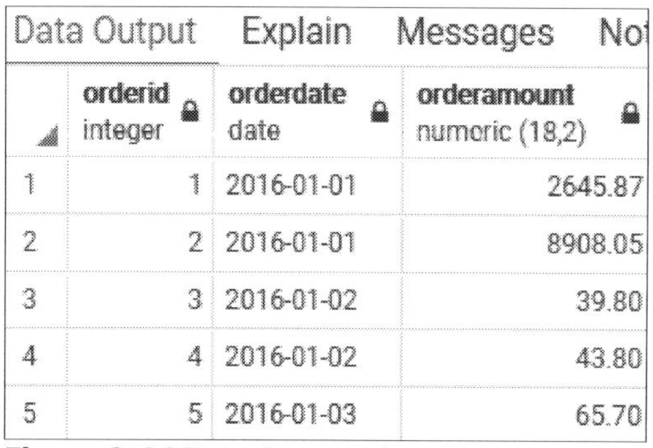

	orderid integer	orderdate date	orderamount numeric (18,2)
1	1	2016-01-01	2645.87
2	2	2016-01-01	8908.05
3	3	2016-01-02	39.80
4	4	2016-01-02	43.80
5	5	2016-01-03	65.70

Figure 2-14 Data Output tab

Explain Tab

The functionality of this tab is beyond the scope of this book.

Messages Tab

This tab is used to view information about the query that was just run. The number of rows that the query retrieved is also displayed. As shown in Figure 2-15, 9,772 rows were retrieved.

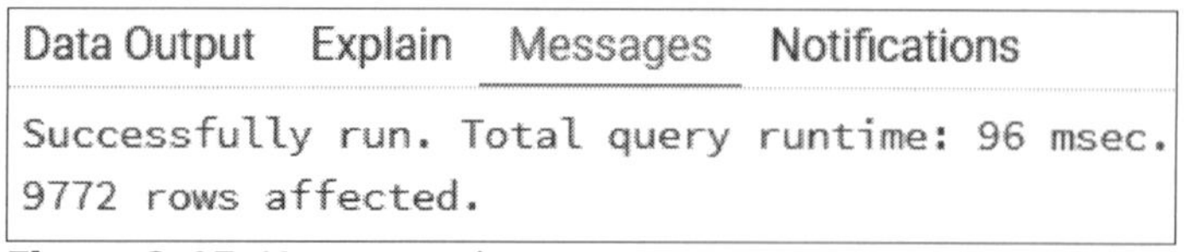

Figure 2-15 Messages tab

If there is an error, the error message is displayed on this tab.

The code/syntax that generated the error is underlined on the Query Editor tab, as illustrated in Figure 2-16.

Syntax errors are covered later in this chapter.

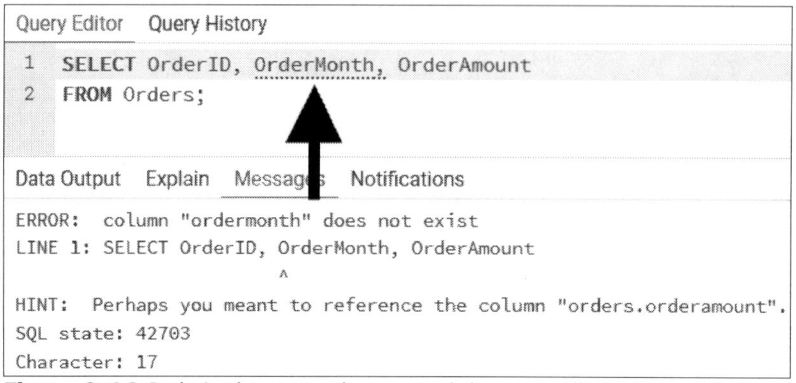

Figure 2-16 Code in the query that caused the error, illustrated

Notifications Tab

This tab, shown in Figure 2-17, will display asynchronous messages that are received from the server.

Figure 2-17 Notifications tab

Scratch Pad

This window has its own panel. It is used to hold code (often referred to as snippets), that you may have the need to use in more than one query. The content that is placed in this window, sadly is only available when pgAdmin is open. The contents of this window cannot be saved. I would like to have the option of being able to save the contents placed in this window, like you can save snippets in MySQL.

I sometimes use this window to store date formatting code. However, since the contents can't be saved, I use software that is similar to Notepad and just leave the software open. Not as convenient, but as least I can save my snippets of code. <smile>

If this window is closed, you can right-click next to the Query History tab ⇒ Add Panel ⇒ Scratch Pad, as shown in Figure 2-18. This option does not place the window back in it's original position. Instead, the window floats on top of the Query Editor window.

Figure 2-18 One way to display the Scratch Pad

The other option is to save the changes to the query, then refresh (Press the F5 key) the web page. I find this method easier and it puts the Scratch Pad window back to where it was, as shown earlier in Figure 2-10.

Query Editor Toolbar

Figure 2-19 shows the Query Editor toolbar. Table 2-1 explains the buttons.

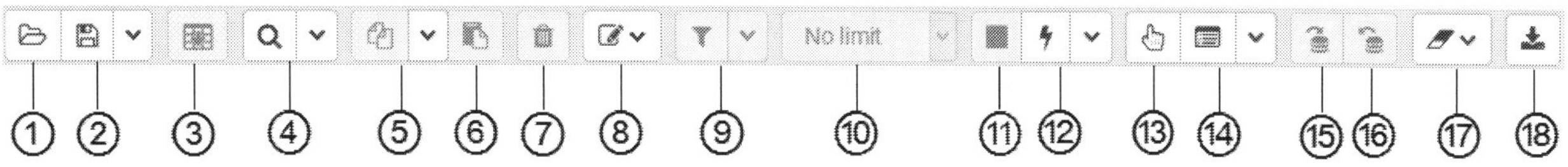

Figure 2-19 Query Editor toolbar

Button	Description
①	The **OPEN FILE** button, opens the dialog box shown in Figure 2-20. It is used to open an existing file that has a query. In this book, you will use this option to open an existing .sql query file that you have created, to save it with a new file name, to use it as the starting point for a new query.
②	The **SAVE** button [See Figure 2-54 for the button options] will save an existing file or save an existing file with a new name. If you wanted to save a file in a specific folder on the C drive, follow these steps: Click the Save button ⇒ Double-click on the C drive icon ⇒ Click on the folder that you want to save the file in ⇒ Click after the last slash \ in the **FILE NAME FIELD** at the top of the dialog box ⇒ Type in the name of the file and the extension .sql, as shown in Figure 2-21.
③	The **SAVE DATA CHANGES** button is enabled when changes have been made to the data. (1)
④	The **FIND** button is used to search or replace the contents of the Query Editor window. Clicking the arrow for this button, displays the menu options shown in Figure 2-22.
⑤	The **COPY** button is used to copy what is selected in the Data Output tab. (1)
⑥	The **PASTE** button is used to paste the copied row of data to a new row, on the Data Output tab. (1)
⑦	The **DELETE** button is used to mark rows on the Data Output tab that you want to delete. The marked rows are deleted, when the Save Data Changes button is clicked. (1)
⑧	The first two options on the **EDIT** button drop-down list, shown in Figure 2-23, are used to format the code. The last three options are used to add or remove the code (the symbol) to or from the lines of code that you have selected. Truth be told, it is easier to just type the comment symbol manually.
⑨	The **FILTER** button is used to set the filter and sort criteria for the data that is retrieved from a query, when the data is viewed in the View/Edit data mode. (1)
⑩	The **LIMIT** button is used to select the maximum number of rows that are retrieved and displayed. "No Limit" is the default. Figure 2-24 shows the other options that are available. This option is helpful if you are using tables that have tens of thousands of rows, or more. Limiting the number of rows, will return a smaller result set. This option is enabled when you are viewing or editing the data in a table. [Right-click on a table in the Browser panel ⇒ View/Edit Data ⇒ Select one of the options]
⑪	The **CANCEL QUERY** button is used to stop the query when it is running.
⑫	The **EXECUTE/REFRESH** button is used to run the query. You can also press the **F5** key to run a query. Any options that are checked on the drop-down list, shown in Figure 2-25, are automatically processed. To complete the queries in this book, neither option is required to be checked.
⑬	The **EXPLAIN** button is used to view the explanation plan for the query. (1)
⑭	The **EXPLAIN ANALYZE** button is used to run/generate an explanation plan for the current query. (1)
⑮	The **COMMIT** button is used to save the transaction. (1)
⑯	The **ROLLBACK** button is used to undo/rollback the transaction. (1)
⑰	The **CLEAR** button displays the options shown in Figure 2-26. The options are used to erase/remove the contents of the Query Editor window or the contents on the Query History tab.
⑱	The **DOWNLOAD AS CSV** button is used to download the result set of the current query to a CSV file. Figure 2-29 shown later, are the options that you can set to customize how the data is added to the CSV file. (1)

Table 2-1 Query Editor toolbar buttons explained

(1) Using this option is beyond the scope of this book.

Execute/Refresh Button
In my opinion, it would have been nice if the developers that designed the toolbar would have known that most queries that are created are run, and put this button in a better location on the toolbar (perhaps after the Save button), instead of in some random location in the middle of the toolbar. It would also be great if a different icon was used, as they used the same icon for the Query Tool button on the Browser panel.

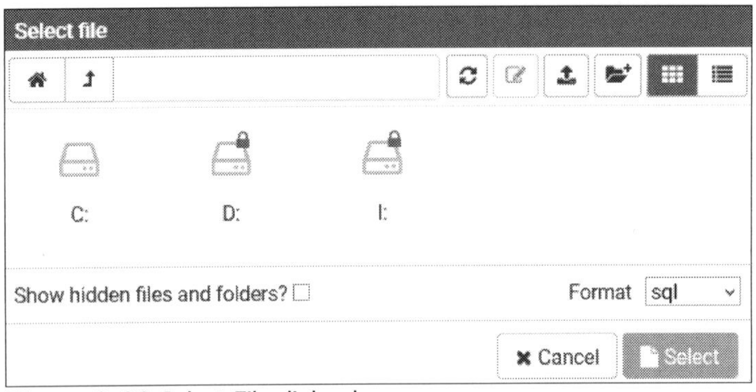

Figure 2-20 Select File dialog box

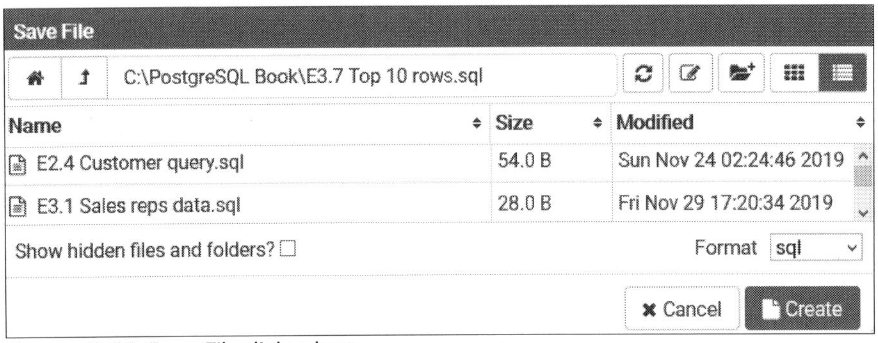

Figure 2-21 Save File dialog box

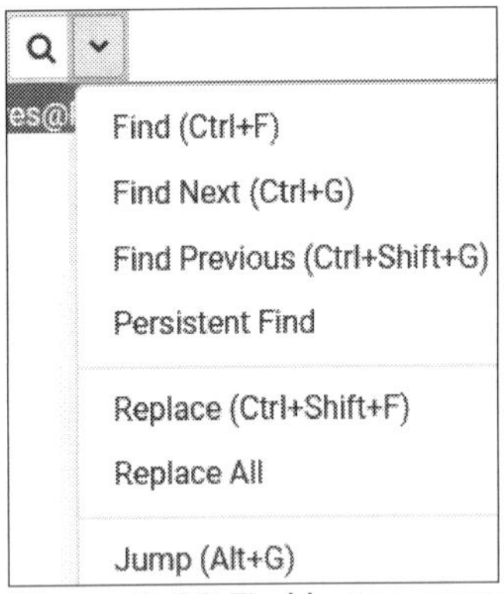

Figure 2-22 Find button menu options

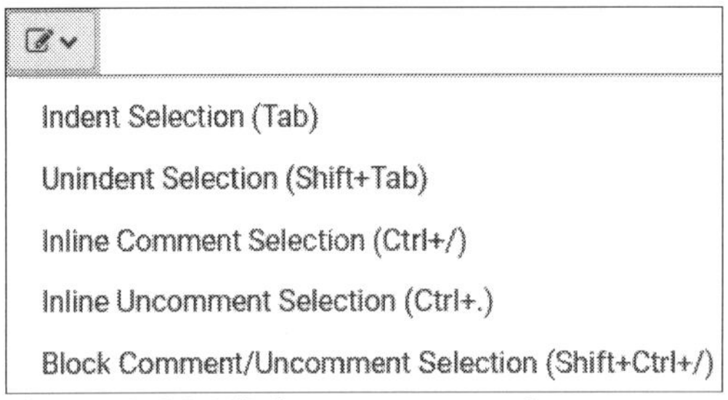

Figure 2-23 Edit button menu options

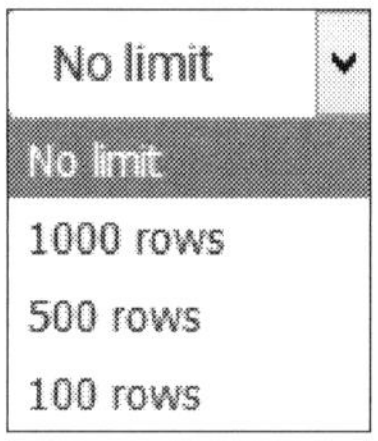

Figure 2-24 Limit button menu options

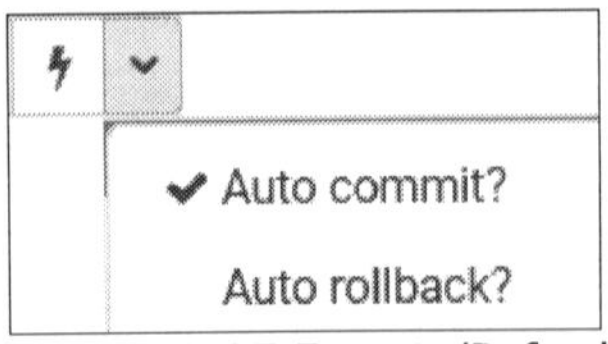

Figure 2-25 Execute/Refresh button menu options

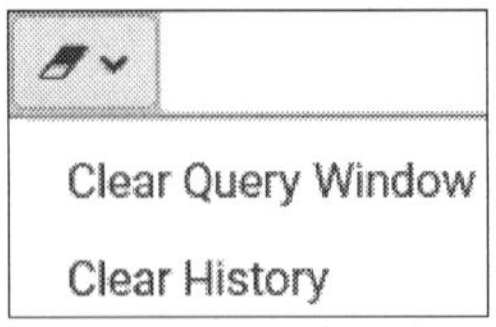

Figure 2-26 Clear button menu options

Customizing pgAdmin

For the most part, the default options that are selected, will support most of your needs. It is a good idea though, to at least see what options you can change. The next few sections, show you where the options are. Don't worry, I am not going to bore you by covering all of the options. <smile> I am only covering the options that I think you may want or need to change at some point.

Preferences Dialog Box

The options on the dialog box shown in Figure 2-27 are used to customize pgAdmin. [File menu ⇒ Preferences, opens this dialog box.] The query related options, that you may want or need to change, are covered below.

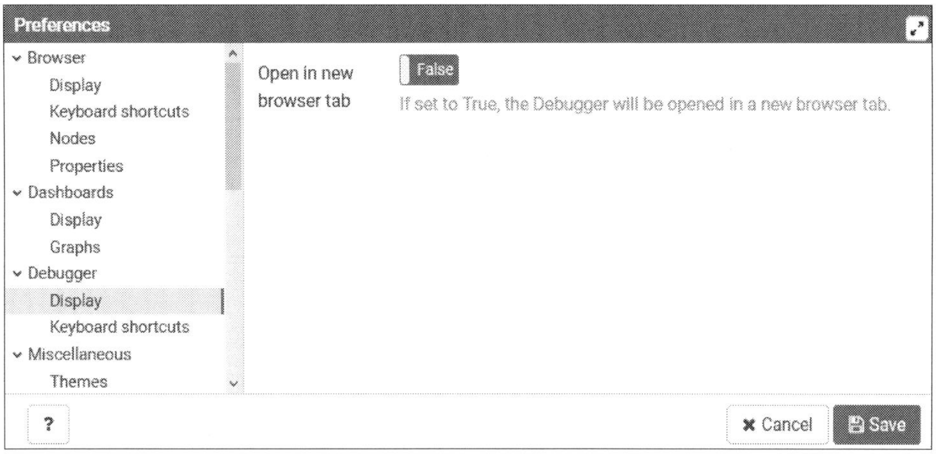

Figure 2-27 Preferences dialog box

Browser Nodes Options

As shown earlier in Figure 2-4, the Browser panel displays a lot of nodes. If seeing all of the nodes gets on your nerves, you can hide some of the ones that you know that you will not use, on this screen. The Nodes screen is not shown.

Debugger Display Option

The option shown above in Figure 2-27 is used to select whether or not the Debugger window will open on a new tab.

Themes

At the time that this book went to print, there was one theme named Standard, which is the default and a beta theme named Dark.

Query Tool Preferences

The options in this section of the Preferences dialog box are for the queries that you will create and run. For now, it is probably best to read about the options, then after you have created a few queries, come back here and see if there is an option for what is getting on your nerves. <smile>

Auto Completion

The option shown in Figure 2-28, is used to select whether or not keywords should be in all capital letters in the query. Using upper case letters for keywords is an SQL standard, but not a requirement. Having the keywords in upper case, makes it easy to recognize them in a query.

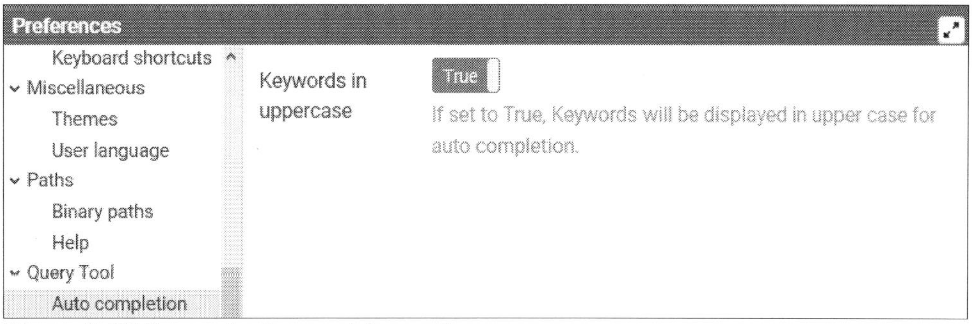

Figure 2-28 Keyword auto completion option

CSV Output

The options shown in Figure 2-29 are used to select how data will be formatted, when it is exported from PostgreSQL to a .csv file.

The **REPLACE NULL VALUES WITH OPTION** is free form. This means that you can type in what you want to be added to a field that does not have any data.

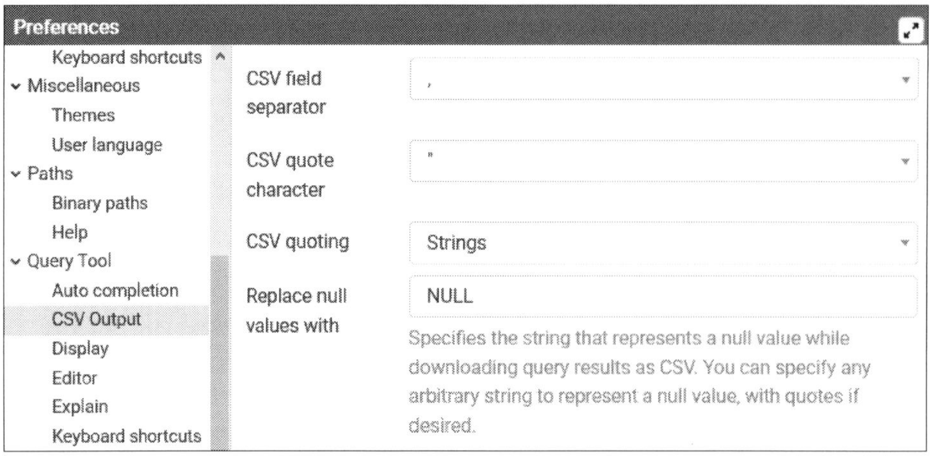

Figure 2-29 CSV Output options

Display

The options shown in Figure 2-30 are used to select what happens when a new instance of the Query window is opened on a new tab.

I changed the **QUERY INFO NOTIFIER TIMEOUT** option from 5 seconds, as shown in the figure, to 10 seconds.

I did this because I wanted to have enough time to see how many rows each query returns, without having to display he Messages tab, just to have to see how many rows the query returned.

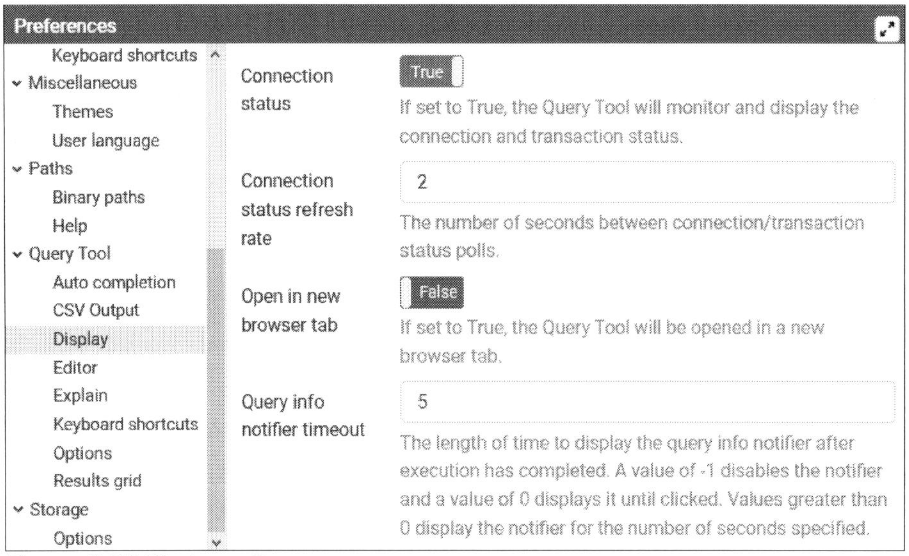

Figure 2-30 Display options

Editor

The options shown in Figure 2-31 are used to select whether or not sets of parentheses are highlighted, in the query.

If the **CODE FOLDING OPTION** is set to False, it will improve the editors performance if you are working with tables that have a lot of data.

The **FONT SIZE OPTION** is used to increase/decrease the font size that is used in the editor.

By default, the **INSERT BRACKET PAIRS OPTION** will automatically add a set of parentheses, brackets [ ] or quotes, in the editor when you type the first one in.

If the **PLAIN TEXT MODE OPTION** is set to True, keywords and code folding will be disabled.

The **TAB SIZE OPTION** is used to select the number of spaces to use, to indent a line of code in the query, when the tab key is pressed.

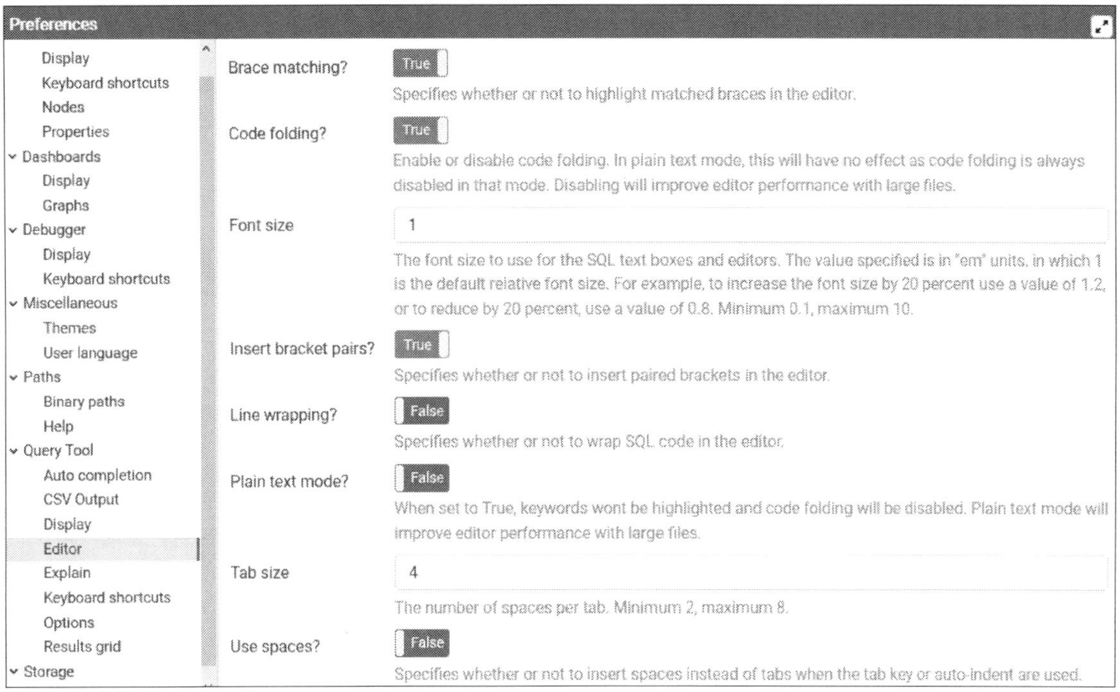

Figure 2-31 Editor options

Explain

The options on this screen are beyond the scope of this book.

Keyboard Shortcuts

The options on this screen are used to change the default shortcut keys.

Options

The options shown in Figure 2-32 are used to select what should happen when the data or the query has changed.

When set to True, the **AUTO COMMIT OPTION** will automatically save any changes that have been made to the data, if the query runs and does not generate an error.

When set to True, the **AUTO ROLLBACK OPTION** will automatically remove and changes that were made to the data, if the query fails.

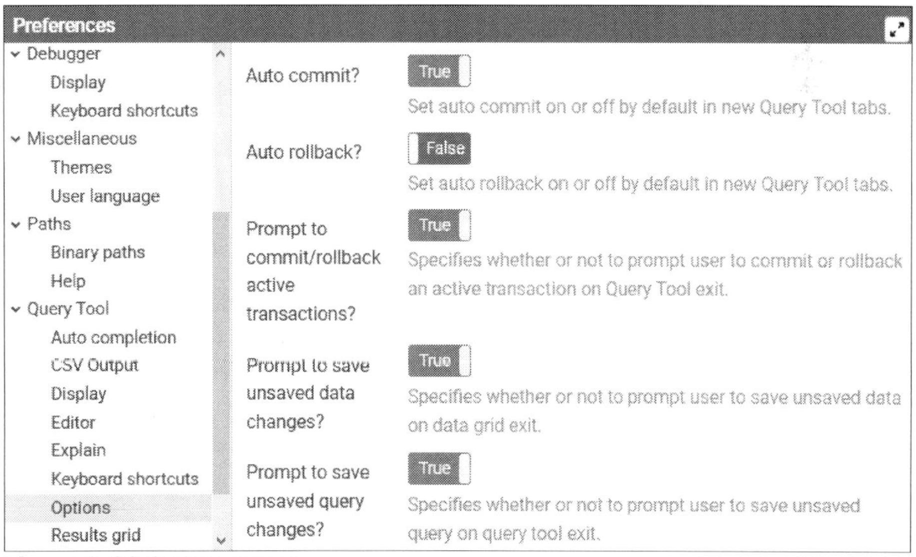

Figure 2-32 Options screen

When you are first learning how to create queries that change the data in a table, it may be a good idea to set the **AUTO COMMIT** option to False. That will give you a chance to view the changed data to make sure that the changes are correct. Keep in mind that just because a query does not generate an error, that does not mean that the query produced the result that you were expecting.

Results Grid

The options shown in Figure 2-33 are used to customize the Data Output section of the Query Editor, which displays the data that was retrieved by the query.

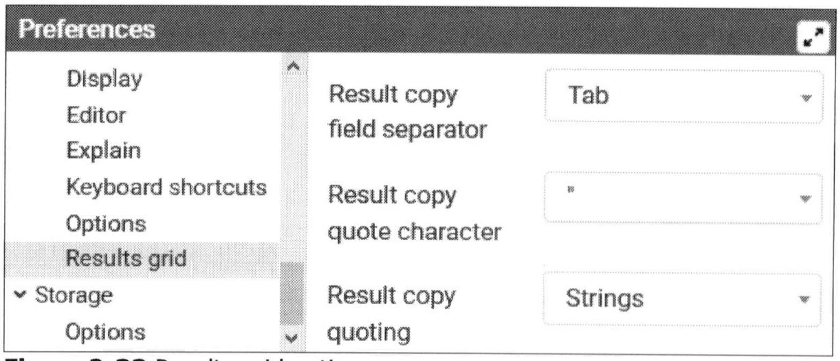

Figure 2-33 Results grid options

Exercise 2.2: Create A Database

In this exercise, you will create a database. It will be used in the next exercise to restore the database that you downloaded. This database will be used in the rest of this book.

1. In the Browser panel, right-click on the Databases node ⇒ Create ⇒ Database.

2. In the Database field, type `sqldata`, as shown in Figure 2-34 ⇒ Click Save. The database will be created.

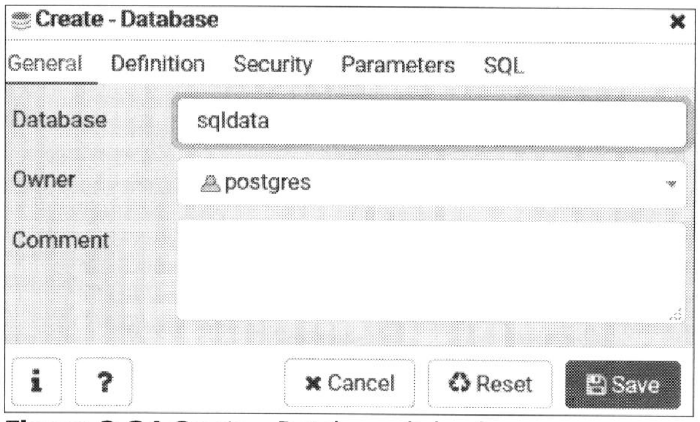

Figure 2-34 Create - Database dialog box

Exercise 2.3: Restore A Database

In this exercise, you will restore the database that you downloaded in Chapter 1, to the sqldata database that you created in the previous exercise.

1. Right-click on the sqldata database ⇒ **RESTORE**, as shown in Figure 2-35.

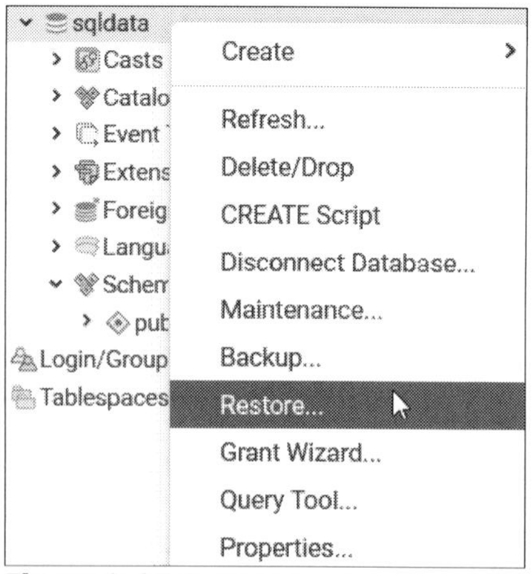

Figure 2-35 Option to restore the database

2. Click the button at the end of the **FILENAME FIELD** ⇒ Navigate to the folder that you created for this book ⇒ Select the **SQLDATA.TAR** file.

3. Click the Select button.

4. Select **POSTGRES** from the **ROLE NAME** drop-down list.

   You should have the options shown in Figure 2-36.

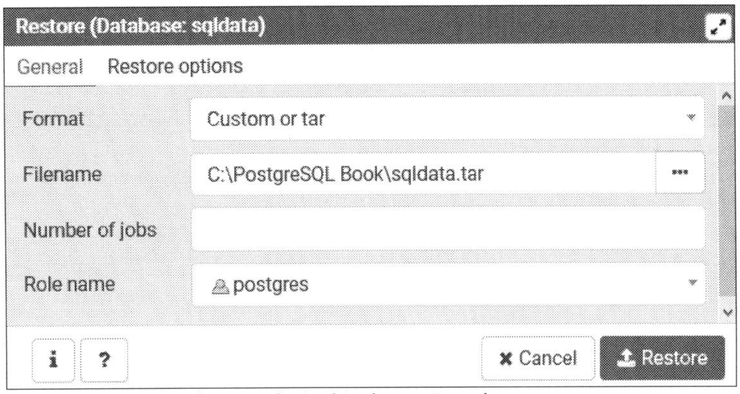

Figure 2-36 Database selected to be restored

5. At the top of the Restore dialog box, click on the **RESTORE OPTIONS** tab.

6. Change the following options to Yes: **DATA** and **VERBOSE MESSAGES**, as illustrated in Figure 2-37 ⇒ Click the **RESTORE BUTTON**.

   When the restore is complete, you should see that the sqldata database has 14 tables, as shown in Figure 2-38.

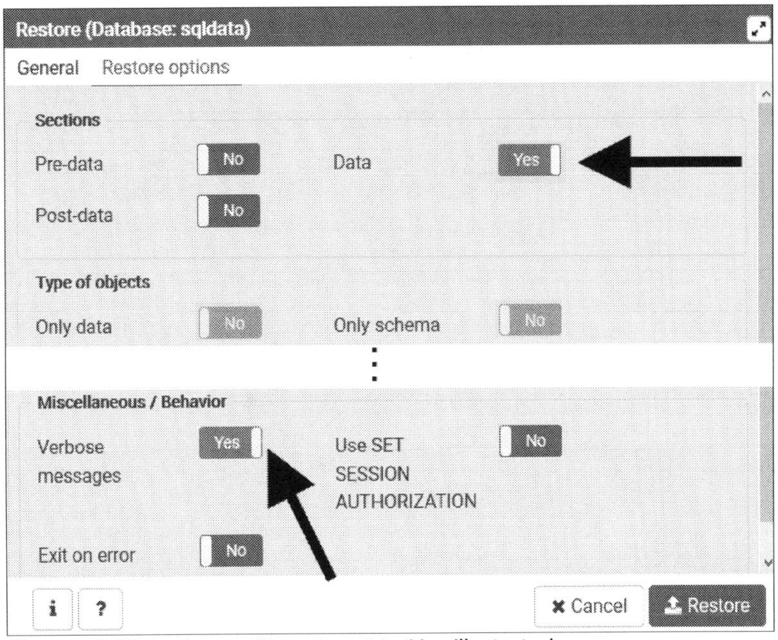

Figure 2-37 Restore options to set to Yes illustrated

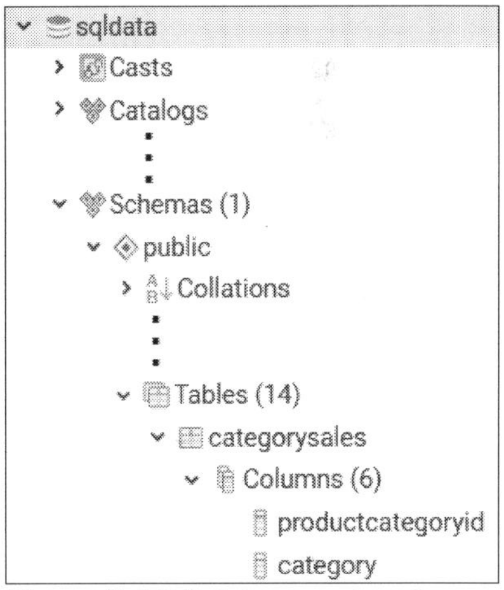

Figure 2-38 Database restored

> As shown above in Figure 2-38, PostgreSQL defaults to all lower case letters for the table and column names. When creating queries, you can type the table and field names in all lower case, as shown in the figure. You can also type the names in the query, in mixed cases, as shown below in Exercise 2.4, step 2. I find mixed cases, easier to read. You can use whatever style you like. Just be consistent.

> **Using The Query Tool**
> Before opening this tool, make sure that the database that you want to create the query for is selected in the Browser panel, as shown above in Figure 2-38. If the database that you want to use is not selected, close or save all open query windows ⇒ In the Browser panel, click on the database that you want to create the query for ⇒ Reopen the Query Editor.
>
> The way to ensure that you have connected to the correct database is to look at the label for the query window, right below the Query Editor toolbar. The first part of the tab name displays the database name, as illustrated in Figure 2-39. Notice at the top of the figure (in the upper right corner), that there is also a query window open for the postgres database. That is fine, as long as you are aware of which query window is currently available.

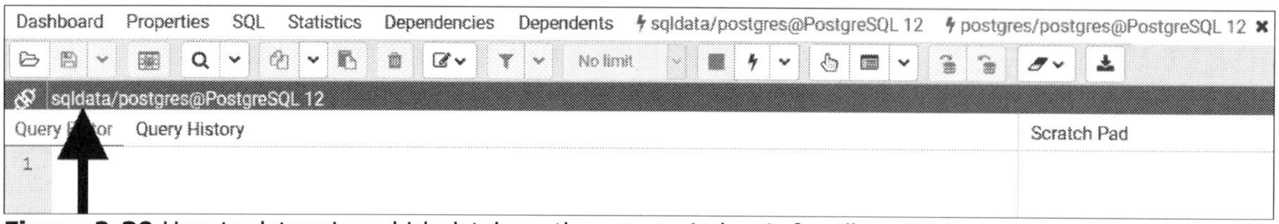

Figure 2-39 How to determine which database the query window is for, illustrated

> **Closing A Query Tab**
> There are two ways to close a query tab, as explained below.
> ① Click on the query tab that you want to close, as shown at the top of Figure 2-39 ⇒ Click the X button (Close the currently active panel tab) in the upper right corner of the tab.
> ② Right-click on the query tab that you want to close, as shown at the top of Figure 2-39 ⇒ Select **REMOVE PANEL**, as shown in Figure 2-40.

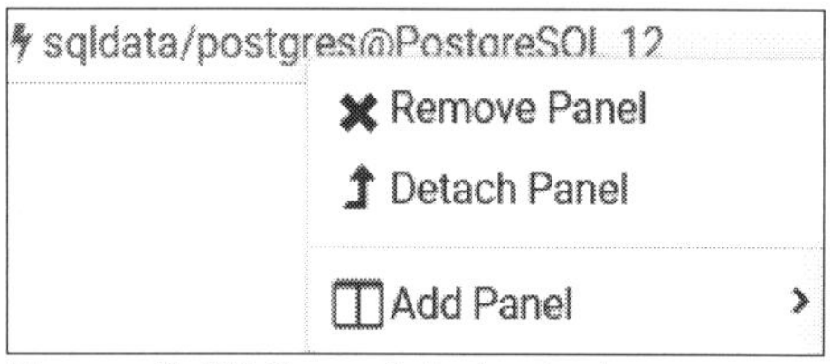

Figure 2-40 Query tab shortcut menu

> While you are typing in the query, pgAdmin will automatically color code the statements. For example, the following clauses are changed to purple: SELECT, FROM, WHEN, GROUP BY, ORDER BY and HAVING.

Exercise 2.4: Create A Query

Now that you have had a chance to see where some features and options are and what they do, it is time to create a query.

1. Open a new query window.

2. In the query window, type
```
SELECT CustomerID, FirstName, LastName
FROM Customers;
```

3. Run the query.

   You should see the results shown in Figure 2-41.

   555 rows were returned, as indicated in Figure 2-42.

	customerid integer	firstname character v	lastname character var
1	1	Chris	Christianson
2	2	Christine	Manley
3	3	Gary	Jannis
4	4	Alexander	Mast
5	5	Patrick	Reyess

Figure 2-41 Result of the query

Figure 2-42 Message displaying how many rows were returned

4. On the Query Editor toolbar, click the Save button ⇒ Navigate to and select the PostgreSQL Book folder ⇒ Type `E2.4 Customer query.sql`, as the file name ⇒ Click the **CREATE** button.

   If you look at the bottom of the query window, you will see a message that indicates that the file has been saved, as shown in Figure 2-43. By default, this message is only displayed for 5 seconds.

   If you look above the query toolbar, you will see that the tab name has changed to the query name, as shown in Figure 2-44.

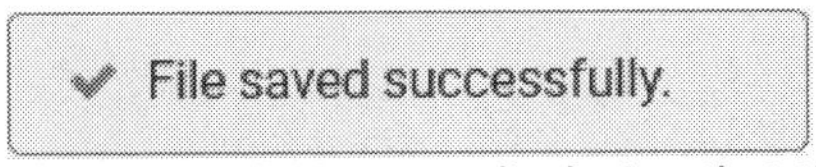

Figure 2-43 Message displaying that the query file was saved

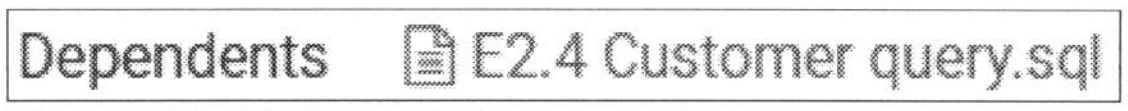

Figure 2-44 Query tab renamed

Open Query Windows
As shown in Figure 2-44, you see the Tabbed Browser window menu. To the right of the Dependents tab you should see the tab for Exercise 2.4 query. If you open two or more query windows, you will see tabs for them. Out of all of the SQL Editors that I have used, this is by far the worst layout in my opinion, for open query windows, that I have seen. For starters, the default name for the query window is way too long. Why the query editor could not have it's own row for query tabs is beyond comprehension. Figure 2-45 and 2-46 show the query window from other editors. They show the default tab name and a tab for a query that has been saved. Both are easier to read in my opinion.

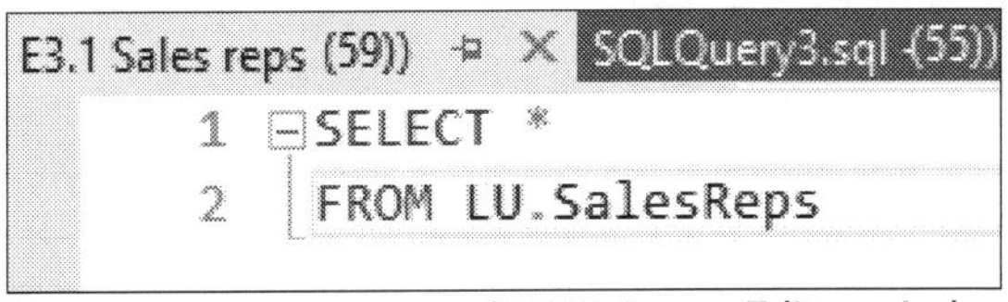

Figure 2-45 SQL Server/SSMS Query Editor window

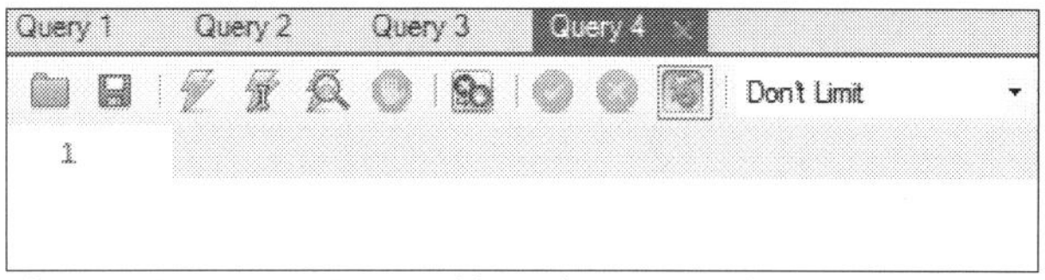

Figure 2-46 MySQL Workbench Query Editor window

Hopefully, now you see what I am talking about. It's like there was little to no thought of what would be appealing and would work for people that create queries on a regular basis. The same goes for the fact that the Query Editor toolbar **DOES NOT** have a button to open a new query window. If you are speechless, you are in good company. <smile>

Query File Extension
Not surprisingly, the file extension for query files is **.SQL**. I was horrified to discover that pgAdmin does not automatically add the **.SQL** file extension to the file name that you type in, when saving the file. I have never seen software, other then SQLite Studio, that does not automatically add an extension to a new file that is being saved. Have you?

Handling Syntax Errors

While not the most pleasant thing to happen, you will create queries that have syntax errors. It could be that you left out a comma or spelled a field name or keyword wrong. Most errors are caused by syntax, that is incorrect.

The bottom of Figure 2-47 shows an error, which says that the column CustomerIDx is not in the table.

If you look on the first line of the query in the figure, you will see this field. Once you fix the error, run the query again.

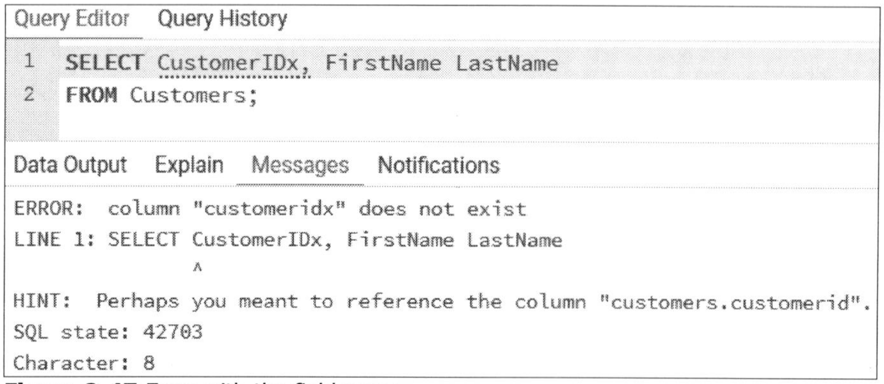

Figure 2-47 Error with the field name

Figure 2-48 shows the query after the CustomerIDx field name was corrected and the data that was returned. Notice that no error was detected.

Also notice that the First Name field is not displayed on the Data Output tab. Something is wrong!

If you look on the first line of the query, you will see that a comma is missing between the name fields.

THIS IS WHY YOU REALLY HAVE TO PAY ATTENTION TO THE DATA THAT IS RETURNED. JUST BECAUSE A QUERY RETURNS DATA, DOES NOT MEAN THAT THE DATA THAT IS RETURNED, IS CORRECT.

Figure 2-48 Result of fixing the field name problem

Exercise 2.5: Viewing Data In The Database

It helps to view some of the data that you will use to create queries from, especially if you are not already familiar with the data. Doing so will give you a better idea of what data is in the tables.

1. In the Browser panel, expand the SQLdata database folder ⇒ Expand the Tables folder.

2. Right-click on the Orders table ⇒ Select View/Edit Data ⇒ First 100 Rows. This will display up to 100 rows of data in the table, as shown in Figure 2-49. The figure does not show all of the columns in the table.

   As shown, there are column names (fields) that end with **ID**.

   These columns will be used to link (create a relationship) to another table in the database.

   For example, the CustomerID field shown in the figure, is used to create a relationship with the Customers table.

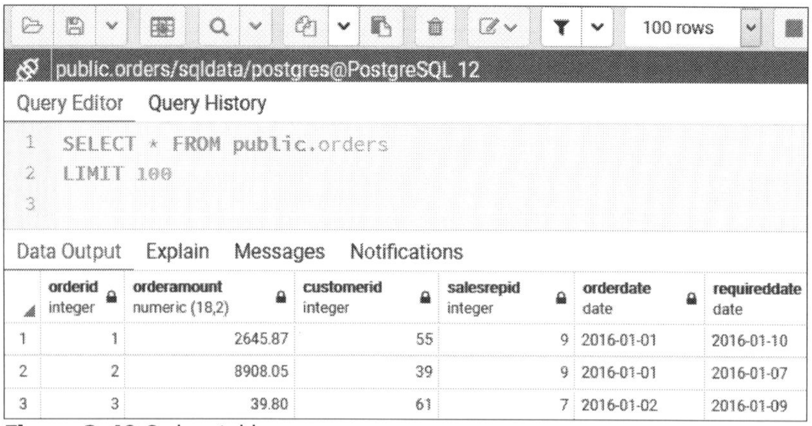

Figure 2-49 Orders table

Understanding Nulls

It is very possible that all rows of data do not have data in every column. When that is the case, the column (cell) will be empty, as shown in Figure 2-50.

This only happens if the field is not required to have data entered. **NULL** is not a value. It is a placeholder, if you will, for a missing value in a field.

	productid integer	productname character varyi	size character	color chara
30	3304	ATB Lock	[null]	[null]
31	3305	Mini Lock	[null]	[null]
32	4101	Crochet Glove	small	[null]
33	4102	Crochet Glove	medium	[null]

Figure 2-50 Table with null values in pgAdmin

> **Where Is Auto Completion?**
> One thing that I found interesting is that while pgAdmin has auto complete, it only appears if you type in the Windows shortcut, Ctrl + Space bar key combination. While this works, as shown in Figure 2-51, it's just not the same, as when auto completion happens automatically, as you type.

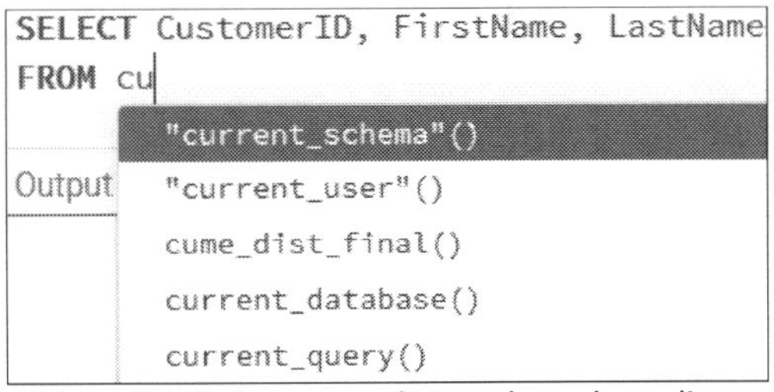

Figure 2-51 Auto completion drop-down list

Tables In The Practice Database

If you haven't already, at some point, you will receive query requests from various departments, most of which either have their own database or a specific set of tables, in a database. This means that you have to "learn" about a lot of data in a relatively short period of time. Using the database in this book is no exception. To help you get up to speed quickly, this section briefly covers the database and the tables in it.

Figure 2-52 shows the tables and their relationships (as needed), that you will use to create the queries in this book. All of the tables in the database, are not shown in this figure. The type of data stored in the tables that you will use most, are explained below the figure. Keep in mind that in a production database, some of these tables would have several more columns. I tried to keep the tables as small as possible, for learning purposes.

While the database used in this book is small, in terms of the number of tables and rows of data, compared to the databases used in most companies, that was done on purpose. I did it to help you become familiar with the tables and data. On your own, even if the database that you use, has 50 tables or more, you may find that you will only need a subset of those tables to create 10 or more queries. For example, if you need to create 10 queries that need to use marketing data, there may only be five tables in the entire database that store marketing data. And if you are really lucky, all of the marketing tables will have a unique schema or start with the same three or four letters, which makes it much easier for you to find the tables that you need.

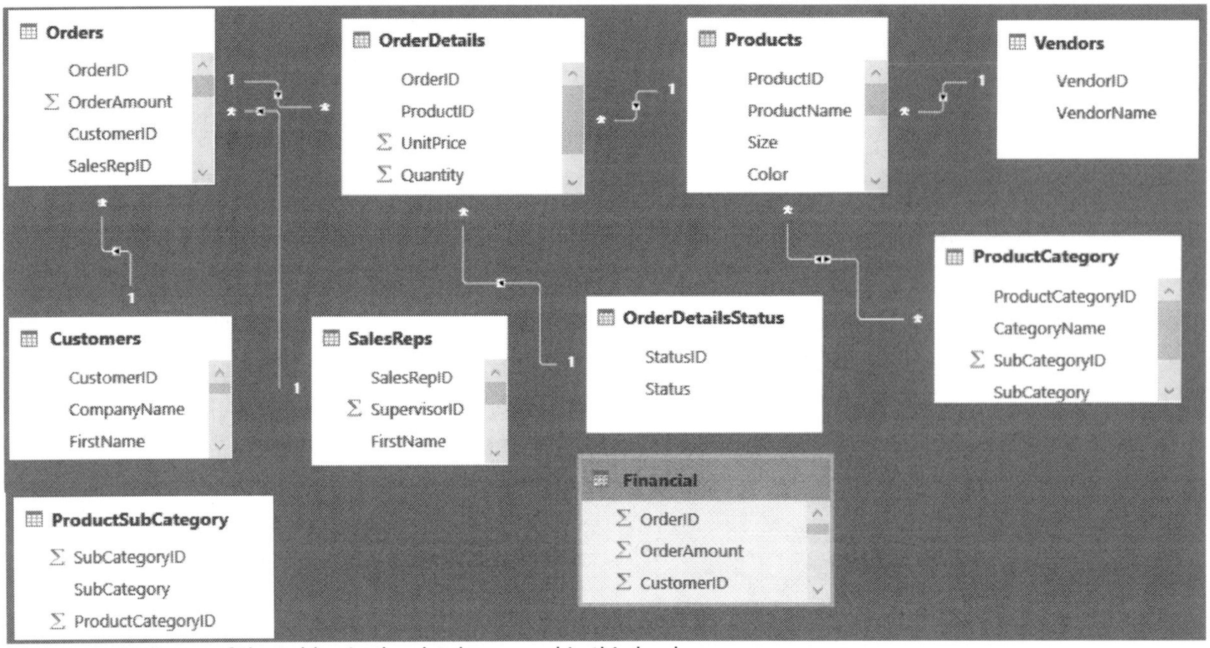

Figure 2-52 Some of the tables in the database used in this book

Category Sales stores the sales for each product category in the Product Category table, for the years 2016 through 2018.

Customers stores information including customer names and addresses of people that have placed an order.

Financial includes values like net sales, direct costs and gross margin.

Invoices stores billing information for customer orders.

Orders stores what is known as the "header" information for an order. This includes the order number, customer number, order date and sales rep number.

Order Details stores what is known as the "detail" information for an order. Fields in this table include the order number, item number, quantity ordered, and item price. There is one record in this table for each item that every customer orders.

Order Details Status contains the options for where in the order process, each item in the Order Details table is.

Products stores all of the products that the company sells. Fields include the product number, product name and vendor number.

Product Category contains the categories for all of the products.

Product Sub Category contains all of the subcategories for each product category.

Regions contains a list of regions in the USA.

Sales Reps stores information for each sales rep, including their name and position. This table doubles as the Employee table.

Store Inventory stores the quantity on hand for each product, by store.

Vendors contains the company name that each product comes from. Yes, at some point, I will add more columns to this table, but for the needs of this book, the company name for each vendor is enough. <smile>

Script Files

A script file contains the code for a query. It can also contain the code to create a database, tables and views. This type of script file can also add data to a table. Most of the time, when a file is called a script file, it is referencing a file that manipulates or creates data.

Exercise 2.6: Run A Query Using A Script File

As covered in the previous section, there are generally two types of script files. In this exercise, you will use an existing query file, as the starting point for a new query.

1. Open the E2.4 file.

2. Add the Country field to the end of the SELECT clause, as shown in Figure 2-53.

```
SELECT CustomerID, FirstName, LastName, Country
FROM Customers;
```

Figure 2-53 Field added to an existing query

3. Click the arrow for the Save File button ⇒ Select the **SAVE AS** option, shown in Figure 2-54.

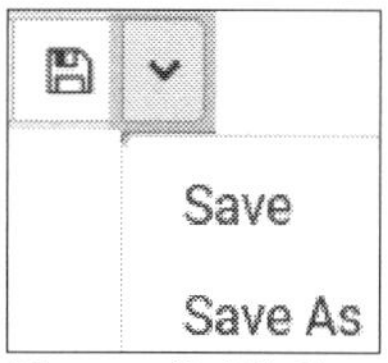

Figure 2-54 Save File button options

4. Type `E2.6 Modified E2.4 query`, as the file name.

5. Run the query. You should see the Country field in the result. Compare this to the result shown earlier in Figure 2-41.

Summary

This chapter covered a variety of topics including learning about the pgAdmin workspace and restoring a database. You also learned about the tables in the database that will be used in this book. The primary goal was to get you acquainted with pgAdmin, because you will use it to create queries. Speaking of queries . . .

It's time to create more queries!

CREATING SINGLE TABLE QUERIES

After reading this chapter and completing the exercises you will:

- ☑ Know what data types are supported in PostgreSQL
- ☑ Have a better understanding of the SELECT statement
- ☑ Be able to create basic queries

CHAPTER 3

Overview

This chapter is an introduction to creating queries. The focus of this chapter is on retrieving columns and rows of data from a single table. While the techniques covered in this chapter use a single table, the same techniques are also used in queries that retrieve data from more than one table. Other techniques covered in this chapter, include learning about the data types, using a column alias, handling null values, calculated fields and more.

This chapter covers the foundation topics that will help you in later chapters. The one fundamental technique that is not covered in this chapter is creating filters. That is because Chapter 4 is dedicated to filtering data.

What Is A Query?

In the SQL world, a query is any SQL statement. More times then not though, the term query is used to refer to the code that is written to retrieve data from tables and views in one or more databases. Queries are created to retrieve data that will answer a question. For example, "Which customers ordered a blue hat in November 2018?"

PostgreSQL Data Types

I know that you are probably anxious to start creating queries, but you need to know about and understand why a fields data type is important when creating queries.

Each column in a table has a data type. The data type defines the type of data that can be stored in a column.

For example, a column that contains customer names would have a string data type. A column that contains dates would have a date data type.

The Data type column in Figure 3-1 shows the data types for some of the columns in the Sales Reps table.

To open this dialog box, right-click on the table ⇒ Properties ⇒ Columns tab.

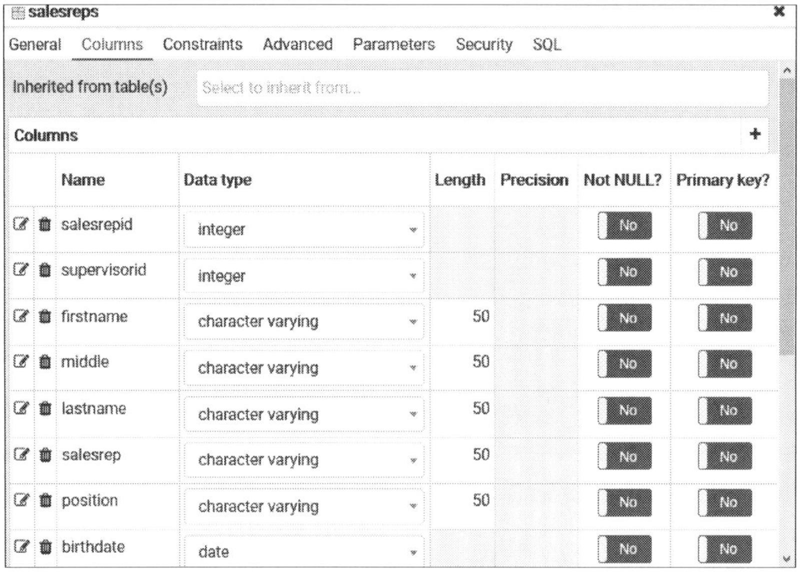

Figure 3-1 Data types for the Sales Reps table

There are several categories of data types. Even if on your own, you will not be creating databases or tables, it is important to know about the data types, because you can run into problems when creating queries that need a calculation. That is because some functions require fields to have a certain data type. Below are the categories of data types covered in this book and the table that they are covered in.

☑ **String** Stores text based data. [See Table 3-1]
☑ **Numeric** Stores numeric data. [See Table 3-2]
☑ **Date** and **Time** Stores dates, times or both. [See Table 3-3]

> Data types are the rules, if you will, that define what data can be saved in a column. This restricts the data in a column. The data type is what checks and allows data to be saved or not saved, in a column. For example, if a column has a date data type, you cannot enter your first name in the field. Data types also determine how the data in the column can be sorted.

String Data Types

This is the most commonly used data type. This data type stores text values like product name, sales territory and city. While US zip codes are numeric, the column should use a string data type because zip codes and phone numbers for that matter, are not used in calculations. Also, if the zip code column has a numeric data type, the zip codes that start with zero, like 07652, would not save the zero. It would only save 7652. You may see string data types referred to as a **CHARACTER** (which is how PostgreSQL refers to them) or **TEXT DATA TYPE**. They are one in the same and the names can be used interchangeably. There are two types of string data types as explained below.

① **FIXED LENGTH** This data type is used when the column should only allow a specific maximum number of characters, like 35 characters for a city name.

② **VARIABLE LENGTH** This data type is used when you do not want a specific maximum number of characters, to be set. As indicated in Table 3-1, variable length data types actually have a maximum number of characters.

Why Use Fixed Length Data Types?
I know what you are thinking. Why use a fixed length data type? The answer is short and sweet. To avoid causing performance issues. An example is that fixed length fields can be sorted faster then variable length fields. Variable length fields cannot be indexed.

String Data Types	Description
CHAR(n)	This is a fixed length character string. If the data entered in the field is less than the number of characters allocated for the field, PostgreSQL pads the rest of the field with spaces. Currently, this data type is not used as much as the other two string data types. (1)
TEXT	This is a variable length character data type and has an unlimited length. This data type has more features then the CHAR and VARCHAR data types. You do not have to specify a length. This data type does not pad or remove spaces. While PostgreSQL states that this data type is unlimited, it has a maximum length of 1GB.
VARCHAR(n)	This is a variable length character string. If the data entered in the field is less than the number of characters allocated for the field, PostgreSQL does not pad the rest of the field with spaces. (1)

Table 3-1 String data types explained

(1) (n) is the maximum number of characters that you want the field to store.

While you may be tempted to use the string data type for all fields, when creating a table, it is not a good idea. One of the biggest problems is that string data types, sort the values in the field, one character at a time, starting from the left.

For example, if the values in the field are 1, 2, 5 and 11, that is probably the order that you would expect them to be displayed in, when sorted. If the field has a string data type, the values will be sorted and displayed in this order. 1, 11, 2, 5. If you see numeric values that are not sorted properly, the data type probably needs to be changed to a numeric data type. And dare I say that changing a data type **AFTER** a table has data, can present problems that you would not believe, including losing data.

Numeric Data Types

As you may have guessed, this data type stores numeric values. As covered in Table 3-2, some numeric data types only support whole numbers. These are known as **INTEGER DATA TYPES**. Other data types support numbers that have decimal places. These are known as **FIXED POINT** and **FLOATING POINT DATA TYPES**. All of these data types support positive and negative numbers, including zero.

Currency Values
PostgreSQL does not have a specific data type for currency values. Use the DECIMAL data type.

Numeric values should not be enclosed in quotes, when used in a query. However, when a function is used to select or extract part of a numeric value, the extracted value becomes text.

Numeric Data Types	This Data Type Supports . . .
BIGINT	Whole numbers between -9,223,372,036,854,775,808 and 9,223,372,036,854,775,807. (2)
DECIMAL	Decimal numbers up to 131072 digits before the decimal point and up to 16383 digits after the decimal point. (3)
DOUBLE PRECISION	15 decimal digits precision. (4)
INTEGER	Whole numbers between -2,147,483,648 and 2,147,483,647. (2)
NUMERIC	Decimal numbers up to 131072 digits before the decimal point and up to 16383 digits after the decimal point. (3)
REAL	6 decimal digits precision. (4)
SMALLINT	Whole numbers between -32768 and 32767. (2)

Table 3-2 Numeric data types explained

(2) This is an integer data type.
(3) This is a decimal fixed point data type. These data types can be used interchangeably. The reason that I use Decimal is because it indicates that the field can store a decimal value and other SQL databases, use the Decimal data type.
(4) This is a decimal floating-point data type.

Signed vs Unsigned Attributes
SQL supports two types of attributes, as explained below. As needed, specify one of the attributes in the query.

The **SIGNED ATTRIBUTE** allows negative values to be stored in the field.
The **UNSIGNED ATTRIBUTE** prevents negative values from being stored in the field. PostgreSQL does not support this attribute.

Date And Time Data Types

Table 3-3 explains the date and time data types.

Date & Time Data Types	This Data Type . . .
DATE	Only stores the date.
TIME	Only stores the time.
TIMESTAMP	Stores the date and time.
TIMESTAMPZ	Stores the date, time and time zone.
INTERVAL	Stores a value that represents a unit of time, like four hours or four days. This value is used for filtering other date or time fields or for calculations.

Table 3-3 Date and Time data types explained

Boolean Data Type

In PostgreSQL, this data type represents/uses True, False or NULL. In other SQL databases, this data type is an integer that uses zero, 1 or NULL and also supports Yes, and No values because internally, they are converted to and saved as 0 or 1. You may know this as a **BOOLEAN FIELD**.

Examples vs Exercises

From here through the rest of this book, you will see examples (which have this heading, Example #) and exercises. Examples are used to explain or demonstrate a concept. It is not a requirement to create or save the queries in the examples. The exercises are the queries that you should create and save.

Learning To Create Queries

For some, learning to create queries can be intimidating. **LEARNING TO CREATE QUERIES CORRECTLY TO ANSWER A QUESTION, REQUIRES TIME, PATIENCE, DEDICATION AND ATTENTION TO DETAIL.** SQL is a robust language and has a lot of features and options. As you go through the exercises in this book, take your time and try to understand how the concepts that you are learning can be applied to queries that you will create on your own. It is possible to go through this entire book in a few days, if you already have some experience creating queries using another SQL database.

The reality is that you will make some mistakes along the way. If you have a fear of making mistakes, this is the time to let go of the fear, because the fear will prevent you from learning. It is also normal to initially get confused on what to do next. Even though you may not understand why you are being instructed to do something, the steps in each exercise will allow you to achieve the expected result. This is how you will begin to build a foundation for creating queries on your own.

One mistake that many people make is trying to run before they crawl, if you know what I mean. While the query exercises and examples in this book, do not require you to understand the raw data used to create the queries, on your own, you will find it easier to know which function(s) to use, if you understand the data that you are using.

Creating effective queries **REQUIRES** knowing what data is stored in what table and how the tables are related to each other. Without knowing this and not having an above average understanding of the data, increases the chance of not retrieving the correct rows of data, which will cause problems.

The first time that a concept or technique is presented, a lot of information is provided. Each subsequent time that you have to perform the same task, less and less information (aka hand holding) will occur. As you will see, there are a lot of repetitious tasks involved in creating queries. These are the tasks that less and less information will be provided for, as you go through this book. The purpose behind this learning technique is to allow you to rely more on your knowledge, instead of flipping through this book months from now, to find the answer.

In my opinion, to create a query, the first thing that you have to get right is to understand what the question is asking for. Once you understand the question, you have to translate that into the SQL language. This is how the database knows what data to retrieve.

The way to learn SQL is by creating the queries in this book. Just reading what the SQL functions do and looking at the query results in this book, really won't cut it. That is because on your own, you will not have a foundation to draw from, to know whether or not a query produces the expected values. As you will see, just because a query does not generate an error, does not mean that it is retrieving the correct data. I am not saying this to be mean. I just know what it takes to learn SQL, or any programming language for that matter. Completing the exercises, will let you get a feel for what it is like to create the queries that you need, on your own.

One thing that I found troubling when I use to teach programming courses, is that many students wanted to and did rush through the basics, to get to the "cool stuff". Because they rushed, they found out that much of the so called cool stuff, required using the basics, so the applications that they designed, which included queries, had major flaws, which caused the application and/or reports to not work correctly. Needless to say, their grades reflected this and they were not happy campers. Take from this life lesson, what you will.

If you think that I created all of the query examples and exercises in this book correctly on the first try, you are sadly mistaken. <smile> Sometimes, just getting the syntax right for longer queries, can stop you for 10 plus minutes. Typos are not your friend.

Creating Queries

Queries are created to answer a question, even if the request is not worded in question format. Below are some examples of questions and statements, that queries can be created for.

- ☑ Display all orders in September 2018.
- ☑ How many orders did each sales rep have in 2017?
- ☑ Display the Order ID, Customer ID and Order Date fields from the Orders table.
- ☑ Which products sold more than 5,000 units in 2018?

SQL Statements

SQL statements consist of clauses. Some clauses are required (SELECT and FROM) and some are optional (WHERE, GROUP BY, HAVING and ORDER BY). There are more clauses, but these are the most used.

SQL statements consist of basic English terms. These terms are known as **KEYWORDS**, a **CLAUSE** or **ARGUMENT**. Each SQL statement contains one or more keywords. The SELECT statement is the most used SQL statement. The SELECT statement is used to query tables and apply logic as needed, to ensure that only specific data is returned.

Honestly, what these words are called, depends on who is writing the content and the context that they are using the word in. I think this is because many people know more than one language and the same word is not known as the same thing in each language. For example, in one language the word TOP is called a function and in another language it is called an argument. What is mostly consistent is that the word, regardless of what it is defined as, works the same way, from one SQL database to another. My advice is not to get hung up on what the word is defined as. Instead, just learn what the word does.

Table 3-4 lists the order that the most used clauses have to be used in, in a query.

> **Creating SQL Statements**
> SQL statements are not case sensitive. That means that you can type SELECT, Select or select, and the result is the same. Many programmers and developers, including yours truly, prefer to use all uppercase letters for keywords and functions. Doing this makes it easier to read the code. The best thing that you can do is to pick a convention for the case that you want to use and stick to it.

Clause	Required	This Clause Is Used To . . .
SELECT	Yes	List the columns, including expressions that you want the query to return. This is the primary clause in an SQL statement.
FROM	Most of the time.	List the tables and views that have the columns that are used in the query. This is the next most important clause in an SQL statement. While rare, you can type the data in the query, opposed to using data in a table.
WHERE	No	Create filters to select the rows that are returned from the table or view. This clause uses an expression that must evaluate to true, false or unknown. Comparison or Boolean operators are often used in the expression. (5)
GROUP BY	No	Select the columns or expressions to create the groups for. When aggregate functions are used on the SELECT clause, they are intended to create summary information (for example, a count of this or a total of that).
HAVING	No	Filter the groups that are created by the GROUP BY clause. This clause is similar to the WHERE clause, in that is also uses an expression that has to evaluate to true, false or unknown. (5)
ORDER BY	No	Sort the rows of data returned by the query, in ascending or descending order. More than one column can be sorted on. If this clause is not used in a query, most of the time, the rows will be returned in the same order that they were added to the table.

Table 3-4 Order that the clauses are used in SQL statements

(5) If the WHERE or HAVING clause is not used in a query, all of the rows in the data set will be returned.

SELECT Statements

The SELECT statement is the most used statement in SQL. That is because it is used to retrieve data from tables. It is the statement that drives the answer to the question, that the query must answer. This is where the phrase "querying the database" comes from. A SELECT query is used to query one or more tables, apply logic (as in create calculations or filter data) and return a data set.

To retrieve data from a database, you have to specify what you want to retrieve and what table or view has the data that you want to retrieve. For example, the query below will retrieve one column (Company Name) from the Customers table. Part of the result is shown in Figure 3-2.

```
SELECT CompanyName
FROM Customers;
```

	companyname character varying (75)
1	City Cyclists
2	Pathfinders
3	Bike-A-Holics Anonymous
4	Psycho-Cycle
5	Sporting Wheels Inc.

Figure 3-2 Result of the query

As you will see, the SELECT statement has several arguments that are used to better define the data that you want to retrieve. While the SELECT statement may be the best known and most used statement that queries data, it is not the only one. The CASE statement is also used to query data.

What may not be obvious now, is that while most of the time, a SELECT statement retrieves data from a table or view, that is not a requirement. SELECT statements can also return values from variables, literals and more. For example, the SELECT statement below does not return data from a table, as shown in Figure 3-3.

SELECT 'HELLO';

	?column? text
1	HELLO

Figure 3-3 Result of the SELECT statement

The data that a query returns is called a **RESULT SET** or **DATA SET**. The data returned, is displayed on the **DATA OUTPUT TAB**, below the Query Editor window.

Keywords

A keyword is a word that has a pre-defined meaning and action in SQL. One way to think of keywords is that they have the same functionality as a macro, because they have code, that when run, completes a task or performs an action.

Queries made up of keywords. These words are used to perform SQL operations, for lack of a better word. These keywords are reserved words and should not be used to name databases, tables, views, fields or any other object that you create, in a database. Many of these keywords are functions. Other examples of keywords are LIMIT and NULL. While SQL keywords are not case sensitive, the common practice is to type them in all upper case letters.

SQL was designed around a set of keywords. The keywords are combined to create commands, which tell the query what to do. A keyword can be more than one physical word. For example, GROUP BY is a keyword, even though it is defined as a clause. Don't ask. I honestly don't know how or why different groups of people have different categories for the same word. Like I said earlier, just learn what the words do. <smile>

SQL Query Syntax

If you have used other programming languages, you know that each language has its own syntax. SQL is no different. Understanding the syntax terms explained below, will help make learning SQL a little easier. Some SQL functions are similar to Excel functions. Each SQL function has its own syntax (the rules that you have to follow to use the function in a query). The explanation of the terms below are for the syntax. These terms can have a different meaning, when used in a different context.

① **EXPRESSION** Is used to define a constant, a reference to a column, a literal or Boolean test.
② **OPERATORS** Dictate what to do with the values in the expression, like add them together or compare one value to another. The operators that SQL supports are covered throughout the rest of this book.
③ **FUNCTIONS** Are pre-built formulas that perform a variety of math, logic tests, time based calculations and more.
④ **VALUES** Is the actual data in the column or data that you hard code (type in) in the query. The values can come from other columns in the same table or from a different table, that is available in the query.

SQL Syntax
While currently not a requirement, a semi colon should go at the end of a query. You should check with your IT department to see whether or not they require it.

SELECT Clause Arguments

The SELECT clause has a set of **ARGUMENTS/KEYWORDS** that can be used to define the rows that are returned. These arguments are typed on the SELECT clause line, or on a line below the SELECT clause line, before the FROM clause line. The arguments that you will use most, are explained below.

① **ALL** This keyword is used to indicate that rows that have duplicate data can be returned. This argument is the default and is usually not typed in.
② **DISTINCT** Is used to indicate that the only rows that can be returned, are rows that have a unique value in the field specified. NULL values in the field are considered equal, when the DISTINCT argument is used. When used, this argument replaces or overrides the ALL argument.
③ * (asterisk) Use this argument when you want the query to return all of the columns in the table or view.
④ **<SELECT_LIST>** Is used to list the specific columns from the table or view that you want to retrieve. Each column or expression in the list must be separated by a comma. If more than one table is used, you may have to **QUALIFY THE COLUMN NAME**, by typing the table name before the column name. This is only needed when the same column name is in more than one table, that is used in the query. The database name may also have to be typed in with the table and column name.

⑤ **EXPRESSION** An expression can be any of the following: a function, a constant value, a subquery, or any combination of column names, functions or constant values, that are joined/connected by operators.

Scalar Expressions

A **SCALAR EXPRESSION** is one that when evaluated, returns a single value or a column reference, in the evaluation context. The majority of calculated fields that you will create in this book, are scalar expressions.

FROM Clause

This clause is used to specify what table(s) or view(s) the data is in, that you need to create the query. The SELECT statement shown below in Example #1, will return all fields and rows in the Orders table.

Example #1 Display Data In A Table

The query shown in Figure 3-4 will return all of the data in the Orders table. This query answers the question, "Show me all of the columns and rows in the Orders table".

```
SELECT *
FROM Orders;
```

Figure 3-4 Query that displays all of the data in a table

SELECT and FROM are the keywords in the SQL statement.

The first line in the figure is the SELECT clause. It says to select all of the columns and rows in the table or view, listed on the FROM clause. The preferred technique is to explicitly type in the column names, instead of typing SELECT *.

The second line is the FROM clause. It states which table to get the records from. Figure 3-5 shows some of the fields and rows that were returned, when the query was run.

	orderid integer	orderamount numeric (18,2)	customerid integer	salesrepid integer	orderdate date	requireddate date	shipdate date	shipperid integer
1	1	2645.87	55	9	2016-01-01	2016-01-10	2016-01-03	4
2	2	8908.05	39	9	2016-01-01	2016-01-07	2016-01-04	1
3	3	39.80	61	7	2016-01-02	2016-01-09	2016-01-14	4
4	4	43.80	9	3	2016-01-02	2016-01-09	2016-01-03	3
5	5	65.70	66	3	2016-01-03	2016-01-15	2016-01-16	4

Figure 3-5 Data returned from the query in Example #1

Wildcard Characters
The asterisk * is a wildcard character. As you saw in Example #1, it returned all of the columns in the table, in the order that they are in the table. While this is an easy way to return all of the columns in a table, from a code perspective, it can often slow down performance. I have noticed a performance hit, especially when this wildcard character is used in a query that is run from an application. Later in this chapter, you will learn another way to add all of the columns in a table to the query. Even better, it is done with a few mouse clicks and no typing! Wildcard characters are covered in more detail in Chapter 4.

Learn To Talk To Yourself

Yes, I know how this sounds, but please hear me out. This technique will help you translate the question that you need to answer, into SQL. I call this "pseudo code" because you write the query without having to use the correct syntax. For example, instead of using words or phrases like what, who, list or show me, use the word "SELECT". Then answer what you need to select. In Example #1 above, what you want to select is all columns. At this point your query looks like this. SELECT *.

The next thing that you need to answer is where is what you want to select. The data could be in a table or view. Now the query looks like the one shown earlier in Figure 3-4. If you need specific orders, like orders in 2018, this WHERE clause would be added to the query. WHERE date_part('year', OrderDate) = '2018'

When you first start creating queries on your own and get stumped, cheat and talk to yourself. Then look at the clauses in Table 3-4 to determine which ones you need to include in the query, to retrieve the correct data.

Example #2 Select Specific Data

The previous example used a query that displayed all of the data in the Orders table. The query in this example, selects specific records to display. This query answers the question "Show me a count of orders for sales rep #2, for each year". The query uses several clauses to answer this question. Don't worry. Over the next few chapters, the code in this query will make a lot more sense.

```
SELECT SalesRepID, date_part('year', OrderDate) AS OrderYear, COUNT(*) AS OrderCount
FROM Orders
WHERE SalesRepID = '2'
GROUP BY SalesRepID, date_part('year', OrderDate)
HAVING COUNT(OrderID) > 1
ORDER BY date_part('year', OrderDate);
```

Figure 3-6 shows the result. This query selects records where the Sales Rep ID field equals 2. A count of orders is created. This count is grouped by year. The result displays the Sales Rep ID, Order Year and Order Count columns.

	salesrepid integer	orderyear double pre	ordercount bigint
1	2	2014	2
2	2	2015	6
3	2	2017	7

Figure 3-6 Data returned from a query that uses several clauses

While this query is more complex, then the one in Example #1, the same technique of talking to yourself can be applied. The difference is that you would have to ask the person that is requesting the query to tell you which fields they wanted to see. That is because the way that the question is written, the fields are not specified. For example, is the Sales Rep ID value ok, or do they need to see the Sales Reps name?

More than likely, you can figure out a good portion of what this query does, without understanding all of the code. Notice that there is no row for the order year 2018 in the figure, even though there is data in the Orders table for 2018. In this query, this means that the sales rep did not have more than one order in that year. In another query, with different requirements, not displaying a count for the year 2018 could mean something entirely different.

This query filters the Orders table to only select orders that are for sales rep #2. These records are then counted and grouped, based on the year of each order.

PostgreSQL does not support functions like YEAR, MONTH and QUARTER, that other SQL databases support. Instead, you have to use the date_part function to select which part of a date that you want to use, as shown in Figure 3-7 below. This function is covered in Chapter 9.

Understanding The Order That The Clauses Are Processed In

What you may find interesting is that the order that the clauses are used in, in a query, is not the order that they are processed in. In most programming languages, the lines of code are processed in the order that they are written in.

Newsflash! SQL does not follow that process. Believe it or not, the clauses are processed in the order listed to the right. Compare this order to the order that the clauses are used in above, in the query in Example #2.

① FROM
② WHERE
③ GROUP BY
④ HAVING
⑤ SELECT
⑥ ORDER BY

When I first learned this, I was a bit shocked. Mainly because queries **MUST** start with the SELECT statement, as shown earlier in Example #2. This means that the query shown in Example #2, actually looks like the one shown in Figure 3-7, when it is processed.

```
FROM Orders
WHERE SalesRepID = '2'
GROUP BY SalesRepID, date_part('year', OrderDate)
SELECT SalesRepID, date_part('year', OrderDate) AS OrderYear, COUNT(*) AS OrderCount
HAVING COUNT(OrderID) > 1
ORDER BY date_part('year', OrderDate)
```

Figure 3-7 Order that the clauses are actually processed in

When you stop and think about it though, the order that the clauses are processed in, makes sense. I say that because the table needs to be selected first, so that the query knows which table has the fields used in the query. The WHERE clause filters the records by selecting records that meet the criteria. This reduces the number of records that the other clauses have to process. This is a good thing because it allows the query to run faster.

Because the tables used in this book do that have a lot of records, you should not encounter a performance issue. If the tables had millions of records, you could very well notice that some queries take a while to run.

Exercise Tips
Below are some tips that will hopefully make creating queries easier.

1. Make sure that the SQLdata database is selected, each time that you open PostgreSQL. If it isn't selected, click on it in the Browser panel.

2. Unless stated otherwise, open a new query window before starting step 1, of an exercise. Because the query window tabs are on the same menu bar as the Dashboard, Properties etc. tabs, (which truly gets on my nerves <smile>), I found it easier to open several query windows at one time and use the one on the far right first. When I finish creating a query, I will close that window and use the next tab. This kept the Dashboard tab from appearing when I closed a query window. Doing this is optional.

3. It is not a requirement to type each clause on a new line, as shown earlier in Figure 3-4. The query shown in Figure 3-8, returns the same result. Typing each clause on a new line, just makes the query easier to read, especially for longer queries, as shown earlier in Example #2.

4. Once you finish typing the query, save it, then run it. Save the queries that you create, in the folder for this book. Remember to type `.sql` at the end of the query file name.

5. The **QUERY HISTORY TAB** displays the last 20 queries that were run, as long as you do not clear the history file. This tab can make it easier to find a previous query that you created, and open it in a new query window to use as the starting point for a new query window.

6. While I type the query using upper and lower case letters, that is not a requirement. I do it to make the code easier to read. You can type the code in all lower case letters if you want.

```
1  SELECT * FROM Orders;
```

Figure 3-8 Query typed on one line

Exercise 3.1: Display Sales Rep Data

In this exercise, you will create a query that displays the data in the Sales Reps table.

1. Create this query.

```
SELECT *
FROM SalesReps;
```

2. Run the query. You should see the data shown in Figure 3-9. You will see more columns then shown in the figure. 15 rows were returned.

	salesrepid integer	supervisorid integer	firstname character v	middle characte	lastname character v	salesrep character varying (5	position character varying (50)	birthdate date
1	1	5	Nancy	A	Davolio	Nancy Davolio	Sales Representative	1972-12-08
2	2	[null]	Andrew	[null]	Fuller	Andrew Fuller	Vice President, Sales	1969-02-19
3	3	5	Janet	E	Leverling	Janet Leverling	Sales Representative	1971-08-30
4	4	5	Margaret	I	Peacock	Margaret Peacock	Sales Representative	1973-09-19
5	5	2	Steven	[null]	Buchanan	Steven Buchanan	Sales Manager	1975-03-04

Figure 3-9 Sales Rep data

> **The Order That Rows Are Returned In**
> It is very possible that the order that rows are shown in the figures in this book, is not the order that you will see them in on your computer. That is fine, as long as you have the same number of rows. Don't worry, nothing is wrong. This can happen when the query results are not explicitly sorted. Usually, data that is not sorted by using code in the query, will be displayed in the order that it was added to the table. The queries in this chapter are pretty basic. I include the number of rows that the query, should have returned. That way, even if your data is not displayed in the same order, as shown in this book, you will know that your query is working correctly.

3. Save the query as `E3.1 Sales reps data.sql`.

   Can you believe that typing a few words, returned and displayed all of the columns and rows in a table?

> If some of the code in a query is selected/highlighted, as shown in Figure 3-10, when you click the Execute/Refresh (Run) button, only the highlighted portion of the code will be run. This probably isn't what you want to have happen, so make sure that no code in the query is selected, before you run the query. The exceptions would be if you are testing a **SUBQUERY** or part of a query that uses the **UNION** or **UNION ALL OPERATOR**. The Union operators can run a specific part of a query.

```
SELECT OrderID, CustomerID, OrderDate
FROM Orders
WHERE CustomerID IN(
  SELECT CustomerID
  FROM Customers
  WHERE State = 'CA' )
ORDER BY OrderID;
```

Figure 3-10 Subquery portion of the code selected

SQL Style Layout

You can pretty much use any layout that you want, to type in a query. For example, if the SQL statement is short, you can type it all on one line, as shown earlier in Figure 3-8 or you can type it on multiple lines, as shown earlier in step 1 in Exercise 3.1. This is my preference because I like each primary clause to be on it's own line, as shown in Figure 3-10 above. The longer the query, the more blank lines I add. <smile>

The requirement is that keywords must be separated by one of the following: A space, a line, a break (press the Enter key) or a tab character (Press the Tab key). The best advice that I can give you is to make the code as easy to read as possible.

Exercise 3.2: Return Multiple Columns

In this exercise, you will create a query that returns more than one column from the Sales Reps table. To save key strokes, you can save Exercise 3.1 with a new name, and use it as the starting point for the new query, then add the new part of the query. Doing this is optional because you can type the query from scratch.

1. Save the E3.1 query as `E3.2 Return multiple columns.`

2. Modify the query, so that it looks like this one.

```
SELECT SalesRepID, FirstName, LastName
FROM SalesReps;
```

3. Run the query.

   You should see the result shown in Figure 3-11. 15 rows were returned.

	salesrepid integer	firstname character v	lastname character
1	1	Nancy	Davolio
2	2	Andrew	Fuller
3	3	Janet	Leverling

Figure 3-11 Multiple columns returned

What Is A Column Alias?

A column alias, is a name that you create, to use in the query instead of the column name in the table. Using an alias does not change the field name in the underlying table. It only changes the name that is displayed when the query is run. One way to understand an alias, is that an alias is a way to temporarily rename a field or an alias is used to create a name for a new column of data (a calculated field), that is not stored in a table. An alias is used with a column in the table for a few reasons, as explained below.

- ☑ The column name in the table is not descriptive enough to have meaning, when displayed on a report. For example, Order ID is not as descriptive as Order Number.
- ☑ The column name in the table is too long to type over and over again, in the query.

A column alias can be used with the ORDER BY clause. A column alias cannot be used with the WHERE, GROUP BY or HAVING clause.

The query shown earlier in Example #2, created two alias columns. In that query, the Order Year and Order Count are the alias column names.

> The **KEYWORD "AS"** is not required, when creating a column alias. While the query in Example #2 included the word "AS", to denote an alias name, it is not required. The query below does not use the keyword AS. As shown in Figure 3-12, the result still displays the alias name. I use AS in the queries in this book. You do not have to type the word if you don't want to, to complete the exercises in this book. Using the AS keyword just makes it easier to recognize that the field will be displayed with a different column heading.
>
> ```
> SELECT MAX(RetailPrice) HighestPrice
> FROM Products;
> ```

	highestprice numeric
1	2939.85

Figure 3-12 Result of a query that does not use "AS" to denote an alias column name

> While the alias name shown above in Figure 3-12, is one word, an alias name can be created using multiple words with spaces. To create this type of alias name, the words must be enclosed in double quotes. The other option is to use an underscore between the words to replace the spaces like this, highest_price.

Exercise 3.3: Create A Column Alias

In this exercise, you will create an alias for the Sales Rep ID column.

1. Save the E3.2 query as `E3.3 Create a column alias.`

2. Click after the Sales Rep ID column in the query ⇒ Press the space bar ⇒ Type `AS "Sales Rep Nbr".`

   Figure 3-13 shows the alias name. Compare this to the result shown earlier in Figure 3-11.

	Sales Rep Nbr integer	firstname character var	lastname character
1	1	Nancy	Davolio
2	2	Andrew	Fuller

Figure 3-13 Result of a query that uses an alias name

Removing Duplicate Rows From The Result Set

At some point, you could create a query that returns duplicate rows of data. Sometimes, this means that there really are rows that have the same data in the table and other times it means that the way that the query was created, allows for duplicate data to be returned.

First, I want to say that well constructed tables should not have duplicate rows of data. Usually, the result set will have a column that has duplicate data, which isn't a problem, as long as the column is not a key field, in the primary table. The query in Example #3 demonstrates duplicate data in a column, which is what you will encounter, more often than duplicate rows of data.

Example #3 Duplicate vs Redundant Data

The query below returns duplicate values in the Position column, as shown in Figure 3-14. Technically, this is not duplicate data because more than one person can have the same position/title. Instead, this is redundant data. In some instances, the problem is that you only want each position to be returned once.

```
SELECT Position
FROM SalesReps;
```

	position character varying (50)
1	Sales Representative
2	Vice President, Sales
3	Sales Representative
4	Sales Representative

Figure 3-14 Column with redundant data

Selecting Distinct Values

Use the **DISTINCT KEYWORD** to only return unique values in a column. Most of the time, you will use the DISTINCT keyword with one field, but it can be used with more fields. This keyword suppresses duplicate values in the column(s) used in the query.

As you know, by itself, the SELECT clause returns all rows. There will be times that you do not want or need every occurrence of a value, as shown in Figure 3-15. When you know that is the case, use the DISTINCT keyword in the query.

	orderdate date
1	2016-01-01
2	2016-01-01
3	2016-01-02
4	2016-01-02
5	2016-01-03
6	2016-01-03

Figure 3-15 List of order dates in the Orders table

Example #4 DISTINCT Keyword

The query below will suppress records based on the values in the Order Date column in the Orders table. I use this keyword when I need to create a query that will be used as a list of values for a parameter field, on a data entry screen or a report. For example, if I needed a list of distinct order dates from the Orders table, I would create the query shown below.

```
SELECT DISTINCT OrderDate FROM Orders;
```

The query used to retrieve the data shown above in Figure 3-15 returned 9,772 rows. It is the same query shown above, minus the DISTINCT keyword. Adding the DISTINCT keyword to the query, as shown in the query above, returns 1,695 rows. The Orders table has several records that have the same order date. For values displayed in a parameter field, each date only needs to be displayed once, in the parameter field drop-down list.

Exercise 3.4: Find Distinct Values In A Column

In this exercise, you will create a query that creates a list of unique values in the Position column. If you look at the results from Exercise 3.1, you will see that more than one person has the same position/title.

1. Create this query.
```
SELECT DISTINCT Position
FROM SalesReps;
```

2. Save the query as `E3.4 Column of unique values.`

   Figure 3-16 shows the list of unique positions.

	position character varying (50)
1	Inside Sales Coordinator
2	Marketing Director
3	Advertising Specialist
4	Vice President, Sales
5	Sales Manager
6	Sales Representative
7	Marketing Associate
8	Business Manager

Figure 3-16 Result of selecting distinct values

Example #5 Use The DISTINCT Keyword With Multiple Columns

The query shown below will suppress rows, based on the values in the three fields (meaning a row will be suppressed when the values in the three columns are the same as the values in another row in the table). This query will display three columns from the table. When the DISTINCT keyword is placed before all of the columns on the SELECT clause, as shown in the query below, it is applied to all of the columns. This query returns 6,605 rows, as shown in Figure 3-17.

SELECT DISTINCT SalesRepID, OrderDate, ShipVia FROM Orders;

What you will notice is that the same value can appear in the column more than once. What you will not see is the same values in all three columns on more than one row. For example, the combination of values on row 1 (6, 4/20/2017, Parcel Post) will not be on any other row returned by the query. Each row retrieved, has a set of distinct values from every other row that is returned.

	salesrepid integer	orderdate date	shipvia character
1	6	2017-04-20	Parcel Post
2	1	2018-03-22	Parcel Post
3	7	2018-04-30	UPS
4	4	2014-09-16	UPS

Figure 3-17 Result of DISTINCT keyword applied to multiple columns

Be careful when using multiple columns with the DISTINCT keyword, because you can suppress rows that you do not mean to suppress.

How To Suppress Duplicate Records
The query in Example #6 below, will suppress duplicate records in the Orders table. Keep in mind that the table used in the query may not have duplicate records. If there are no duplicate records, using the DISTINCT keyword will not prevent the rest of the query from working as expected.

Example #6 Use The DISTINCT Keyword To Suppress Duplicate Records

The query in the previous example suppressed records based on the values in three columns. The query below will suppress records in the Orders table, when the values in all columns in a record, match all of the values, in all of the columns, in a different row. In the Orders table, the chances of all columns in two or more records, having the same data, is pretty slim. If nothing else, the value in the Order ID field should be different because it is automatically generated. If you run this query, **ALL OF THE ROWS** in the Orders table are returned. This means that the Orders table does not have duplicate rows of data.

SELECT DISTINCT * FROM Orders;

What Is An Expression?

An expression is an operation that uses string data, numbers or dates. The expression can use values in a column, literal (a constant) values or a combination of both. Expressions can also be used to filter data, as well as, slice and dice the data, like you can do in Excel. You may know expressions as a **CALCULATED FIELD**.

Types Of Expressions

The majority of expressions that you will create, will fall into one of the types explained below.

① **CONCATENATION** Combines two or more columns or literals into one string field. For example, an expression that uses a mix of text and data from a table, like 'Customer Name ' || CustomerName. This is known as **CONCATENATING FIELDS**. It is not a requirement to use an alias with this type of expression.
② **MATH** Uses operators to perform basic math calculations, like addition, subtraction and multiplication. For example, an expression that calculates a value, like Qty * Price AS LineItemTotal.
③ **DATE AND TIME** Add and subtract values from dates, as well as extract part of a date field. For example, an expression that calculates the number of days, between the Order Date and the Shipped Date.

Creating Calculations

While a large part of creating queries consists of selecting, filtering, sorting, grouping and formatting data, there is often some math involved. Oh, please don't boo me. <smile> I would not be doing my job if I did not include calculations, as part of learning how to create queries. If you have created formulas in Excel, you are already familiar with many of the calculations that will be covered in this book. The two biggest differences are:

① Column names are used in a query, instead of cell numbers, that Excel uses in formulas.

② Calculations in a query are automatically applied to every row in the table, without any intervention on your part, meaning that you do not have to "fill in" the calculation in each row, like you do in Excel.

Truth be told, my initial outline for this book was to have a chapter dedicated to creating calculations, but I decided that it was better to include calculations throughout this book, because I know many people do not like math. Just like people put kale in a fruit smoothie. You know its there, but because you can't see or taste it, it is not so bad after all. Hopefully, the calculations will not be so bad after all. <smile>

What Is A Calculated Field?

A calculated field creates a new field on the fly (meaning that the data for the new field is not already stored in a table). A calculated field is an expression, that may or may not use a function. You can create as many calculated fields in a query, as needed.

For all practical purposes, an expression and a calculated field are one in the same. I think some people say that they are different because a calculated field always involves math. An expression may or may not involve math. As you may have guessed, I use the terms "expression" and "calculated field" interchangeably. <smile> Both are used when the data in the database is not exactly in the format that you need or when data that you need does not exist in the database at all. Just know that whichever term you use, the end result is the same. Calculated field examples include the following:

☑ You need to display the city, state and zip code as one field on a report, but they are stored in three fields in the table.
☑ You need a total for a column of data in a table.
☑ You need to display text with data in a field.

Handling NULL Values

SQL refers to fields that are empty or are missing data as a **NULL VALUE**. As shown in Figure 3-18, the rows do not have a value in the Color column. That is why you see [null] in the column. These are null values. Working with fields that have null values can be tricky, especially when a field with a null value is combined with other fields or used in some types of calculations.

	productid integer	productname character varyi	size character	color chara
1	1101	Crochet Glove	xtra small	[null]
2	1102	Crochet Glove	small	[null]
3	1103	Crochet Glove	medium	[null]
4	1104	Crochet Glove	large	[null]

Figure 3-18 Rows that do not have a value in the Color column

For example, if you created an expression that combined the city, state and zip code fields. If any of those fields did not have a value in any row in the table, the query would not produce the outcome that you are probably expecting.

My guess is that you think that the query would return data and just skip the null values. For example, the rows that do not have a city, the expression would just combine the state and zip code. If only it was that easy. <smile> Figure 3-9 shown earlier, shows that the Middle field has at least two rows that have a null value. As you will learn, creating an expression with a field that has null values, defaults to null. The solution is to check for null values in the expression. Throughout the rest of this book, I cover more examples of null value situations that you may encounter on your own.

In SQL, a null is a placeholder for a missing or unknown value. Null does not represent a blank space or a zero. A blank space is a valid character. Zero is a valid number. Often, a null value is a data entry (human) error, in a field that is not required. In Figure 3-18, the null values are probably a data entry error because gloves have a color. It could be that when the record was created, the color of the gloves were unknown or the person that created the record left the Color field empty by mistake.

The biggest problem of nulls is when the column is used in a calculation. That is because nulls always evaluate to and display null, in the result column. Needless to say, a null changes the result of the calculation.

Combining Columns Of Data

Expressions (calculated fields) can be created to combine data from two or more columns. This is known as **CONCATENATION**. The concatenate operator is two vertical bars ||, which is also known as a **DOUBLE-PIPE**.

At some point, you may have the need to display the data that is in two or more columns, as one column. For example, display the first name, middle initial and last name as one column. To concatenate columns, a double pipe (||) is added between the columns. The result displays the data from the concatenated columns as one column.

CONCAT Function
The SQL standard includes the **CONCAT FUNCTION** to concatenate fields. PostgreSQL supports this function. This function is covered in Chapter 8.

Using An Alias When Creating A Calculated Field
More than likely, you will want to use an alias for each calculated field that you create. Otherwise, the heading for the field will be displayed, as shown in Figure 3-19. Another reason to create an alias name is because if the column needs to be referenced by other software, like a report writing tool, an unnamed column cannot be referenced.

	?column? text
1	Sterling Heights, MI 48358
2	DeKalb, IL 60148
3	Blacklick, OH 43005
4	Huntsville, AL 35818

Figure 3-19 Calculated field without an alias

Example #7 Combine The First And Last Name Columns

This query combines the values in the first and last name columns. Figure 3-20 shows the result.

```
SELECT FirstName || " || LastName AS FullName
FROM Customers;
```

Notice that an alias name was created and used to display the data from the two columns that were combined. In Figure 3-20, that there is no space between the first and last names. Adding an empty string value between columns that will be concatenated, will make the data easier to read. A string can support almost any character that is enclosed in single quotes. The query below uses a space as the string (the ' ' in the code) between the fields. The result is shown in Figure 3-21.

```
SELECT FirstName || ' ' || LastName
  AS FullName
FROM Customers;
```

	fullname text
1	ChrisChristianson
2	ChristineManley
3	GaryJannis

Figure 3-20 Result of combining two columns

	fullname text
1	Chris Christianson
2	Christine Manley
3	Gary Jannis

Figure 3-21 Result of adding a space between the columns that are combined

Exercise 3.5: Create A Query That Uses A Field With Null Values

In this exercise, you will create a query that has an expression that has a field with null values.

1. Create this query.

```
SELECT FirstName || ' ' || Middle || ' ' || LastName
  AS FullName
FROM SalesReps;
```

2. Save the query as `E3.5 Field with null values`.

Your result should look like the one shown in Figure 3-22. Does the result of this query surprise you?

It seems that the query returns all values combined or does not return any value. Yet, if you look in the Sales Reps table, you will see that the First and Last Name fields have data. You would expect that at least the fields that have data, would be displayed. Sorry, but that is not how concatenation works, when null values are involved.

	fullname text
1	Nancy A Davolio
2	[null]
3	Janet E Leverling
4	Margaret I Peacock
5	[null]

Figure 3-22 Result of an expression that uses a field with NULL values

On your own, the bigger issue is now you have to figure out which column(s) have a null value. In this exercise, you know that it is the Middle field that has null values, because Figures 3-20 and 3-21 above, returned the first and last name, without a problem and the result of Exercise 3.1, displayed the Null value in some rows for the Middle field. But in case you missed those clues, there are two options to figure out which column is causing the problem, as explained below. <smile>

① View the data in the columns, that you want to combine and look at all of the values.

② Use the **COALESCE** function in the query.

If you are familiar with **IF . . . THEN . . . ELSE STATEMENTS**, or the **NVL FUNCTION** in Oracle, or the **ISNULL FUNCTION** in SQL Server or the **IFNULL FUNCTION** in MySQL, you understand how the COALESCE function works.

COALESCE Function

This function uses two or more arguments and returns the first non null argument value in the list. If all of the arguments are NULL, this function returns NULL. The COALESCE function is used to provide a default value to replace a NULL value, when displayed.

Exercise 3.6: One NULL Values Solution

As you learned in the previous exercise, querying data that has null values can return unexpected results. This exercise will show you one way to fix the problem, shown above in Figure 3-22. In this exercise, the null value in a column will be replaced with a space. The query in this exercise will use the COALESCE function to check whether or not the Middle field is null.

Yes, you could create a query that only checks the value in the Middle field and the query would work right up to the time there is a record where either the first or last name field does not have data. Then, you would have the result shown above in Figure 3-22. That is the $50,000 a year solution. The $100,000 a year solution is to check all three fields to ensure that all three fields can be combined. In Chapter 4, you will learn another solution.

1. Create this query.

```
SELECT (COALESCE(FirstName,'') || ' ' ||
  COALESCE(Middle,'') || ' ' ||
  COALESCE(LastName, '')) AS FullName
FROM SalesReps;
```

2. Save the query as `E3.6 Use the COALESCE function.`

   Your query result should look like the one shown in Figure 3-23.

   Now you can see that some sales reps do not have a middle initial. In this exercise, the query uses the COALESCE function to replace null values with an empty string. This result is much better, then the one shown above in Figure 3-22.

	fullname text
1	Nancy A Davolio
2	Andrew Fuller
3	Janet E Leverling
4	Margaret I Peacock
5	Steven Buchanan

Figure 3-23 Result of using the COALESCE function

PS and by the way, NULL values exist in fields that are not required to have data. On your own, you should add the COALESCE function to all fields that are not required. The easiest way to tell which fields could have null values, is to view the table(s) that the fields are in, on the Columns tab on the Properties dialog box for the table. If the value in the **NOT NULL? COLUMN** is set to NO, as shown earlier in Figure 3-1, the field is not required to have data.

Example #8 More On NULL Values

The previous exercise provided a solution for a field that is known to have NULL values. The query in this example will check to see if the Payment Type field is NULL. If it is not null, the value in the Payment Type field will be displayed.

If the field is null, '** Ask Rep #' and the sales reps id number will be displayed in place of the payment type, as shown in Figure 3-24.

```
SELECT OrderID, OrderDate, OrderAmount,
  COALESCE(PaymentType, '** Ask Rep # ' ||
    SalesRepID) Payment
FROM Orders;
```

	orderid integer	orderdate date	orderamount numeric (18,2)	payment character varyi
2	2	2016-01-01	8908.05	** Ask Rep # 9
3	3	2016-01-02	39.80	Credit Card
4	4	2016-01-02	43.80	Credit Card
5	5	2016-01-03	65.70	Credit Card
6	6	2016-01-03	27.00	Check
7	7	2016-01-03	6839.10	Check
8	8	2016-01-04	9612.47	** Ask Rep # 3

Figure 3-24 Result of displaying alternate text

LIMIT Clause

Earlier in this chapter, you learned that the DISTINCT keyword returns rows that have a unique value in a column, thus reducing the number of rows that are returned. The LIMIT clause works in a similar way, in that it reduces the number of rows returned. If you are familiar with the term "**TOP N FUNCTIONALITY**" from other software, the LIMIT clause in PostgreSQL works in a similar way, because you can select the number of rows that will be returned.
The LIMIT clause does not have all of the functionality that the TOP keyword in SQL Server supports.

Example #9 LIMIT Clause

The query below will return five records from the Orders table. The reality is that you have no way to predict what records the query will retrieve. That is because new rows of data can be added to a table or existing rows in the table could be edited in a way that causes them to no longer meet the LIMIT clause criteria or rows could be deleted.

You could run this query again six hours from now and see five different rows. This may say strange, this early in the learning process, but the way that you think data will be returned, may not be the way that it is returned. You have to add code to the query, to specify how you want the data to be returned.

```
SELECT LIMIT 5 * FROM Orders;
```

When the rows are not sorted, you can't predict which rows will be returned. Most of the time though, rows are returned in the order that they were added to the table. Chapter 5 introduces sorting and will include more on the LIMIT keyword.

If you want to return rows starting from a specific row number and want to specify how many rows to return, use the following syntax: LIMIT 3, 5. This tells PostgreSQL to skip the first three rows and start at row 4 and return the next 5 rows.

Exercise 3.7: Use The LIMIT Clause

In this exercise, you will learn how to use the LIMIT clause to return a specific number of rows from a table.
The query that you will create, will return 10 records (Yes, the infamous Top 10), from a table.

1. Create the query shown below.

```
SELECT OrderID AS OrderNumber, OrderDate, OrderAmount, PaymentType
FROM Orders
LIMIT 10;
```

2. Save the query as `E3.7 Top 10 rows.`

   You should see the rows shown in Figure 3-25. Yes, I know what you are thinking, "The top 10 of what?"

   Without sorting the data, there is no way to determine which rows will be returned or what the rows returned, mean.

   The LIMIT clause does not sort data. The query needs sort functionality added to it, so that the intended TOP N rows are returned. Sorting is covered in Chapter 5.

	ordernumber integer	orderdate date	orderamount numeric (18,2)	paymenttype character vary
1	1	2016-01-01	2645.87	Check
2	2	2016-01-01	8908.05	[null]
3	3	2016-01-02	39.80	Credit Card
4	4	2016-01-02	43.80	Credit Card
5	5	2016-01-03	65.70	Credit Card
6	6	2016-01-03	27.00	Check
7	7	2016-01-03	6839.10	Check
8	8	2016-01-04	9612.47	[null]
9	9	2016-01-04	40.50	[null]
10	10	2016-01-04	4304.10	Cash

Figure 3-25 Top 10 rows returned

It is possible that the specific number of rows that you want to return cannot be returned. This can happen in one of two ways:
① You enter a number larger then the number of rows in the table. For example, the table has 19 rows and you request the top 25 rows. At most, only the 19 rows in the table will be returned.
② When the query has filter criteria that reduces the number of available rows, to a number that is less than the number of rows that you specified in the query. For example, you want to see the top 25 rows, but the filter criteria in the query, reduces the number of available rows to 20. Only those 20 rows will be returned.

Mathematical Operators

Earlier in this chapter, calculated fields/expressions were introduced. In this section, you will learn how to create queries using the mathematical operators covered in Table 3-5.

Operator	This Operator Is Used To Create An Expression That . . .
+	Adds the values in the fields together.
-	Subtracts the value in one field, from the value in another field or subtracts a constant value from a value in a field.
*	Multiplies the values in two fields or multiplies the value in one field, by a constant value.
/	Divides the value in one field, by the value in another field, or divides the value in a field by a constant value.
%	Divides two numbers, but returns the remainder of a division calculation. You may know this operator as the **MOD FUNCTION** or the **MODULO OPERATOR**.
^	Raises the base number to an exponent. This is the **EXPONENTIATION OPERATOR**.
|/	Calculates the square root of a number. This is the **SQUARE ROOT OPERATOR**. You can also use the **SQRT(N) FUNCTION**.
||/	Calculates the cube root of a number. This is the **CUBE OPERATOR**.
!	Calculate the factorial of a number. This is the **FACTORIAL OPERATOR**.

Table 3-5 Mathematical operators explained

Example #10 Calculate The Invoice Total

The query below will add the values in the Subtotal, Shipping and Sales Tax fields to calculate the invoice total. Figure 3-26 shows the result.

```
SELECT InvoiceID, InvoiceDate, FirstName
  || ' ' || LastName AS CustomerName,
  Subtotal + Shipping + SalesTax
    AS InvoiceTotalAmount
FROM Invoices;
```

	invoiceid integer	invoicedate date	customername text	invoicetotalamount numeric
1	740	2018-06-01	Chris Christianson	49.50
2	741	2018-06-01	Ron Cunningham	527.83
3	742	2018-06-01	Pavel Ropoleski	118.58
4	743	2018-06-01	Ian Kelly	19.25

Figure 3-26 Result of the calculated field

Exercise 3.8: Create An Expression That Creates A New Column Of Data

In this exercise, you will create an expression (calculated field) that calculates the Order Total Amount. This expression adds the value in two fields together, as shown on the second line of the query.

1. Create this query.

```
SELECT OrderID, OrderAmount, ShippingAmount,
  OrderAmount + ShippingAmount AS OrderTotalAmount
FROM Orders;
```

2. Save the query as `E3.8 Calculate the order total amount.`

   Figure 3-27 shows the result. 9,772 rows were returned. If only shipping amounts were this reasonable today. <smile>

	orderid integer	orderamount numeric (18,2)	shippingamount numeric (18,2)	ordertotalamount numeric
1	1	2645.87	26.46	2672.33
2	2	8908.05	89.08	8997.13
3	3	39.80	0.40	40.20
4	4	43.80	0.44	44.24
5	5	65.70	0.66	66.36

Figure 3-27 Result of the Order Total Amount calculation

Exercise 3.9: Create An Expression To Calculate The Line Item Total

In this exercise, you will create an expression that calculates the Line Item Total by multiplying the value in the Unit Price field by the value in the Quantity field. The result of this calculation provides the actual cost of the product, that is ordered. The Line Item Total is also known as the Extended Price.

1. Create this query.

```
SELECT ProductID, UnitPrice, Quantity,
  UnitPrice * Quantity AS "Line Item Total"
FROM OrderDetails;
```

2. Save the query as `E3.9 Calculate the line item total.`

   Figure 3-28 shows the result.

	productid integer	unitprice numeric(1	quantity integer	Line Item Total numeric
1	1101	14.50	1	14.50
2	1102	14.50	2	29.00
3	7038	479.85	2	959.70
4	1103	14.50	3	43.50
5	7039	479.85	1	479.85

Figure 3-28 Result of the Line Item Total calculation

Adding Comments To A Query

You may have a need to add a comment to a query. Often, comments are used to document a query or explain why the query was created. If a query is created for a specific report, adding the report name as a comment would be helpful. There are two ways to indicate that a line in the query is a comment, as explained below. While both options can be used in the same query, try to just use the same one in a query.

① Type `--` (two hyphens without a space between them), then type the comment. The text cannot wrap to a new line. If the comment needs more than one line, type `--` on the next line, then continue typing the comment, as shown in Figure 3-29. When you have finished typing the comment, press the Enter key.

② Type `/*`, then type the comment. Using this option lets the comment wrap to another line, without having to type the symbols on each line. This comment option can also be used for a comment that is only one line. When you have finished typing the comment, type `*/`. This ends the comment. Figure 3-30 shows an example of a multi line comment. Notice that the comment starts on line 5 and ends on line 6.

```
-- This is the comment
SELECT CustomerID, FirstName, LastName, JobTitle
FROM Customers

-- The line below will search for all job titles
-- that ends with the word "Manager"

WHERE JobTitle LIKE '%Manager'
```

Figure 3-29 Comments created using hyphens

```
/* This is the comment. */
SELECT CustomerID, FirstName, LastName, JobTitle
FROM Customers

/* The line below will search for all job titles
   that ends with the word "Manager" */

WHERE JobTitle LIKE '%Manager'
```

Figure 3-30 Comment that wraps to another line

Another Way To Create A Query That Retrieves All Of The Columns In A Table

In Exercise 3.1, you used the * (asterisk) to return all of the columns in the table. While that works as expected, it does not provide the ability to create an alias for a column. If you needed to return more than three or four columns from a table, you may find using the steps below easier then typing each column name in the query.

1. Right-click on the table name in the Browser panel ⇒ **SCRIPTS** ⇒ **SELECT SCRIPT**.

2. You will see a query like the one shown in Figure 3-31.

   From here, you can modify the query as needed.

   You can delete the columns that you do not need and format columns as needed. You can also add other clauses to the query.

```
SELECT vendorid, vendorname
    FROM public.vendors;
```

Figure 3-31 Result of using the SELECT SCRIPT option on the Browser panel

Summary

This chapter introduced you to the basics of the SELECT statement and creating queries that only used one table. You learned that there are more clauses in addition to the FROM and DISTINCT clauses that can be used in a SELECT statement. They are covered in the next two chapters. You learned how queries are logically processed, which is a different order then you type the clauses on the SELECT statement.

While the queries in this chapter only retrieved data from one table, the skills that you learned can be used with any SELECT statement, regardless of the number of tables that are needed to retrieve all of the data. Have no fear, before you know it, you will be creating queries that use two or more tables. I feel that it is important to start slow and learn the basics of creating queries before jumping into creating queries that use multiple tables. The "basics" include creating filters, grouping and sorting data, as covered earlier in Table 3-4.

You also learned how to create a column alias. You were introduced to NULL values, calculated fields and combining data from two or more columns.

As you know, SQL uses a set of keywords that complete a variety of tasks. To be able to create queries, it is imperative that you learn as many of the keywords as possible and their limitations, if applicable. Additionally, on your own to create queries that return the correct data, it is also imperative that you know what tables the fields are in, that you need. You also need to know the range of data (the smallest and highest number or date) that a field can have, and especially, whether or not the field can have NULL values.

Creating Single Table Queries

From a data perspective, creating queries is similar to creating reports. By that I mean that the first two steps are the same, for both. Those steps are listed below. These are the first two tasks that you need to do **BEFORE** you start to create a query or report.

① Understand what the query needs to accomplish. Another way to say it, is what question does the query need to answer.
② Make a list of the fields and the tables that they are in, that are needed to create the query.

Not understanding the data that you are using to create queries, means that you really don't know if the query is returning the correct rows of data. And that can be a career ending move. What do you think will happen if business decisions are made on only a partial amount of data, because the query that you created, did not return all of the data that it should have? I'll just say this. I use to remind my staff that their paycheck depended on them getting it right the first time, not a month later. No, I am not trying to scare you or make you mad. I just want you to be cognizant of the implications of not creating queries correctly and to double and triple check the data that is returned.

Just because a query returns data, does not mean that the data that is returned, is the correct data that was requested by the business owner or user. This is probably the number 1 mistake that new query and report designers make. If you do not understand the request, the chances of creating a query that returns the correct rows and has the appropriate calculations, are slim to none.

I can also tell you that a lot of new query designers run into problems because they do not fully grasp the concept of joining tables, which is covered in Chapters 6 and 7. If the wrong join type is used, you are just about guaranteed that the data returned by the query is wrong and is often missing rows of data.

As this is the first chapter that you created a lot of queries in, I hope that you did not run into a lot of problems. A lot of ground was covered and hopefully, you are at least somewhat comfortable creating queries. It probably isn't in my best interest to bring this up, but I hope that you survived the exercises that had math calculations. <smile>

While the database used in this book does not have a lot of tables, you may find that on your own, that the database that you use, has a lot of tables. When first starting out, this can make it difficult and time consuming to find the fields that you need. If that is the case, you can ask the IT department if anyone has created a table layout like the one shown in Chapter 2, Figure 2-52. Another option is to keep the columns for each table that you need to use, displayed in the Browser panel.

As you create longer and longer queries, you may find it helpful to include blank lines between statements or clauses. Blank lines do not alter the functionality of the query. They just make the code easier to read.

If you are brand new to creating queries, especially if you do not have an IT background, one of the best things that you can do, is to seek out someone that has experience creating queries, to help you when you have a question. The worst thing that you can do, in my opinion, is to think that you have all of the skills needed, to create all queries correctly. If you cannot find someone like this to be your mentor, the next best solution is to post questions on the PostgreSQL mailing list, discussed in Chapter 1. There is a lot of help available online. Please don't be afraid or embarrassed to ask for help.

FILTER DATA

After reading this chapter and completing the exercises, you will know how to use the WHERE clause and its operators, to filter data. As you will see, the operators provide a variety of ways to return the subset of data that you need.

CHAPTER 4

Overview

Companies are collecting more and more data at a very fast rate. The majority of the time, people only need to analyze or view a portion of the data that is stored. The goal of filtering the data is to return specific data from a database. Most of the time, the requirements for the query, do not need all of the rows of data in a table.

Surprisingly, this chapter picks up where the previous chapter left off. <smile> The previous chapter showed you how to create queries. Almost all of the queries that you created returned all of the rows in a table. This chapter introduces the filter techniques that are needed to enhance the queries that you created in the previous chapter, so that you can return data that will answer a question, that requires specific data. If you have used the filter options in Excel, you are familiar with the filter process, because SQL has many of the same filter operators. While not as fascinating as most magic tricks, you do get to make data disappear in this chapter. <smile>

The SELECT statement has several clauses. So far, the SELECT and FROM clauses were the only clauses covered. That was by design, because I felt that understanding the various ways to retrieve columns, including customizing them, is important. That is the foundation of creating queries.

After I created the outline for this book and listed the majority of topics that I wanted to cover, I quickly realized that the WHERE clause, which is used to filter data, needed its own chapter. So, here we are.

As you will see, there is often more than one way to create a filter to return the same data. Additionally, some data types have their own filter requirements. While some will say that technical logic skills are required to create queries, I say that understanding the data and understanding the question that you are creating the query for, is equally important, as the logic skills. One of the best ways to know if the query returned the correct data, is by looking at, at least a subset of the data in the table. Viewing all of the data in a table, on the Data Output tab is usually sufficient.

This is an example. Suppose the question that you are trying to answer is "Show me the orders that are from customers in the south region, during the second quarter of 2018?" Display the following fields: Region ID, Order ID, Customer ID, Customer First Name, Customer Last Name, Order Date and Order Amount. The list below are the items (fields) required to answer this question. This is the logic that is needed (aka understanding the question).

① A field that has region information for customers.

② The Order date, to be able to only return orders for the second quarter of 2018.

The following is the "understanding the data" portion (of creating a query) that I was talking about. The filter criteria that needs to be created in the query, to answer the question. Once you look at the data, you will know the names of the fields that will answer this question.

Quiz For This Chapter
By the time that you get to the end of this chapter, you should be able to create a query that selects the required fields and has the filter criteria that was discussed, two paragraphs above. By the time that you get to the end of Chapter 6, you should be able to modify the query to include the region criteria and customers name.

WHERE Clause

Unlike the tables in the database used in this book, tables in databases in the real world, usually have a lot of records. It is rare that you will have the need to retrieve all of the records in a table. Most of the time, you only need a subset of the records. The ability to retrieve specific records is known as filtering data.

The WHERE clause is used to filter the rows of data in a table. This is how you find the specific data that you are looking for. The criteria that you create, determines the rows that are returned. The WHERE clause has several operators that will make creating the filter criteria easier. I say this because I suspect that you are already familiar with at least half of the operators that are available.

The WHERE clause is added to the SELECT statement to create the filter criteria. If you have used the drop-down list on a column in Excel and filtered the data on the spreadsheet, you will be familiar with many of the WHERE clause operators that are covered in the next section.

This clause is used to create the filter criteria that the data has to meet in order to be returned. The majority of queries that have been created so far in this book returned all or almost all of the records in a table. Believe it or not, there are a lot of options when it comes to filtering data.

The WHERE clause checks the column to see if it has the value specified or is in the range specified, then filters (keeps or rejects) the record, based on whether or not the value passed the filter test.

Many of the queries that you will create on your own, will require using the WHERE clause. Rarely, will there be a need to retrieve all of the rows in a table, like the majority of examples and exercises in Chapter 3 did.

The WHERE clause is very powerful. You can be as specific as you need to be when creating the filter criteria, because the goal of the WHERE clause is used to only retrieve the rows that you need. Below is the general format that you use to create the filter criteria.

COLUMN NAME Is the column that has the data that you are looking for.
OPERATOR How you want to select the data. [See WHERE Clause Operators]
VALUE The data that you want to find.

WHERE Clause Operators

These operators are used to create comparisons, perform logic tests or evaluations, using the WHERE clause. Table 4-1 explains the more popular operators that PostgreSQL supports.

Operator	This Operator Retrieves Rows That Have A Value That . . .
=	Is equal to the value specified on the WHERE clause. It checks to see if the two values are equal. (1)
<> or !=	Is not equal to the value specified on the WHERE clause. It checks to see if the two values are not equal. (1)
>	Is greater than the value specified on the WHERE clause. It checks to see if the value to the left of the operator is greater than the value to the right of the operator. (1)
>=	Is greater than or equal to the value specified on the WHERE clause. It checks to see if the value to the left of the operator is greater than or equal to the value to the right of the operator. (1)
<	Is less than the value specified on the WHERE clause. It checks to see if the value to the left of the operator is less than the value to the right of the operator. (1)
<=	Is less than or equal to the value specified on the WHERE clause. It checks to see if the value to the left of the operator is less than or equal to the value to the right of the operator. (1)
IS NULL	Has a NULL value in the field specified on the WHERE clause. (2)
BETWEEN	Is in the range of values specified on the WHERE clause. The range is specified by using the AND operator with the BETWEEN operator. (2)
AND	Matches all of the conditions listed with this operator. This operator is used to filter on more than one column. This operator can also use more than one condition. All of the conditions must evaluate to true for the record to be returned. It checks to see if **ALL** Boolean expressions are true. (2)
OR	Matches one of the conditions listed with this operator. This operator is used to filter on more than one column or more than one value in the same column. Only one of the conditions needs to evaluate to true for the record to be returned. It checks to see if **ANY** Boolean expression is true. (2)
IN	Matches one of the values listed with this operator. This operator is used to specify two or more conditions. As long as there is a match, the record will be returned. This operator uses a comma delimited list of valid values, that has to be enclosed in parentheses. (2)
NOT	Is not one of the values listed with this operator. This operator is used to specify two or more conditions. As long as there is no match, the record will be returned. This operator can be used with the IS NULL, BETWEEN, IN, LIKE and ILIKE operators, to exclude rows of data. (2)
LIKE/ILIKE	Matches a value in the search criteria. These operators use wildcard characters to look for text patterns. This is a text operator. (2)

Table 4-1 WHERE clause operators explained

(1) This operator is also known as a **COMPARISON OPERATOR**.
(2) This operator is also known as a **LOGICAL OPERATOR**.

LIKE Operator vs ILIKE Operator
The **LIKE OPERATOR** is case sensitive and is part of the ANSI SQL standard. The **ILIKE OPERATOR** is case insensitive and is only available is PostgreSQL. It is not part of the ANSI SQL standard.

When needed, more than one operator can be used with the WHERE clause.

Below are examples of questions that a query can answer, by creating filter criteria. The answer to these questions are specific and require filter criteria.

- ☑ Which customers placed an order in September 2015?
- ☑ Which customers are in Canada?
- ☑ Did any sales reps have sales over $100,000 in February 2018?
- ☑ Show me a list of customers that placed an order over $25,000 in 2019.
- ☑ Which products are missing a size or color?

How The WHERE Clause Works

The WHERE clause has a search condition that it uses as the filter. This is how rows are selected to be included or excluded from the result. The search criteria is applied to every row in the table. As you will learn, criteria can be and often is, created for more than one field. Some of the example questions listed above, require that filter criteria be created for more than one field.

The expression that is created on the WHERE clause can use literal values (aka hard coded values that you type in), columns in a table or functions, just like expressions for other clauses. Before you can create the filter criteria, you need to answer the following questions.

① Which column has the data that needs to be tested?
② What is the value or values that the data in the column will be tested against?
③ What operator should be used to test the data?

Which Operator Should I Use When The Filter Requires Multiple Values For The Same Field?
As you saw in Table 4-1, there are options to select "IS" (include) and "IS NOT" (exclude). This means that you have the option to include the values in the result or to exclude the values from the result.

For example, you need to find all products that come in one of five colors. It is best to create a filter that lists the colors that you want included, or is it best to list the values (colors) that should be excluded. If you create a filter of what you do not want, what happens when a new color is added for a product? As the new color is not listed in the exclude filter criteria, in this scenario, records that have the new color will be retrieved.

This is where logic skills become important. You have to think about this when you are creating the query, because the decision that you make can effect the query results down the road, when new data is added to a table. If you know for sure that you only need to know about the five colors, include them in the filter.

Some will say to select the option (include or exclude) that requires less typing. Maybe this is just how my brain works, but I prefer to see the values that will be returned in the query, then to see the values that will not be returned.

However, this is a decision that needs to be made on a query by query basis and on an individual by individual basis (aka your decision). I just want you to keep this in mind, as you are in the beginning stages of learning to create queries, especially if you do not have an IT programming background. No, that is not shade, I just know that people without an IT background, usually do not have the technical skills to consider a wide variety of options about how new data that is added to a table, in the future, can cause existing queries to no longer retrieve the expected and correct data. The example of whether or not to list the five colors or list the colors that should not be included, is a good example of the "logic" that is required. You have to think of the potential pitfalls of queries that you create, and address them as needed.

WHERE Clause Tips
① When creating filter criteria for a column that has a string data type, the value that you are searching for must be enclosed in single quotes, as shown later in Example #1.
② Columns that are used on the WHERE clause, **DO NOT** have to be added to the SELECT clause <select_list> argument. The column just has to be in one of the tables on the FROM clause. This means that you can filter data on a column that is not displayed in the result.
③ When creating filter criteria that has a range, the specific values used to create the range, do not have to exist in the column used to create the filter criteria.

Comparison Operators

This is the most popular type of operator and is probably the easiest to create and understand. These operators compare one value to another value.

While it is easy to use these operators to compare numeric and date values, often you will have to give more thought when comparing data that has the string data type. Things that you have to know and keep in mind for fields that have the string data type, are listed below. Not being aware of these items, makes it easy to **NOT** retrieve the rows that you are expecting.

☑ What determines the comparison for string fields is the **COLLATING SEQUENCE** used by the database. The collating sequence determines the order that characters are sorted in. In addition to the collating sequence having an impact on how the data is sorted, it also has an impact on how the comparison operators work.
☑ How string data is sorted from low to high, depends on the SQL database and how the database was configured.
☑ Databases that use the ASCII collating sequence, sort numbers before letters and uppercase characters before lowercase characters.
☑ If the database has the case insensitive option enabled, lower and uppercase letters are equal.

On your own, if you did not create and configure the database, these are questions that you will have to ask the owner of the database, unless there is documentation.

Using The Equal To Operator

This operator is used to check if the value in a field is equal to (the same as) the value listed on the WHERE clause. This operator can also be used with the **JOIN CLAUSE**, to create a relationship (link) between tables.

Example #1 Select Customers In The USA

The WHERE clause in the query shown below, does not return all of the records in the Customers table. It only retrieves records that have USA in the Country column. Figure 4-1 shows the result. The Customers table has 555 rows. This query returned 377 rows.

```
SELECT CustomerID, CompanyName, Country
FROM Customers
WHERE Country = 'USA';
```

Notice that the value being checked for, USA, is in single quotes, in the query. That is the requirement when using data in a string field.

	customerid integer	companyname character varying (75)	country characte
1	1	City Cyclists	USA
2	2	Pathfinders	USA
3	3	Bike-A-Holics Anonymous	USA

Figure 4-1 Customers in the USA

This is an example of why you need to know and understand data types, even if you do not have to create and populate the tables.

> **Creating Filter Criteria For String Values**
> Most of the time, when you create filters for string values, you are checking for an exact match. When you only need to check a field for one value, the = sign is a good choice. When you need to check for multiple values, in the same field, the IN operator is a good choice.

Exercise 4.1: Find The Orders For A Sales Rep

In this exercise, you will create a query that will display all of the orders for sales rep 9.

1. Create this query.

```
SELECT OrderID, SalesRepID, OrderAmount
FROM Orders
WHERE SalesRepID = 9;
```

2. Save the query as
   `E4.1 Orders for sales rep 9.`

   Figure 4-2 shows the result. 1,602 rows were returned. This is the number of orders that sales rep #9 has taken.

	orderid integer	salesrepid integer	orderamount numeric (18,2)
1	1	9	2645.87
2	2	9	8908.05
3	20	9	659.70
4	25	9	43.80

Figure 4-2 Orders for sales rep 9

Displaying Fields Used With The WHERE Clause
It is not a requirement to display the fields used to create the filter in the final output of the query. Most people display the fields used on the WHERE clause when testing the query, then remove them from the SELECT clause, when the testing is over, unless they are needed. Displaying the field used to create the filter criteria, is optional. The field(s) used to create the filter criteria are displayed in this book, for the majority of the queries, so that you can see that the query is working as expected.

Using The Is Not Equal To Operator

This operator is used to select rows that do not have the value specified on the WHERE clause. Another way to explain Is Not Equal To is "Find all rows, except the rows that have the following value".

Example #2 Different Ways To Select All Sales Reps Except One

Both queries below will select all of the sales reps, except sales rep #2. Figure 4-3 shows the rows that both queries retrieve. The Sales Reps table has 15 rows. Both queries return 14 rows. Notice that there is no record for Sales Rep ID 2 in the figure.

```
SELECT SalesRepID, SalesRep
FROM SalesReps
WHERE SalesRepID <> 2;
```

```
SELECT SalesRepID, SalesRep
FROM SalesReps
WHERE SalesRepID != 2;
```

Notice that the criteria in both queries, is not enclosed in quotes. That is because the Sales Rep ID field is numeric.

	salesrepid integer	salesrep character varying
1	1	Nancy Davolio
2	3	Janet Leverling
3	4	Margaret Peacock
4	5	Steven Buchanan
5	6	Michael Suyama
6	7	Robert King
7	8	Laura Callahan
8	9	Anne Dodsworth
9	10	Albert Hellstern
10	11	Tim Smith
11	12	Caroline Patterson
12	13	Justin Brid
13	14	Xavier Martin
14	15	Laurent Pereira

Figure 4-3 All sales reps except sales rep 2

Creating Filter Criteria For Numeric Values
What you will find is that the majority of the filters that you will create for numeric values are comparison in nature, opposed to whether or not the value in the column, is equal to the value in the filter, like you do for columns that have text values.

While the **BETWEEN OPERATOR** is used to find rows that have a value in a column, that fall within the clearly defined range of values specified with the BETWEEN operator, many of the other operators covered earlier in Table 4-1, actually allow for a range of values. For example, the Less than operator creates a range from zero through the number before the number that you type with the Less than operator. If this is the filter criteria < 222, the range of values is all rows with a value from 0 to 221.99 in the column. If you wanted to use the BETWEEN operator, you would type BETWEEN 0 AND 221.99.

Using The Greater Than Operators

As covered in Table 4-1, there are two greater than operators. The differences between > and >=, is explained below in Example #3.

Example #3 Understanding The Difference Between The > And >= Operators

In Exercise 4.2, you will create a query that checks to see if the value in a field is greater than the value specified on the WHERE clause. The difference between the two operators is whether or not you need to include the value specified on the WHERE clause, as one that meets the filter criteria.

The query on the left shown below, retrieves products that have a Unit Cost that is greater than $411.09. This query will not return any products that have a Unit Cost of $411.09, as shown in Figure 4-4. This query returned 20 rows.

The query on the right, will return all of the records that the query on the left retrieves, plus any records that have a Unit Cost of $411.09, as shown in Figure 4-5. This query returned 33 rows. Notice the two rows at the bottom of the figure, that have the Unit Cost value, that was used in the query. That is the difference between using the equal sign and not using it.

```
SELECT ProductID, ProductName, UnitCost
FROM Products
WHERE UnitCost > 411.09;
```

```
SELECT ProductID, ProductName, UnitCost
FROM Products
WHERE UnitCost >= 411.09;
```

Currency Values
As shown above in both queries, currency values can include cents, when needed to create the filter criteria.

	productid integer	productname character varying (50)	unitcost numeric
10	7009	Mountain Bicycle	1919.19
11	7010	Mountain Bicycle mens	793.44
12	7011	Mountain Bicycle ladies	793.44
13	7012	Mountain Bicycle mens	793.44
14	7013	Mountain Bicycle ladies	793.44
15	7014	Mountain Bicycle ladies	793.44
16	9000	Test Product	5500.00
17	9001	Test Product	6250.00
18	9002	Test Product	9199.00
19	9003	Test Product	7199.00
20	9004	Test Product	8375.00

Figure 4-4 Result of the greater than operator query

	productid integer	productname character varying (50)	unitcost numeric (
9	7008	Mountain Bicycle	1919.19
10	7009	Mountain Bicycle	1919.19
11	7010	Mountain Bicycle mens	793.44
12	7011	Mountain Bicycle ladies	793.44
13	7012	Mountain Bicycle mens	793.44
14	7013	Mountain Bicycle ladies	793.44
15	7014	Mountain Bicycle ladies	793.44
16	7015	Mountain Bicycle mens	411.09
17	7016	Mountain Bicycle ladies	411.09

Figure 4-5 Result of the greater than or equal to operator query

I remember when I taught college level introduction Excel classes, students often really did not understand the difference between the greater than and greater than or equal to operators. When I asked why they used > most of the time, when >= should have been used, they really could not explain why, other then the value being checked for was entered on the Auto Filter dialog box in Excel. So they thought that the value was included in what would be filtered.

This just let me know that there are a lot of spreadsheets out there, that when filtered, are not being filtered correctly. Yes, that was a scary moment. It is also why I include a lot of examples in the books that I write, that are on topics that I "discovered", caused a lot of my students problems. This is also why in Chapter 3, I wrote a section called "Learning To Create Queries", in which I said that learning to create queries correctly, requires time, patience, dedication and attention to detail. Not truly understanding the difference between > and >=, is an example of what I am referring to. Take from this, what you will.

Exercise 4.2: Find Orders Over $15,000

The WHERE clause that you will create in this exercise, will return orders that have an order amount that is greater than $15,000.

1. Create this query.

```
SELECT OrderID, OrderDate, OrderAmount
FROM Orders
WHERE OrderAmount > 15000;
```

2. Save the query as `E4.2 Orders over 15000.`

Figure 4-6 shows some of the rows that were returned. The Orders table has 9,772 rows. This query returned 21 rows.

Notice that the value on the WHERE clause does not have quotes around it. That is because the data type of the Order Amount column is numeric.

The important thing to take away from this exercise is that filtering data does not always require an exact match.

	orderid integer	orderdate date	orderamount numeric (18,2)
1	704	2016-07-07	17658.81
2	716	2016-07-07	17658.81
3	728	2016-07-07	17658.81
4	885	2016-07-24	17305.93

Figure 4-6 Orders that are over $15,000

Numeric Values On The WHERE Clause
Numeric values that you type in on this clause **CANNOT** be formatted. This means that you have to type the number without a comma or dollar sign. Typing a comma will generate an error. Typing a decimal point is fine, as shown earlier in the queries in Example #3.

Exercise 4.3: Use The Greater Than Or Equal To Operator

The query that you will create in this exercise will select records that have a Last Years Total Order Amount greater than or equal to $20,000.

1. Create the query shown below.

```
SELECT CustomerID, CompanyName, LastYearsTotalOrderAmount
FROM Customers
WHERE LastYearsTotalOrderAmount >= 20000;
```

2. Save the query as `E4.3 Greater than or equal to.`

Figure 4-7 shows the result. 204 rows were returned.

	customerid integer	companyname character varying (75)	lastyearstotalorderamount numeric (18,2)
1	1	City Cyclists	20045.27
2	2	Pathfinders	26369.63
3	4	Psycho-Cycle	52809.11
4	5	Sporting Wheels Inc.	85642.56

Figure 4-7 Order Amount >= to $20,000

Example #4 Using The > Or >= Operator With Non Numeric Values

In Exercise 4.3, you used the >= operator with a numeric value. Most of the time, that is how the operator is used. I did want to let you know that these operators can also be used with a column that has a string data type. When used with a string column, these operators take into account alphabetic order. By that I mean, the rows that are returned will have values less than or greater than (depending on the operator that you select) the string value that you use.

The query below will return rows with a company name that is greater than or equal to Off Road Bikes. Figure 4-8 shows the result. All of the company names returned, are alphabetically greater than or equal to the filter criteria.

```
SELECT CustomerID, CompanyName
FROM Customers
WHERE CompanyName >= 'Off Road Bikes';
```

	customerid integer	companyname character varying (75)
1	2	Pathfinders
2	4	Psycho-Cycle
3	5	Sporting Wheels Inc.
4	6	Rockshocks for Jocks

Figure 4-8 Result of the >= operator used with a string field

Using The Less Than Operators

As you have probably guessed, the less than operators work the opposite of the greater than operators. Actually, the greater than and less than operators can be used interchangeably, to produce the same result.

Example #5 Use Different Less Than Operators To Achieve The Same Result

The queries in this example will demonstrate how the less than and less than or equal to operators can be used to return the same records.

The first query below, retrieves all rows that have a QtyOnHand value that is less than 201.
The second query, retrieves all rows that have a QtyOnHand value that is less than or equal to 200.
The same concept also applies to the greater than operators.

```
SELECT ProductName, QtyOnHand
FROM Products
WHERE QtyOnHand < 201;

SELECT ProductName, QtyOnHand
FROM Products
WHERE QtyOnHand <= 200;
```

Both of the queries above, return the rows shown in Figure 4-9.

The difference between these queries is the value on the WHERE clause. < 201 and <= 200 are two ways of saying the same thing.

This works because the Qty On Hand field only supports whole numbers. If the field supported decimal numbers, the value 200, would have to be changed to 200.99, to retrieve the same rows.

	productname character varying (50)	qtyonhand integer
1	Crochet Glove	123
2	Lycra Glove	111
3	Youth Helmet	57
4	Youth Helmet	41
5	Anatomic Mens Saddle	34
6	Gellite Mens Saddle	39
7	Comfort Ladies Saddle	30
8	Gelflex ATB Mens Saddle	30
9	Gelflex Ladies Saddle	34
10	Mountain Bicycle	39
11	Mountain Bicycle	41
12	Mountain Bicycle	57
13	Mountain Bicycle	111
14	Mountain Bicycle	123

Figure 4-9 Result of both less than operator queries

IS NULL Operator

The IS NULL operator checks to see if a field has a value. Keep in mind that NULL indicates that the information is missing or unknown. Most of the time, this operator is used to check the field specified on the WHERE clause to see whether or not it has a value. Fields that do not have a value are considered "empty". When the IS NULL operator is used alone, it returns a value of True or False (Boolean). If the value in the field is null, the row will be returned. This operator has similar functionality to the **IFNULL FUNCTION**, that **MYSQL** supports.

> NULL values means that the field is empty. Fields that have a 0 (zero) are not empty. If someone pressed the space bar in the field, the field is **NOT EMPTY**. When this is the case, the record will not be selected, when using the COALESCE function or the IS NULL operator. If you need to find fields that have a space, you have to search for ' '.

Example #6 Use The IS NULL Operator To Find Missing Values

The query below will return a list of all products that do not have a value in the Size column. Figure 4-10 shows the result. 77 rows were returned.

```
SELECT ProductName, Size
FROM Products
WHERE Size IS NULL;
```

	productname character varyir	size chara
1	Chain Lock	[null]
2	U Lock	[null]
3	XL U Lock	[null]

Figure 4-10 Result of using the IS NULL operator

Exercise 4.4: Use The IS NULL Operator With A String Field

In Chapter 3, Exercise 3.6, you used the COALESCE function to combine the values in the First Name, Middle and Last Name columns. That worked as expected. The query that you will create in this exercise is not a replacement for that query. The query that you will create, will check the Middle column to find rows that do not have a value in this column.

1. Create this query.

```
SELECT FirstName, Middle, LastName
FROM SalesReps
WHERE Middle IS NULL;
```

2. Save the query as `E4.4 Records with a null value.`

   Figure 4-11 shows some of the seven rows that were returned.

	firstname character v	middle characte	lastname character
1	Andrew	[null]	Fuller
2	Steven	[null]	Buchanan
3	Robert	[null]	King
4	Anne	[null]	Dodsworth
5	Tim	[null]	Smith

Figure 4-11 Result of using the IS NULL operator with a string field

Example #7 Use The IS NULL Operator With A Numeric Field

The query below checks to see if the Unit Cost field is null. If it is, the row is returned. Figure 4-12 shows the result.

```
SELECT ProductID, UnitCost
FROM Products
WHERE UnitCost IS NULL;
```

	productid integer	unitcost numeric
1	9005	[null]
2	9006	[null]
3	9007	[null]
4	9008	[null]

Figure 4-12 Products that do not have a Unit Cost value

NULL Values And The Equal Sign
In Example #7, the Unit Cost field was filtered to return rows if the field is NULL. While it may seem that this code, WHERE Unit Cost = NULL, is the equivalent of using IS NULL, it is not. This code will not return any data. This may cause some people to think that the field does not have any empty values, even though that is not the case. The reason the WHERE clause code above will not return any data is because "NULL" is not stored in the table.

Creating Filter Criteria That Has More Than One Condition

So far, all of the filter criteria that you have learned to create, only needed one condition to answer the question. As you may have guessed, many queries will need more than one condition to return the correct data. The AND and OR operators are used to combine two or more conditions. When the query requires three or more filter conditions, parentheses may be needed to indicate the order that the conditions should be processed in.

Using The AND Operator

This operator is used to combine or append multiple filter criteria on the WHERE clause. Using the AND operator means that the filter criteria before and after this operator must evaluate to true, for the row to be returned. If either of the conditions evaluates to false, the row will not be returned. While the query in Example #8 below, only uses the AND operator once, the AND operator can and often is used more than once, when more filter conditions are needed.

Example #8 AND Operator

The WHERE clause in this query has two conditions. The AND operator joins them. This query will only return rows that meet both conditions. The query below will return all orders that have an order amount greater than $500 and the Sales Rep ID = 9.

```
SELECT OrderID, SalesRepID, OrderAmount
FROM Orders
WHERE SalesRepID = 9 AND OrderAmount > 500;
```

Figure 4-13 shows the result. 910 rows were returned. More than likely, Sales Rep 9 took orders that were $500 or less, but those records will not be returned by this query.

	orderid integer	salesrepid integer	orderamount numeric (18,2)
1	1	9	2645.87
2	2	9	8908.05
3	20	9	659.70
4	40	9	844.90

Figure 4-13 Result of using the AND operator

Example #9 AND Operator Used More Than Once In A Query

The query below uses the AND operator multiple times to append four filter conditions that the row must meet, to be returned. In addition to demonstrating how to use the AND operator more than once, this example also demonstrates how to filter on both text and numeric data in the same query.

```
SELECT SalesRepID, OrderAmount, PaymentType, ShipVia
FROM Orders
WHERE SalesRepID = 9 AND PaymentType = 'Credit Card' AND OrderAmount > 7500 AND ShipVia = 'Parcel Post';
```

Figure 4-14 shows some of the 6 rows that were returned. Each row that was returned, meets all of the criteria, which is what should happen.

	salesrepid integer	orderamount numeric (18,2)	paymenttype character varyi	shipvia character va
1	9	8819.55	Credit Card	Parcel Post
2	9	9187.30	Credit Card	Parcel Post
3	9	8846.55	Credit Card	Parcel Post
4	9	8846.55	Credit Card	Parcel Post

Figure 4-14 Result of using multiple AND filter criteria

Exercise 4.5: Find All Products That Are Missing A Size And Color Value

In this exercise, you will use the **IS NULL** and **AND** operators to find all products that do not have a size and color value. Both conditions have to be met for the record to be returned.

1. Create this query.

```
SELECT ProductName, Size, Color
FROM Products
WHERE Size IS NULL AND Color IS NULL;
```

2. Save the query as `E4.5 Missing product size & color`.

Figure 4-15 shows the result. Out of the 127 rows in the Products table, 20 rows were returned.

Keep in mind that not all products require a size or color. By that I mean, that in the context of this exercise, that is fine that there are products that do not have data in these fields. For products like shoes or clothes, not having a size or color would be a problem.

	productname character varyir	size chara	color chara
1	Chain Lock	[null]	[null]
2	U Lock	[null]	[null]
3	XL U Lock	[null]	[null]
4	ATB Lock	[null]	[null]

Figure 4-15 Products missing the size and color

Exercise 4.6: Find Orders With A Missing Payment Type

In this exercise, you will create a query that will return all orders for sales rep #6, that do not have a payment type.

1. Create this query.

```
SELECT SalesRepID, OrderAmount, PaymentType
FROM Orders
WHERE SalesRepID = 6 AND PaymentType IS NULL;
```

2. Save the query as `E4.6 Payment Type IS NULL`.

Figure 4-16 shows the result.
876 rows were returned.

	salesrepid integer	orderamount numeric (18,2)	paymenttype character vary
1	6	950.97	[null]
2	6	959.70	[null]
3	6	3479.70	[null]
4	6	1529.70	[null]

Figure 4-16 Orders with a missing payment type for sales rep 6

Example #10 Incorrect Use Of The AND Operator

When creating a query that uses the AND operator, make sure that the same field is not used twice on the WHERE clause with the = (equal) operator. Creating a query like the one shown below, will not return any rows, as shown in Figure 4-17. That is because each field in the table, only stores one value.

The WHERE clause in this query is checking to see if the value in the Job Title field is equal to Accountant **AND** equal to Engineer. At best, the value in the field can only be equal to one of those values.

```
SELECT FirstName, LastName, JobTitle
FROM Customers
WHERE JobTitle = 'Accountant' AND JobTitle
  = 'Engineer';
```

	firstname character v	lastname character va	jobtitle charact

Figure 4-17 Result of a query that did not return any rows

The AND and OR operators are used to combine WHERE clauses.

Using The OR Operator

Like the AND operator, the OR operator is used to append multiple filter conditions. The difference between the two operators is that when the OR operator is used, a record only needs to match one of the filter criteria conditions to be retrieved. It is possible that rows will meet each filter criteria. When that is the case, the row is still only returned once. The OR operator can be used more than once on the WHERE clause. As you will learn later in this chapter, both operators can and often are used on the same WHERE clause.

Example #11 OR Operator

The query below will return all rows that meet one of these filter conditions: The Sales Rep ID is 9 or the Order Amount is greater than $5,000. Figure 4-18 shows the result. 2,605 rows were returned.

```
SELECT OrderID, SalesRepID, OrderAmount
FROM Orders
WHERE SalesRepID = 9 OR OrderAmount > 5000;
```

	orderid integer	salesrepid integer	orderamount numeric (18,2)
1	1	9	2645.87
2	2	9	8908.05
3	7	6	6839.10
4	8	3	9612.47

Figure 4-18 Result of using the OR operator

Example #12 OR Operator Used With The Same Field

The OR operator can be used with the same field to select (or not select) rows that have one of the values specified. The query below will select rows where the company is in one of three states.

```
SELECT CompanyName, State
FROM Customers
WHERE State = 'FL' OR State = 'OK' OR State = 'SD';
```

Figure 4-19 shows the result. 20 rows were returned. All of the companies returned, are in one of the states listed in the query, which is what is expected.

	companyname character varying (75	state chara
1	Wheels and Stuff	FL
2	Extreme Cycling	FL
3	Hangin' Two	OK
4	Off Road Bikes	SD

Figure 4-19 Companies in one of three states

Exercise 4.7: OR Operator Used More Than Once With Different Fields

The query in Example #12 demonstrated how to use the OR operator with the same field. The query that you will create in this exercise, uses the OR operator to combine four filters. Rows will be returned if any of the following conditions are true: The Sales Rep ID = 2 or 9, the Order Amount is >= $20,000 or the Shipping Amount is < $10.

1. Create the query shown below.

```
SELECT OrderID, SalesRepID, OrderAmount, ShippingAmount
FROM Orders
WHERE SalesRepID = 2 OR ShippingAmount < 10 OR SalesRepID = 9
  OR OrderAmount >= 20000;
```

2. Save the query as
   `E4.7 Use multiple OR operators.`

   Figure 4-20 shows the result. 6,246 rows were returned. You will see that each row matches at least one of the filter criteria on the WHERE clause.

	orderid integer	salesrepid integer	orderamount numeric (18,2)	shippingamount numeric (18,2)
1	1	9	2645.87	26.46
2	2	9	8908.05	89.08
3	3	7	39.80	0.40
4	4	3	43.80	0.44

Figure 4-20 Result of using multiple OR operators

Exercise 4.8: Use The AND And OR Operators

So far, the exercises have used one or the other operator, but not both. This exercise will use both operators in the same query. You will add criteria to the E4.5 query to also return rows that have a Quantity On Hand value that is greater than or equal to 2,500. This means that a record only has to match one set of criteria to be returned.

1. Save the E4.5 query as `E4.8 Use the AND & OR operators.`

2. At the end of the SELECT clause, add the QtyOnHand field.

3. At the end of the WHERE clause, type `OR QtyOnHand >= 2500.`

   Figure 4-21 shows the result. 54 rows were returned.

   Compare these results to the ones shown earlier in Figure 4-15.

   As you will see later in this chapter, while this query returned data, it probably does not process the data the way that you think it does.

	productname character varyin	size character	color charact	qtyonhand integer
1	Vertigo Helmet	medium	black	7043
2	Chain Lock	[null]	[null]	2204
3	U Lock	[null]	[null]	2205
4	XL U Lock	[null]	[null]	7040
5	ATB Lock	[null]	[null]	2206
6	Mini Lock	[null]	[null]	3305
7	Crochet Glove	small	[null]	7036

Figure 4-21 Result of using the AND and OR operators

Example #13 Using The <> And != Operators

> When you create filter criteria to select rows that do not have a specific value in a field, rows that have a NULL value in that field are not returned. This means that you have to decide whether or not rows that have a NULL value should or should not be returned. Actually, you should ask the person or group of people that requested or will use the query, what they want. Both options are demonstrated in this example. When creating this type of filter criteria, you need to verify and ensure that all rows with a NULL value in the field that the filter criteria is for, are returned when the query is run.

As stated in the warning above, when creating filter criteria that uses the not equal to operator, you may not be retrieving all of the rows that you should. That is because the Not Equal operator does not take into account, fields that have a NULL value.

In the query shown below, you would expect that the rows that do not have "medium" in the Size column would be returned. If you run this query, 26 rows are returned, as shown in Figure 4-22.

```
SELECT ProductName, Size
FROM Products
WHERE Size <> 'medium';
```

	productname character varyin	size character
1	Crochet Glove	xtra small
2	Crochet Glove	small
3	Crochet Glove	large
4	Crochet Glove	extra large

Figure 4-22 Result of the not equal to operator filter criteria

None of the rows that have NULL in the Size column were returned. You need to decide if this is acceptable or not.

If this is not acceptable and you need to include rows that have NULL in the Size column in the result, the query above needs to be modified, as shown below. When the modified query below is run, 103 rows are returned, as shown in Figure 4-23.

SELECT ProductName, Size
FROM Products
WHERE Size <> 'medium' OR Size IS NULL;

	productname character varying	size charac
19	Vertigo Helmet	large
20	Chain Lock	[null]
21	U Lock	[null]
22	XL U Lock	[null]
23	ATB Lock	[null]
24	Mini Lock	[null]
25	Crochet Glove	small

Figure 4-23 Result of the IS NULL operator added to the filter criteria

While both queries above used <>, you can also use the != operator and the result would be the same.

The moral to this example is that when creating filter criteria, you need to decide whether or not rows with null values in any of the fields that are used to create filter criteria should be returned, as part of the result set.

AND vs OR Operators

Now that you have used both operators, a recap is in order, to help make sure that you are clear on what each operator brings to the table, as they say.

- ☑ By default, the AND operator narrows the search, because both filter conditions must be met for the row to be returned.
- ☑ By default, the OR operator will return more rows than the AND operator will, because only one of the conditions has to be met.

AND And OR Operator Precedence
The AND operator has precedence over the OR operator. This means that the criteria surrounding the AND operator is processed first, regardless of where the AND operator is physically located on the WHERE clause. After that, the filter criteria is processed from left to right. This means that if the AND operator comes before the OR operator, parentheses may not be necessary. However, for readability and to be on the safe side, it is best to use parentheses to ensure that the filter criteria is processed the way that you intend it to.

Order Of Evaluation

You may know the order of evaluation as the **ORDER OF PRECEDENCE**. Both terms refer to the same process. While the WHERE clause supports using the AND and OR operators, using both in the same query can be a problematic. One problem occurs when either operator has two or more conditions for the same field.

Like most SQL databases, PostgreSQL processes AND operators first and then processes OR operators.

Table 4-2 shows the order of evaluation for operators. Example #14 explains the problem of using the AND and OR operators in the same query in detail, and how to correct it.

Order	Operator
1	+ (positive sign), - (negative sign)
2	* (multiplication), / (division)
3	+ (addition), (subtraction)
4	=, <>, <, <=, >, >=, IS NULL, BETWEEN, IN, LIKE
5	NOT
6	AND
7	OR

Table 4-2 Operator order of evaluation

Example #14 Understanding The Order Of Evaluation

The goal is to create a query that retrieves orders for sales reps 2 and 5, that have an order amount that is greater than or equal to $2,500. Both of the queries listed below have all of the criteria to return the correct data. As you will see, they are processed differently, due to the order that the AND and OR operators are actually processed in, opposed to the physical order that they appear, in the query.

Query Option 1
SELECT OrderID, SalesRepID, OrderAmount
FROM Orders
WHERE SalesRepID = 2 OR SalesRepID = 5 AND OrderAmount >= 5000;

Query Option 2

```
SELECT OrderID, SalesRepID, OrderAmount
FROM Orders
WHERE OrderAmount >= 5000 AND SalesRepID = 2 OR SalesRepID = 5;
```

How Parentheses On The WHERE Clause Are Processed

You can use as many sets of parentheses as needed. You can also embed one set of parentheses in another set of parentheses. It should not be a surprise that there is an order of evaluation for parentheses, used on the WHERE clause. The order is explained below.

① Filter criteria in parentheses is processed before filter criteria that is not in parentheses.

② If there are two or more sets of parentheses on the WHERE clause, they are processed from left to right. This means that you have to place each set of filter criteria in a specific order, to achieve the expected result.

③ If the WHERE clause has embedded parentheses, the parentheses are processed from the inner most set of parentheses first, to the outermost set.

How The Queries Are Processed

This section explains how each of the queries in Example #14 above, are processed.

Query Option 1

Step 1: The query processes Sales Rep ID = 5 and Order Amount >= 5000 together first, meaning return all rows that meet both of these conditions.

Step 2: The query then processes the Sales Rep ID = 2 criteria, meaning it retrieves all orders for sales rep 2, whether or not the Order Amount is >= 5000.

This query retrieves the rows shown in Figure 4-24. 21 rows were returned. While the query correctly only selected rows for sales reps 2 or 5, some of the order amounts are less than $5,000, for sales rep 2, which is a problem, based on the requirements for the query.

Query Option 2

Step 1: The query processes the Order Amount >= 5000 and Sales Rep ID = 2 together, meaning return all order amounts >= 5000 for sales rep 2. Notice that the first row for sales rep 2, in Figure 4-25, has a value over $5,000. If you created this query on your own, you would see that the other rows returned for sales rep 2 also have a value over $5,000. This alone could let you think that the query returned the correct rows.

Step 2: The query then retrieves all rows where the Sales Rep ID = 5, whether or not the Order Amount for the row is >= 5000.

This query retrieves the rows shown in Figure 4-25. 24 rows were returned. While the query correctly only selected rows for sales reps 2 or 5, some of the order amounts are less than $5,000, for sales rep 5, which is a problem.

	orderid integer	salesrepid integer	orderamount numeric (18,2)
1	2448	2	8908.05
2	2451	5	9612.47
3	2461	2	659.70
4	2464	5	11465.42
5	2483	2	2996.65

Figure 4-24 Rows returned from the query in Option 1

	orderid integer	salesrepid integer	orderamount numeric (18,2
1	2448	2	8908.05
2	2451	5	9612.47
3	2464	5	11465.42
4	2476	5	844.90
5	2486	5	1758.79

Figure 4-25 Rows returned from the query in Option 2

Solution

In this scenario, the expected result is that all order amounts are >= 5000, for both sales reps. The problem is that the wrong operators were processed together. The solution is to place parentheses around the operator, which in this example, is the OR operator. The parentheses force that part of the query to be processed first, because parentheses have a higher order of evaluation than the AND and OR operators.

Below are the revised queries. The parentheses for the sales rep criteria will be processed first, regardless of where it is, physically on the WHERE clause. Then from that list, select the rows that have an order amount >= 5000, which, in this example is what you want. Both revised queries below, return the seven rows shown in Figure 4-26. As you can see, there is a big difference between returning seven rows versus returning over 20 rows.

Query Option 1 Revised
SELECT OrderID, SalesRepID, OrderAmount
FROM Orders
WHERE (SalesRepID = 2 OR SalesRepID = 5)
AND OrderAmount >= 5000;

Query Option 2 Revised
SELECT OrderID, SalesRepID, OrderAmount
FROM Orders
WHERE OrderAmount >= 5000 AND (SalesRepID = 2
OR SalesRepID = 5);

	orderid integer	salesrepid integer	orderamount numeric (18,2
1	2448	2	8908.05
2	2451	5	9612.47
3	2464	5	11465.42
4	2524	5	6729.55
5	2801	5	8159.40
6	6996	5	8412.45
7	7090	2	5179.98

Figure 4-26 Correct result for both queries

In case you are wondering why the query in Exercise 4.8 covered earlier, worked without using parentheses, even though it uses the AND and OR operators, it works because different fields were used for both AND conditions. The queries in Example #14 used the same field (Sales Rep ID) for both filter conditions.

Example #15 Understanding Parentheses Placement

As you learned in the previous example, parentheses are used to determine which criteria are processed together. While the solution examples in that section placed the parentheses around the same criteria (the Sales Rep ID criteria), that is not always a requirement. You are free to place the parentheses around the criteria that you need processed together.

The two queries below have the same filter criteria. They produce different results because of where the parentheses are placed.

Figure 4-27 shows the result of Query 1. It returns 1,925 rows. This query selects rows that have a Sales Rep ID =1 and the Ship Via field is equal to Parcel Post. Then all of the rows that have the Ship Via value equal to Pickup are also returned.

Figure 4-28 shows the result of Query 2. It returns 613 rows. This query selects rows that have the Ship Via value of Parcel Post or Pickup. From that list, rows that have the Sales Rep ID = 1 are kept and displayed.

As you can see, the results that the queries produced are quite different, even though all of the filter criteria is the same. What a difference parentheses make!

Query 1
SELECT OrderID, SalesRepID, OrderAmount, ShipVia
FROM Orders
WHERE (SalesRepID = 1 AND ShipVia = 'Parcel Post') OR ShipVia = 'Pickup';

Query 2
SELECT OrderID, SalesRepID, OrderAmount, ShipVia
FROM Orders
WHERE SalesRepID = 1 AND (ShipVia = 'Parcel Post' OR ShipVia = 'Pickup');

	orderid integer	salesrepid integer	orderamount numeric (18,2)	shipvia characte
1	5	3	65.70	Pickup
2	12	7	701.54	Pickup
3	28	9	101.70	Pickup
4	35	3	67.80	Pickup

Figure 4-27 Result of Query 1

	orderid integer	salesrepid integer	orderamount numeric (18,2)	shipvia character va
1	36	1	8229.76	Pickup
2	38	1	101.70	Pickup
3	43	1	727.50	Parcel Post
4	75	1	10384.96	Pickup

Figure 4-28 Result of Query 2

Example #16 Add Parentheses To The Query In Exercise 4.8

The way that the query in Exercise 4.8 is written, it is difficult to know which portion of the WHERE clause is processed first, because it uses the AND and OR operators. While the Order Of Evaluation section explained that the AND operator is processed first and then the OR operator is processed, it is still a good programming technique to place parentheses around the filter criteria that you want processed together. It is not a good idea to just type the criteria using the AND operator first. That would just be something else that you would have to remember to always do.

If you go back and read the introduction for Exercise 4.8, you will see that I did not specify one way or the other, how the criteria should be processed. As is, the criteria is ambiguous. By that I mean, should the query require the Size and Color columns to be null for the row to be returned or can the Color column be null or the Qty On Hand be >= 2500, for the row to be returned. Adding parentheses will remove the ambiguity.

The query in Exercise 4.8 has been revised to include parentheses, as shown. This will ensure that the size and color have to be null or the Qty On Hand is >= 2500 for the row to be returned. This query returns the same 54 rows that Exercise 4.8 returned.

```
SELECT ProductName, Size, Color, QtyOnHand
FROM Products
WHERE (Size IS NULL AND Color IS NULL) OR
  QtyOnHand >= 2500;
```

This query has the parentheses around the last two filter conditions. The query returns 39 rows, as shown in Figure 4-29. This query returns rows where either the (Color is null or Qty On Hand is >= 2500) and the Size is null. This means that all rows returned have to meet the Size IS NULL filter criteria and one of the filter conditions that are in parentheses.

```
SELECT ProductName, Size, Color, QtyOnHand
FROM Products
WHERE Size IS NULL AND (Color IS NULL
  OR QtyOnHand >= 2500);
```

When you compare the results of this query, to the results shown earlier in Figure 4-21, you will see that some rows are the same and some are different.

On your own, you would need to ask the person that requested the query, to clarify how they want the filter criteria grouped.

Hopefully, between the queries in this example and the queries in the previous example, you are starting to see how important it is to put the parentheses in the correct place.

	productname character varying (5(	size chara	color character va	qtyonhand integer
4	ATB Lock	[null]	[null]	2206
5	Mini Lock	[null]	[null]	3305
6	Mtn Lock	[null]	[null]	4106
7	Rhino Lock	[null]	[null]	7042
8	Titan Lock	[null]	[null]	5201
9	Road Bicycle ladies	[null]	satin silver	3305
10	Road Bicycle ladies	[null]	forest blue	3305

Figure 4-29 Result of parentheses added around different filter criteria

Using The BETWEEN Operator

The BETWEEN operator is used to create a range of values by specifying the lowest and highest values for the filter criteria, that the value in the field must fall in, for the record to be returned. The two values must be separated by the keyword AND, as shown in Example #17.

Example #17 BETWEEN Operator

This query will select all customers whose Last Years Total Order Amount is between $10,000 and $20,000. Figure 4-30 shows the result. 60 rows were returned.

```
SELECT CustomerID, CompanyName, LastYearsTotalOrderAmount
FROM Customers
WHERE LastYearsTotalOrderAmount BETWEEN 10000 AND 20000;
```

	customerid integer	companyname character varying (75)	lastyearstotalorderamount numeric (18,2)
1	7	Poser Cycles	10923.00
2	16	Hercules Mountain Bikes	18000.00
3	18	Bikes and Trikes	12000.00
4	27	The Great Bike Shop	15218.09

Figure 4-30 Result of using the BETWEEN operator

Creating A Query That Uses A Range
It is not a requirement to use values that are in the table for the beginning and ending range values.

Exercise 4.9: Find Orders In A Specific Order Amount Range

This exercise will show you how to create a query that finds orders that have an order amount that falls within a range.

1. Create this query.

```
SELECT OrderID, OrderDate, OrderAmount
FROM Orders
WHERE OrderAmount BETWEEN 2500 AND 5000;
```

2. Save the query as `E4.9 Orders in a specific order amount range.`

   Figure 4-31 shows the result. 1,083 rows were returned.

	orderid integer	orderdate date	orderamount numeric (18,2)
1	1	2016-01-01	2645.87
2	10	2016-01-04	4304.10
3	29	2016-01-10	3086.71
4	41	2016-01-13	3977.26

Figure 4-31 Order amounts between $2,500 and $5,000

BETWEEN Operator Tip
What may not be obvious is that the two values used with this operator, are also included as acceptable values in the range of values. For example, in Exercise 4.9 above, the values 2500 and 5000 are included in the range. This means that any row that has either of these values as the order amount, will be returned.

Exercise 4.10: Emulating The BETWEEN Operator

The query that you will create in this exercise, is a way to get the same result as using the BETWEEN operator that was covered in Example #17.

1. Create the query shown below.

```
SELECT CustomerID, CompanyName, LastYearsTotalOrderAmount
FROM Customers
WHERE LastYearsTotalOrderAmount >= 10000 AND LastYearsTotalOrderAmount
  <= 20000;
```

2. Save the query as `E4.10 Emulate the BETWEEN operator.`
   You should see the same rows, as shown earlier in Figure 4-30.

   While effective, using this option requires you to type the field name twice. It also isn't as clear, at least to me, that the query is creating a range of values, like the BETWEEN operator does. The choice is yours.

Example #18 Use Calculated Values With The BETWEEN Operator

The query below uses an expression that calculates the highest value in the range. The range that the Invoice Total must be in, is the Subtotal (the lowest value) and Subtotal + 40 (the highest value). This will filter the data. Figure 4-32 shows the result.

```
SELECT InvoiceID, InvoiceTotal, Subtotal
FROM Invoices
WHERE InvoiceTotal BETWEEN Subtotal AND Subtotal + 40;
```

	invoiceid integer	invoicetotal numeric (18,2	subtotal numeric
1	740	49.50	45.00
2	742	118.58	107.80
3	743	19.25	17.50
4	745	70.87	64.42

Figure 4-32 Result of using a calculation to filter data

> **Date Fields In PostgreSQL**
> While PostgreSQL supports a few date formats like MM/DD/YYYY, the ISO Standard (International Organization for Standardization), for dates is YYYY-MM-DD. This is the format used in this book because it is supported in all SQL databases. This makes queries that use date fields portable from one SQL database to another. This is also the only date format that SQLite databases support. Chapter 9 covers using date fields in detail.

Exercise 4.11: Use The BETWEEN Operator To Create A Date Range Filter

In Exercise 4.9, the query used the BETWEEN operator to find orders with an order amount, in a range. The query that you will create in this exercise will find orders with an order date in one range and a ship date in a different date range.

1. Create this query.

```
SELECT OrderID, OrderDate, ShipDate
FROM Orders
WHERE (OrderDate BETWEEN '2018-09-19' AND '2018-09-29')
  AND (ShipDate BETWEEN '2018-09-21' AND '2018-09-30');
```

2. Save the query as `E4.11 BETWEEN operator with a date range.`

Figure 4-33 shows the result. 33 rows were returned.

All of the rows returned have an order date and ship date in the corresponding range specified on the WHERE clause.

	orderid integer	orderdate date	shipdate date
1	4490	2018-09-19	2018-09-21
2	4491	2018-09-19	2018-09-29
3	4492	2018-09-19	2018-09-21
4	4493	2018-09-19	2018-09-28

Figure 4-33 Result of using the BETWEEN operator to create a date range

Example #19 Using The BETWEEN Operator With Text Values

When this operator is used with text values, it creates an alphabetical range. For this type of query to work correctly, the lowest letter, alphabetically, **MUST** be entered first, with the BETWEEN operator. Entering H before E would not return any rows. The query below will return all customers whose last name starts with a letter between E through H. Figure 4-34 shows the result of using the BETWEEN operator with a text column.

```
SELECT CustomerID, FirstName, LastName
FROM Customers
WHERE SUBSTRING(LastName, 1, 1) BETWEEN 'E'
  AND 'H';
```

The **SUBSTRING FUNCTION** retrieves the number of characters specified with the function, starting at the beginning of the column. This function is the equivalent of using the **LEFT FUNCTION**.

	customerid integer	firstname character v	lastname character
1	23	Annie	Harper
2	24	Tony	Garneau
3	25	Zach	Fabro
4	31	Richard	Grewal

Figure 4-34 Customers whose last name starts with a letter between E and H

Using The IN Operator

This operator checks the value in a field to see if it matches any of the values in the IN operator list. Yes, this operator works the same as the **OR OPERATOR**, when it is only used with one field to check for multiple values. The difference, in my opinion, is that the IN operator requires less typing. I don't know about you, but that makes me happy. <smile> Like the OR operator, the IN operator also uses parentheses. The values in the list must be separated by commas. The IN operator is used to type in two or more values that you want to filter on. You do not have to type the values on the same line. Below are the syntax requirements for the IN operator.

① All of the values must be enclosed in a single set of parentheses.
② Each value, except the last, must be followed (separated) by a comma.
③ Text values must be enclosed in single quotes.

Example #20 Use The IN Operator With A Numeric Field

The query below checks to see if the Region ID is one of four values. If there is a match, the row will be returned. Figure 4-35 shows the result. 37 rows were returned.

```
SELECT CustomerID, CompanyName, RegionID
FROM Customers
WHERE RegionID IN (2, 10, 19, 24);
```

	customerid integer	companyname character varying (7	regionid integer
7	59	The Biker's Path	10
8	118	Tony's Better Bikes	24
9	123	One Track Mind	2
10	129	Tears For Gears	19

Figure 4-35 Customers in one of four regions

The IN operator (in Example #20 above), translates to "Is the Region ID equal to 2 or 10 or 19 or 24?" Notice that I used the word "or". The logic and reason is because the Region ID field only stores one value for each customer.

The customer cannot be in multiple regions at the same time. Understanding how this operator works is important, especially when the query requires multiple filter conditions. As with a lot of options in SQL, it is very easy to return the wrong data and not even know it.

Example #21 Emulating The IN Operator

This query uses the OR operator to emulate the IN operator query, shown above in Example #20. This query returns the same records. Which of these queries would you rather type? <smile>

```
SELECT CustomerID, CompanyName, RegionID
FROM Customers
WHERE RegionID = 2 OR RegionID = 10 OR
  RegionID = 19 OR RegionID = 24;
```

IN Operator vs OR Operator

As you saw in Examples #20 and #21, both operators can create the same result. In addition to less typing, the IN operator has the advantages explained below.

- ☑ The IN operator runs faster than the OR operator, because there is more than one OR operator that has to be processed. There is one OR operator for each value.
- ☑ The order of evaluation is easier to manage when the IN operator is used, because there are fewer operators.
- ☑ The IN operator is easier to read, when there is a long list of values to check for.
- ☑ The IN operator supports having its own SELECT statement. This means that a subquery can be created using the IN operator. Subqueries are covered in Chapter 11.

Exercise 4.12: Find Products In Specific Categories

In this exercise, you will create a query that retrieves products that are in one of three categories.

1. Create this query.

```
SELECT ProductID, ProductName, ProductCategoryID
FROM Products
WHERE ProductCategoryID IN (1, 3, 5);
```

2. Save the query as `E4.12 Products in specific categories.`

   Figure 4-36 shows the products that meet the criteria. 60 rows were returned.

	productid integer	productname character varying (	productcategoryid integer
16	4105	Lycra Glove	5
17	4106	Lycra Glove	5
18	7000	Mountain Bicycle	1
19	7001	Mountain Bicycle	1

Figure 4-36 Products in one of three product categories

Example #22 Using The IN Operator With A String Field

While the IN operator examples and exercises so far, were demonstrated with numeric fields, the IN operator can also be used with fields that have a string data type. The query below retrieves customers in one of three states. Figure 4-37 shows the result. 64 rows were returned.

```
SELECT CompanyName, State
FROM Customers
WHERE State IN ('CA', 'IL', 'FL');
```

	companyname character varying (75)	state charact
1	Pathfinders	IL
2	Sporting Wheels Inc.	CA
3	Rowdy Rims Company	CA
4	Hercules Mountain Bikes	IL

Figure 4-37 Customers in CA, IL or FL

Using String Data That Has An Apostrophe
If string data that you need to search for has an apostrophe in it, like Cyclist's Trail, you have to add a single quote before the apostrophe, like this, 'Cyclist' 's Trail.

Exercise 4.13: Create Multiple Sets Of Filter Criteria

The query that you will create in this exercise has the following filter criteria.

① All products that have a Unit Cost > 350 and a Retail Price > 500.

② Or products in the product categories 5 or 6, that have a size of medium or large.

Yes, this query has a lot of filter criteria. While the chances of having to create a query with this specific criteria may seem unrealistic, trust, you will get requests for a data set with equally complex business needs and "interesting" requirements. <smile>

When you have this much criteria, it is helpful to create one set of filter criteria and make sure that it works, BEFORE adding another set of filter criteria, to the query. This is especially helpful when you are first learning to create queries. The first three lines in the query below, creates some of the filter criteria. These three lines return 28 rows.

1. Create the query shown below.

```
SELECT ProductID, ProductName, Size, UnitCost, RetailPrice,
  ProductCategoryID
FROM Products
WHERE (UnitCost > 350 AND RetailPrice > 500)
OR
 (Size IN ('medium', 'large') AND ProductCategoryID IN (5, 6));
```

2. Save the query as `E4.13 Multiple sets of filter criteria.`

Figure 4-38 shows the result. 52 rows were returned.

Each row meets at least one set of the filter criteria. Notice that each set of filter criteria is enclosed in parentheses and that there is a set of embedded parentheses.

	productid integer	productname character varyir	size character	unitcost numeric (	retailprice numeric (18	productcategoryid integer
1	1103	Crochet Glove	medium	7.27	14.50	5
2	1104	Crochet Glove	large	7.27	14.50	5
3	1109	Lycra Glove	medium	4.29	16.50	5
4	1110	Lycra Glove	large	4.29	16.50	5

Figure 4-38 Result of multiple sets of filter criteria

Using The NOT Operator

This operator works the opposite of the **IN OPERATOR**, that was covered earlier in this chapter. The filter criteria used in this operators list, is used to **EXCLUDE ROWS** that have one of the values listed. The NOT operator is placed right before another operator on the WHERE clause. There is no advantage that I am aware of to use the NOT operator, to create a basic filter, other then it being easier to read then using several <> or != operators. The NOT operator is more helpful when creating a complex filter.

Having said that, the NOT operator can be used with comparison operators (except the ones that have "NOT" in the definition). For example, the following two WHERE clauses produce the same result.

WHERE ProductID <> 2
WHERE NOT ProductID = 2

The reason that the NOT operator should not be used with comparison operators that have "NOT" in the definition is because the two NOT operators will cancel each other out, like a double negative.

Example #23 Use The NOT Operator With A Numeric Field

The query shown below is the same query that was used earlier in Example #20. The only difference is that the NOT operator is used with the IN operator. This means that the query will return the rows that the query in Example #20, did not retrieve.

```
SELECT CustomerID, CompanyName, RegionID
FROM Customers
WHERE RegionID NOT IN (2, 10, 19, 24);
```

Figure 4-39 shows the result. 340 rows were returned.

	customerid integer	companyname character varying (75)	regionid integer
1	1	City Cyclists	12
2	3	Bike-A-Holics Anonymous	13
3	4	Psycho-Cycle	31
4	5	Sporting Wheels Inc.	48

Figure 4-39 Customers that are not in one of the regions listed in the query

Exercise 4.14: Find Products That Are Not In Specific Sub Categories

The query that you will create in this exercise will return records that are not in the sub categories, listed in the query.

1. Create this query.

```
SELECT ProductID, ProductName, SubCategoryID
FROM Products
WHERE SubCategoryID NOT IN (1, 9, 10, 27);
```

2. Save the query as `E4.14 Products not in specific sub categories.`

   Figure 4-40 shows the result.
   82 rows were returned.

	productid integer	productname character varyi	subcategoryid integer
11	2206	Pro Helmet	6
12	3301	Chain Lock	7
13	3302	U Lock	11
14	3303	XL U Lock	11

Figure 4-40 Products that are not in the specific sub categories

Using The NOT Operator With A String Field
Not (no pun intended) to be outdone, the NOT operator can also be used with a field that has a string data type. The query shown earlier in Example #22 has the syntax for a string field.

Using The WHERE Clause To Compare Columns

So far, the filter criteria that you have created, compared values in a field, to literal values that are hard coded on the WHERE clause. That type of comparison is not the only type of comparison criteria that can be created. You can also compare the value in one column to the value in another column.

Exercise 4.15: Compare The Values In Numeric Columns

In this exercise, you will create filter criteria to see if the value in the Qty On Hand column is less than the value in the Reorder Level column. The Reorder Level column contains the quantity that specifies when the product should be reordered. If the Qty On Hand value is less than the Reorder Level value, the product needs to be reordered.

1. Create this query.

```
SELECT ProductName, QtyOnHand, ReorderLevel
FROM Products
WHERE QtyOnHand < ReorderLevel;
```

2. Save the query as
   `E4.15 Compare values in columns.`

   Figure 4-41 shows the result.

   13 rows were returned. These are the products that need to be reordered.

	productname character varying	qtyonhand integer	reorderlevel integer
1	Crochet Glove	456	500
2	Crochet Glove	123	500
3	Lycra Glove	111	250
4	Lycra Glove	222	250

Figure 4-41 Products that need to be reordered

Using The LIKE Operator

While I specifically reference the LIKE operator, the **ILIKE OPERATOR** has the same functionality.

This operator filters data differently then the other operators that have been covered in this chapter, so far. The other operators did one of the following:

☑ Compared a value in a field, to a range of values.
☑ Checked to see if the value in a field matches the value listed on the WHERE clause.
☑ Checked to see if the value is equal to, less than or greater than the value specified in the query.

As you have seen, those options provide a lot of ways to filter data, when you know what the values are, that you are looking for. There may be times though, when you need to create a filter, but do not know all of the specifics or want to search the contents of a field for specific data.

For example, you need to create a query that will display a list of customers whose last name starts with the letter A or customers whose birthday is in September. These are the types of queries that the LIKE operator and wildcards are designed to handle. That is because the LIKE operator matches the data in a field to the pattern that you type in. The LIKE operator is used to check whether or not a character string matches the pattern that you specify, in the query.

This type of filter searches the field that you specify, for the portion or pattern of the value that you know. The pattern that you are looking for is what you put in quotes after the word LIKE on the WHERE clause.

Technically, LIKE is a predicate, not an operator. However, the result of a query is the same. I just wanted to let you know, in case you see LIKE referenced as a predicate, in some documentation.

Using The ILIKE Operator

The benefit that I have found using the ILIKE operator instead of the LIKE operator in searches, is that because it is not case sensitive, it does not exclude rows of data from being retrieved, if the value in the field has a different case, then the one that you type in as the filter criteria. For example, if you capitalize the search criteria in the query and the data is not capitalized, the row will still be retrieved.

Wildcard Characters

To perform this type of search (a pattern search), wildcard characters are used to fill in, if you will, the part of the value that you don't know or don't need to know, depending on how you look at it. Another way to put it is that a wildcard search is used to find a value that is only part of the value in the field. Wildcard characters can be used any place in the search pattern. These characters **MUST BE** used with the LIKE operator. The wildcard characters that are used with the LIKE operator, are explained below.

☑ **PERCENT SIGN %** This wildcard character represents any size string, meaning that it matches any number (zero or more) of characters. For example, find all products that start with the word Helmet. This is probably the most used wildcard character. This wildcard character is often used with the underscore wildcard character.
☑ **UNDERSCORE _** This wildcard character only matches one character, no more or no less. It can be used anywhere in the search pattern. It can also be used several times, to create the search criteria.

LIKE Operator Wildcard Search Criteria
Below are some features of wildcard characters that you need to be aware of.

① The search criteria, which comes after the word LIKE, must be enclosed in single quotes.
② The **BRACKETS [ ]** wildcard character is not supported in PostgreSQL with the LIKE operator. I wanted to let you know in case you have used another SQL database that supports this wildcard character, with the LIKE operator.
③ The wildcard search could be case sensitive. By default, most PostgreSQL installations are **CASE INSENSITIVE**. If the configuration has been changed, you may find that the search is **CASE SENSITIVE**. The best thing to do when typing in the search criteria, is to type the column name, using the same case, as it is saved in the table.

Example #24 Using The LIKE Operator With The Percent Sign Wildcard Character

The query shown below will search the Product Name field and return rows that have "Helmet", anywhere in the field. Notice that the % sign is placed before and after the text that is being searched for. This is how you indicate to search the entire field.

```
SELECT ProductID, ProductName
FROM Products
WHERE ProductName LIKE '%Helmet%';
```

Figure 4-42 shows some of the 23 rows that were returned. Each row returned, has the word Helmet in the Product Name column.

	productid integer	productname character varyir
5	2205	Pro Helmet
6	2206	Pro Helmet
7	2207	Vertigo Helmet
8	2208	Vertigo Helmet

Figure 4-42 Products that have "Helmet" in the name

Dealing With Trailing Spaces In A Search
Trailing spaces in a field used in a search, can present a problem. For example, in the query in Example #24 above, if in the Product Name field, there was more than one space after the word 'Helmet', in some rows, and the search criteria was LIKE '%Helmet', the rows that have two or more spaces after the word, would not be returned because of the additional spaces. The search criteria in the query, in Example #24 will handle this and return rows where there are two or more spaces after the word, because there is a percent sign after the search criteria.

Example #25 Using The LIKE Operator With The Underscore Wildcard Character

The query shown below will search the Company Name field and return records where the second letter in the Company Name field is the lower case letter a. If the second letter is an uppercase A, this query will not retrieve the record. If you also need to return records with an uppercase A, you have to add a clause to search for it also, or use the ILIKE operator. Notice that the percent wildcard character is also used in the query. Figure 4-43 shows some of the 88 records that were returned.

```
SELECT CustomerID, CompanyName
FROM Customers
WHERE CompanyName LIKE '_a%'
  OR CompanyName LIKE '_A%';
```

Notice that the company name in row 9 has an uppercase A, as the second letter.

	customerid integer	companyname character varying (75)
7	55	Tandem Cycle
8	58	Making Tracks
9	64	SAB Mountain
10	67	Paris Mountain Sports

Figure 4-43 Company names that have the letter a, as the second letter

Exercise 4.16: Find Job Titles That Start With The Word "Sales"

In this exercise, you will use the percent sign wildcard character to search the Job Title field to return rows that have a title that starts with the word "Sales".

1. Create this query.

```
SELECT CustomerID, FirstName, LastName, JobTitle
FROM Customers
WHERE JobTitle LIKE 'Sales%';
```

2. Save the query as `E4.16 Job titles that start with the word sales.`

   Figure 4-44 shows the result.

   69 rows were returned. This is the number of customers that have a sales related job.

	customerid integer	firstname character v	lastname character var	jobtitle character varying (50
5	107	Henri	De Montigny	Sales Manager
6	108	Claude	Antoine	Sales Representative
7	110	Daniel	Beauchamp	Sales Manager
8	111	Stan	Delaware	Sales Agent

Figure 4-44 Job titles that start with the word "Sales"

Example #26 Find Manager Job Titles

The query in this example will find all customers whose job title ends with the word "Manager". Notice in the query below, that the percent sign is before the word Manager. Figure 4-45 shows the result. The rows returned are the customers that have a management position.

```
SELECT CustomerID, FirstName, LastName,
  JobTitle
FROM Customers
WHERE JobTitle LIKE '%Manager';
```

	customerid integer	firstname character v	lastname character var	jobtitle character varying (5
1	1	Chris	Christianson	Sales Manager
2	5	Patrick	Reyess	Technical Manager
3	10	Anthony	Shoemaker	Project Manager
4	16	James	Sergent	Technical Manager

Figure 4-45 List of Manager job titles

Example #27 Using A Wildcard Character To Exclude Data

So far, all of the LIKE operator examples and exercises covered creating queries that would include rows that matched the criteria. The same wildcard characters can be used to exclude rows of data. This is accomplished by adding the NOT operator before the LIKE operator, as shown in the query below.

```
SELECT FirstName, LastName, JobTitle
FROM Customers
WHERE JobTitle NOT LIKE '%Manager';
```

Figure 4-46 shows the result. None of the rows returned, have the word Manager at the end of the Job Title field.

	firstname character v	lastname character	jobtitle character varying (50
1	Christine	Manley	Sales Representative
2	Gary	Jannis	Accountant
3	Alexander	Mast	Business Analyst
4	Heather	Davis	Consultant

Figure 4-46 Result of the LIKE operator used to exclude data

> **Percent Wildcard Character And NULL Values**
> While it may seem like the percent wildcard character can handle all search patterns and filter criteria, the search pattern that it cannot handle is null values. If the percent wildcard is used to check for null values, no rows will be returned.

Exercise 4.17: Use The Underscore Wildcard Character To Filter Data

The query that you will create in this exercise will use the underscore character to filter on the last three characters in the Invoice Number field, which is the region code. The underscore character will be used to match the first seven characters in the Invoice Number field. This query will return invoices that have the region code S21.

1. Create the query shown below. There are seven underscore characters on the last line of the query.

```
SELECT InvoiceID, InvoiceNumber, InvoiceTotal
FROM Invoices
WHERE InvoiceNumber LIKE '_______S21';
```

2. Save the query as `E4.17 Use the underscore wildcard character.`

   Figure 4-47 shows the result. 35 rows were returned.

   As you can see, the invoice numbers returned, have S21 at the end of the field. Yes, the % wildcard character could have been used, but I needed a way to demonstrate the underscore wildcard character. <smile>

	invoiceid integer	invoicenumber character varying	invoicetotal numeric (18,2
1	747	7471666S21	11729.03
2	753	7531672S21	111.87
3	759	7593074S21	37.29
4	767	7673079S21	6467.67

Figure 4-47 Invoices table filtered by the region code

Example #28 Alternate Option To Using The Percent Wildcard Character

As covered in the previous section, if there is an alternative to using the wildcard characters, use it. The first query below, uses the percent wildcard character to return all customers whose last name starts with the letter E.
The second query retrieves the same 15 rows shown in Figure 4-48, by using a function.

Percent wildcard character query

```
SELECT FirstName, LastName
FROM Customers
WHERE LastName LIKE 'E%';
```

Alternate query that produces the same result

```
SELECT FirstName, LastName
FROM Customers
WHERE SUBSTRING(LastName, 1, 1) = 'E';
```

	firstname character v	lastname character
1	Donald	Edwards
2	Jerry	Esler
3	Dave	Elkins
4	Kent	Estes

Figure 4-48 Customers whose last name starts with the letter E

While the LIKE operator is powerful and may seem like the "cool" operator to use, keep the following in mind.

- ☑ If there is another operator or function that can create the criteria that you need, use it instead of the LIKE operator, as demonstrated above in Example #28.
- ☑ Using a wildcard character at the beginning of the search criteria, like the one shown earlier in Example #26, takes longer to process, then when the wildcard character is placed in another location in the search criteria.
- ☑ While useful, wildcard searches in general, take longer to process then the other filter operators covered in this chapter.

REGEXP Operator

While similar to the LIKE operator, the **REGEXP OPERATOR** takes searching for string patterns to the next level. It is more robust and is used to create complex string patterns, that are known as **REGULAR EXPRESSIONS**. The REGEXP operator has the same drawbacks that the LIKE operator has, as explained above.

Creating Filter Criteria For Boolean Fields

Boolean fields have their own data type, appropriately named, **BOOLEAN**. This data type only stores the values 0 (zero) or 1. Filters can be created for Boolean fields. What you have to keep in mind is that even though the Boolean field may display Yes/No or True/False, depending on the software that you are using to view the data, these values cannot be used in the filter criteria. They are not the values that are stored in the table.

The values that are stored in the table are 0 and 1. These are the values that many SQL databases support. This is because the Boolean data type is numeric. Instead of using Yes/True or No/False to create the filter criteria, you have to use 1 for Yes and True and 0 for No and False. As you may have seen, PostgreSQL supports TRUE and FALSE, which makes life a little easier. While I type the Boolean values in all capital letters, that is not a requirement.

Example #29 Create A Filter For A Boolean Field

The query below creates filter criteria to return a list of all orders that have not been shipped. Figure 4-49 shows the result.

SELECT OrderID, OrderAmount, Shipped
FROM Orders
WHERE Shipped = 'FALSE';

	orderid integer	orderamount numeric (18,2)	shipped boolean
1	356	47.00	false
2	357	125.70	false
3	364	125.70	false
4	365	83.80	false

Figure 4-49 List of orders that have not been shipped

Exercise 4.18: Find Products That Have Been Retired

The query that you will create in this exercise, will return a list of products that have been retired. The Retired Product field has the Boolean data type.

1. Create this query.

```
SELECT ProductName, RetiredProduct
FROM Products
WHERE RetiredProduct = 'TRUE';
```

2. Save the query as `E4.18 List of retired products.`

   Figure 4-50 shows some of the 12 products that have been retired.

	productname character varying (50)	retiredproduct boolean
1	Crochet Glove	true
2	Pro Helmet	true
3	U Lock	true
4	Adult Helmet	true

Figure 4-50 List of retired products

Using Dates To Filter Data

Dates are an integral part of queries, because many reports are date driven. Like all of the queries that you have created in this chapter, queries that use dates, also use the WHERE clause and the operators covered earlier in Table 4-1.

As you have seen, in some of the figures in this chapter, dates are displayed in the following format: year, month, day. When using dates in a query, the dates must be enclosed in single quotes. As covered earlier, right before Exercise 4.11, you learned that the ISO Standard for typing dates is 'YYYY-MM-DD' (including the dashes).

Example #30 Date Format

The query below will return all orders that have a date that is greater than September 19, 2016, as shown in Figure 4-51.

SELECT OrderID, OrderDate, OrderAmount
FROM Orders
WHERE OrderDate > '2016-09-19';

	orderid integer	orderdate date	orderamount numeric (18,2)
1	1594	2016-09-20	5236.05
2	1595	2016-09-20	5236.05
3	1596	2016-09-20	5236.05
4	1597	2016-09-21	3777.33

Figure 4-51 Orders placed after September 19, 2016

Exercise 4.19: Find Orders On A Specific Date

In this exercise, you will create a query that will find all orders for 9/19/2016.

1. Save the E4.9 query as `E4.19 Orders on a specific date.`

2. Change the WHERE clause to `WHERE OrderDate = '2016-09-19'.`

   Figure 4-52 shows the result. 15 rows were returned.

	orderid integer	orderdate date	orderamount numeric (18,2
1	1579	2016-09-19	46.50
2	1580	2016-09-19	2553.45
3	1581	2016-09-19	803.50
4	1582	2016-09-19	46.50

Figure 4-52 Orders for a specific date

Exercise 4.20: Find Orders Shipped After A Specific Date

In this exercise, you will create a query that will find all orders that were shipped on or after 9/19/2016.

1. Save the E4.19 query as `E4.20 Orders shipped on or after a specific date.`

2. On the SELECT statement line, add the Ship Date field, after the Order Date field.

3. Change the WHERE clause to `WHERE ShipDate >= '2016-09-19'.`

   Figure 4-53 shows the result. 3,888 rows were returned.

	orderid integer	orderdate date	shipdate date	orderamount numeric (18,2
1	1464	2016-09-12	2016-09-19	2412.92
2	1470	2016-09-12	2016-09-19	2412.92
3	1476	2016-09-12	2016-09-19	2412.92
4	1482	2016-09-12	2016-09-19	2412.92

Figure 4-53 Orders shipped on or after 9/19/2016

Exercise 4.21: Find Orders In A Date Range

In this exercise, you will create a query that will find all orders that are in a date range. The query will return all orders in 2018.

1. Save the E4.19 query as `E4.21 Orders in a date range.`

2. Change the WHERE clause to `WHERE OrderDate BETWEEN '2018-01-01' AND '2018-12-31'.`

   Figure 4-54 shows the result. 1,863 rows were returned.

	orderid integer	orderdate date	orderamount numeric (18,2
1	3563	2018-01-01	851.77
2	3564	2018-01-01	1025.40
3	3565	2018-01-02	5219.55
4	3566	2018-01-02	59.70

Figure 4-54 Orders placed in 2018

Example #31 Use Two Date Ranges To Filter Data

In Exercise 4.21 you created a date range for a specific year. For comparison analysis reporting purposes, you may have the need to display data for two or more years on a chart. This query adds another year of filter criteria.

```
SELECT OrderID, OrderDate, OrderAmount
FROM Orders
WHERE OrderDate BETWEEN '2018-01-01' AND '2018-12-31'
   OR (OrderDate BETWEEN '2016-01-01' AND '2016-12-31');
```

As you learned earlier in this chapter, parentheses are necessary when you need specific filter criteria grouped together. While only one set of parentheses is needed in this example, you could add them around both sets of filter criteria, if that makes it easier for you to understand the filter criteria.

Doing that does not change the functionality of the query. The same rows will be returned. Figure 4-55 shows the result. All of the 4,309 rows returned, have an order date in 2016 or 2018.

	orderid integer	orderdate date	orderamount numeric (18,2)
2444	2444	2016-12-30	789.15
2445	2445	2016-12-30	5879.70
2446	2446	2016-12-31	2644.20
2447	3563	2018-01-01	851.77
2448	3564	2018-01-01	1025.40

Figure 4-55 Orders in 2016 or 2018

Exercise 4.22: Find Orders That Are Not In The Date Range

In this exercise, you will create a query that will find orders outside (not in the range) of the date range specified in the query. This query is the opposite of the query created in Exercise 4.21. Therefore, this query will return all orders that were not placed in 2018.

1. Save the E4.21 query as `E4.22 Orders not in the date range`.

2. Change the WHERE clause to
`WHERE OrderDate < '2018-01-01' OR OrderDate > '2018-12-31'`.

   Notice that the OR operator, instead of the AND operator, was used to create the query. That is because the Order Date only needs to meet one of the filter criteria options.

   A date cannot be less than and greater than, at the same time, if the dates on the WHERE clauses are entered correctly. All of the orders returned, will not have a date in 2018. You should see the orders shown in Figure 4-56. 7,909 rows were returned.

	orderid integer	orderdate date	orderamount numeric (18,2)
1	1	2016-01-01	2645.87
2	2	2016-01-01	8908.05
3	3	2016-01-02	39.80
4	4	2016-01-02	43.80

Figure 4-56 Orders not in the date range

Example #32 Alternate Query To The One Used In Exercise 4.22

This query will return the same rows as the query in Exercise 4.22. Notice that this query uses two operators "NOT BETWEEN".

```
SELECT OrderID, OrderDate, OrderAmount
FROM Orders
WHERE OrderDate NOT BETWEEN '2018-01-01' AND '2018-12-31';
```

Exercise 4.23: Find Orders That Meet Date And Non Date Filter Criteria

So far, all of the date queries that you have created only had to meet date criteria. There will be times when a query needs to meet more than date criteria. The query that you create in this exercise will find records that have an order date greater than or equal to 9/19/2016 and have an order amount that is greater than or equal to $5,275.

1. Save the E4.22 query as `E4.23 Date & non date filter criteria`.

2. Change the WHERE clause to `WHERE OrderDate >= '2016-09-19' AND OrderAmount >= 5275`.

   Figure 4-57 shows the result. 410 rows were returned.

	orderid integer	orderdate date	orderamount numeric (18,2
1	1604	2016-09-22	5617.93
2	1607	2016-09-22	6125.20
3	1609	2016-09-22	5617.93
4	1612	2016-09-22	6125.20

Figure 4-57 Result of a query with multiple filter criteria

Example #33 Using More Than Two Filter Criteria Conditions

The date examples and exercises so far, have only used one or two filter criteria requirements. More filter criteria can be used. For example, adding criteria that the Payment Type must be a check, to the query in Exercise 4.23. The query below will accomplish this. Figure 4-58 shows the result. 165 rows were returned.

```
SELECT OrderID, OrderDate, OrderAmount,
  PaymentType
FROM Orders
WHERE OrderDate >= '2016-09-19'
  AND OrderAmount >= 5275
  AND PaymentType = 'Check';
```

	orderid integer	orderdate date	orderamount numeric (18,2)	paymenttype character varyi
1	2002	2016-11-04	5498.88	Check
2	2003	2016-11-04	5879.70	Check
3	2005	2016-11-04	5498.88	Check
4	2006	2016-11-04	5879.70	Check

Figure 4-58 Result of a query with three filter criteria requirements

Exercise 4.24: Find Orders In Specific Years

In Exercise 4.21, you learned how to create a query that returned orders for one year, using the BETWEEN operator. While you could have added more criteria to also return orders for another year, as shown earlier in Example #31, there is an easier way.

In this exercise, you will create a query that retrieves orders placed in 2016 or 2018. I am jumping ahead a few chapters now, by also using the **DATE_PART FUNCTION**. This function is used to extract the year from a date field.

1. Create this query.

```
SELECT OrderID, OrderDate, OrderAmount
FROM Orders
WHERE date_part('year', OrderDate) IN ('2016', '2018');
```

2. Save the query as `E4.24 Orders in 2016 or 2018.`
   Figure 4-55, shown earlier, shows the result for this query. The same 4,309 rows were returned.

Exercise 4.25: Compare Values In Date Columns

Earlier in Exercise 4.15, you learned how to compare values in numeric columns. In this exercise, you will create filter criteria to select orders that were shipped late. In this exercise, orders are considered to be shipped late, if the Ship Date is greater than the Required Date.

1. Create this query.

```
SELECT OrderID, OrderAmount, RequiredDate, ShipDate
FROM Orders
WHERE ShipDate > RequiredDate;
```

2. Save the query as `E4.25 Orders that were shipped late.`

   Figure 4-59 shows the orders that were returned.
   36 rows were returned.

   As shown, the Ship Date is after the Required Date.

	orderid integer	orderamount numeric (18,2)	requireddate date	shipdate date
1	3	39.80	2016-01-09	2016-01-14
2	5	65.70	2016-01-15	2016-01-16
3	6	27.00	2016-01-10	2016-01-23
4	2404	74.50	2016-01-04	2016-12-25

Figure 4-59 Orders that were shipped late

Exercise 4.26: Filter Data Using A Calculation

In this exercise, you will create a query that filters the data based on the result of a calculation. The query will return orders that have an order total >= $7,500.

1. Create this query.

```
SELECT OrderID, OrderAmount,
 OrderAmount + ShippingAmount AS OrderTotal
FROM Orders
WHERE OrderAmount + ShippingAmount >= 7500;
```

2. Save the query as `E4.26 Filter data based on a calculation.`

Figure 4-60 shows the result. 508 rows were returned. I included the calculation on the SELECT clause to be able to confirm that the calculation was working as expected. Doing this is not a requirement.

	orderid integer	orderamount numeric (18,2)	ordertotal numeric
1	2	8908.05	8997.13
2	8	9612.47	9708.59
3	23	11465.42	11580.07
4	26	9446.27	9540.73

Figure 4-60 Result of using a calculation to filter data

CASE Function

This function returns a value based on the conditions that you set up in the query. The CASE function is used to create conditional logic. If you have used the **IF FUNCTION** (IF ... Then ... Else) or the **IIF FUNCTION** (in other software), you are already familiar with how the CASE function works. PostgreSQL currently does not support the IF or IIF function.
As you will see, there are two ways to use the CASE function. The CASE function is used to create two or more conditions, and what should happen when a value in a field, matches a condition. This is accomplished by testing the data in one column and selecting what to do with the result of the test. I don't know for sure, but I suspect that the most popular clause that the CASE function is used on, is the SELECT clause.

The CASE function can also be used as a way to group or reclassify rows of data, based on a value in a field, just like the GROUP BY clause can. The way that groups can be created using the CASE function, has more functionality than the GROUP BY clause. The CASE function creates a **SCALAR EXPRESSION**. This means that it can be used wherever scalar expressions can also be used in a query. The CASE function can also be used with the following clauses: WHERE, the ON clause of a JOIN, ORDER BY and HAVING. There are two ways that the CASE function can be used, as explained below.

① **SIMPLE** This option is used to compare a value or scalar expression to a list of possible values and return the value for the first match found in the list. The simple CASE function compares the input expression on the CASE clause to the expressions on the **WHEN/THEN CLAUSES**. When a matching expression is found on a WHEN clause, for the input expression, the corresponding expression on the THEN clause is returned. Unlike the searched CASE function option discussed below, the order of the WHEN clauses is not important, because equal to is the only condition that can be used in a simple search.

This option is best suited to be used with a column that has a limited number of values that need to be checked and those values do not change on a frequent basis. That is because if new values are added, the query will have to be updated to include the new values. Multiple WHEN/THEN clauses can be used. (3)

The syntax for the simple CASE function is:

```
CASE input expression
  WHEN expression 1 THEN result 1
 [WHEN expression 2 THEN result 2]
 [ELSE result expression]
END
```

② **SEARCHED** This option is more flexible than the simple option, because it is used to compare a value to a range of values, instead of the "equal to" requirement of the single value or expression, that the simple option, discussed above uses. With the searched option, you can test for less than, greater than, BETWEEN, EXISTS or IN. If you have used software like Power BI Desktop or SQL Server Analysis Services (SSAS) and created DAX expressions that created "buckets" for rows of data to be grouped on or reclassified, it is the same concept as the searched CASE function option.

When using the search CASE function, the order of the WHEN clauses is important. That is because the CASE function returns the expression for the first test that evaluates to true. As I said earlier, the search CASE function has more flexibility, then the simple CASE function option. For example, each condition can be based on a different expression or column. A **SUBQUERY** can be used to return data from another table. (3)

The syntax for the searched CASE function is:

```
CASE
 WHEN condition 1 THEN result 1
 [WHEN condition 2 THEN result 2]
 [ELSE result]
END
```

(3) If there is no match for the value in the list of WHEN clauses, the CASE function returns the value on the **ELSE CLAUSE**. If the CASE expression does not have an ELSE clause, the ELSE clause is implied and defaults to ELSE NULL.

While this may not seem like a filter, the **WHEN CLAUSE** used in the CASE statement is filtering the data. The difference between the WHERE clause that you have used in this chapter and the WHEN clause, is that the WHERE clause returns the row if the value in the field meets the condition. In addition to meeting the condition on the WHEN clause, the WHEN clause also creates a new column and adds the value for the corresponding **THEN CLAUSE**, to the new column for each row that meets the criteria.

Using Parentheses With A CASE Statement
While the CASE function does not require parentheses, they can be used. You can use them to make the CASE statement easier to understand.

Simple CASE Function vs Searched CASE Function
The simple CASE function **COMPARES** the expression on each WHEN clause.
The searched CASE function **TESTS** the expression on each WHEN clause.

Keep in mind that for both CASE expressions (simple and searched), the expression evaluation stops when the query finds the first WHEN clause that is true and returns the corresponding THEN expression. Both **CASE** expressions also support using the ELSE clause, for rows that do not meet any of the WHEN clause conditions.

How The Simple CASE Function Works

The expression on the CASE clause is compared to the expression on the WHEN clauses. If an expression on the WHEN clause matches the expression on the CASE clause, the expression on the corresponding THEN clause is returned.

In Example #34, if the value in the Status ID field (on the CASE clause) equals 5, the value 'Out Of Stock' is returned by the CASE function. The THEN clause option is how the rows are grouped or reclassified.

The simple version of the CASE function is a good option to use when an ID field has a short list of options, as you will see in Example #34. It is also a good option if you only want to select a few of the values from a field to query on.

Example #34 Simple CASE Function

The query in this example checks the value in the Status ID field, against the values on the WHEN clauses. Figure 4-61 shows the result.

While this example does not use the ELSE clause (at the end of the CASE statement), the ELSE clause is used to enter what should be returned if the value in the Status ID field does not match any of the values on the WHEN clauses. Using the ELSE clause is optional. If it is not used and there is no match, NULL will be displayed.

```
SELECT OrderID, ProductName, StatusID,
CASE StatusID
  WHEN 0 THEN 'No status'
  WHEN 1 THEN 'Product Allocated'
  WHEN 2 THEN 'Product Invoiced'
  WHEN 3 THEN 'Product Shipped'
  WHEN 4 THEN 'Product On Order'
  WHEN 5 THEN 'Out Of Stock'
END AS Status
FROM OrderDetails INNER JOIN Products
  ON OrderDetails.ProductID = Products.ProductID;
```

I don't know about you, but seeing the word NULL in the result is not very helpful or informative. I would use something like ELSE '** No status found for item **', to let the reader know that the line item may have a problem.

	orderid integer	productname character varying (50	statusid integer	status text
55	27	Crochet Glove	2	Product Invoiced
56	27	Road Bicycle ladies	1	Product Allocated
57	28	Crochet Glove	9	[null]
58	28	Road Bicycle ladies	0	No status

Figure 4-61 Result of a simple CASE function query

How The Searched CASE Function Works

The searched CASE function has more flexibility then the simple CASE function. For example, the searched option can be used to test for conditions other than equal to, like less than. Another example is that each condition can use a different expression or column. Getting the order of the criteria correct, **IS CRUCIAL** to displaying the correct results, when using the searched option. That is because the first condition that evaluates to true is selected.

The searched version of the CASE function is used when any of the following are true: You need to create more complex comparisons, use more than one field to compare on, or the comparison needs to occur on the WHERE, JOIN or HAVING clause.

Example #35 Use The CASE Function To Swap Values

Figure 4-62 shows four of the 15 rows that were returned from the query.

The value "*Status Not Listed*" means that the value in the Status field was a value other then S or M. It could also mean that the field is NULL.

```
SELECT SalesRep,
CASE Status
  WHEN 'S' THEN 'Single'
  WHEN 'M' THEN 'Married'
ELSE '* Status Not Listed *'
END
AS "Single/Married"
FROM SalesReps;
```

	salesrep character varying (5(	Single/Married text
1	Nancy Davolio	Married
2	Andrew Fuller	* Status Not Listed *
3	Janet Leverling	Married
4	Margaret Peacock	Single

Figure 4-62 Sales reps marital status

Exercise 4.27: Create Product Categories Using The CASE Function

While products already have a category in the database used in this book, the query that you will create in this exercise will show you how to create categories for the products, on the fly. Categories will only be created for the accessory products. The other products will be categorized as a non accessory product, using the **SIMPLE** form of the CASE function.

1. Create this query.

```
SELECT ProductID, ProductName, ProductCategoryID,
CASE ProductCategoryID
  WHEN 5 THEN 'Gloves for women'
  WHEN 6 THEN 'Helmets for children'
  WHEN 7 THEN 'Bicycle Locks'
  WHEN 8 THEN 'Saddles for everyone'
ELSE 'Not An Accessory'
END AS NewCategoryName
FROM Products;
```

2. Save the query as `E4.27 CASE function product categories.`

   Figure 4-63 shows the result. 127 rows were returned.

	productid integer	productname character varying (50)	productcategoryid integer	newcategoryname text
45	5302	Rhino Lock	7	Bicycle Locks
46	5303	Titan Lock	7	Bicycle Locks
47	5207	Youth Helmet	6	Helmets for children
48	5208	Youth Helmet	6	Helmets for children

Figure 4-63 New product categories created

Exercise 4.28: Use The CASE Function With Numeric Values

The previous exercise used the CASE function with a string value. This exercise will show you how to use the CASE function with a numeric value. This query uses the **SEARCHED** form of the CASE function.

1. Create the query shown below.

```
SELECT OrderID, SalesRepID, OrderAmount,
CASE
  WHEN OrderAmount < 500 THEN 'Less than $500'
  WHEN OrderAmount BETWEEN 500 AND 1000 THEN 'Between $500 and $1000'
  WHEN OrderAmount > 1000 THEN 'Over $1,000'
ELSE 'Is not in the range'
END AS "Order Amount Category"
FROM Orders;
```

2. Save the query as `E4.28 CASE function using numeric values.`

Figure 4-64 shows the result. All 9,772 rows in the Orders table were returned.

The WHEN clauses in this exercise, account for all values, in the Order Amount field. This means that all rows with a value in the Order Amount field will match one of the WHEN clause conditions.

	orderid integer	salesrepid integer	orderamount numeric (18,2)	Order Amount Category text
9	9	3	40.50	Less than $500
10	10	6	4304.10	Over $1,000
11	11	4	1583.15	Over $1,000
12	12	7	701.54	Between $500 and $1000

Figure 4-64 Result of the CASE function used with numeric values

If the first WHEN clause was changed to < 100, you would see that the ELSE clause would be applied to rows where the Order Amount is between $100.00 and $499.99, as shown in Figure 4-65.

	orderid integer	salesrepid integer	orderamount numeric (18,2)	Order Amount Category text
19	19	4	296.87	Is not in the range
20	20	9	659.70	Between $500 and $1000
21	21	7	6891.94	Over $1,000
22	22	3	46.50	Less than $500

Figure 4-65 Orders not in the range of any of the WHEN clauses

Syntax Difference Between Simple And Searched CASE Statements
Notice in Exercise 4.27 that the field being searched, was added next to the CASE function and in Exercise 4.28, the field being searched, is listed with each WHEN clause. This is how you can tell the difference between simple and searched CASE statements.

WHEN Clause Order For The CASE Function
When setting up the criteria for the WHEN clause for numeric values, they need to be put in an order that each record can only match the criteria for one WHEN clause. Example #36, explains this in more detail.

Example #36 Selecting The Correct Order For WHEN Clause Criteria In A Searched CASE Query

This query will assign a discount for a future order, based on the last order.

How this query works, is explained below.

```
SELECT OrderID, SalesRepID, OrderAmount,
CASE
  WHEN OrderAmount >= 10000 THEN '10% discount'
  WHEN OrderAmount >= 5000 THEN '15% discount'
  WHEN OrderAmount >= 2500 THEN '20% discount'
ELSE '25% discount'
END AS "Discount Amount"
FROM Orders;
```

Because the Order Amount field is evaluated for each record, it will only match one of the WHEN statements when the query is set up correctly. For example, if the order amount is $3,000, the query will stop processing after the third WHEN statement, in the query above. If the order amount is $6,500, the query will stop processing after the second WHEN statement, as shown in Figure 4-66.

The order that you place the criteria values in for the order amount, is very important. If the statements in the query above, were in a different order, the query would not return the correct result. That is because it is possible that the order amount would meet the criteria of another statement, that it is not intended to meet.

For example, if the >=2,500 portion of the query was before the >=10,000 portion of the query, as shown in this query, and the order amount is $6,500, the formula would stop processing after the first WHEN statement, because $6,500 is >=2,500. That is not the outcome that you want though, as shown in Figure 4-67.
You really want the $6,500 order to receive a 15% discount.

```
SELECT OrderID, SalesRepID, OrderAmount,
CASE
  WHEN OrderAmount >= 2500 THEN '20% discount'
  WHEN OrderAmount >= 10000 THEN '10% discount'
  WHEN OrderAmount >= 5000 THEN '15% discount'
ELSE '25% discount'
END AS "Discount Amount"
FROM Orders;
```

The rule of thumb is to put numeric criteria in high to low order, when using the same operator. The ELSE statement is the "catch all" statement. Sometimes you may need to print or display a message on the report because the data is outside of the range of data that you need to report on. In the first query above, the customer would receive a 25%

discount off of their next order, if their last order was less than $2,500, as shown in Figure 4-66. In this scenario, the company is going to offer larger discounts to customers that placed smaller orders, in hopes of having them place a larger order, the next time that they order.

	orderid integer	salesrepid integer	orderamount numeric (18,2)	Discount Amount text
4902	4902	4	10629.23	10% discount
4903	4903	7	2294.55	25% discount
4904	4904	6	2530.95	20% discount
4905	4905	1	5935.70	15% discount

Figure 4-66 Result of the WHEN clauses in the correct order

	orderid integer	salesrepid integer	orderamount numeric (18,2)	Discount Amount text
4902	4902	4	10629.23	20% discount
4903	4903	7	2294.55	25% discount
4904	4904	6	2530.95	20% discount
4905	4905	1	5935.70	20% discount

Figure 4-67 Result of the WHEN clauses in the wrong order

Summary

In this chapter, you learned how to use the WHERE clause with the SELECT statement, to filter the data in a table. This was accomplished by using the WHERE clause operators. Some of the ways that data can be filtered, are finding rows that have a value less than the value specified on the WHERE clause and finding rows that have a value in the range specified in the filter criteria.

This chapter also covered combining WHERE clauses, by using the AND and OR operators. You learned about the order of evaluation and how to resolve an issue if presented with one. The **CASE FUNCTION** was also covered. As you learned, it is an alternative to using the **IIF FUNCTION**, which is not supported in PostgreSQL. Both are used to create conditional logic, which can be used to group data.

While the filters that you learned how to create in this chapter were only applied to one table, filters can also be created for any field in a table that has been linked to (using a JOIN clause) in the query. You will see this in Chapter 6.

Even just learning how to create and apply filters to one table, you have come a long way since the end of Chapter 3, where you learned how to select tables and columns. The fun continues in the next chapter, where you will learn about more clauses that are used with the SELECT statement.

Creating queries to check for NULL values was covered and demonstrated several techniques that can be used. As you know, some fields can look empty, but really aren't. That is because someone could have pressed the space bar or typed in a comma or quote in the field. Sadly, pressing the space bar in a field that is not required, means that the field has a value.

> The following code will check for a space in the field. WHERE UnitCost = ' '. Rows that are returned by this code will not be returned with code that checks for NULL values. You may want to include this code when you are checking for NULL values, to make sure that the query is really returning all rows that do not have a value.

If you think that the rows returned are not correct, one thing that you should do, is test the columns used to create the filter criteria, to see if they have NULL values. Remember that rows with a NULL value are not returned, unless the OR operator is used and another filter condition is created that checks for null values and evaluates to true.

You learned about the order of evaluation. If the rows returned do not look right, check to see if the data is being processed correctly. By that I mean, display the table(s) of data, and walk through the calculation or filter criteria, using the data from the tables to see if the calculation is processing the data in the correct order. You may find that the parentheses are not in the correct location, in the query.

An important thing to keep in mind when creating filter criteria is that you need to figure out if it is easier to have the list of values for the filter criteria include or exclude rows of data. By that I mean, is the list of values to include, longer or shorter then the list of values to exclude. If the include list is shorter, use that list of values. If not, use the exclude list of values. For example, if you need to retrieve orders in 2016, 2017 and 2019 and that list is shorter then the list of all of the years in the table, you would create the filter criteria to include those years, opposed to excluding all other years.

As needed, write down (yes, with a pen or pencil and paper) all of the tasks that the filter criteria needs to accomplish, BEFORE actually creating the query. This is especially true for queries that need to use the AND and OR operators, because the placement of parentheses in the filter criteria is crucial, as they effect the order of evaluation, which means that the result of the filter criteria will be wrong and not retrieve the rows that you are expecting. It is important to understand how parentheses alter the order that filter criteria is processed in. The reason is because they can change the rows of data that are returned. You should find this helpful, at least for the first three to six months or so, that you are on your own, creating queries.

Being able to combine filter conditions or create code that forces some filter criteria to be applied and not others is very helpful. Being able to create a filter on part of the data in a field may seem daunting at first. But after a minute or two, you will see that it is possible.

Perhaps the most tricky type of filter to create is one that needs to include or exclude rows that have a NULL value in a field. One way to confirm that the query is retrieving the rows that you expect, is to look at the actual data.

You learned that some operators include rows and other operators exclude rows of data. You have the option of selecting which way you want the data to be processed. The end result is to return the correct rows of data in the most **EFFICIENT** way. Did you think that there were so many options available to filter data? <smile>

As covered, there are a lot of options to filter data. Perhaps the most important option is to create filter criteria that processes data quickly. By that I mean that the order that filter criteria is processed in, determines how long the query takes to run. The first condition processed should be the one that excludes the most rows of data. Doing this means that each additional filter condition starts with a smaller subset of data that it has to process. And that is a good thing, in terms of processing data faster. For example, if there is criteria that selects a date or date range, this criteria will exclude a lot of rows. Another example of criteria to put first, would be filter criteria for a specific sales rep. Hopefully, this chapter provided enough filter criteria examples and exercises to get you thinking about the types of filter criteria that you will need to create for your own data.

Have no fear, this is not the last that you will use filters, in this book. <smile> Several of the exercises and examples in the rest of this book have filter criteria. One thing that I hope you learned, is that in many instances, more than one operator can be used to create the same filter criteria. Select the one that you understand the best. That way, should something not work as expected, it should be easier for you to resolve the issue.

This chapter covered a lot of ground, as they say. In addition to learning how to create basic filter criteria, you also learned how to create multiple sets of filter criteria and how to use wildcard characters to search the data and a lot more. What you will probably discover on your own, is that a large number of queries that you will need to create are complex, opposed to basic. Just take your time.

Who knew that the word "WHERE" could be so powerful! <smile>

But before you go to the next chapter, do you think that you have learned enough to be able to create a query that will answer part of the question that I discussed in the "Overview" section of this chapter? [See the tip on page 4-2]

Try creating the query now. Figure 4-68 shows the result of the portion of the query that you should be able to create now. 505 rows were returned.

	orderid integer	customerid integer	orderdate date	orderamount numeric (18,2)
1	3843	65	2018-04-01	29.00
2	3844	51	2018-04-02	8015.01
3	3845	37	2018-04-02	3544.12
4	3846	56	2018-04-02	29.00

Figure 4-68 Partial result of the query presented earlier in this chapter

How Groups Are Created

One of the topics covered in the next chapter is creating groups. From experience, I know that for some, the concept of grouping is hard to visualize, so I figured that I would start explaining it now.

When using the GROUP BY clause, you are saying "Take all of the rows that have the same value in a column and combine them into one row and then use an aggregate function to calculate a summary value". The field(s) that are used to create the summary value do not have to be from the same table, as the column that is used to create the group.

While you can, I do not usually see the value of using the column that is being grouped on, in the calculation that creates the summary value. You may find that the opposite is true for the data that you are using.

What Types Of Queries Can I Create?

There are two general types of queries, as explained below.

① **QUERIES THAT RETURN DETAIL ROW INFORMATION**. By detail, I mean that the rows returned have a lot of columns of data and any calculations that are created are processed at the row level. This type of query does not have calculations for a group of rows, like sub or grand totals. All of the queries created up to this point, in this book, are in this query category.

② **SUMMARY QUERY** This type of query initially returns rows of data, just like the detail row queries, discussed above. Usually, fewer columns are used to create a summary query. This type of query groups and sorts the detail rows into categories, and creates totals of some type, for the groups. The data that this type of query returns, only displays the pertinent columns and their totals. An example is order totals by state and year. The left column in the result would list all of the states. Across the top of the result table would be the year or years that totals were created for. The middle of the table would have the total for each state, for each year. This type of query is also known as a **CROSSTAB** or **PIVOT TABLE** query, because that is the layout that the data returns, is displayed in.

Another summary query layout would be a list of products and a count of the number of each product sold. This count could also be divided to display the count by year or state. You will start to learn how to create this type of query in the next chapter.

CREATING ADVANCED SINGLE TABLE QUERIES

After reading this chapter and completing the exercises, you will be able to use the ORDER BY, GROUP BY and HAVING clauses with the SELECT statement.

CHAPTER 5

Overview

As you know, there are several key clauses that are used with the SELECT statement to retrieve data. The FROM and WHERE clauses have been covered. Now, it is time to tackle the three remaining clauses, that are most used. They are the ORDER BY, GROUP BY and HAVING clauses.

The GROUP BY clause is used to create sub totals and grand totals. These totals are usually based on a group or category of data. This chapter introduces you to the SQL code that is required to group data, so that you can create meaningful totals. As you will see, this clause and the aggregate functions, go hand in hand. Most of the time, the HAVING clause is used with the GROUP BY clause.

SELECT Statement Clauses

Table 5-1 is a refresher on the primary clauses that are used to create a query. They are listed in the order that they must be used in. It is important to remember the order that they go in.

Clause	Required?	This Clause Is Used To . . .
SELECT	Yes	Select columns and create expressions.
FROM	Only when you need to select data from a table or view, which is most of the time.	List the table(s) or view(s) that the fields used in the query are in.
WHERE	No	Create filters for the detail rows of data.
GROUP BY	Only when creating aggregate calculations for a group.	List the field(s) that will be used to create the group(s).
HAVING	No	Create filters for the groups.
ORDER BY	No	Sort the data.

Table 5-1 SELECT statement clauses explained

Sorting The Data In A Query

By default, the data returned from the query is not sorted. This means that the rows that are returned are displayed in the order that they are processed in, which may or may not be the physical order that they are in, in the table. The data can be sorted on more than one column. Columns that are sorted on, do not have to be displayed in the query result. In a way, sorting data is like grouping data, because all records that have the same value in the column(s) used in the sort, are placed together. You will learn how to sort alphabetically and numerically, in ascending and descending order.

The column that is designated as the primary key for the table has an index, known as a **CLUSTERED INDEX**. Sometimes, data will be returned in the order of the clustered index primary key, but there is no guarantee that will happen every time. Therefore, when you need rows returned/displayed in a specific order, you have to state the sort order that you want, by using the ORDER BY clause.

ORDER BY Clause

This is the clause that is used to sort the data that is retrieved by the query. If a sort order is not added to this clause for a field, the field is automatically sorted in ascending order. If you want to specify the ascending sort order, type ASC, after the field name. Having said that, there really is no need to specify an ascending sort order because that is the default. By default, the ORDER BY clause sorts text in alphabetical order, numbers in lowest to highest order and dates in sequential order, from earliest to most recent.

To sort in descending order type DESC, after the field name. **ASC** and **DESC** are keywords. The data can be sorted alphabetically or numerically. You have created a lot of queries in the previous chapters. The data that was returned in many of those queries, would be easier to understand, if the data was sorted.

The way that the ORDER BY clause sorts data depends on the collating sequence that the database software uses. The **COLLATING SEQUENCE** determines the **ORDER OF PRECEDENCE** for each character in the character set (based on the language). For example, the collating sequence determines whether or not case matters. The case determines if lowercase letters are sorted before uppercase letters. In the **ASCII COLLATING SEQUENCE**, numbers are sorted before letters and uppercase letters are sorted before lowercase letters.

ORDER BY Clause Tips

① Column names and aliases used on the ORDER BY clause, must be listed in the **<SELECT_LIST>**, if the SELECT statement uses any of the following keywords: DISTINCT, **EXCEPT**, **INTERSECT** or UNION.

② By default, when sorting in ascending order, special characters or symbols are returned first (like the index in this book), then numeric values and last, but not least, letters (text).

③ The ORDER BY clause cannot be used to create a view, subquery or derived table.

④ If you need to sort in descending order on multiple columns, each column must have its own DESC keyword.

Yes, I know that there seems to be a lot of rules to sorting data. The good news is that most of the sorting that you will do, will be selecting the ascending or descending order. I would not be doing my job well, if I only discussed sorting in ascending and descending order.

Example #1 Sort Data In Ascending Order

Figure 5-1 shows three columns of data, that were returned by using the first two lines of code in the query shown below. By looking at the data shown in Figure 5-1, it is difficult to tell if or how the data is sorted. If anything, it could be sorted on the Customer ID field. You could display the fields in the order that the data is sorted by, to make it easier to see the sort order. Doing that is more valuable for the person creating the query (aka you), then the person using the data to create a report. That could be you or someone else.

This query will sort the data on the Last Name field, in ascending order, as shown in Figure 5-2.

```
SELECT CustomerID, FirstName, LastName
FROM Customers
ORDER BY LastName;
```

	customerid integer	firstname character v	lastname character var
1	1	Chris	Christianson
2	2	Christine	Manley
3	3	Gary	Jannis
4	4	Alexander	Mast

Figure 5-1 Data not sorted

	customerid integer	firstname character va	lastname character
1	169	Elan	Abbibi
2	72	Paolo	Accorti
3	163	Paja	Al Majid
4	259	Alex	Alvarez

Figure 5-2 Data sorted in ascending order by last name

Example #2 Use The ASC Keyword

Notice that the query in Example #1 did not specify ascending or descending as the sort order. That is because ascending is the default, so it does not have to be typed in.

This query specifies the sort order. It displays the rows, in the same order, as shown above in Figure 5-2. Using the ASC keyword is optional.

```
SELECT CustomerID, FirstName, LastName
FROM Customers
ORDER BY LastName ASC;
```

Example #3 Sorting In Descending Order

The query below will sort the data shown above in Figure 5-1, in descending order by the Last Name field. Figure 5-3 shows the result of sorting on the Last Name field, in descending order.

```
SELECT CustomerID, FirstName, LastName
FROM Customers
ORDER BY LastName DESC;
```

	customerid integer	firstname character v	lastname character
1	224	Fang	Zhou
2	225	Fan	Zhang
3	513	Bob	Zarcalister
4	140	Bob	Zarcalister

Figure 5-3 Data sorted in descending order by last name

Exercise 5.1: Sort The Data In The Products Table

In this exercise, you will sort the data in the Products table, in ascending order, on the Product Name column.

1. Create this query.

```
SELECT ProductID, ProductName
FROM Products
ORDER BY ProductName ASC;
```

2. Save the query as `E5.1 Sort in ascending order on 1 column.`

   Figure 5-4 shows the result.

	productid integer	productname character varying (50)
6	5206	Adult Helmet
7	5402	Anatomic Ladies Saddle
8	5401	Anatomic Mens Saddle
9	3304	ATB Lock

Figure 5-4 Result of data sorted on the Product Name column

Example #4 Another Way To Sort Data

The ORDER BY clause supports using a number instead of the column name to indicate the column to sort on. The number corresponds to the position of the column on the SELECT clause. It can be used with the ASC or DESC keyword.

This query sorts the data shown earlier in Figure 5-1, in descending order on the Last Name column. The (3) represents the position of the field, on the SELECT clause, that you want to sort on. This query sorts the data the same as the query in Example #3.

```
SELECT CustomerID, FirstName, LastName
FROM Customers
ORDER BY (3) DESC;
```

> While the sort option shortcut discussed above will save you some typing, if the order of the fields is changed on the SELECT clause, the data will be sorted on the new field that is in the third position on the SELECT clause. If you look at queries that were created by other people, you will know what this number means. Need I say that this is a shortcut that you probably should not use. <smile>

Example #5 Sorting On Multiple Columns

As shown earlier in Figure 5-3, there are multiple customers with the same last name. The sort would be more effective if the First Name column was also sorted. Sorting on two or more columns is sometimes referred to as a **NESTED SORT**. That is because the second column that is sorted on, is sorted within the values in the first column, that is sorted on, and so on.

The query below sorts the data by the last name in descending order and the first name in ascending order. The result is shown in Figure 5-5. Notice that there is a comma between the fields that are being sorted on.

```
SELECT CustomerID, FirstName, LastName
FROM Customers
ORDER BY LastName DESC, FirstName ASC;
```

	customerid integer	firstname character v	lastname character
4	140	Bob	Zarcalister
5	458	Donald	Zarcalister
6	127	Aaron	Zalapski
7	501	Aaron	Zalapski

Figure 5-5 Data sorted on two columns

> **Tips For Sorting On Multiple Columns**
>
> ① A comma should not be added after the last column on the ORDER BY clause.
>
> ② When you sort on two or more columns, the sorting is processed in the order that the fields are listed in, from left to right, on the ORDER BY clause.
>
> ③ The DESC keyword is only applied to the column name that precedes this word. This means that if there are two columns on the ORDER BY clause, that you want to sort in descending order, you have to add the DESC keyword after both columns.
>
> ④ Only sort data when necessary, especially if the data set that is being sorted is large. The reason is because sorting requires a lot of processing resources and can cause the query to run slow.

Exercise 5.2: Sort On Two Columns

In this exercise, you will create a query that sorts on the first and last name columns, using the sort order that is most used to sort names.

1. Create this query.

```
SELECT CustomerID, LastName, FirstName
FROM Customers
ORDER BY LastName ASC, FirstName ASC;
```

2. Save the query as `E5.2 Sort on last & first names.`

   Figure 5-6 shows the result of the sort, that you were expecting to see, compared to the sort result shown earlier in Figure 5-5.

	customerid integer	lastname character	firstname character
6	273	Anderson	Elizabeth
7	145	Anderson	Sandra
8	285	Anderson	Sandra
9	166	Andover	Jerry

Figure 5-6 Data sorted on the last and first name columns

Exercise 5.3: Sort On Three Columns

In this exercise, you will create a query that sorts on the State, City and Company Name fields.

1. Create this query.

```
SELECT State, City, CompanyName
FROM Customers
ORDER BY State, City, CompanyName;
```

2. Save the query as `E5.3 Data sorted on 3 columns.`

   Figure 5-7 shows the result. Within each state, the cities are sorted in alphabetical order.

   Within each city, the company names are sorted in alphabetical order.

	state charac	city character va	companyname character varying (75
13	AL	Huntsville	Royal Cycle
14	AL	Huntsville	The Great Bike Shop
15	AL	Monroe	Globe Bike
16	AL	Seattle	Kangeroo Trikes
17	AR	Bellevue	One Track Mind
18	AR	Little Rock	Bikefest

Figure 5-7 Data sorted on three columns

Example #6 Sorting On A Numeric Field

The query below will sort the data on the Last Years Total Order Amount column, in descending order. Figure 5-8 shows the result of the sort.

SELECT CompanyName, LastYearsTotalOrderAmount
FROM Customers
ORDER BY LastYearsTotalOrderAmount DESC;

	companyname character varying	lastyearstotalorderamount numeric (18,2)
1	Paradise Sports	500000.00
2	BBS Pty	500000.00
3	Fahrkraft Rder	500000.00
4	Royal Cycle	500000.00
5	Peddles of Perth	401000.00

Figure 5-8 Data sorted on numeric values

Exercise 5.4: Sort On Numeric And String Data

The query in Example #6 sorted the data on a numeric column. In this exercise, you will enhance that query by also sorting on the Company Name column.

1. Create this query.

```
SELECT LastYearsTotalOrderAmount, CompanyName
FROM Customers
ORDER BY LastYearsTotalOrderAmount DESC, CompanyName;
```

2. Save the query as
   `E5.4 Sort on numeric & string data.`

   Figure 5-9 shows the result. 555 rows were returned.

   You will only notice the Company Name sort when there are two or more rows that have the same numeric value.

	lastyearstotalorderamount numeric (18,2)	companyname character varying
1	500000.00	BBS Pty
2	500000.00	Fahrkraft Rder
3	500000.00	Paradise Sports
4	500000.00	Royal Cycle
5	401000.00	Peddles of Perth
6	401000.00	SAB Mountain

Figure 5-9 Data sorted on numeric and string values

Exercise 5.5: Sort On Two Numeric Fields

While I could not think of a real world example of sorting on two numeric fields, does not mean that there isn't one. This exercise will sort the first numeric field in descending order and the second numeric field will be sorted in ascending order.

1. Create this query.

```
SELECT ProductName, ReorderLevel, QtyOnHand
FROM Products
ORDER BY ReorderLevel DESC, QtyOnHand;
```

2. Save the query as
   `E5.5 Sort on 2 numeric columns.`

   Figure 5-10 shows the result of the sort.
   127 rows were returned.

   Because the Reorder Level field was sorted in descending order, the rows that have a null value in the field are displayed first. By default, when sorted, null values are displayed at the end of the result.

	productname character varying (5(	reorderlevel integer	qtyonhand integer
11	Test Product	[null]	[null]
12	Test Product	[null]	[null]
13	Road Bicycle ladies	3500	4101
14	Road Bicycle ladies	3500	4102
15	Road Bicycle	3500	4103

Figure 5-10 Data sorted on two numeric fields

Sort Values By Using The LIMIT Clause

In Chapter 3, you learned how to use the **LIMIT CLAUSE** to return a specific number of rows. If you remember, I asked the question "The top 10 of what?". For the LIMIT clause to work as expected, the query needs to use the ORDER BY clause. The field used on the ORDER BY clause is what answers the top N of what, question.

When the LIMIT clause is used with the ORDER BY clause, the rows returned is limited to the first N number of rows based on the field used on the ORDER BY clause. Otherwise, the LIMIT clause returns the first N number of rows in any order.

While the correct number of rows are returned, the rows were not in any specific order, in the exercise in Chapter 3. For the rows that are returned to have any meaning, the data needs to be sorted. The exception that comes to mind is if only one row is requested to be returned, as demonstrated in Example #7.

Example #7 Find The Largest Order Total

The query below finds the customer that had the largest order total amount last year. Figure 5-11 shows the result. As expected, only one row was returned.

```
SELECT FirstName, LastName, LastYearsTotalOrderAmount
FROM Customers
ORDER BY LastYearsTotalOrderAmount DESC
LIMIT 1;
```

	firstname character	lastname character	lastyearstotalorderamount numeric (18,2)
1	Victoria	Ashworth	500000.00

Figure 5-11 Result of the query

Example #8 Select The Top 10 Rows By Order Amount

The query in Example #7 was designed to only return the top row. You may be thinking that there really was no need to sort one record. The query below will return the top 10 rows, based on the Last Years Total Order Amount value.

```
SELECT FirstName, LastName, LastYearsTotalOrderAmount
FROM Customers
ORDER BY LastYearsTotalOrderAmount DESC
LIMIT 10;
```

Figure 5-12 shows the top 10 rows.

Notice that many of the rows have the same value in the last column.

Also notice that the first four rows have the same value, as shown above in Figure 5-11. Interesting, huh?

	firstname character	lastname character va	lastyearstotalorderamount numeric (18,2)
1	Dave	Flynn	500000.00
2	Victoria	Ashworth	500000.00
3	Sven	Hoffman	500000.00
4	Bruce	Hyde	500000.00
5	Karen	Toh	401000.00
6	Claus	Main	401000.00
7	Elizabeth	Kawa	301568.22
8	Dwight	Mallel	301568.22
9	Glenda	Donnatelli	301568.22
10	Marie	Bertrand	300000.00

Figure 5-12 Top 10 rows

As shown above in Figure 5-12, there are several rows that have the same order amount value. PostgreSQL does not have the equivalent of the WITH TIES argument that SQL Server supports, which forces all records with the same value in the field being sorted on, to be returned, regardless of how many rows were selected to be returned. For example, the query at the end of this section was created in T-SQL/SQL Server. It is the same query, as the one in Example #7. Figure 5-13 shows the result.

Not having this argument limits (no pun intended) the functionality of the **LIMIT CLAUSE**. By that I mean that if there are multiple rows that have the same value in the field that is being used to sort on, the LIMIT clause may not return all of the rows, because this clause only has functionality to return a specific number of rows.

For example, as shown earlier in Figure 5-11, only one row, out of the four that have the same total order amount was returned. The query in Example #7 requested the top 1 records based on the value in the Last Years Total Order Amount field. Figure 5-12 shows the four rows with the same order amount. When that is the case, you do not know that there are more rows that have the same value, thus making the returned data inaccurate.

T-SQL query that created the result shown in Figure 5-13.

```
SELECT TOP(1) WITH TIES FirstName, LastName, LastYearsTotalOrderAmount
FROM Customers
ORDER BY LastYearsTotalOrderAmount DESC;
```

	FirstName	LastName	LastYearsTotalOrderAmount
1	Sven	Hoffman	500000.00
2	Victoria	Ashworth	500000.00
3	Bruce	Hyde	500000.00
4	Dave	Flynn	500000.00

Figure 5-13 Result of the T-SQL query

Bottom N Functionality

Most of the time, you need to find the rows with the largest value in a field. There will be times when you need to find the lowest values in a field. Some programming languages have a BOTTOM N function to handle this type of query. SQL does not. No worries. You can use the LIMIT clause and sort the rows in ascending order. Just keep in mind that all of the limitations that the LIMIT clause has, still apply when it is used to find the lowest or smallest values.

Example #9 Find The Bottom Rows

This query will return the 10 rows with the lowest values in the Total Order Amount field.

```
SELECT FirstName, LastName, LastYearsTotalOrderAmount
FROM Customers
ORDER BY LastYearsTotalOrderAmount
LIMIT 10;
```

Figure 5-14 shows the result. It would be helpful to add a comment to this query to explain that it will return the bottom n rows, because a month from now, you will probably not remember that is what the query should accomplish.

Don't act like I am the only one that would not remember this. <smile>

	firstname character v	lastname character var	lastyearstotalorderamount numeric (18,2)
1	Donna	Cogswell	27.00
2	Phil	Franklyn	27.00
3	Martin	Caledonia	27.00
4	Bob	Tuque	27.00
5	Janice	Pierson	27.00
6	Barry	Wilcox	33.90
7	Michael	Cartman	33.90
8	John	Camel	33.90
9	David	Manon	35.00
10	Russ	Clemmens	35.00

Figure 5-14 Bottom 10 rows

Example #10 Use The OFFSET Argument With The LIMIT Clause

The LIMIT clause has an **OFFSET ARGUMENT** that is used to select how many rows to skip, before returning rows. The default value for this argument is zero. Using this argument is optional.

Figure 5-15 shows the first 10 orders (rows) in the Orders table. The query below, skips the first two rows in the table, then selects the next five rows.

```
SELECT OrderID, OrderAmount
FROM Orders
LIMIT 5 OFFSET 2;
```

Figure 5-16 shows the result.

	orderid integer	orderamount numeric (18,2
1	1	2645.87
2	2	8908.05
3	3	39.80
4	4	43.80
5	5	65.70
6	6	27.00
7	7	6839.10
8	8	9612.47
9	9	40.50
10	10	4304.10

Figure 5-15 Part of the Orders table

	orderid integer	orderamount numeric (18,2)
1	3	39.80
2	4	43.80
3	5	65.70
4	6	27.00
5	7	6839.10

Figure 5-16 Rows retrieved using the OFFSET argument

Use The ORDER BY Clause With The WHERE Clause To Sort Data

Using the WHERE clause with the ORDER BY clause will sort the rows that have been filtered by the WHERE clause. The WHERE clause can also be used to filter the rows returned by the LIMIT clause.

Example #11 Sort Data That Has Been Filtered

Sorting data that has been filtered, is no different then sorting data that has not been filtered. This query will sort the data on the Company Name field. The WHERE clause filters the data to only return customers in the USA. Figure 5-17 shows the result.

```
SELECT CustomerID, CompanyName, Country
FROM Customers
WHERE Country = 'USA'
ORDER BY CompanyName;
```

	customerid integer	companyname character varying (75)	country charact
1	132	7 Bikes For 7 Brothers	USA
2	413	7 Bikes For 7 Brothers	USA
3	425	Against The Wind Bikes	USA
4	133	Against The Wind Bikes	USA

Figure 5-17 Customers in the USA, sorted by Company Name

Exercise 5.6: Sort The Orders For A Specific Sales Rep

In this exercise, you will create a query that filters the data for a specific sales rep and sorts the data on the Order Amount column.

1. Create this query.
```
SELECT OrderID, SalesRepID, OrderAmount
FROM Orders
WHERE SalesRepID = 9
ORDER BY OrderAmount DESC;
```

2. Save the query as `E5.6 Orders for sales rep 9 sorted.`

   Figure 5-18 shows the result. 1,602 rows were returned.

	orderid integer	salesrepid integer	orderamount numeric (18,2)
1	7534	9	17658.81
2	4202	9	17658.81
3	728	9	17658.81
4	7522	9	17658.81

Figure 5-18 Orders for sales rep 9 sorted

Exercise 5.7: Sort The Filtered Data On Two Columns

In this exercise, you will modify an existing query and sort the data on two columns. This will make the data easier to understand.

1. Save the E4.3 query as `E5.7 Sort filtered data on 2 columns.`

2. On the first line, move the Company Name field to the end of the row.

3. Add this ORDER BY clause. `ORDER BY LastYearsTotalOrderAmount DESC, CompanyName.`

   Figure 5-19 shows the result. 204 rows were returned.

   All of the rows that have the same total order amount, also have the company names sorted. This makes the data a little easier to read.

	customerid integer	lastyearstotalorderamount numeric (18,2)	companyname character varying
1	71	500000.00	BBS Pty
2	74	500000.00	Fahrkraft Rder
3	286	500000.00	Paradise Sports
4	283	500000.00	Royal Cycle
5	276	401000.00	Peddles of Perth
6	64	401000.00	SAB Mountain

Figure 5-19 Rows sorted by total order amount and company name

Exercise 5.8: Filter The Top 10 Rows

In Exercise 3.7, you created a query that returned the top 10 rows. In this exercise, you will modify that query to sort on the Order Amount field and filter the results by the Payment Type. This means that the rows returned will have to meet the payment type filter criteria.

1. Save the E3.7 query as `E5.8 Filter a top 10 query.`

2. Add this WHERE clause. `WHERE PaymentType = 'Check'`

3. Sort the data on the Order Amount field in descending order.

   Figure 5-20 shows the result.

   This query returns the top 10 orders, based on the order amount and the payment type criteria.

	ordernumber integer	orderdate date	orderamount numeric (18,2)	paymenttype character vary
1	2968	2017-07-07	17658.81	Check
2	4202	2018-07-07	17658.81	Check
3	5574	2014-07-07	17658.81	Check
4	7546	2015-07-07	17658.81	Check
5	2865	2017-06-15	15492.32	Check
6	3760	2018-03-02	14741.15	Check
7	4021	2018-05-26	14039.10	Check
8	2514	2017-01-26	12913.80	Check
9	2714	2017-04-18	11867.20	Check
10	3910	2018-04-18	11867.20	Check

Figure 5-20 Result of top 10 rows filtered

Exercise 5.9: Sort Data That Is In A Date Range

In Exercise 4.21, you created a query that returns orders for a particular year. The data would be easier to understand if it was sorted by the Order Date and Order Amount fields.

1. Save the E4.21 query as `E5.9 Sort data in a date range.`

2. Add this ORDER BY clause to the query.
   `ORDER BY OrderDate, OrderAmount DESC`

   Figure 5-21 shows the result. 1,863 rows were returned.

   The order amount is sorted in descending order, for each order date. This will let you see the largest order amounts for each day first.

	orderid integer	orderdate date	orderamount numeric (18,2)
2	10414	2018-01-01	1439.55
3	3564	2018-01-01	1025.40
4	3563	2018-01-01	851.77
5	3565	2018-01-02	5219.55
6	3568	2018-01-02	3842.55

Figure 5-21 Orders sorted by order date and order amount

Exercise 5.10: Find The Top 10 Orders In 2018

In this exercise, you will modify an existing query to find the top 10 orders in 2018.

1. Save the E5.9 query as `E5.10 Top 10 orders in 2018.`

2. On a new line at the bottom of the query, type `LIMIT 10.`

3. On the ORDER BY line, delete the Order Date field.

   Figure 5-22 shows the top 10 orders in 2018.

	orderid integer	orderdate date	orderamount numeric (18,2)
1	4202	2018-07-07	17658.81
2	4261	2018-07-24	17305.93
3	4087	2018-06-15	15492.32
4	3760	2018-03-02	14741.15
5	4021	2018-05-26	14039.10
6	3910	2018-04-18	11867.20
7	4247	2018-07-21	11759.40
8	4015	2018-05-23	11553.00
9	4503	2018-09-23	11316.60
10	3619	2018-01-15	10886.79

Figure 5-22 Top 10 orders by order amount in 2018

Example #12 Using The ORDER BY Clause With A Column Alias

A column alias name can be used to sort on, just like a column name. This query will sort the data by using the alias name.

```
SELECT OrderID, OrderAmount AS OrderTotal
FROM Orders
ORDER BY OrderTotal DESC;
```

Exercise 5.11: Sort Using An Expression

The previous example showed you how to sort using the alias name. What is probably not obvious, is that you can sort using an expression. It is not a requirement that the result of the expression be used in the query, but often it is. The only downside in my opinion, is that from a code perspective, it can be a little confusing to know which column in the query result, is the one being sorted on. In this exercise, you will modify an existing query, to sort using an expression.

1. Save the E3.8 query as `E5.11 Sort on an expression.`

2. Create this ORDER BY clause.

```
ORDER BY OrderAmount
  + ShippingAmount DESC
```

Figure 5-23 shows the result.

	orderid integer	orderamount numeric (18,2)	shippingamount numeric (18,2)	Order Total Amount numeric
18	897	17305.93	173.06	17478.99
19	4087	15492.32	154.92	15647.24
20	7308	15492.32	154.92	15647.24
21	2865	15492.32	154.92	15647.24

Figure 5-23 Result of a query sorted by using an expression

Example #13 Calculations That Return NULL Values

When performing calculations, it is possible that some rows do not have data in all of the columns used in the calculation. This can return unexpected results. When adding the values in columns, if one of the columns does not have a value, the result of the calculation will be NULL. This may or may not be what you want.

This query adds the values in two columns.

```
SELECT ProductID, ProductName, UnitCost, ShippingCost,
  UnitCost + ShippingCost AS TotalProductCost
FROM Products;
```

Figure 5-24 shows the result. Notice that some rows do not have a shipping cost. Those rows return a Total Product Cost of NULL.

This is because SQL makes the entire calculation invalid for the row. If this is not what you want to have happen, the next exercise will show you how to fix this potential issue.

	productid integer	productname character varying (50)	unitcost numeric (	shippingcost numeric (18,2)	totalproductcost numeric
115	7054	Touring Bicycle Child	86.29	7.75	94.04
116	9000	Test Product	5500.00	[null]	[null]
117	9001	Test Product	6250.00	[null]	[null]
118	9002	Test Product	9199.00	[null]	[null]
119	9003	Test Product	7199.00	[null]	[null]
120	9004	Test Product	8375.00	[null]	[null]
121	9005	Test Product	[null]	[null]	[null]

Figure 5-24 Result of adding the values in two fields

Exercise 5.12: Modify The NULL Values Calculation

In this exercise, you will modify the query shown above in Example #13, to replace a NULL value in the Shipping Cost field with a zero. This will allow the calculation to be processed and not return a NULL value for the Total Product Cost, when the Shipping Cost is NULL. On your own, you will have to decide what to do, on a query by query basis.

1. Create the query shown below.

```
SELECT ProductID, ProductName, UnitCost, ShippingCost,
  UnitCost + COALESCE(ShippingCost,0) AS TotalProductCost
FROM Products;
```

2. Save the query as `E5.12 Fix the null values calculation.`

Figure 5-25 shows the result of adding a check for NULL values to the Shipping Cost field. By adding the COALESCE function to a numeric field, you can set (convert) the value that you want, if the field is NULL. Most of the time, setting a numeric field to zero is the best solution. More than likely, the Shipping Cost field should have data or at the very least, a zero should be in the field.

While the calculation in this query did not cause an error with the COALESCE function, in other types of calculations (like division), a null value can cause an error. The COALESCE function portion of the formula translates to "If the Shipping Cost field has a NULL value, replace the NULL value with a zero". This **WILL NOT** display a zero in the column. The zero is only used in the calculation.

Compare the values in the Total Product Cost column, starting with Product ID 9000 in this figure, to the same rows shown above in Figure 5-24.

You will see that some of the products now have a value in the last column.

The result of modifying the query allows the total cost to be calculated, as expected.

	productid integer	productname character varying (50)	unitcost numeric (	shippingcost numeric (18,2)	totalproductcost numeric
115	7054	Touring Bicycle Child	86.29	7.75	94.04
116	9000	Test Product	5500.00	[null]	5500.00
117	9001	Test Product	6250.00	[null]	6250.00
118	9002	Test Product	9199.00	[null]	9199.00
119	9003	Test Product	7199.00	[null]	7199.00
120	9004	Test Product	8375.00	[null]	8375.00
121	9005	Test Product	[null]	[null]	[null]

Figure 5-25 Result of checking for null values in the Shipping Cost field

The same COALESCE expression, should be added to the Unit Cost field, so that the last two rows in the figure above would be calculated properly.

How Null Values Are Displayed

I have discussed null values a lot so far. This is one more topic about null values that you need to know. When a field that has null values is used to sort on, depending on the database configuration, the rows that have a null value will either appear at the top of the rows returned or at the bottom of the rows returned. The ANSI SQL standard, does not specify one way or the other. For example, by default SQL Server and MySQL display rows that have a null value in the field being sorted on, at the top of the rows returned.

In PostgreSQL, by default, the rows with a null value in the field being sorted on, are displayed last. Fortunately, the ANSI SQL standard does support adding **NULLS FIRST** or **NULLS LAST** to the ORDER BY clause, to indicate where you want the rows with null values to be displayed.

Figure 5-26 shows the result of this query, which does not specify where the rows with a null value should appear.

```
SELECT VendorID, Size, COUNT(*) AS ProductCount
FROM Products
GROUP BY VendorID, Size
Order BY VendorID;
```

Figure 5-27 shows the result of this query, which specifies where the rows with a null value should appear.

```
SELECT VendorID, COUNT(*) AS ProductCount
FROM Products
GROUP BY VendorID, Size
Order BY VendorID NULLS FIRST, Size NULLS FIRST;
```

	vendorid integer	size chara	productcount bigint
23	111	[null]	4
24	112	[null]	5
25	113	[null]	8
26	114	[null]	14
27	[null]	[null]	12

Figure 5-26 How null values are displayed by default

	vendorid integer	size character va	productcount bigint
1	[null]	[null]	12
2	100	extra large	2
3	100	large	2
		⋮	
14	103	small	2
15	104	[null]	5
16	104	large	3
17	104	medium	5

Figure 5-27 Null values displayed by the sort order specified

If you think about it, in PostgreSQL, you only need to use NULLS FIRST, because the sort order defaults to NULLS LAST automatically.

Grouping Data

This chapter introduces you to the GROUP BY clause. The GROUP BY clause is often used to create totals (counts, sums etc.) for each group of data. To create these totals, an aggregate function is used. These functions are covered in more detail in Chapter 10. Groups can also be filtered. The rest of this chapter focuses on creating groups.

The primary reason to group data is to create some type of total. Grouping allows data to be divided, so that calculations can be created for each group. When the GROUP BY clause is used, the SELECT statement returns one row per group, instead of the detail rows that have been returned up to this point.

Understanding Groups

Grouping takes detail rows of data that have the same value or a value in the same range of values, in a column together, so that at least one column can be summarized. Grouping data is similar to sorting data. The difference is that grouping allows an expression to be created, that will calculate a total for the detail rows in each iteration of the group. Often, an expression is created using an aggregate function, to calculate a sum, count, average or some other value for the group.

For example, if you needed to analyze sales by state, the group would be created for the State column. All rows that have the same state would be grouped together. There would be a group for each state that is in the table. The expression for the group would be to add (sum) the order amount for each record that is in each iteration (state) group. The summarized data for each group is what will be displayed, when the query is run, not the detail rows that are used to create the group.

Another example would be if you wanted a count of orders by state. The expression for the group would be to count each order, in each state group. If the table that you are using does not have the column of data that you need to group on, you have the two options discussed below.

① Create a relationship to a table that does have the column of data that you need, to create the group.
② Create a calculated field that will add the data that you need to group on.

Aggregating data creates a total of some type for the detail rows in each group iteration. Grouping detail rows in an SQL query is similar to creating a pivot table in Excel. By that I mean that grouping takes the detail rows and rolls them up, if you will, to summarize the detail rows.

Sorting vs Grouping Data

The biggest difference between sorting and grouping records is that sorting displays all of the detail records and grouping displays a summary of the detail records. Another difference is that grouping records allows aggregated calculations to be added to the query. These calculations are often created by using what is known as an **AGGREGATE FUNCTION.**

GROUP BY Clause

This clause takes sorting one step further by creating a summary (a total) for the detail rows that have a common value in the field(s) being grouped on. The GROUP BY clause is used to select how the detail rows that are returned, are grouped. The GROUP BY clause is also used to arrange the rows into groups that are determined by the columns that you add to the GROUP BY clause. This allows aggregate calculations to be performed on the detail rows in each group. The two tasks that are needed to create a GROUP BY clause are explained below.

① You have to decide which field(s) will be used to create a group. The unique values in these fields create the group. For example, the Orders table has a sales rep and order date field. All orders that have the same sales rep and order date could be used to create a group. Each group creates one row that will be displayed in the result.
② You have to decide what other fields need to be displayed on the summary row (the row created by the GROUP BY clause). These are fields that do not need a calculation. These fields can be placed on the GROUP BY clause, after the fields that will be used to create the groups(s), but that is not a requirement. They can be placed on the SELECT clause. Usually, these fields do not have values that make sense to group on, or if they could be grouped on, it would not add value to the data that is returned.

GROUP BY Clause Tips

While I may be getting ahead of myself, by listing these tips before you have actually created a query that groups data, my hope is that you keep these tips in mind while working on the GROUP BY exercises.

① The GROUP BY clause must come after the WHERE clause and before the ORDER BY clause.

② The groups are automatically created for the columns added to the GROUP BY clause. When the GROUP BY clause has more than one column, the data is summarized for the last column listed on the GROUP BY clause. By this I mean that all of the columns listed on the GROUP BY clause are processed together, when the groups are created. This prevents data from being calculated for each column on the GROUP BY clause.

③ If a column that is used to create a group has one or more rows with a **NULL VALUE**, the rows with a null value will cause a new group to be created and will contain a total for the rows that have a null value.

④ Each column listed on the GROUP BY clause, must come from a table, view or be a valid expression, created on the GROUP BY clause, that does not use an **AGGREGATE FUNCTION**.

⑤ The GROUP BY clause can have as many columns as needed. This allows for nested groups (a group within a group) to be created.

⑥ Keep in mind that you cannot use an expression that was created on the SELECT clause, that has an alias, on the GROUP BY clause. The GROUP BY clause only uses columns from a table or view on the FROM clause. You have to repeat the expression on the GROUP BY clause, without the alias. The other option is to create a subquery on the FROM clause and create the calculated columns in the subquery.

Example #14 Understanding How The GROUP BY Clause Works

This clause can be a little tricky to understand or visualize, so I have created three queries to help explain the concept, and walk you through the process of going from displaying detail rows to displaying grouped rows. The goal of the first two queries in this example, is to find out how many orders each customer placed, each year. The WHERE clause filters the data and the query only retrieves rows that meet the WHERE clause criteria. The rows that are displayed, are the ones that are grouped and summarized.

Query 1

The query below returns the Customer ID and Order Year for two customers. Each row represents one order that the customer placed in that year, as shown in Figure 5-28. The figure shows a portion of the data that was returned.

```
SELECT CustomerID, date_part('year', OrderDate) AS OrderYear
FROM Orders
WHERE CustomerID IN (9,19)
ORDER BY CustomerID;
```

	customerid integer	orderyear double pre
75	9	2015
76	9	2015
77	9	2015
78	9	2018
79	19	2016
80	19	2016

Figure 5-28 Customer orders by year

Based on the data shown in the figure, customer 9 placed 3 orders in 2015 and 1 order in 2018. Customer 19 placed 2 orders in 2016.

Keep in mind that these counts are based on the rows shown in the figure, not all of the rows that were returned.

Query 2

The query below adds the GROUP BY clause to Query 1. The result is shown in Figure 5-29. As shown, the GROUP BY clause rearranged the detail rows into groups of unique combinations of the Customer ID and Order Year. Now, there is only one row for each year, for each customer. As shown above in Figure 5-28, customers placed more than one order in the some years.

```
SELECT CustomerID, date_part('year', OrderDate)
  AS OrderYear
FROM Orders
WHERE CustomerID IN (9,19)
GROUP BY CustomerID, date_part('year', OrderDate)
ORDER BY CustomerID;
```

	customerid integer	orderyear double pre
1	9	2014
2	9	2015
	:	
5	9	2018
6	19	2014
	:	
9	19	2017
10	19	2018

Figure 5-29 Orders grouped by Customer ID and year

Query 3

The goal of this query is to group the products by category and provide a count of products in each category.

```
SELECT ProductCategoryID, COUNT(*) AS ProductCount
FROM Products
GROUP BY ProductCategoryID
ORDER BY ProductCategoryID NULLS FIRST;
```

This query displays two columns. The Product Category ID column contains the ID number of the products category. Product Count is a calculated field that is created by the COUNT(*) function. It will count the number of rows (products) that are in each group. This function is explained in more detail, later in this chapter.

The GROUP BY clause groups the product rows by their Product Category ID value. Then the count calculation is performed. Figure 5-30 shows the result.

	productcategoryid integer	productcount bigint
1	[null]	12
2	1	20
3	2	8
4	3	23

Figure 5-30 Count of products grouped by category

Exercise 5.13: Group The Count Of Customer Orders By Year

This exercise picks up where Query 2, in Example #14, left off. The query that you will create in this exercise will create a count of customer orders by year.

1. Create this query.

   As you can see, only one field was added to the query in Query 2, shown above.

```
SELECT CustomerID, COUNT(OrderID) AS OrderCount,
  date_part('year', OrderDate) AS OrderYear
FROM Orders
WHERE CustomerID IN (9,19)
GROUP BY CustomerID, date_part('year', OrderDate)
ORDER BY CustomerID;
```

2. Save the query as `E5.13 Count of customer orders by year.`

   Figure 5-31 shows the result. The same 10 rows were returned. Now, the result of the query has value.

	customerid integer	ordercount bigint	orderyear double pre
1	9	8	2014
2	9	18	2015
3	9	27	2016
4	9	11	2017
5	9	14	2018
6	19	23	2014
7	19	46	2015
8	19	66	2016
9	19	23	2017
10	19	40	2018

Figure 5-31 Count of customer orders by year

Exercise 5.14: Group Last Years Sales By Country And Region

In this exercise, you will create a query that groups on last years sales and region. The query will also create a count of customers and a total sales amount for each region.

1. Create this query.

```
SELECT Country, RegionID,
  COUNT(CustomerID) AS CustomerCount,
  SUM(LastYearsTotalOrderAmount) AS LastYearsTotal
FROM Customers
GROUP BY Country, RegionID
ORDER BY Country, RegionID;
```

2. Save the query as `E5.14 Customers grouped by country & region.`

Figure 5-32 shows the result. 120 rows were returned.

The first two rows in the figure have a NULL value because those countries do not have a region.

	country character varying (75)	regionid integer	customercount bigint	lastyearstotal numeric
65	United Arab Emirates	[null]	1	95900.85
66	United Kingdom	[null]	14	578229.17
67	USA	1	3	12175.95
68	USA	2	3	13411.34

Figure 5-32 Customers grouped by country and region

Example #15 Understanding The COUNT(*) Function

COUNT is an aggregate function that counts the number of rows in the context of the query. There are two ways that the **COUNT FUNCTION** can be used. This example covers using the * wildcard character. The other way was used in Exercise 5.14.

COUNT(*) will initially count all of the rows in the table. If the query has a filter, the rows that the filter discards are also removed from the count.

The query below will create a count of products that a specific vendor has. Figure 5-33 shows the result. Each line in the query is explained below.

```
SELECT COUNT(*) AS ProductCount
FROM Products
WHERE VendorID = 100;
```

	productcount bigint
1	11

Figure 5-33 Product count for one vendor

SELECT COUNT(*) AS ProductCount This code creates a calculated field named Product Count. Product Count is the alias name for the calculated field that the count of rows value will be stored in. This calculation will be used in several GROUP BY examples and exercises in this chapter.

FROM Products This line contains the table name that has the rows that will be counted by the calculated field(s) on the SELECT clause. This table also has the Vendor ID field that is used on the WHERE clause.

WHERE VendorID = 100 This line creates a filter, which restricts the COUNT calculation to only count rows when the Vendor ID field has a value of 100. This query does not need a GROUP BY clause, because it will only return data for one vendor.

Adding a group to this query would let you create any or all of the following queries:

- ☑ A count of products for each vendor.
- ☑ A count of products for one vendor by size.
- ☑ Find vendors that have less than five products.
- ☑ Find vendors that have products that have a retail price over $250.

Example #16 Count A Vendors Products By Size

The query below will create a count of products for a specific vendor, by size.

```
SELECT VendorID, Size, COUNT(*) AS ProductCount
FROM Products
WHERE VendorID = 100
GROUP BY VendorID, Size;
```

Figure 5-34 shows the 6 rows that were returned.

Keep in mind that the goal of this query is to only display products that have a size. That means that it is very possible that vendor 100 has products that do not have a size. If a product has NULL in the Size field, it would not be retrieved by this query.

	vendorid integer	size character va	productcount bigint
1	100	small	2
2	100	extra large	2
3	100	xtra small	2
4	100	medium	2
5	100	petite	1
6	100	large	2

Figure 5-34 Count of vendor products by size

Example #17 Count Products By Size For All Vendors

The query in the previous example created a count of products for one vendor. The query below creates a count of products for all vendors, by size.

SELECT VendorID, Size, COUNT(*) AS ProductCount
FROM Products
GROUP BY VendorID, Size
Order BY VendorID NULLS FIRST, Size;

One difference between this query and the one in Example #16, is that this query does not have a WHERE clause.

	vendorid integer	size character v	productcount bigint
1	[null]	[null]	12
2	100	extra large	2
3	100	large	2
4	100	medium	2
5	100	petite	1

Figure 5-35 Count of all vendors products, by size

Figure 5-35 shows the result. 27 rows were returned. The first row shown in the figure is a count of products that do not have a vendor or size. In the real world, not having a vendor for a product would probably be a problem. <smile>

The values on the last row in the figure, indicate that vendor 102 has five products, that do not have a size. This may or may not be a problem, as all products do not have a size.

Exercise 5.15: Create A Count Of Products For Each Vendor

The query in Example #16 created a product count for one vendor. In this exercise, you will create a query that counts products for all vendors.

1. Create this query.

```
SELECT VendorID, COUNT(*) AS ProductCount
FROM Products
GROUP BY VendorID
Order BY VendorID NULLS FIRST;
```

2. Save the query as `E5.15 Vendor product count.`

   Figure 5-36 shows the result. 16 rows were returned.

   The query created a group for each vendor and calculated the number of products each vendor has. The calculation counted each row, for each vendor and kept a running tally. In this query, each vendor is a group. Like the query in Example #17, the first row is a count of products that do not have a vendor.

	vendorid integer	productcount bigint
1	[null]	12
2	100	11
3	101	15
4	102	5

Figure 5-36 Vendor product count

Creating Group Filters

In theory, group filters work like the row filters (the filters that you learned how to create in Chapter 4, that are created on the WHERE clause). The difference is that group filters, are applied to groups, not individual rows in the table. Group filters are used to select which groups to keep or exclude. For example, you only want to see product categories (groups) that have 10 or more products or sales reps that have total sales of at least $25,000 between January and March 2018.

The HAVING clause is used to create group filters. The syntax for the HAVING clause, is the same as the WHERE clause, so are the options, like the operators. This means that the filter criteria that you have learned to create on the WHERE clause can be created on the HAVING clause, and it will be applied to groups. Yeah!

While not necessarily obvious, the GROUP BY clause sorts the data by the field(s) on the HAVING clause, then groups the data. This means that the expression (on the SELECT clause) is only calculated once for each value in the field on the GROUP By clause, instead of each row in the table, individually.

HAVING Clause

The HAVING clause is used to create filter criteria for groups. The HAVING clause filters the groups, that are created by the GROUP BY clause.

As needed, this clause is mostly used with the GROUP BY clause. I say mostly, because the HAVING clause can be used without using the GROUP BY clause. When used alone, the HAVING clause almost works the same way that the

WHERE clause works. The difference is that the fields on the SELECT clause have to use an aggregate function. It is best to use the WHERE clause, instead of the HAVING clause, to filter data, when the GROUP BY clause is not used in the query.

The syntax for this clause is HAVING <search criteria>.
The <search criteria> argument is used to specify one or more conditions that the group or aggregate value must meet to be selected.

Example #18 Using The HAVING Clause

The query below will return all rows in the Order Details table that have a line item total (how much the customer spent on the product) that is >= $10,000. Figure 5-37 shows the result. 429 rows were returned.

```
SELECT OrderID, ProductID, LineItemTotal
FROM OrderDetails
GROUP BY OrderID, LineItemTotal, ProductID
HAVING LineItemTotal >= 10000
ORDER BY OrderID;
```

	orderid integer	productid integer	lineitemtotal numeric (18,2
1	49	7013	15658.65
2	56	7000	29398.50
3	57	7014	13918.80
4	58	7002	29398.50

Figure 5-37 Line item product totals >= $10,000

WHERE Clause vs HAVING Clause

One difference between these clauses is that the WHERE clause filters are applied first, before the data is grouped. The rows that are excluded by the WHERE clause are **NOT** processed by the HAVING clause and are **NOT** included in a group. Another way to say it, is the following steps:

Step 1 - The WHERE clause filters the detail rows before they are grouped.
Step 2 - The GROUP BY clause creates the groups.
Step 3 - The HAVING clause filters the groups.

Because the WHERE and HAVING clauses process different data, both clauses can and often are used in the same query. For example, a query needs to display a list of sales reps that have orders totaling at least $200,000, in September 2016. The WHERE clause should be used to only retrieve orders placed in September 2016. The rows retrieved by the WHERE clause, will be grouped on the Sales Reps name field. The HAVING clause will filter on an expression that used the SUM function to get a total dollar amount of orders, then check to see which sales reps totals are >= $200,000.

The WHERE clause criteria, that is discussed in this example, greatly reduces the rows available to be grouped, which is a good thing. <smile> While this WHERE clause criteria could be done on the HAVING clause, it would create a lot of unnecessary processing to create the group rows, that are returned.

Example #19 Use The WHERE And HAVING Clauses Together

This query will provide a count of products by category, that have a retail price >= 15 and the product category has a product count >= 10. The HAVING clause filters the groups and only selects groups (Product Categories) that have at least 10 products.

```
SELECT ProductCategoryID, COUNT(*) AS ProductCount
FROM Products
WHERE RetailPrice >= 15
GROUP BY ProductCategoryID
HAVING Count(*) >= 10
ORDER BY ProductCategoryID;
```

Figure 5-38 shows the result if the query did not use the HAVING clause. Notice that there are categories with a product count that is less than 10.

	productcategoryid integer	productcount bigint
1	1	20
2	2	8
3	3	23
4	4	4

Figure 5-38 Result of a query without using the HAVING clause

Figure 5-39 shows the result with the HAVING clause. Notice that all product categories that were returned, have a product count >= 10, which is what the query above, was designed to accomplish.

	productcategoryid integer	productcount bigint
1	1	20
2	3	23
3	6	23
4	8	12

Figure 5-39 Result of a query that uses the HAVING clause

HAVING Clause Tips

① An alias name cannot be used on the HAVING clause. Instead, you have to repeat the expression that the alias clause is associated with.

② Most of the time, using the WHERE clause is more efficient then using the HAVING clause.

Exercise 5.16: Create A Valid Expression For The HAVING Clause

In this exercise, you will create a query that displays products that have sold an average quantity of five or more.

1. Create this query.

```
SELECT ProductID
FROM OrderDetails
GROUP BY ProductID
HAVING AVG(Quantity) >= 5
ORDER BY ProductID;
```

2. Save the query as `E5.16 HAVING clause valid expression.`

   Figure 5-40 shows the result. 51 rows were returned.

   Yes, I know that having a query only return one column is not exciting. Please be patient.

	productid integer
1	1109
2	1110
3	2202
4	2206

Figure 5-40 Result of a valid HAVING clause expression

Exercise 5.17: Use The HAVING Clause To Filter The Groups

The query in Exercise 5.15 created a count for all groups (vendors). In this exercise, you will modify that query to only include vendors that have a product count that is less than five. This exercise is similar to the one created in Exercise 5.16.

1. Save the E5.15 query as `E5.17 Filter the groups.`

2. Add this HAVING clause to the bottom of the query. `HAVING COUNT(*) < 5`

   Figure 5-41 shows the result. 2 rows were returned.

   Each group (row) that was returned, has a product count that is less than 5.

	vendorid integer	productcount bigint
1	111	4
2	110	4

Figure 5-41 Groups (vendors) that have less than 5 products

As you saw earlier in Exercise 5.15, there were products that do not have a vendor. The query created in this exercise, did not display any vendors that do not have a count. This should be an indication that something is wrong. There should be at least one vendor that does not have a count. There are two problems with this query, as explained below.

☑ The Products table, may or may not have all of the vendors, so the Vendors table should be used instead of the Products table. That would at least provide a list of all vendors. This would require two tables to be joined, but that has not been covered in this book yet. Hang on. <smile>

☑ The second problem is that using the COUNT(*) function, especially with the < or <= operators can be problematic, because the COUNT(*) function counts all rows, not just rows that have data in a column.

The same problem is covered in Chapter 10, Example #14 and one solution is covered in Exercise 10.15. While the query in this exercise uses the HAVING clause, the solution in Exercise 10.15 does not use this clause.

Exercise 5.18: Filter The Detail Rows Before The Groups Are Created

In this exercise, you will modify an existing query to filter the rows in the table, before the groups are created. This is the processing order. [See Table 5-1] The WHERE clause filter criteria will exclude products that do not have a retail price of at least $250.

1. Save the E5.17 query as `E5.18 Filter detail rows before groups are created.`

2. Add this WHERE clause to the query. `WHERE RetailPrice >= 250`

   Figure 5-42 shows the 4 rows that were returned. This product count only includes vendors that have products that have a retail price >= $250.

   In this query, vendor 106 has one product that meets the criteria. In the results from the query in Exercise 5.17, vendor 106 did not have any products that met the criteria. [See Figure 5-41]

	vendorid integer	productcount bigint
1	105	1
2	106	1
3	111	4
4	110	4

Figure 5-42 Vendors with retail price products >= $250

SUM Function

This function adds up all of the values in a field, to create a total. This function is covered in more detail in Chapter 10.

Exercise 5.19: Group Orders By Sales Rep

In this exercise, you will create a query that groups the orders by sales rep and creates a total sales amount (a sum), for each sales rep.

1. Create this query.

```
SELECT SalesRepID, SUM(OrderAmount) AS RepTotalSalesAmount
FROM Orders
GROUP BY SalesRepID;
```

2. Save the query as `E5.19 Group orders by sales rep.`

   Figure 5-43 shows the result. 14 rows were returned.

   The second column is the total sales amount of each sales reps orders.

	salesrepid integer	reptotalsalesamount numeric
1	4	2644886.34
2	14	44780.21
3	3	2399385.02
4	13	26845.37

Figure 5-43 Orders grouped by sales rep

Example #20 Filter The Detail Rows Retrieved By The Query In Exercise 5.19

The query below filters the rows in the Orders table, to only select rows that have a payment type. Figure 5-44 shows the result. When the values in the Rep Total Sales Amount column are compared to the ones shown above in Figure 5-43, you will see that the values are less. When this is the case, it means that some of the orders, do not have a payment type.

```
SELECT SalesRepID, SUM(OrderAmount)
  AS RepTotalSalesAmount
FROM Orders
WHERE PaymentType IS NOT NULL
GROUP BY SalesRepID;
```

	salesrepid integer	reptotalsalesamount numeric
1	4	1243600.63
2	14	17876.99
3	3	1201992.40
4	13	16120.55

Figure 5-44 Orders that have a payment type, grouped by sales rep

Exercise 5.20: Count, Sum And Group Sales Reps Orders

In this exercise, you will modify the query created in Exercise 5.19, to include a count of orders for each sales rep and to only create a group for sales reps that have at least 1,000 orders.

1. Save the E5.19 query as `E5.20 Count sum & group orders.`

2. Add the COUNT expression below, to the SELECT statement, before the SUM expression.

   ```
   COUNT(*) AS NbrOfOrders.
   ```

   Figure 5-45 shows the result. 14 rows were returned.

   As you can see, there are sales reps that do not have at least 1,000 orders. That is because the count needs to be filtered at the group level.

	salesrepid integer	nbroforders bigint	reptotalsalesamount numeric
1	4	1568	2644886.34
2	14	20	44780.21
3	3	1516	2399385.02
4	13	18	26845.37

Figure 5-45 Count of orders added to the query

Filter The Groups

In this part of the exercise, you will create a filter that selects groups (sales reps) that have at least 1,000 orders.

1. Save the E5.20 query as `E5.20-2 Filter the groups.`

2. Add this HAVING clause to the query.

   ```
   HAVING COUNT(*) >= 1000
   ```

   Figure 5-46 shows some of the 6 rows that were returned.

   These are the sales reps that have at least 1,000 orders, as indicated by the values in the Nbr Of Orders column.

	salesrepid integer	nbroforders bigint	reptotalsalesamount numeric
1	4	1568	2644886.34
2	3	1516	2399385.02
3	7	1788	3263593.66
4	9	1602	3120245.83

Figure 5-46 Sales reps with at least 1,000 orders

Exercise 5.21: Total And Group Last Years Sales By State

In this exercise, you will create a query that calculates the total sales for last year, for each state in the USA.

1. Create the query shown below.

   ```
   SELECT State, SUM(LastYearsTotalOrderAmount) AS LastYearsTotal
   FROM Customers
   WHERE Country = 'USA'
   GROUP BY State
   ORDER BY State;
   ```

2. Save the query as `E5.21 Last years sales grouped by state.`

   Figure 5-47 shows the result. 50 rows were returned.

   These are the total sales for last year, for each state in the USA.

	state charac	lastyearstotal numeric
1	AK	36683.90
2	AL	207998.81
3	AR	16439.10
4	AZ	142631.65

Figure 5-47 Last years sales, grouped by state

Example #21 Sort By Last Years Total Amount

The query in Exercise 5.21, displays the data sorted by the state abbreviation. That is fine, but you may have a need to display the same data sorted on the Last Years Total column. This would let you see which states have the largest totals at the top of the report.

If you replaced the ORDER BY clause in Exercise 5.21 with this one, `ORDER BY LastYearsTotal DESC`, the sort order would be changed.

Figure 5-48 shows the data sorted in descending order on the Last Years Total field. The values in this column are the same as the values before the data was sorted.

	state charac	lastyearstotal numeric
1	IL	1035517.07
2	VA	957573.61
3	CA	835192.65
4	PA	825954.86

Figure 5-48 Last years total sorted in descending order

Exercise 5.22: Group And Count Products In Specific Categories

In this exercise, you will create a query that groups products by their product category and provides a count of products in each category. Only specific product categories will be selected.

1. Create this query.

```
SELECT ProductCategoryID, COUNT(*) AS ProductsInCategory
FROM Products
GROUP BY ProductCategoryID
HAVING ProductCategoryID IN (1, 3, 5, 8)
ORDER BY ProductCategoryID;
```

2. Save the query as `E5.22 Group & count products by category.`

Figure 5-49 shows a count of products in each category. 4 rows were returned, which is what is expected, because the filter selected four product categories.

While this query produces the correct output, it would be more helpful to see the product category name, instead of the ID number. That is coming in the next chapter, because the product category name is stored in another table.

	productcategoryid integer	productsincategory bigint
1	1	20
2	3	23
3	5	17
4	8	12

Figure 5-49 Products grouped and filtered by category

Example #22 Alternate Way To Group And Count Products In Each Category

Earlier in this chapter, I said that the HAVING clause has the same options as the WHERE clause. The query below produces the same output as the query that you created in Exercise 5.22, as shown in Figure 5-50. I purposely did not give the count expression an alias name, so that you could see that it is not a requirement to give expressions an alias.

```
SELECT ProductCategoryID, COUNT(*)
FROM Products
WHERE ProductCategoryID IN (1, 3, 5, 8)
GROUP BY ProductCategoryID
ORDER BY ProductCategoryID;
```

	productcategoryid integer	count bigint
1	1	20
2	3	23
3	5	17
4	8	12

Figure 5-50 Result of alternate query to group and count products in a category

Sorting And Grouping

At the beginning of this chapter, you learned how to sort rows by using the ORDER BY clause. The ORDER BY clause has the following characteristics:

- ☑ The ORDER BY clause is not required.
- ☑ Sorts the data that the query returns, both detail rows and group rows.
- ☑ You can sort on any column, whether or not the column is used in the query. The column just has to come from a table or view used in the query.

The GROUP BY clause has the following characteristic:

☑ The groups that are created may not be in the order that you are expecting. When that is the case, add the ORDER BY clause to sort the groups.

Keep in mind that while most of the time, the GROUP BY clause will put the groups in the order that you are expecting, there is no guarantee, that this will happen all the time. In other words, don't count on the GROUP BY clause to sort the data, the way that you want it sorted.

Just because the data is grouped one way, does not mean that you want the result sorted the same way. By that I mean, the GROUP BY clause sorts the data that is being grouped on. For example, in Exercise 5.22, the data is grouped on the Product Category ID field. You may need to have the data in that query, sorted on the Products In Category field.

Therefore, even though it is not required, it is a good idea to always use the ORDER BY clause when using the GROUP BY clause, even if the field on the ORDER BY clause is the same as the one on the GROUP BY clause. Using the ORDER BY clause is the only way to ensure that the data is sorted the way that you want it to be sorted.

Example #23 Sort On The Sales Reps Total Sales Amount

In Exercise 5.19, you created a query that grouped orders by sales rep and created a total sales amount field. As shown earlier in Figure 5-43, the data is not sorted on either column. The query in that exercise was modified to sort the data on the Rep Total Order Amount column, as shown below.

The result is shown in Figure 5-51.
14 rows were returned.

```
SELECT SalesRepID, SUM(OrderAmount)
  AS RepTotalSalesAmount
FROM Orders
GROUP BY SalesRepID
ORDER BY RepTotalSalesAmount DESC;
```

	salesrepid integer	reptotalsalesamount numeric
1	7	3263593.66
2	9	3120245.83
3	6	3034952.37
4	4	2644886.34

Figure 5-51 Result of sorting the data retrieved in Exercise 5.19

Exercise 5.23: Group Sales By Category And Year

In this exercise, you will create a query that will display the sales total for each category, by year.

1. Create this query.

```
SELECT Category, SalesYear, SUM(Sales) AS SalesTotal
FROM CategorySales
GROUP BY Category, SalesYear
ORDER BY Category, SalesYear;
```

2. Save the query as `E5.23 Sales grouped by category & year.`

   Figure 5-52 shows the result. 24 rows were returned.

   The data is grouped by category, then sales year (within each category). There is one row for each category and sales year combination of data.

	category character varying	salesyear numeric	salestotal numeric
1	Bicycle Locks	2016	463850.80
2	Bicycle Locks	2017	304558.20
3	Bicycle Locks	2018	327298.50
4	Children's Bicycle	2016	12028.50

Figure 5-52 Sales grouped by category and year

Exercise 5.24: Group And Sort Sales By Category And Sub Category

In this exercise, you will modify the query created in Exercise 5.23, by adding another column to group on. This will divide the total sales for each category.

1. Save the E5.23 query as `E5.24 Group by category sub category & sales year.`

2. On the SELECT, GROUP BY and ORDER BY lines, add the Sub Category field, after the Category field.

As shown in Figure 5-53, the Bicycle Locks category has a lot of sub categories.

If you added the sales total for every row with the sales year 2016, in the Bicycle Locks category, they would be equal to the total on the first row, shown above in Figure 5-52. 87 rows were returned.

	category character varyi	subcategory character vary	salesyear numeric	salestotal numeric
1	Bicycle Locks	ATB Lock	2016	59721.20
2	Bicycle Locks	ATB Lock	2017	7293.00
3	Bicycle Locks	ATB Lock	2018	32556.30
4	Bicycle Locks	Chain Locks	2016	46341.40

Figure 5-53 Sales total grouped on three columns

Exercise 5.25: Group And Sort Orders By Date

In this exercise, you will create a query that groups the orders by order date and creates a total order amount for each day that there are orders. The orders will be filtered for a specific date range.

1. Create the query shown below.

```
SELECT OrderDate, SUM(OrderAmount) AS TotalOrderAmountForTheDay
FROM Orders
WHERE OrderDate BETWEEN '2018-01-01' AND '2018-01-31'
GROUP BY OrderDate
ORDER BY OrderDate;
```

2. Save the query as `E5.25 Group & sort orders by date`.

Figure 5-54 shows the order totals for the first four days in January 2018.

31 rows were returned. One row for each day in January that has orders.

If there were three days in January that did not have any orders, a row would not be returned for those three dates.

	orderdate date	totalorderamountfortheday numeric
1	2018-01-01	5611.27
2	2018-01-02	13506.06
3	2018-01-03	15119.22
4	2018-01-04	31847.95

Figure 5-54 Daily order totals

Example #24 Create A Valid Expression To Sort On

This query calculates the average line item total for each product that has been sold. The data will be grouped by the Product ID and sorted by the Product ID and the average line item total for the product.

Figure 5-55 shows the result. 115 rows were returned.
The result shows the average order amount for each product.

In reality, the data in this query does not need to be sorted on the expression because the data is grouped. That automatically means that there will only be one value per group.

There are instances where you will need to sort using an expression.

```
SELECT ProductID,
  ROUND(AVG(LineItemTotal), 2)
    AS AverageLineTotal
FROM OrderDetails
GROUP BY ProductID
ORDER BY ProductID, AVG(LineItemTotal);
```

	productid integer	averagelinetotal numeric
1	1101	53.80
2	1102	57.17
3	1103	69.44
4	1104	71.41

Figure 5-55 Valid ORDER BY clause expression

Exercise 5.26: Find The Top 3 Sales Reps

In Exercise 5.20, you created a query that calculated a count of orders and total sales amount, grouped by sales rep. In this exercise, you will modify that query to display the top 3 sales reps, based on the value in the Rep Total Sales Amount field.

1. Save the E5.20 Count sum & group orders query as `E5.26 Top 3 sales reps.`

2. Add the `LIMIT 3` criteria to the end of the query.

3. Sort the data by the Rep Total Sales Amount column, in descending order.

   Figure 5-56 shows the top 3 sales reps, based on the values in the Rep Total Sales Amount column.

	salesrepid integer	nbroforders bigint	reptotalsalesamount numeric
1	7	1788	3263593.66
2	9	1602	3120245.83
3	6	1578	3034952.37

Figure 5-56 Top 3 sales reps

Exercise 5.27: Find The Top 3 Sales Reps In A Date Range

In the previous exercise, you modified a query so that it would retrieve the top 3 sales reps. In this exercise, you will modify that query to select the top 3 sales reps in a date range.

1. Save the E5.26 query as `E5.27 Top 3 sales reps in a date range.`

2. Add filter criteria, using the Order Date field, to select orders in the first quarter of 2018.

   Figure 5-57 shows the three sales reps that meet the date criteria.

	salesrepid integer	nbroforders bigint	reptotalsalesamount numeric
1	9	155	288148.75
2	1	145	255314.24
3	3	139	225838.16

Figure 5-57 Top 3 sales reps in the first quarter of 2018

Exercise 5.28: Group Customers By Region

In this exercise, you will create a query that groups customers in the USA, by region. The query will also create a count of customers in each region and a total of last years order amount, in each region.

1. Create the query shown below.

```
SELECT RegionID, COUNT(*) AS "Number Of Customers In Region",
  SUM(LastYearsTotalOrderAmount) AS "Last Years Sales Total For Region"
FROM Customers
WHERE Country = 'USA'
GROUP BY RegionID
ORDER BY SUM(LastYearsTotalOrderAmount) DESC;
```

2. Save the query as `E5.28 Group customers by region.`

   Figure 5-58 shows the result. 50 rows were returned.

	regionid integer	Number Of Customers In Region bigint	Last Years Sales Total For Region numeric
1	10	28	1035517.07
2	28	16	957573.61
3	48	26	835192.65
4	9	19	792910.36

Figure 5-58 Customers grouped by region

Using The GROUP BY Clause With An Expression

The data that will be grouped, can be grouped by an expression, as long as the expression does not use an aggregate function. This query is not valid because SUM is an aggregate function and it is used on the GROUP BY clause.

```
SELECT OrderID, UnitPrice, Quantity
FROM OrderDetails
GROUP BY SUM(UnitPrice * Quantity);
```

Exercise 5.29: Create A Valid Expression On The GROUP BY Clause

In this exercise, you will create a valid expression for the GROUP BY clause. The query will also calculate the average quantity and line total for each detail row. The rows will be grouped by the result of the Unit Price * Quantity calculation.

1. Create this query.

```
SELECT ROUND(AVG(Quantity), 2) AS AverageQuantity,
  (UnitPrice * Quantity) AS LineTotal
FROM OrderDetails
GROUP BY (UnitPrice * Quantity)
ORDER BY (UnitPrice * Quantity) DESC;
```

2. Save the query as `E5.29 Valid GROUP BY clause expression.`

   Figure 5-59 shows the result. 293 rows were returned.

   The Order Details table has 24,776 rows. This means that a lot of the rows in the Order Details table have the same Unit Price and Quantity values.

	averagequantity numeric	linetotal numeric
1	10.00	29398.50
2	9.00	26458.65
3	8.00	23518.80
4	7.00	20578.95

Figure 5-59 Valid GROUP BY clause expression

Exercise 5.30: Find The Top 10 Regions By Sales

In this exercise, you will modify the E5.28 query to find the top 10 regions by sales.

1. Save the E5.28 query as `E5.30 Top 10 regions by sales.`

2. Add this clause to the query.
   `LIMIT 10;`

   Figure 5-60 shows the top 10 regions, based on last years sales totals.
   10 rows were returned.

	regionid integer	Number Of Customers In Region bigint	Last Years Sales Total For Region numeric
1	10	28	1035517.07
2	28	16	957573.61
3	48	26	835192.65
4	9	19	792910.36
5	17	16	753377.89
6	14	18	667544.00
7	3	7	559117.72
8	15	17	502130.43
9	13	13	470550.54
10	38	4	450106.32

Figure 5-60 Top 10 regions by sales

Exercise 5.31: Calculate The Number Of Orders By Year

In this exercise, you will create a query that groups the orders by year. The query will also calculate a yearly order total and a count of customers by year.

1. Create this query.

```
SELECT date_part('year', OrderDate) AS OrderYear,
  COUNT(DISTINCT CustomerID) AS CustomerCount,
  COUNT(*) AS NumberOfOrders,
  SUM(OrderAmount) AS OrderTotalForTheYear
FROM Orders
GROUP BY date_part('year', OrderDate)
ORDER BY date_part('year', OrderDate);
```

2. Save the query as `E5.31 Count of customers & orders per year.`

   Figure 5-61 shows the result.
   Now, you can easily see the total number of customers, total number of orders and total order amount for each year.

	orderyear double pre	customercount bigint	numberoforders bigint	ordertotalfortheyear numeric
1	2014	296	1282	2304271.58
2	2015	242	3064	5458331.83
3	2016	235	2446	4305080.25
4	2017	181	1116	2041079.99
5	2018	375	1863	3294469.86
6	2019	1	1	5545.42

Figure 5-61 Count and total of orders per year

Exercise 5.32: Group Orders By Sales Rep And Order Year

In this exercise, you will create a query that calculates a total by year, for each sales rep.

1. Create this query.

```
SELECT SalesRepID, date_part('year', OrderDate) AS OrderYear,
  SUM(OrderAmount) AS YearlyTotal
FROM Orders
GROUP BY SalesRepID, date_part('year', OrderDate)
ORDER BY SalesRepID, OrderYear;
```

2. Save the query as `E5.32 Orders grouped by sales rep & year.`

   Figure 5-62 shows the result. 62 rows were returned.

   Each sales rep has one row of data for each year that they have orders. As shown, sales rep 13 has orders in four years and sales rep 14 has orders in three years.

	salesrepid integer	orderyear double prec	yearlytotal numeric
56	13	2014	1919.40
57	13	2015	15451.52
58	13	2017	9055.87
59	13	2018	418.58
60	14	2015	26972.12
61	14	2017	16496.32
62	14	2018	1311.77

Figure 5-62 Orders grouped by sales rep and year

Example #25 Using Parentheses In Queries That Have Math Calculations

As you have learned, parentheses are used to group which portion of the query should be processed together. The same concept applies to queries that have math calculations.

This query subtracts the Direct Costs from the Net Sales, then adds the Sales Costs. Figure 5-63 shows the result.

```
SELECT OrderID, CustomerName, NetSales, DirectCosts, SalesCosts,
  NetSales - DirectCosts + SalesCosts AS GrossProfit
FROM Financial;
```

	orderid integer	customername character varying (75)	netsales numeric (1	directcosts numeric (18,	salescosts numeric (18	grossprofit numeric
1	1000	Pathfinders	25050.00	575.00	200.00	24675.00
2	1001	On The Edge Cyclery	74000.00	1500.00	1000.00	73500.00
3	1002	Spokes for Folks	100250.00	1387.00	2250.00	101113.00

Figure 5-63 Result of a calculation without parentheses

More than likely, you want to subtract the sum of the Direct Costs and Sales Costs from the Net Sales value. The query above does not do that. The query below does, and as shown in Figure 5-64, the Gross Profit amounts are different.

```
SELECT OrderID, CustomerName, NetSales, DirectCosts, SalesCosts,
  NetSales - (DirectCosts + SalesCosts) AS GrossProfit
FROM Financial;
```

Putting parentheses around the cost fields, forces them to be added together, **BEFORE** the result is subtracted from the Net Sales, which is what you want. This is how you force the order of precedence/evaluation.

	orderid integer	customername character varying (75)	netsales numeric (	directcosts numeric (18,	salescosts numeric (18,	grossprofit numeric
1	1000	Pathfinders	25050.00	575.00	200.00	24275.00
2	1001	On The Edge Cyclery	74000.00	1500.00	1000.00	71500.00
3	1002	Spokes for Folks	100250.00	1387.00	2250.00	96613.00

Figure 5-64 Result of the calculation with parentheses

If you find that the calculation portion of the query is hard to understand, because it is all on one line, maybe the layout to the right, will make it easier to understand. This layout lets you see the part that is processed first (the part in parentheses).

```
SELECT NetSales -
  (DirectCosts + SalesCosts)
   AS GrossProfit
```

Exercise 5.33: Calculate The Sales To Cost Ratio

The query that you will create in this exercise is similar to the second query in Example #25 above. The query will create what is often called the Cost of goods sold. It calculates the gross profit (which is what the last query in Example #25 calculated) divided by the Retail Price (in this data set, the Retail Price is the Sales Price). To calculate the ratio, the result that is calculated in the parentheses is divided by the Retail Price.

1. Create the query shown below.

```
SELECT ProductID, ProductName,
(RetailPrice - (UnitCost + ShippingCost))/RetailPrice AS SalesToCostRatio
FROM Products;
```

2. Save the query as `E5.33 Sales to cost ratio.`

Figure 5-65 shows the result. 127 rows were returned.

The first calculation processed is the Unit Cost + Shipping Cost. That is the total cost to produce the product.

That amount is then subtracted from the Retail Price. This value (known as the gross margin) is divided by the Retail Price, which is the ratio value shown in the last column.

	productid integer	productname character varyir	salestocostratio numeric
1	1101	Crochet Glove	0.43241379310344827586
2	1102	Crochet Glove	0.43241379310344827586
3	1103	Crochet Glove	0.42965517241379310345
4	1104	Crochet Glove	0.42965517241379310345

Figure 5-65 Result of the sales to cost ratio calculation

Summary

In this chapter you learned about three clauses that are used in a SELECT statement. As you saw, they add a lot of functionality to queries.

The ORDER BY clause is used to sort the data that the query retrieves, in a variety of ways. This is very helpful when the data will be used to create a report (especially in a pivot table or matrix layout), or a chart (like a bar chart), that needs the data displayed in a certain order.

The ORDER BY clause allows the data to be sorted in ascending or descending order. Using this clause with the WHERE clause adds more functionality to the queries. On my own, I type ASC in the code, so that when I look at the code later, I know exactly what is going on. As you gain experience, sometimes you miss the easy things, which can often be the problem that you are having with the data returned from the query. To avoid that, as much as possible, I type the default values in the query, even though that is not a requirement.

The GROUP BY clause is used to display detail rows of data in a summarized format. This clause groups the detail rows on at least one field and produces a total of some type, for each group.

The HAVING clause is used to filter the groups that are created. This filter is in addition to filters on the WHERE clause.

Quiet as it's kept, this chapter introduced **SUMMARY QUERIES**. They allow an unlimited number of detail rows to be summarized. This topic is covered in more detail in Chapter 10. This chapter also introduced you to two aggregate functions: COUNT and SUM. They were used to create totals for the groups.

I tried to show you a variety of ways of how to group data on numeric and string fields. Hopefully, when you are creating queries on your own, that need to group data and you get stuck (hey, it happens), there will be a query in this chapter or another chapter later in this book, that has an example that you can use.

This chapter covered a lot of ground. And to think, all of this was accomplished by only using one table per query. In the next chapter, things really get wild, because the wait is over. You will learn how to join tables!

CREATING QUERIES THAT USE MULTIPLE TABLES

After reading this chapter and completing the exercises, you will have an understanding of the join type options and how to join tables. This will let you retrieve data from multiple tables in the same query.

CHAPTER 6

Joining Tables

The previous three chapters focused on creating queries that only used one table. Hopefully, those chapters made you comfortable with the basics of creating queries. As you saw, many of the queries had to display ID field values, in attempts of having the data that was returned, make sense.

SQL databases are created in a relational format, which stores the data in two or more tables. Each of the ID fields in the database used in this book, indicates that there is additional related data stored in another table in the database. When tables are linked together, you have access to more data. Joining tables provides the ability to use data from two or more tables. This provides a more complete view of the data.

As you may have guessed by the title of this chapter, we are moving to the next level of creating queries, because you will learn how to use two or more tables to create a query. Hopefully, you remember what you learned about relationships, earlier in this book, because this is the chapter where that knowledge is needed. The good thing is that all of the clauses, keywords and concepts covered in the previous three chapters are available when the query retrieves data from two or more tables.

Things are about to change, because this chapter covers linking (joining) tables, so that fields from two or more tables can be used in the same query. This will enable you to create queries that display the sales reps name that is stored in one table, along with the order information that is stored in another table. Yes, I know what you may be thinking "Why have the data in separate tables, only to have to learn how to join them to use the data?" The primary answer, as discussed in an earlier chapter, is to not have the same data in multiple tables.

The focus of this chapter is to show you how to join tables. Think back to Chapter 1, where I discussed "virtual joined tables". Without joining tables, the result of the queries will seem incomplete, as you have seen in previous chapters. The same figure used in Chapter 1, is also shown in Figure 6-1, because it illustrates what the data in two tables looks like, if you could see it, once the tables are joined. Creating joins is probably the most powerful feature in SQL.

As you will see in this chapter and the next one, is that there are several join type options. Understanding how each join type connects the tables and how the join types select the data, is critical to retrieving the correct rows of data. Equally important in my opinion, is understanding the data in the tables that will be joined and what you need to retrieve.

For example, do you need to retrieve all of the orders and look up the region name or do you need to only retrieve rows from the Orders table that have a matching row in the Regions table? While these two scenarios may sound similar, they will not retrieve the same rows of data. Usually, the latter scenario will retrieve fewer rows from the Orders table.

While the focus of this chapter is learning to create joins, to retrieve data from tables, joins are also used to create views and stored procedures (stored procedures are beyond the scope of this book).

If you recall, in the Chapter 3 summary, I discussed how problematic it is, not understanding the join type options. This chapter and the next one are probably the most important chapters for you to understand. Not understanding the data set that each join type returns, means that the rest of the query may not retrieve the correct rows of data.

As covered in previous chapters, you learned that even when only retrieving data from one table, it isn't that difficult to get into trouble and not retrieve the correct data. Sadly, those issues do not go away when tables are joined. If anything, it can be harder to find the problem. As I have said before, when you are on your own, **TAKE YOUR TIME**.

Hopefully, you have completed many of the query exercises in previous chapters, as they will be used in this chapter and throughout the rest of this book, as the starting point for new queries.

> As you know, the WHERE clause is used to filter data. When you stop and think about it, joining tables is a way to filter data, because the join type is used to select which rows from which tables to retrieve. Thinking of joins as a filter, like you have done for the WHERE clause up to this point, may be helpful. As you will see, each join type selects records differently.

Join Types

There are several types of joins that can be created. These different types of links are called **JOIN TYPES**. Each join type will retrieve different sets of rows from the same tables, which you will see in Figures 6-2 through 6-5. There are three primary types of joins: INNER, OUTER and CROSS. As you will see, each of these join type categories use different logical query processing. For example, an inner join has two phases, a filter and **CARTESIAN PRODUCT**. An outer join has three phases, a filter, Cartesian product and **ADD OUTER ROWS**. A **CROSS JOIN** has one phase, a Cartesian product. The JOIN table operator uses two input tables. **INNER** joins are the most common.

Joining tables (creating a relationship) is not permanent. Joins are recreated each time the query is run. The two main types of joins, are explained below. Both join type categories filter the rows of data in the tables.

① **INNER JOINS** The record set (records that are returned) only contains records that have a matching record in both tables. An important fact to keep in mind is that inner joins act like a filter because rows are only returned (from both tables) if there is a matching value in the field that is used to join the tables. This automatically filters the data.

② **OUTER JOINS** The record set contains all records from one table (usually the primary table) and the matching records from the other table (usually the child table). This join category filters data because only a subset of data from one table (the table on the right), in a LEFT OUTER JOIN is returned. Sometimes, the join filters the data the way that you need it to be filtered, without you creating any filter criteria. OUTER JOINS are covered in Chapter 7.

Join operators are processed/evaluated from left to right. As needed, parentheses can be used to group the joins.

The first two join types that are explained in Table 6-1, are the join types that are the most used in SQL databases. The join type descriptions in the table reference left and right tables. In the Orders and Order Details tables scenario, shown below in Figure 6-1, the Orders table is the **LEFT** table and the Order Details table is the **RIGHT** table.

The "matching" explained in Table 6-1 is usually done on primary key fields.

Join Type	How Records Are Selected . . .
INNER JOIN	Selects records that have a matching value in a field, in both tables, as shown in Figure 6-2.
LEFT OUTER	Selects all records from the table on the left and only matching records in the table on the right, as shown in Figure 6-3. (1)
RIGHT OUTER	Selects all records from the table on the right and only matching records from the table on the left, as shown in Figure 6-4. This join type works the opposite of the LEFT OUTER join type. (1)
FULL OUTER	Selects all records from both tables whether or not there are matching records in the other table, as shown in Figure 6-5. The same result can by achieved by using the **UNION OPERATOR**. FULL OUTER joins are also known as a **UNION JOIN TYPE**. (1)
Self Join	[See Recursive Join]
CROSS JOIN	[See CROSS JOIN]

Table 6-1 Join types explained

(1) Using the word OUTER in the query is optional.

Join Type Examples

When walking through these examples, compare the data in each example to the data shown in Figure 6-1.

Naturally, there are exceptions to how tables are joined. By that I mean that there can be instances where two primary or two lookup tables can be joined.

Orders				Order Details		
Order ID	Order Date	Order Amount	Cust ID	Order ID	Product ID	Quantity
1000	01/02/2015	$263.99	48	1000	43	4
1000	01/02/2015	$263.99	48	1000	76	2
1001	01/02/2015	$322.45	57	1001	76	3
1001	01/02/2015	$322.45	57	1001	10	2
1002	01/03/2015	$196.00	3			
1003	01/04/2015	$124.99	48	1003	10	1
				1004	25	3

Figure 6-1 Virtually joined tables

The figures in this section **ONLY** display the data that would be returned, based on the join type that is selected. This is why it is important to understand linking and join types. The arrows between the tables represent the direction of the flow of the data. While the examples only show joins between two tables, joins can and often are created between three or more tables.

INNER JOIN Example

In Figure 6-2, the record for Order ID 1002 in the Orders table would not be returned in an INNER join because there is no related record in the Order Details table.

Orders			
Order ID	Order Date	Order Amount	Cust ID
1000	01/02/2015	$263.99	48
1001	01/02/2015	$322.45	57
1003	01/04/2015	$124.99	48

Order Details		
Order ID	Product ID	Quantity
1000	43	4
1000	76	2
1001	76	3
1001	10	2
1003	10	1

Figure 6-2 INNER join record set

LEFT OUTER JOIN Example

In Figure 6-3, the record for Order ID 1004 would not be returned from the Order Details table in a LEFT OUTER join because there is no related record in the Orders table.

Orders			
Order ID	Order Date	Order Amount	Cust ID
1000	01/02/2015	$263.99	48
1001	01/02/2015	$322.45	57
1002	01/03/2015	$196.00	3
1003	01/04/2015	$124.99	48

Order Details		
Order ID	Product ID	Quantity
1000	43	4
1000	76	2
1001	76	3
1001	10	2
1003	10	1

Figure 6-3 LEFT OUTER join record set

RIGHT OUTER JOIN Example

In Figure 6-4, the record for Order ID 1002 in the Orders table would not be returned in a RIGHT OUTER join because there is no related record in the Order Details table.

Orders			
Order ID	Order Date	Order Amount	Cust ID
1000	01/02/2015	$263.99	48
1001	01/02/2015	$322.45	57
1003	01/04/2015	$124.99	48

Order Details		
Order ID	Product ID	Quantity
1000	43	4
1000	76	2
1001	76	3
1001	10	2
1003	10	1
1004	25	3

Figure 6-4 RIGHT OUTER join record set

FULL OUTER JOIN Example

In Figure 6-5, all records would be returned from both tables in a FULL OUTER join, whether there is a related record in the other table or not. This means that when there is no matching Order ID in one table, when displayed, that row will have missing data.

Orders			
Order ID	Order Date	Order Amount	Cust ID
1000	01/02/2015	$263.99	48
1001	01/02/2015	$322.45	57
1002	01/03/2015	$196.00	3
1003	01/04/2015	$124.99	48

Order Details		
Order ID	Product ID	Quantity
1000	43	4
1000	76	2
1001	76	3
1001	10	2
1003	10	1
1004	25	3

Figure 6-5 FULL OUTER join record set

Recursive Join

In addition to the inner and outer join types, there is another join type called **RECURSIVE JOIN**. (This join type is also known as a **SELF-JOIN**.) This join type is not always obvious when looking at the table structure. A recursive join occurs when the same data is stored in two different fields (usually primary key fields) in the same table. This is not the same as a parent/child (also known as a master/detail) relationship, because this type of relationship does not require two tables to create the link, like the Orders and Order Details tables do. No link is required to use the recursive join type.

An example of a recursive join is in the table shown in Figure 6-6. In the real world, this table would be the Employees table. I renamed it to make it easier to understand scenarios used in this book.

The Supervisor ID field in the table contains the Sales Rep ID of another record in the same table. This is because supervisors are also employees. As shown, four employees (sales reps) have the number 5 in the Supervisor ID field. This is because they all have the same supervisor, Steven Buchanan, whose Employee ID, is number 5.

Recursive joins are often used to create **HIERARCHICAL REPORTS**. An example of this type of report would be a report that displays a list of managers and the people in their department.

	salesrepid integer	supervisorid integer	firstname character \	middle characte	lastname character v:	salesrep character varying (5(	position character varying (50)	birthdate date	hiredate timestamp without tir	salary numeric (1
1	1	5	Nancy	A	Davolio	Nancy Davolio	Sales Representative	1972-12-08	1993-04-16 00:00:00	40000.00
2	2	[null]	Andrew	[null]	Fuller	Andrew Fuller	Vice President, Sales	1969-02-19	2011-08-30 00:00:00	90000.00
3	3	5	Janet	E	Leverling	Janet Leverling	Sales Representative	1971-08-30	2005-09-19 00:00:00	33000.00
4	4	5	Margaret	I	Peacock	Margaret Peacock	Sales Representative	1973-09-19	2003-07-25 00:00:00	35000.00
5	5	2	Steven	[null]	Buchanan	Steven Buchanan	Sales Manager	1975-03-04	2005-11-11 00:00:00	50000.00
6	6	5	Michael	R	Suyama	Michael Suyama	Sales Representative	1963-07-02	2015-05-02 00:00:00	30000.00

Figure 6-6 Part of the Sales Reps table

CROSS JOIN

This type of join is also known as a **CARTESIAN PRODUCT**. This join type joins every row in one table to every row in another table. This will display all possible row combinations. This happens when no relationship has been created between the tables or if the query does not have a **WHERE CLAUSE**. [See Tables Without A Relationship] Technically, a CROSS JOIN works like an INNER JOIN, where the join criteria is either not included in the query, or it always evaluates to True.

Another way to explain a cross join is that because it does not have to find matches between the key fields in the tables, there is no need or reason to create a join using the ON keyword. This will be demonstrated in Exercise 6.1.

What Is A Cartesian Product?
This phase matches all of the rows in one table with all of the rows in another table. For example, if the Orders table shown earlier, has 100 rows and the Order Details table has 1,000 rows, the result of the query will display 100,000 rows (100 x 1000).

Tables Without A Relationship

If you added the Orders and Order Details tables to a query but did not join them, the query would not know which record in the Orders table matches which record(s) in the Order Details table.

The result of the scenario discussed in the tip box above, would be that each order record would be displayed (matched) with each of the records in the Order Details table. Figure 6-7 shows some of the rows that would be returned.

When a query uses more than one table, this is usually not what you want. This is known as a **CROSS OR CARTESIAN JOIN**.

Orders			
Order ID	Order Date	Order Amount	Cust ID
1000	01/02/2015	$263.99	48
1000	01/02/2015	$263.99	48
1000	01/02/2015	$263.99	48
1000	01/02/2015	$263.99	48
1000	01/02/2015	$263.99	48
1000	01/02/2015	$263.99	48
1001	01/02/2015	$322.45	57
1001	01/02/2015	$322.45	57
1001	01/02/2015	$322.45	57
1001	01/02/2015	$322.45	57
1001	01/02/2015	$322.45	57
1001	01/02/2015	$322.45	57
:			
1003	01/04/2015	$124.99	48

Order Details		
Order ID	Product ID	Quantity
1000	43	4
1000	76	2
1001	76	3
1001	10	2
1003	10	1
1004	25	3
1000	43	4
1000	76	2
1001	76	3
1001	10	2
1003	10	1
1004	25	3
:		
1004	25	3

Figure 6-7 Result of tables that are not joined

Exercise 6.1: Create A Cross Join Query

In this exercise, you will create a query that produces the result of a cross join query.

1. Create this query.

```
SELECT SalesRep, Position, OrderDate, OrderAmount,
  ShippingAmount
FROM SalesReps, Orders
ORDER BY OrderDate;
```

2. Save the query as `E6.1 Cross join query`.

Figure 6-8 shows the result.

146,580 rows were returned.

	salesrep character varying (5	position character varying (50)	orderdate date	orderamount numeric (18,2)	shippingamount numeric (18,2)
1	Nancy Davolio	Sales Representative	2014-01-01	2645.87	26.46
2	Nancy Davolio	Sales Representative	2014-01-01	8908.05	89.08
3	Andrew Fuller	Vice President, Sales	2014-01-01	8908.05	89.08
4	Janet Leverling	Sales Representative	2014-01-01	8908.05	89.08

Figure 6-8 Result of a cross join query

As discussed earlier, in a cross join, the number of rows returned is the number of rows in one table multiplied by the number of rows in the other table.

The Sales Reps table has 15 rows and the Orders table has 9,772 rows. 15 x 9,772 = 146,580. As shown, each row in the Sales reps table is joined with each row in the Orders table. I guess that there may be a need to create this type of query, but I honestly can't think of such a need.

Earlier, you learned what a schema is in PostgreSQL. The schema discussed below is a different topic, that uses the same word.

What Is A Star Schema?

Chapter 1 covered relationships and relational databases, which is also known as a data model. Now that you are familiar with data models, it is time to clearly define what the data model will be used for. If this book represented the real world, the data model used in this book would be used for analyzing and reporting on data. The schema types for data models are:

① **STAR** Has one level of **CHILD TABLES**.
② **SNOWFLAKE** Can have multiple levels of child tables. Some people say that this schema can cause performance issues because of the increased number of relationships. My advice is to try it and see for yourself. It may also be the only option, depending on the tables that are in the data model, that you are using.
③ **CONSTELLATION** Is used when there is more than one fact table.

My personal preference is the Star schema because it handles large data sets. That, and it is easy to understand.

A **FACT TABLE** is the parent or primary table in the data model. The fact table usually has some or all of the following characteristics:

① It has measurable data, meaning that the data, in the table, will answer a question. For example, the Orders table has an Order Amount field, which would be used to answer, which five states have the most sales.
② Other tables are linked to it. The fact table usually has the most ID fields.
③ It has one or more date fields, which confirm when something happened, like when the order was placed or the date of each basketball game.
④ Fact tables often have more rows of data, then any other table in the data model. Date tables are not included when determining which table is the fact table, because a date table does not contain data that will be analyzed. A date table is often used in a data model. This book does not cover date tables.

The primary table is surrounded by the other tables in the data model, forming, you guessed it, a star, as shown in Figure 6-9. This is also known as **DIMENSIONAL MODELING** because it describes the logical way that data should be structured, to obtain the best performance. The Orders table is the fact table in this figure. It is not a requirement to arrange the tables in this layout, when using software that has functionality to display tables and relationships.

On your own, if you are not sure which table is the fact table, create the relationships for the tables and see which table has the most relationships. More than likely, the table with the most relationships to other tables is the fact table.

The other tables (known as the **DIMENSION TABLES**, **LOOKUP TABLES** or **CHILD TABLES**) in the schema contain supporting data, if you will, that provide additional information about a field in the fact table.

For example, in Figure 6-9, the Customer table contains information on who placed each order. The Order Details table contains the items for each order. Notice that each dimension table is linked to the fact table and none of the dimension tables are linked to each other.

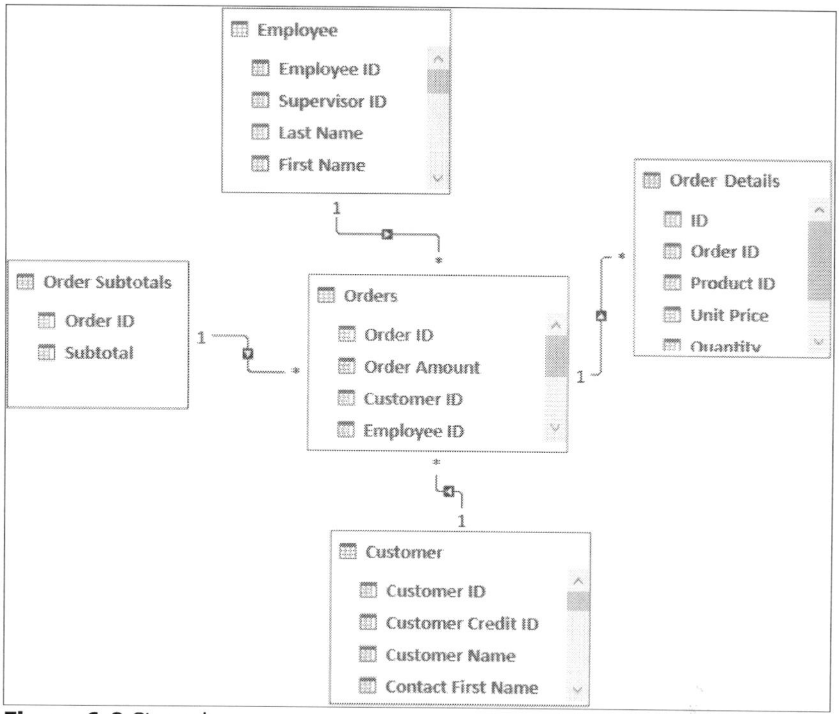

Figure 6-9 Star schema

Dimension tables can be linked to each other. An example would be adding a Products table to the schema shown above in the figure. It would be linked to the Order Details table, using the Product ID field. That would allow the product name to be returned and displayed on a report. If the schema rules were strictly followed, adding a relationship to the Products table would make the Star schema shown in Figure 6-9, a Snowflake schema, because the Products table does not have a direct relationship with the Orders **FACT TABLE**.

What Is Normalization?

There are two normalization strategies, as explained below:

① **DENORMALIZATION** is the process of combining several tables (usually small tables) into one big table. While this causes the new table to have redundant data, it is done on purpose, because it allows the queries to process faster against the table(s) in the data model. This is sometimes the strategy behind the reason that some views are created.

② **NORMALIZATION** is the process of removing redundancy in the data model. It works the opposite of denormalization. It takes a large table and turns it into two or more smaller tables. If a value occurs more than once in a column, it is only saved once in the table. The other occurrences of the value in the column are replaced with a reference to the first occurrence of the value.

After the tables have been added the data model, the next step is to determine if the tables are set up to run in the most efficient way. This is known as **NORMALIZING THE DATA MODEL**. This process organizes the data to make querying data more efficient. The goal of normalization is to ensure that other then key fields, the same data is not stored in more than one table. As the person creating queries, all of this has already been done for you. But it is a concept that you need to understand, because it goes towards helping you understand table structures.

When you join tables in a normalized database, the join is sometimes referred to as **DENORMALIZATION**. That is because denormalization is an important component of building SQL relational data warehouses, like the star schema that was discussed earlier in this chapter.

Creating Joins

This chapter covers joining tables, using the INNER join type. This is known as a basic join. While it may be called "basic", joining two tables using the INNER join type will handle a large percent of your needs. Think back to the queries that you created in Chapter 4. The majority of them, if not all of them displayed an "ID" field. Displaying a customer name, instead of the Customer ID value is more appropriate for reports.

In Chapter 5, you were introduced to creating expressions (also called calculations or calculated fields). They were limited to the fields in one table. When you can use two or more tables in one query, there are more fields available to select from, to create calculations. So, call it what you want, but joining two tables will allow you to greatly enhance the queries that you create. So far, the queries that you have created, have only listed one table on the FROM clause. When you join tables, additional tables can be listed on the FROM clause, by using additional keywords.

To create a join, you have to specify all of the tables that are needed to create the query. You also have to state how the tables are related. This is usually done by using a key field in the table. As you will see, there are two ways that a join can be created, as explained below.

① Use the FROM clause and the **ON CLAUSE**. The ON clause is used to create the condition for how the tables should be joined. It works with the WHERE clause.
② Use the join type keyword (INNER, LEFT OUTER, etc) with the WHERE clause.

While there are two ways to create a join, there are variations on how each option can be used.

Join Tips
① You will see that the fields used to join tables in this book, have the same name. On your own, you may not find that to be the case for all tables. Don't let that through you, as it is not a requirement for the fields that are used to join tables, to have the same name.
② The most efficient joins are those created on fields that have been indexed.
③ While the joins in each query in this book use the same join type, that is not a requirement. If needed, you can mix and match join types, so to speak, in the same query. If you need to do this, my advice is to test the joins individually, to make sure that they retrieve the correct rows.

Because all of the queries that you have created so far only use one table, there is another requirement of joining tables that you need to know about. That is the concept of **QUALIFYING COLUMN NAMES**. As you learned, the foreign key must have the same or compatible data type as the primary key of the table that it will be joined to. Usually, the primary key and the foreign key columns have the same name. While this makes it easier to know which field to use to join tables on, it does present a problem.

The problem is that the database does not know which table to retrieve the field from, when the fields have the same name. The solution is to include the table name with the field name, to create the join. For example, if you want to join the Customers and Orders tables, the field that the tables would be joined on, is the Customer ID field. To reference this field in the Customers table, you would type Customers.CustomerID. To reference the Customer ID field in the Orders table, you would type Orders.CustomerID.

INNER JOINS

As covered earlier, INNER joins apply two logical query processing phases. First, a Cartesian product is applied between the two input tables, like a cross-join. Then it filters rows, based on the criteria that you specify. INNER joins in PostgreSQL use the SQL-92 syntax, as explained below.

SQL-92 SYNTAX When using this syntax, list the table names on the FROM clause, adding the INNER JOIN keyword between the table names. This join type is also known as an **EXPLICIT INNER JOIN**. Using the keyword INNER is optional, because an inner join is the default. The **ON CLAUSE** is used to specify the join condition/filter. The WHERE clause is not used to join tables in this syntax. The WHERE clause can still be used to create other filter criteria, like you have already created in this book.

In addition to the SQL-92 syntax, there is also **SQL-89 SYNTAX**. This join type is also known as an **IMPLICIT INNER JOIN**. The reason that I am bringing this to your attention is because you may come across it in some documentation, or if you have created queries using a SQL Server database, you may already be familiar with it.

How Not To Join Tables

The SQL-92 syntax is less prone to errors than the SQL-89 syntax, used in the query in Example #1 below.
For example, the first query below uses the SQL-89 syntax and does not generate an error. Because this query does not fail and returns data, you may not notice the logic error. What's worse, is that the person that uses the data retrieved from the query will be using incorrect data, because the join condition is not specified (which is a logic error)

in the query. While this query is short, you may be able to catch this problem. However, if the query is more complex and/or has more than one table, it is more difficult to see the problem.

```
SELECT SalesReps.SalesRepID, SalesRep, OrderID
FROM SalesReps, Orders;
```

This query uses the SQL-92 syntax and should generate an error, but it doesn't, in some SQL databases (like MySQL). It does in PostgreSQL. The reason that it should generate an error is because the join condition (how to link the tables) was not included.

```
SELECT SalesReps.SalesRepID, SalesRep, OrderID
FROM SalesReps INNER JOIN Orders;
```

Both of the queries above, create a **CARTESIAN PRODUCT**, as explained earlier, because neither query has a complete join condition.

When more than one table or view is listed on the FROM clause, the table operators are processed from left to right. This means that the second table is treated as the left input to the third table and so on.

Using INNER JOIN vs JOIN
Instead of typing INNER JOIN, you can just type the word JOIN. Both return the same result. I use the full name in this book to make it easier for you to know which join type the query is using.

Example #1 Using The FROM Clause To Join Tables With SQL-89 Syntax

The query below displays the fields shown in Figure 6-10, which shows three fields from the Products table.

```
SELECT ProductName, Size, SubCategoryID
FROM Products
WHERE SubCategoryID IS NOT NULL;
```

	productname character varyi	size character va	subcategoryid integer
3	Crochet Glove	medium	5
4	Crochet Glove	large	5
5	Crochet Glove	extra large	5
6	Lycra Glove	petite	9

Figure 6-10 List of products and their Sub Category ID

Each product has a sub category. The products that do not have a sub category are not displayed. This will be covered later in this chapter. It would be helpful to see the sub category name.

The query below adds the Product Sub Category table to the query on the FROM clause. The Sub Category field from the Product Sub Category table is added to the SELECT clause. Notice that the tables that will be joined, are on the FROM clause, separated by a comma. The WHERE clause joins the tables on the Sub Category ID field. This is the SQL-89 syntax way of joining tables.

```
SELECT ProductName, Products.SubCategoryID,
  SubCategory
FROM Products, ProductSubCategory
WHERE Products.SubCategoryID =
  ProductSubCategory.SubCategoryID;
```

This query will only return rows where there is a match on the Sub Category ID field in both tables. Figure 6-11 shows the result.

	productname character varying (50)	subcategoryid integer	subcategory character varying (50)
14	Touring Bicycle	2	Touring Bicycle (Romeo)
15	Touring Bicycle Child	4	Children's Bicycles
16	Touring Bicycle Child	4	Children's Bicycles
17	Crochet Glove	5	Crochet Gloves

Figure 6-11 Result of joined tables

Notice the following in the query:

- ☑ On the SELECT and WHERE clauses, the Sub Category ID field is fully qualified (it includes the table name). This has to be done, when the same field name exists in two or more tables used in the query. Including the table name is how SQL knows which table the field is in, that you want to use.
- ☑ On the FROM clause, there is a comma between the table names. That is a syntax requirement.
- ☑ The ON clause is not used.
- ☑ The WHERE clause contains the criteria to link the tables. In this query, the value in the Sub Category ID field in both tables must match.

Yes, I know what you are thinking. "Where is the join type specified in the query?" In this example, it is specified on the WHERE clause in the query.

The WHERE Clause Isn't Just For Creating Filter Criteria Anymore

This clause can do double duty. In addition to using the WHERE clause to create filter criteria, it can also be used as part of the code to join tables. For example, the WHERE clause can be used to create an INNER JOIN, as shown above in the second query in Example #1, which used the SQL-89 syntax.

Until this chapter, the WHERE clause was only used to create filter criteria. That hasn't changed. While there is nothing wrong with using the WHERE clause to join tables, it can become complex and in some cases confusing, when the WHERE clause is also used to filter data. If you find that to be the case, you can use the **ON CLAUSE** discussed earlier to define the join. As you will see in the next example, the ON clause is used with the FROM clause. This means that the WHERE clause is free to only be used to create filter criteria, like you have up to this point.

Example #2 Specify The Join Type In The Query

The query in this example uses the **SQL-92 SYNTAX** to join the tables. If you ran this query, you would see that the **INNER JOIN** retrieved the same data that is shown above in Figure 6-11.

```
SELECT ProductName, Products.SubCategoryID, SubCategory
FROM Products INNER JOIN ProductSubcategory
  ON Products.SubCategoryID =
    ProductSubcategory.SubCategoryID;
```

Notice the following:

- ☑ The SELECT clause is the same in this query and the second query in Example #1.
- ☑ The query in this example does not use the WHERE clause to join the tables.
- ☑ The link is created on the FROM clause, using INNER JOIN with the ON clause. The criteria after the ON clause is the same as the WHERE clause criteria in the second query, shown earlier in Example #1. It specifies how to link the tables.

I typed the FROM clause on two lines on purpose, to make it easier to read and understand the code. The first line lists the tables that will be joined. The second line is the criteria for joining the tables. Doing this is optional. Sometimes, I will list each join on it's own line, as shown below. Anything to make the code easier to read. <smile>

```
SELECT ProductName, Products.SubCategoryID, SubCategory
FROM Products
  INNER JOIN ProductSubcategory ON Products.SubCategoryID = ProductSubcategory.SubCategoryID;
```

What you will see is that most of the time, you will use the equal operator to create most joins. As covered earlier, other operators can be used to join tables. For example, you can use the less than operator to create an inner join.

Which Option Should I Use?

The second query in Example #1 and the queries in Example #2, both retrieve the same data and are valid ways to create a query that joins tables. Like many things in life, the easiest option (in this case the second query in Example #1) is usually not the preferred option. Joining tables is no exception. The preferred option is to use INNER JOIN with the ON clause. The choice is yours, unless your company requires a specific way to join tables.

> While **INNER JOINS** may be the most used join type, I think that they filter out the most data, which will cause rows of data that you may need, to not be returned, in many cases. In my opinion, they are best suited for looking up data in a table.

> While the result of the majority of queries in this book display an ID field, it is not necessary, unless the ID field needs to will be displayed on a report.

Exercise 6.2: Retrieve Each Customers Region And Division

In this exercise, you will create a query that retrieves data from the Customers table and looks up region data in another table. This query will only retrieve rows where there is a matching row in both tables. This means that all records in the Customers table may not be returned.

1. Create the query shown below.

```
SELECT CustomerID, FirstName, LastName, RegionName, DivisionName
FROM Customers INNER JOIN Regions
  ON Customers.RegionID = Regions.RegionID;
```

2. Save the query as `E6.2 Customer & Region table data.`

Figure 6-12 shows the result.
377 rows were returned.

The Region Name and Division Name fields are from the Regions table.

	customerid integer	firstname character va	lastname character vary	regionname character var	divisionname character varying
2	2	Christine	Manley	Midwest	East North Central
3	3	Gary	Jannis	Midwest	East North Central
4	4	Alexander	Mast	South	East South Central
5	5	Patrick	Reyess	West	Pacific

Figure 6-12 Fields from the Customers and Regions tables

Exercise 6.3: Retrieve Each Sales Reps Name

In Chapter 5, Exercise 5.32, you created a query that displayed the Sales Rep ID. The results of that query would be easier to understand if the sales reps name was returned. You will also create a count of orders in this exercise. This query will group the orders by sales rep and year.

1. Save the E5.32 query as `E6.3 Add the sales reps name.`
2. On the first line, add the Orders table name to the beginning of the Sales Rep ID field.
3. On the first line, add the Sales Rep field from the Sales Reps table, after the Sales Rep ID field.
4. Create an expression that counts the number of orders and place the field after the Order Year field, on the SELECT statement. Name the field, `NbrOfOrders`.
5. On the GROUP BY and ORDER BY lines, add the Orders table name to the beginning of the Sales Rep ID field.
6. Change the FROM clause to the one shown below.

```
FROM Orders INNER JOIN SalesReps
  ON Orders.SalesRepID = SalesReps.SalesRepID
```

Figure 6-13 shows the result.
62 rows were returned.

I know. Finally, we get to put a name with the Sales Rep ID numbers. <smile>

	salesrepid integer	salesrep character varyin	orderyear double pre	nbroforders bigint	yearlytotal numeric
3	1	Nancy Davolio	2016	390	619317.88
4	1	Nancy Davolio	2017	178	339795.20
5	1	Nancy Davolio	2018	302	537708.75
6	2	Andrew Fuller	2014	2	3374.25

Figure 6-13 Sales rep name added to the query

WHERE Clause vs INNER JOIN
While both will create the same result, in some instances, the rows will be returned in a different order. When you need the rows returned in a specific order, use the **ORDER BY CLAUSE.**

Exercise 6.4: Retrieve The Products Category Name

In this exercise, you will create a query that retrieves each products category name from a different table. This query is similar to the one in Example #2.

1. Create the query shown below.

```
SELECT Products.ProductCategoryID, ProductID, ProductName, CategoryName
FROM Products INNER JOIN ProductCategory ON
  Products.ProductCategoryID = ProductCategory.ProductCategoryID;
```

2. Save the query as `E6.4 Retrieve the category name.`

Figure 6-14 shows the result.
428 rows were returned.

Notice that there are multiple rows for the same product.

	productcategoryid integer	productid integer	productname character varyi	categoryname character varyi
2	5	1101	Crochet Glove	Gloves
3	5	1101	Crochet Glove	Gloves
4	5	1101	Crochet Glove	Gloves
5	5	1102	Crochet Glove	Gloves

Figure 6-14 Result of a query that returned an incorrect number of rows

There is a problem with the number of rows that were returned. The problem is that there are only 127 products in the Products table. So at most, 127 rows should be returned. There could be fewer rows returned, if there are products that do not have a product category.

The rows returned will remind you of a **CROSS JOIN** or a **CARTESIAN JOIN**, even though a valid relationship was created between the tables.

If you look in the Product Category table, you will see multiple rows with the same Product Category ID. That's fine, but this is what caused too many rows to be returned.

The question is how do you modify the query to not retrieve a row for each match in the Product Category table. The answer is you can't, without thinking of some elaborate coding scheme. In this scenario, you need to use a different field in the table to join them. The field must have unique values in one of the tables. As the Products table is suppose to contain all products, regardless of the category, the field with the unique values must be in the Product Category table. Lucky for us, that I knew this when I was creating the tables and data. <smile> The Sub Category ID field is the field that has a unique value for each row in the Product Category table.

3. On the last line in the query, shown above in step 1, change the Product Category ID field in both tables to `SubCategoryID`.

4. Sort the rows on the Product ID field.

Figure 6-15 shows the revised query output.
115 rows were returned. Much better. This means that some products do not have a product category.

On your own, this is something that you need to always be aware of. Just because a query returns data that may "look" right, the data may not be right. Rarely should a query return more rows than the primary table in the query has.

	productcategoryid integer	productid integer	productname character varyir	categoryname character varyir
3	5	1103	Crochet Glove	Gloves
4	5	1104	Crochet Glove	Gloves
5	5	1105	Crochet Glove	Gloves
6	5	1106	Lycra Glove	Gloves

Figure 6-15 Result of the revised query

Exercise 6.5: Find Customers That Placed An Order In June 2018

In this exercise, you will create a query to find customers that placed an order in June 2018.

1. Create the query shown below.

```
SELECT Customers.CustomerID, FirstName || ' ' || LastName AS CustomerName,
  OrderDate, OrderAmount
FROM Customers INNER JOIN Orders
  ON Customers.CustomerID = Orders.CustomerID
WHERE date_part('year', OrderDate) = '2018' AND
  date_part('month', OrderDate) = '06'
ORDER BY OrderDate;
```

To ensure that the data is processed as quickly as possible, the year filter portion of the query needs to go before the month filter, as shown in the query above.

You could have used the BETWEEN operator instead of the criteria on the AND operator. One downside of using the BETWEEN operator in this query is that you have to know how many days are in the month. <smile>

2. Save the query as `E6.5 Customer orders in June 2018.`

Figure 6-16 shows the result. 134 rows were returned. That is how many orders were placed in June 2018.

	customerid integer	customername text	orderdate date	orderamount numeric (18,2)
1	57	Elizabeth Kawa	2018-06-01	67.80
2	4	Alexander Mast	2018-06-01	1138.09
3	31	Richard Grewal	2018-06-01	959.70
4	55	Gordon Bell	2018-06-01	8945.25

Figure 6-16 Customers that placed an order in June 2018

Table Alias

In Chapter 3, the concept of a column alias was introduced. In addition to column name and expressions (calculated fields) being able to use an alias name, tables can also use an alias. This is sometimes done when the query uses more than one table or the table name is long or will be used several times in the query. Using an alias for the table name means that you do not have to type the full table name several times in the query. It may not seem like a big deal, in the queries that have been created so far in this chapter, but they are not using a lot of fields from different tables or all of the SELECT clauses that are available.

A table alias is defined on the FROM clause and/or on the JOIN clause. Usually, the first letter of the table name is used as the alias, like c for the Customers table or P for the Products table. If the table name has two or more words, like Product Category, the alias could be pc. Once the alias is defined in the query, it **MUST BE** used everywhere, in place of the table name, in the rest of the query.

Unlike a column alias, which appears in the result when the query is run, a table alias is not displayed in the result. That is because a table alias is only available while the query in running.

If you do not like to type, a table alias, and column alias for that matter, will become your friend. Just do yourself a favor and use white space in the query, so that the code is easy to read.

Table Alias Tips
Below are some things to keep in mind when creating a table alias name.

☑ Try to make the alias name something that relates to the table name. This will make it easier to remember which table the alias is for. The other option is to create a comments section at the beginning of the query and list which table, each abbreviation represents.
☑ Using the keyword AS is optional, when defining the table alias name.
☑ You do not have to create an alias for every table in a query. If you only need an alias for one table, that is fine.

Example #3 Using A Table Alias

The first query below is the original query. The second query uses table alias names.

SELECT Products.ProductCategoryID, CategoryName, COUNT(*) AS ProductsInCategory
FROM Products INNER JOIN ProductCategory ON
Products.SubCategoryID = ProductCategory.SubCategoryID
GROUP BY Products.ProductCategoryID, CategoryName;

SELECT P.ProductCategoryID, CategoryName, COUNT(*) AS ProductsInCategory
FROM Products AS P INNER JOIN ProductCategory AS PC ON P.SubCategoryID = PC.SubCategoryID
GROUP BY P.ProductCategoryID, CategoryName;

Exercise 6.6: Count Products In Each Category

In this exercise, you will create a query that is similar to the one shown above in Example #3. The difference is that this query will sort the data. You will also get to try out the table name alias feature.

1. Create the query shown below.

```
SELECT P.ProductCategoryID, CategoryName, COUNT(*) AS ProductsInCategory
FROM Products AS P INNER JOIN ProductCategory AS PC
  ON P.SubCategoryID = PC.SubCategoryID
GROUP BY P.ProductCategoryID, CategoryName
ORDER BY CategoryName;
```

2. Save the query as `E6.6 Count products in each category.`

   Figure 6-17 shows some of the 8 rows that were returned, one for each category.

   How do you like using table aliases?

	productcategoryid integer	categoryname character varying (	productsincategory bigint
1	7	Bicycle Locks	8
2	4	Children's Bicycle	4
3	5	Gloves	17

Figure 6-17 Count of products in each product category

Exercise 6.7: Use The WHERE Clause To Join Tables And Filter Data

So far in this chapter, the WHERE clause has not been used to join tables. Even though the WHERE clause can be used to join tables, it can still be used to filter data, like you have done in previous chapters. When used for both, put the table join clause first, then add the filter criteria. The filter criteria must start with the word AND (the operator). Otherwise, it will not be executed for rows that match the join criteria on the WHERE clause.

The query that you will create in this exercise is similar to the one in Exercise 6.2. The difference is that in addition to joining tables, filter criteria is used to select customers that are in specific regions. The join is needed to be able to display the region name.

1. Create the query shown below.

```
SELECT CustomerID, CompanyName, Customers.RegionID, RegionName
FROM Customers, Regions
WHERE Customers.RegionID = Regions.RegionID
  AND Customers.RegionID IN (2, 10, 19, 24);
```

2. Save the query as `E6.7 Join tables & filter data on the WHERE clause.`

   Figure 6-18 shows the result. 37 rows were returned. The first line of the WHERE clause joins the tables. The second line is the filter criteria.

	customerid integer	companyname character varying (75)	regionid integer	regionname character va
6	44	Our Wheels Follow Us Everywhere	10	Midwest
7	59	The Biker's Path	10	Midwest
8	118	Tony's Better Bikes	24	South
9	123	One Track Mind	2	Northeast

Figure 6-18 Result of joining tables and filtering data

Exercise 6.8: Find Orders In A Date Range

In this exercise, you will create a query that finds orders in the first quarter of 2018 and displays the sales reps name, instead of their ID number.

1. Create this query.

```
SELECT OrderID, SalesRep, OrderDate, OrderAmount
FROM Orders INNER JOIN SalesReps
  ON Orders.SalesRepID = SalesReps.SalesRepID
WHERE OrderDate BETWEEN '2018-01-01' AND '2018-04-30'
ORDER BY OrderAmount DESC;
```

2. Save the query as `E6.8 Retrieve orders from a date range.`

   Figure 6-19 shows the result. 831 rows were returned.

   The data is sorted in descending order by the values in the Order Amount field.

	orderid integer	salesrep character varying (	orderdate date	orderamount numeric (18,2)
1	3760	Robert King	2018-03-02	14741.15
2	3910	Nancy Davolio	2018-04-18	11867.20
3	3619	Janet Leverling	2018-01-15	10886.79
4	10417	Janet Leverling	2018-01-03	10798.95

Figure 6-19 Orders from a date range

Exercise 6.9: Filter Sub Categories

In this exercise, you will modify the query that created the results shown earlier in Figure 6-11. You will add filter criteria to exclude some sub categories.

1. Create the query shown below.

```
SELECT ProductName, Products.SubCategoryID, SubCategory
FROM Products INNER JOIN ProductSubCategory
  ON Products.SubCategoryID = ProductSubcategory.SubCategoryID
WHERE Products.SubCategoryID NOT IN (18, 20, 22, 25);
```

2. Save the query as `E6.9 Filter the sub categories.`

   Figure 6-20 shows the result. 105 rows were returned.

   If you scroll down the results, you will not see a row that has one of the four Sub Category ID's, listed in the query.

	productname character varying (50)	subcategoryid integer	subcategory character varyin
27	Pro Helmet	6	Pro Helmet
28	Chain Lock	7	Chain Locks
29	Gelflex Ladies Saddle	8	Ladies Saddles
30	Comfort Ladies Saddle	8	Ladies Saddles

Figure 6-20 Result of sub categories being filtered

Exercise 6.10: Count Customers In Each Region

In this exercise, you will create a query that calculates a count of customers in each region.

1. Create this query.

```
SELECT RegionName, COUNT(*) AS CountOfCustomersInRegion
FROM Customers INNER JOIN Regions
  ON Customers.RegionID = Regions.RegionID
WHERE Country = 'USA'
GROUP BY RegionName
ORDER BY RegionName;
```

2. Save the query as `E6.10 Customer count by region.`

   Figure 6-21 shows the result. This query has a filter to only select rows where the Country = 'USA'.

   Currently, the Regions table only has regions for the USA, but that will not stop data from being entered in the Region ID field in the Customers table, for customers that are not in the USA.

	regionname character vary	countofcustomersinregion bigint
1	Midwest	125
2	Northeast	71
3	South	90
4	West	91

Figure 6-21 Count of customers in each region

> This is where understanding the data that you are using to create queries for, is critical. Without this knowledge of the data, it is very easy to miss, not including this filter criteria. While the Customers table in this database, currently does not have bad data in the Region ID field, somewhere in the future, it could. If that happens, the counts in the result, will be wrong.

Exercise 6.11: Create Two Groups

In this exercise, you will create a query that creates a count of customers in each division. Each division is in a region. This query is similar to the query in the previous exercise. The difference is that this query groups on two fields.

1. Create the query shown below. If you want, you can use a copy of the query from Exercise 6.10 and make changes to it.

```
SELECT RegionName, DivisionName, COUNT(*) AS CountOfCustomersInDivision
FROM Customers INNER JOIN Regions
  ON Customers.RegionID = Regions.RegionID
WHERE Country = 'USA'
GROUP BY RegionName, DivisionName
ORDER BY RegionName, DivisionName;
```

2. Save the query as `E6.11 Group on 2 fields.`

   Figure 6-22 shows the result. 9 rows were returned.

   If you add the counts for each division that has the same region name, you will see that the total for the region, is the same as the total shown above in Figure 6-21. For example, the total for the two Midwest rows, equals 125. This is the same value shown above in Figure 6-21.

	regionname character vary	divisionname character varying (5	countofcustomersindivision bigint
1	Midwest	East North Central	73
2	Midwest	West North Central	52
3	Northeast	Mid-Atlantic	36
4	Northeast	New England	35
5	South	East South Central	21
6	South	South Atlantic	54

Figure 6-22 Data grouped on two columns

Example #4 Group On Three Fields

This query is similar to the one in Exercise 6.11. The difference is that this query groups on three fields: Region Name, Division Name and State. Figure 6-23 shows the result. 50 rows were returned.

```
SELECT RegionName, DivisionName, Regions.State,
  COUNT(*) AS "Count Of Customers Per State"
FROM Customers, Regions
WHERE Customers.RegionID = Regions.RegionID
  AND Country = 'USA'
GROUP BY RegionName, DivisionName, Regions.State
ORDER BY RegionName, DivisionName, Regions.State;
```

	regionname character vary	divisionname character varying (5(	state character v	Count Of Customers Per State bigint
1	Midwest	East North Central	Illinois	28
2	Midwest	East North Central	Michigan	14
3	Midwest	East North Central	Ohio	13
4	Midwest	East North Central	Wisconsin	18

Figure 6-23 Result of creating groups for three columns

Exercise 6.12: Add The Vendor Name To An Existing Query

In Chapter 5, Exercise 5.15, you created a query that grouped the products by the Vendor ID. In this exercise, you will modify that query to include the vendor name, which is in a different table.

1. Save the E5.15 query as `E6.12 Add the vendor name.`

2. Add the Vendors table to the FROM clause ⇒ Add the ON clause to the link on the Vendor ID field.

3. On the GROUP BY line, add the Products table name to the Vendor ID field.

4. Add the Vendor Name field to the SELECT clause, after the Vendor ID field and to the end of the GROUP BY clause.

   Figure 6-24 shows the result.

	vendorid integer	vendorname character varying	productcount bigint
1	100	Active Outdoors	11
2	106	Vesper	5
3	110	Romeo	4
4	104	Titan	13

Figure 6-24 Vendor name added to the result

Joining Three Or More Tables

So far, the queries that you have created in this chapter only joined two tables. There will be times when you need to join more than two tables. When creating a query that uses multiple tables, one of the most important things to remember is that starting with the join from the third table on, each table must be joined to a table that is already joined in the query.

Example #5 Join Three Tables

The query below joins the following tables: Customers, Orders and Order Details. The result is shown in Figure 6-25.

```
SELECT Customers.CustomerID, Orders.OrderID, RegionID, CompanyName, OrderAmount, ProductID, Quantity
FROM Customers INNER JOIN Orders ON Customers.CustomerID = Orders.CustomerID
  INNER JOIN OrderDetails ON Orders.OrderID = OrderDetails.OrderID;
```

How The Query In Example #5 Works

Step 1 The Orders table is joined to the Customers table, using the Customer ID field.

Step 2 The Order Details table is added with a second INNER JOIN and joined to the Orders table, using the Order ID field.

Step 3 The fields on the SELECT clause are returned from the three tables. As you will see later in this chapter, more than three tables can be joined.

	customerid integer	orderid integer	regionid integer	companyname character varying (75)	orderamount numeric (18,2)	productid integer	quantity integer
3	55	1	41	Tandem Cycle	2645.87	7038	2
4	39	2	15	Wheels Inc.	8908.05	1103	3
5	39	2	15	Wheels Inc.	8908.05	7039	1
6	61	3	31	Benny - The Spokes Person	39.80	1104	4

Figure 6-25 Result of joining three tables

The next three exercises will show you how to create what is known as **COMPLEX FILTERS**. They are considered complex because the queries use more than two tables and/or have more than two filter conditions.

Exercise 6.13: Add A Third Table To The Query

In this exercise, you will add a third table to a query. The third table will be used to lookup the sub category name.

1. Create the query shown below.

```
SELECT ProductID, ProductName, CategoryName, PSC.SubCategory
FROM Products AS P
INNER JOIN ProductCategory AS PC ON P.SubCategoryID = PC.SubCategoryID
INNER JOIN ProductSubCategory AS PSC ON PSC.SubCategoryID =
   PC.SubCategoryID;
```

2. Save the query as `E6.13 Three tables used in the query`.

Figure 6-26 shows the result. 115 rows were returned.

The Product ID and Product Name columns are in the Products table.

The Category Name column is in the Product Category table. The Sub Category column is in the Sub Category table.

	productid integer	productname character varyi	categoryname character varyin	subcategory character vary
49	3303	XL U Lock	Bicycle Locks	U Lock
50	3304	ATB Lock	Bicycle Locks	ATB Lock
51	3305	Mini Lock	Bicycle Locks	Mini Lock
52	4101	Crochet Glove	Gloves	Influx Crochet

Figure 6-26 Result of looking up product related data

Exercise 6.14: Find Customer Orders In 2017 Or 2018

In this exercise, you will create a query that has the following criteria.

☑ Customer Type is Online.
☑ Order placed in 2017 or 2018.
☑ Sort on these columns: Customer Last Name, First Name and Order Date.

1. Create the query shown below.

```
SELECT Customers.CustomerID, Customers.LastName, Customers.FirstName,
  OrderDate, OrderAmount, SalesRep, CustomerType
FROM Customers
  INNER JOIN Orders ON Customers.CustomerID = Orders.CustomerID
  INNER JOIN SalesReps ON Orders.SalesRepID = SalesReps.SalesRepID
WHERE CustomerType = 'Online' AND
  date_part('year', OrderDate) IN ('2017', '2018')
ORDER BY Customers.LastName, Customers.FirstName, OrderDate;
```

2. Save the query as `E6.14 Orders in 2017 or 2018`.

Figure 6-27 shows the result. 1,460 rows were returned.

The way that the data is sorted, lets you see how many orders each customer placed and in what year.

	customerid integer	lastname character v	firstname character v	orderdate date	orderamount numeric (18,2)	salesrep character varying	customertype character varyi
1	259	Alvarez	Alex	2018-09-01	3120.70	Michael Suyama	Online
2	259	Alvarez	Alex	2018-09-01	161.70	Robert King	Online
3	145	Anderson	Sandra	2018-09-01	1457.61	Janet Leverling	Online
4	325	Apple	Elan	2018-04-14	107.80	Anne Dodsworth	Online

Figure 6-27 Orders placed in 2017 or 2018

Intermediate Table Joins

At some point, you may have a need to use data in two tables that do not have a common field that can be linked on. If both of these tables can link to a third table, the third table is the intermediate table. Usually, no fields in the intermediate table will be displayed in the result of the query. One example that comes to mind is when you need to create a **MANY-TO-MANY RELATIONSHIP**.

This type of join requires joining three tables like you have already learned how to do. There are no syntax changes to use a table as an intermediate table join.

Exercise 6.15: Create An Intermediate Table Join

In this exercise, you will create a query to join the Products and Product Category tables. This will let you display the Product Category for each product. You will use the Product Sub Category table as the intermediate table to link to the Product Category table.

Yes, I know that the Products table has the Product Category ID field. So, I need you to pretend that the Products table does not have the Product Category ID field and that the Product Category table does not have the Sub Category ID field. <smile> On your own, the corresponding tables would probably not have these ID fields, so you would have to use an intermediate table to get the data that you need.

1. Create the query shown below.

```
SELECT Products.ProductID, ProductName, QtyOnHand,
  ProductCategory.CategoryName
FROM Products INNER JOIN ProductSubCategory
  ON Products.SubCategoryID = ProductSubCategory.SubCategoryID
INNER JOIN ProductCategory ON
  ProductSubCategory.SubCategoryID = ProductCategory.SubCategoryID
ORDER BY ProductID;
```

2. Save the query as `E6.15 Intermediate table join`.

Figure 6-28 shows the result. 115 rows were returned.

The Category Name column is from the Product Category table. The other columns in the figure are from the Products table.

No columns from the Product Sub Category table were selected to be returned. That is by design.

	productid integer	productname character varyi	qtyonhand integer	categoryname character varyir
9	1109	Lycra Glove	387	Gloves
10	1110	Lycra Glove	333	Gloves
11	1111	Lycra Glove	393	Gloves
12	2201	Pro Helmet	444	Helmets

Figure 6-28 Result of an intermediate table join

Exercise 6.16: Count The Number Of Sub Categories

In Exercise 6.6, you created a query that calculated the number of products in each category. In this exercise, you will modify that query by adding a count of sub categories for each category. This requires adding a third table to the query. As each sub category can have more than one product, the count for the Sub Category ID field has to be distinct.

1. Save the E6.6 query as `E6.16 Add sub category count`.

2. Add lines 2, 6 and 7, shown in Figure 6-29, to the query.

```
1 SELECT P.ProductCategoryID, CategoryName,
2   COUNT(DISTINCT PSC.SubCategoryID) AS SubCategoryCount,
3   COUNT(*) AS ProductsInCategory
4 FROM Products AS P INNER JOIN ProductCategory AS PC
5   ON P.SubCategoryID = PC.SubCategoryID
6 INNER JOIN ProductSubCategory AS PSC
7   ON PSC.SubCategoryID = PC.SubCategoryID
8 GROUP BY P.ProductCategoryID, CategoryName
9 ORDER BY CategoryName;
```

Figure 6-29 Changes to make to the query

Figure 6-30 shows the result.

The same 8 rows that were returned in Exercise 6.6, are returned in this exercise.

Now, you can see how many sub categories each category has, in addition to how many products are in each sub category.

	productcategoryid integer	categoryname character varying(	subcategorycount bigint	productsincategory bigint
1	7	Bicycle Locks	7	8
2	4	Children's Bicycle	2	4
3	5	Gloves	4	17
4	6	Helmets	4	23
5	1	Mountain Bicycle	3	20
6	3	Road Bicycle	3	23
7	8	Saddles	3	12
8	2	Touring Bicycle	2	8

Figure 6-30 Sub Category count added to the query

Example #6 To GROUP BY Or Not To GROUP BY, That Is The Question

A primary goal in Chapter 5 was to show you how to use the GROUP BY clause to be able to create sub totals, totals, counts and more. Sometimes, the GROUP BY clause is used, but there are no aggregate calculations. If you find that you are creating groups that do not have aggregate calculations, you can create the same results without using the GROUP BY clause. The query below creates the effect of groups, without using the GROUP BY clause and displays the data shown in Figure 6-31.

```
SELECT CategoryName,
  ProductSubCategory.SubCategory
FROM ProductCategory
  INNER JOIN ProductSubCategory
    ON ProductCategory.SubCategoryID =
      ProductSubCategory.SubCategoryID
ORDER BY CategoryName,
  ProductSubCategory.SubCategory;
```

	categoryname character varying	subcategory character varying
6	Bicycle Locks	Titan Lock
7	Bicycle Locks	U Lock
8	Children's Bicycle	Children's Bicycles
9	Children's Bicycle	Nicos Child

Figure 6-31 GROUP BY look, without the GROUP BY clause

This query uses the GROUP BY clause to create the results shown above in Figure 6-31. If you create this query, you will see that the results are the same. Using the GROUP BY clause has no value, because the query does not have an aggregated column.

```
SELECT CategoryName,
  ProductSubCategory.SubCategory
FROM ProductCategory INNER JOIN ProductSubCategory
  ON ProductCategory.SubCategoryID =
    ProductSubCategory.SubCategoryID
GROUP BY CategoryName, ProductSubCategory.SubCategory;
```

This means that using the GROUP BY clause is just creating overhead processing, which can make the query run slower then necessary.

The query below creates a count of products, so the GROUP BY clause is needed. Figure 6-32 shows the result. I added the ORDER BY clause so that the rows would be displayed in the same order as the previous two queries, in this example.

```
SELECT CategoryName, ProductSubCategory.SubCategory,
  COUNT(ProductID) AS ProductCount
FROM ProductCategory INNER JOIN ProductSubCategory
  ON ProductCategory.SubCategoryID =
    ProductSubCategory.SubCategoryID
INNER JOIN Products ON Products.ProductCategoryID =
  ProductCategory.ProductCategoryID
GROUP BY CategoryName, ProductSubCategory.SubCategory
ORDER BY CategoryName, ProductSubCategory.SubCategory;
```

	categoryname character varying	subcategory character varying(5	productcount bigint
6	Bicycle Locks	Titan Lock	8
7	Bicycle Locks	U Lock	8
8	Children's Bicycle	Children's Bicycles	4
9	Children's Bicycle	Nicos Child	4
10	Gloves	Crochet Gloves	17

Figure 6-32 Result of adding an aggregated column to the query

Exercise 6.17: Creating Joins That Use Multiple Fields

This isn't very common today, but it is possible that at some point, you may come across a table that cannot be joined by only using one field. If that is the case, tables can be joined by using two or more fields.

In this exercise, the query that you will create, will join the Products and Product Category tables on the Product Category ID and Sub Category ID fields. Yes, I know that these tables can be joined on one field, in this database, but I need to demonstrate this concept. Where is your sense of adventure? <smile>

1. Create the query shown below. The last two rows of the query, create the joins using two columns.

```
SELECT CategoryName, SubCategory, ProductName, QtyOnHand
FROM Products
  INNER JOIN ProductCategory ON
  Products.ProductCategoryID = ProductCategory.ProductCategoryID
    AND Products.SubCategoryID = ProductCategory.SubCategoryID;
```

2. Save the query as `E6.17 Tables joined using 2 fields.`

   Figure 6-33 shows the result. 115 rows were returned.

	categoryname character varying (	subcategory character varying (50)	productname character varying (50)	qtyonhand integer
51	Road Bicycle	Road Bicycle (Nicos Adult)	Road Bicycle	4103
52	Children's Bicycle	Children's Bicycles	Touring Bicycle Child	7042
53	Children's Bicycle	Children's Bicycles	Touring Bicycle Child	7042
54	Children's Bicycle	Nicos Child	Mountain Bicycle Child	7041

Figure 6-33 Result of joining tables on two fields

Exercise 6.18: Use Joins To Filter Data

Earlier in this chapter, I discussed that joining some tables can filter data the way that you need it filtered, without creating any filter criteria. The joins in the query that you will create in this exercise will filter the data, the way that it needs to be filtered. The query will create a list of products by category, that have been sold. In this scenario, it does not matter, if the product is currently in stock or has been discontinued.

1. Create the query shown below.

```
SELECT DISTINCT Products.ProductID, CategoryName, ProductName
FROM OrderDetails INNER JOIN Products ON
  Products.ProductID = OrderDetails.ProductID
INNER JOIN ProductCategory ON
 ProductCategory.ProductCategoryID  = Products.ProductCategoryID
ORDER BY CategoryName;
```

2. Save the query as `E6.18 Use joins to filter data.`

   Figure 6-34 shows the result. 115 rows were returned. There are 127 rows in the Products table. That means that there are products that have not sold.

   While I am not a mind reader, I suspect that while you were typing the code for this query, you were wondering why three tables were needed to find this information?

	productid integer	categoryname character varying (	productname character varying (50)
6	5301	Bicycle Locks	Mtn Lock
7	5302	Bicycle Locks	Rhino Lock
8	5303	Bicycle Locks	Titan Lock
9	7051	Children's Bicycle	Mountain Bicycle Child

Figure 6-34 Result of the joins that filter data

The Order Details table has a list of all products that have been sold. The Products table has the product name, but does not store whether or not the product has been sold.

The Product Category table has the category name, but not the product name.

The DISTINCT clause was used to only retrieve each product once. Remember that many products are purchased by many customers. The DISTINCT clause also filters data.

Summary

The primary goal of this chapter was to introduce the concept of joining tables, the join type options that are available and how to use them.

I think that the most important take away from this chapter is to make sure that you fully understand the goal of the query. That is because the goal of the query will help you eliminate some join types. Much of this process depends on whether or not rows that do not find a match in the other table need to be returned. In many instances, you will find that there are two join types that can be used to retrieve the correct rows of data.

The concept of normalization was covered. The normalization process of separating different types (or categories) of data into their own tables, explains and answers the question, "Why are there separate tables?" In Chapter 1, I said that knowing how to use **VLOOKUP** in Excel would be helpful. That is because that function is used to retrieve data in one sheet, from another sheet in a workbook. Joining tables is the same concept.

As covered in the INNER JOINS section, not including the join condition in the query creates a Cartesian product, which most of the time, is not the result that you want. The important concept to keep in mind is that using the INNER JOIN keyword with the **ON CLAUSE**, is the preferred inner join option to use.

As you learned, it is very easy to select the wrong join type and not even realize it. On your own, most of the queries that you will create, will need data from at least two tables, unless views have been created, that have all of the data that you need. Something that you probably were not expecting, was learning how to use two fields to join tables.

An important concept to remember is that the reason that some column names have to be fully qualified, is so that SQL will know which table has the field that you want to use. This happens when both tables have a field with the same name.

In the overview section of Chapter 4, I posted a quiz that by the end of this chapter, you should be able to create a query for. Part of the query could have been created by the time that you completed Chapter 4. Now, you should be able to complete the query, by adding the Region ID field to the query. **HINT:** You have to find the value for the South region. Figure 6-35 shows the first four rows of the result. 12 rows were returned. If you can't create this query on your own, you should probably go back and review Chapter 4 and this chapter to figure out how to create a query, that displays the result shown in Figure 6-35.

	regionid integer	orderid integer	customerid integer	firstname character	lastname character v	orderdate date	orderamount numeric (18,2)
1	3	3965	58	Rosie	Forbes	2018-05-04	3138.15
2	3	4024	58	Rosie	Forbes	2018-05-26	2409.46
3	3	4025	14	Rick	Pratt	2018-05-27	72.90
4	3	4049	58	Rosie	Forbes	2018-06-05	554.35

Figure 6-35 Result for the quiz presented in Chapter 4

USING OUTER JOINS TO LINK TABLES

After reading this chapter and completing the exercises, you will be able to create outer joins to retrieve data from multiple tables.

CHAPTER 7

OUTER JOINS

Unlike INNER joins, which were covered in the previous chapter, OUTER joins only use the **SQL-92 SYNTAX**, which is adding the JOIN keyword between the table name and the join criteria is specified on the **ON CLAUSE**.

In addition to the two logical processing phases (filter and Cartesian product) that inner joins have, outer joins also have the **ADDING OUTER ROWS PHASE**. This logical query processing phase takes the rows that did not find a match in the other table on the ON clause and adds them to the result table that was created by the first two phases of the join. NULLs are added to the rows in the fields from the other table in the join.

A LEFT OUTER JOIN returns all rows from the table on the left whether or not there is a matching row in the table on the right. Any matching rows from the table on the right are returned. For example, if the join is between the Customers and Regions tables and there is no matching record in the Regions table for a customer, the field for the region in the result set (the data displayed after you run the query) will have NULL in those columns. This is how all of the rows in the table on the left are returned, even though the filter phase removed them.

You can also use an OUTER JOIN when you need to join tables and display the missing data in one of the tables. In the previous chapter, you created queries that did not return all of the records in one table. That is because by default, INNER JOINS only return rows that have a match in **BOTH TABLES**. This means that in some queries in the previous chapter, the wrong join type was used, **IF** the query requirements specify that **ALL ROWS** from a table should be returned. While I did that on purpose, it is a way try and get you to see how easy it is to select the wrong join type and not even know it, especially because no error was generated when you ran the query and that the query returned data.

On your own, at the very least, I hope that you get a count of rows for each table that you use and write the counts down. Then, as you are creating queries, especially queries that use more than one table, look at the number of rows that were returned and compare that value to the number of rows in the primary table used in the join query. Doing this should give you an idea of whether or not the number of rows returned in the query, is in the correct range of rows that should be returned, based on the query requirements.

An OUTER JOIN is used to retrieve matched and unmatched rows. This join type will let you see which rows in one table do not have a match in the other table. This is helpful because this join type can be used to find information in the two ways discussed below.

① **FIND MISSING VALUES** An OUTER JOIN can be used to find missing values by testing for NULL values. This will let you create queries to answer the following types of questions:

- ☑ Create a list of customers that have not ordered a bicycle.
- ☑ Show products that do not have a color.
- ☑ Show products have never been ordered.

② **FIND PARTIAL MATCHED INFORMATION** An OUTER JOIN is used to return all rows from one table and any matching rows from another table. This is often done to find (look up) a name for an ID field, that is in the left table, in the query. This will let you create queries to answer the following types of questions:

- ☑ Show all products and any years that they were ordered in.
- ☑ List all sales reps and their number of orders in the South region.
- ☑ Create a list of all customers and any of their orders that include gloves.

Like the inner joins, outer joins are not restricted to using the equal to operator to join tables. You can use any of the comparison operators.

> If a column that is used as a foreign key is not defined as such, null values will be displayed in columns when there is no match for the columns value in the other table.

INNER JOINS vs OUTER JOINS
This explanation may be an easy way to know which join type to select. Use the INNER JOIN to only return matching records from both tables. If there is no match in one of the tables, then no record is returned from either table. Use an OUTER JOIN to return matching records **AND** records that do not match, from the same table.

Basically, before you create the query, you have to decide whether or not you want to return all of the rows in the primary table. The decision is based on what data the query needs to return for the report that will be created from the data. If you are not sure whether or not a LEFT OUTER JOIN or INNER JOIN will affect the query result, create the same query using each of these join types. Then look at the data that is returned and the number of rows that each query returns. INNER and OUTER joins can be used in the same query.

If you are creating the query for someone else, you need to explain this (and probably show them the difference that the join types produce), and ask which data set they need. This is known as CYA.

LEFT OUTER JOIN vs RIGHT OUTER JOIN
The difference is that using the LEFT OUTER JOIN returns all records from the table that is listed **BEFORE** (to the left of) the join operator and only matching rows from the table after the join operator.

The RIGHT OUTER JOIN returns all records from the table listed **AFTER** (to the right of) the join operator and only matching rows from the table before the join operator. Most of the time, it is easier logically, to use the LEFT OUTER JOIN operator. If you think about it, there really isn't a good reason to use the RIGHT OUTER join option.

LEFT OUTER and RIGHT OUTER JOINS produce the same results. The difference is the order that the tables are placed around the join type. These join types can be used interchangeably. A RIGHT OUTER JOIN can be changed to a LEFT OUTER JOIN by changing the order of the tables.

It is not a requirement to use the word "OUTER". Using LEFT JOIN or RIGHT JOIN is fine.

What I do is select the table that I want to return all of the records from and say "Which field(s) in this table, do I need to get or look up data for?" Often, these fields are ID fields, like the Sales Rep ID. In that scenario, I know that the Sales Reps table has to go **AFTER** the join operator, when using a LEFT OUTER JOIN.

Depending on the SQL database flavor, the database can select a different way to process the query. By that I mean that the rows will not be returned in the same order. This isn't a problem. Other then including the ORDER BY clause in the query, there isn't anything that I am aware of, that you can do to change the order that the data is processed in.

OUTER JOIN Examples

In addition to retrieving rows that match, OUTER JOINS also return rows (from the primary table, which is usually on the left) that do not have a match in the other table (the table on the right). Examples of when to use an outer join are listed bellow.

- ☑ Create a list of all customers and display their corresponding region name, if it exists.
- ☑ Calculate how many people in the Customers table, placed an order and include people in the Customers table that have not placed an order. Yes, I know, in the real world there should not be names in the Customers table that have not placed an order. <smile>
- ☑ Create a list of orders that have product A and orders that do not have product B.
- ☑ Create a list of all products, with the quantity that has been sold, including products that have not sold.

Exercise 7.1: Modify The E6.2 Query To Return All Rows

The query in Chapter 6, Exercise 6.2, returned 377 rows from the Customers table. The Customers table has 555 customers. This exercise will show you how to create a query that retrieves all rows from the Customers table, whether or not there is a matching record in the Regions table.

On your own, you have to understand what the requirements are for the data that needs to be retrieved. If you are not 100% sure, you should ask the person that requested the data and clearly explain to them, what the options are.

1. Save the E6.2 query as `E7.1 LEFT OUTER join.`

2. Change the FROM clause to this one. `FROM Customers LEFT OUTER JOIN Regions`

3. Sort the data on the Customer ID field.

   Figure 7-1 shows the result.
   555 rows were returned, as expected.

	customerid integer	firstname character v	lastname character var	regionname character var	divisionname character varying
2	2	Christine	Manley	Midwest	East North Central
3	3	Gary	Jannis	Midwest	East North Central
4	4	Alexander	Mast	South	East South Central
5	5	Patrick	Reyess	West	Pacific

Figure 7-1 All customer records returned

Example #1 RIGHT OUTER JOIN

This join type works in the opposite direction of the LEFT OUTER JOIN. This query produces the same result as the one in Exercise 7.1.

```
SELECT CustomerID, FirstName, LastName, RegionName, DivisionName
FROM Regions RIGHT OUTER JOIN Customers
  ON Customers.RegionID = Regions.RegionID;
```

Understanding OUTER JOIN Filters

The two types of OUTER JOIN filters are explained below.

The filter on the **ON CLAUSE** is not final. By that I mean, the filter on the ON clause does not determine whether or not a row is displayed in the result. This filter determines how to find a matching record in the other table. This filter was used in Exercise 7.1.

Filters on the **WHERE CLAUSE** are processed after the rows are selected and are processed right before the result table is displayed. This filter will be used in Exercise 7.2.

Exercise 7.2: Find NULL Values In A Join

As I'm sure that you know by now, all of the customers in the SQLdata database are not in the USA. If you scroll down the rows returned in Exercise 7.1, to Customer ID 50, you will see a few rows that have NULL in the Region Name and Division Name columns. More than likely, those customers are not in the USA.

To be sure, you would create a query that checks for NULL values. In this scenario, you only have to check for NULL values in one of the columns, because the Regions table has every field filled in. I know because I created the table. <smile> On your own, you would have to confirm this with your equivalent of the Regions table. To be extra safe, you should include the Country field in the query, while testing. Then remove the Country field, once you know that the query is working as expected.

1. Save the E7.1 query as `E7.2 Check for NULL values.`

2. Add the Country field to the end of the SELECT clause.

3. Add this WHERE clause to the query. `WHERE Regions.RegionName IS NULL.`

   Figure 7-2 shows the result.
   178 rows were returned.

   Notice that none of the rows have USA in the Country column, which is what is expected.

	customerid integer	firstname character v	lastname character v	regionname character var	divisionname character vary	country character va
2	50	Davy	Douglas	[null]	[null]	Canada
3	51	Katie	Cronin	[null]	[null]	Canada
4	60	Dave	Elkins	[null]	[null]	Canada
5	64	Claus	Main	[null]	[null]	Switzerland

Figure 7-2 Result of checking for NULL values

The query in Chapter 6, Exercise 6.2, returned 377 rows. This query returned 178 rows. When you add these numbers together, they equal 555, which is the total number of rows in the Customers table. So all customers have been accounted for between the two queries.

Exercise 7.3: Lookup The Category Name For Each Sub Category

The query that you will create in this exercise will return all 29 of the sub categories in one table and look up the category name in another table, for each sub category. It is possible that some sub categories do not have a category. If that is the case, no value will be displayed in the Category Name column.

1. Create the query shown below.

```
SELECT ProductSubCategory.SubCategory, CategoryName
FROM ProductSubCategory LEFT OUTER JOIN ProductCategory
  ON ProductSubcategory.SubCategoryID = ProductCategory.SubCategoryID;
```

2. Save the query as `E7.3 All sub categories & their corresponding category.`

   Figure 7-3 shows the result. All 29 sub category records have a matching category.

	subcategory character varying (50)	categoryname character varying
1	Mountain Bicycle (Decent)	Mountain Bicycle
2	Touring Bicycle (Romeo)	Touring Bicycle
3	Road Bicycles	Road Bicycle
4	Children's Bicycles	Children's Bicycle

Figure 7-3 All sub categories and their category

Other Ways To Join Tables

INNER and OUTER joins also support the **USING CLAUSE** and **NATURAL KEYWORD**, as explained below.

The USING clause can be used instead of the ON clause, to list the field to link on. The difference is that the field name that you want to link on must be the same.

This means that instead of typing ON ProductSubcategory.SubCategoryID = ProductCategory.SubCategoryID, as shown above in Exercise 7.3, type USING(SubCategoryID).

The NATURAL keyword is similar to JOIN . . . USING. The difference is that **ALL** columns that have the same name in both tables will be matched. For example, this means that if both tables have two (or more) columns that have the same name, the NATURAL join keyword will join the tables based on the value of both columns, not just one column, like the USING clause does. In some cases, this can cause a problem. If you want to use the NATURAL keyword, my advice is to look at the field names in the tables that you want to join, to ensure that if there is more than one field that has the same name, that having the tables joined on the second field will still return the rows that you are expecting.

This code demonstrates how to use the NATURAL keyword. It returns the same 29 rows that are returned in Exercise 7.3.

```
SELECT ProductSubCategory.SubCategory, CategoryName
FROM ProductSubCategory Natural JOIN ProductCategory;
```

Exercise 7.4: Lookup Order Detail Records

In this exercise, you will create a query that looks up the detail rows for orders that were placed in 2017 or 2018 that have products with a quantity sold that is >= 5.

1. Create the query shown below.

```
SELECT Orders.OrderID, OrderDate,
  OrderAmount AS TotalOrderAmount, Quantity
FROM Orders LEFT OUTER JOIN OrderDetails
  ON Orders.OrderID = OrderDetails.OrderID
WHERE date_part('year', OrderDate) IN ('2017', '2018') AND Quantity >= 5;
```

2. Save the query as `E7.4 Look up order detail records.`

Figure 7-4 shows the result. 5,125 rows were returned.

Each row represents one item in the Order Details table. For example, the first row tells you that Order ID 2450, has an item that the customer ordered eight of.

	orderid integer	orderdate date	totalorderamount numeric (18,2)	quantity integer
1	2450	2017-01-03	6839.10	8
2	2450	2017-01-03	6839.10	7
3	2451	2017-01-04	9612.47	10
4	2452	2017-01-04	40.50	10

Figure 7-4 Order information from two tables

The Quantity column comes from the Order Details table. When you see the same Order ID on more than one row in the result, that means that there is more than one item on the order, that meets the filter criteria, on the WHERE clause.

There can also be items on the order that have a quantity that is less than 5. Those rows will not be returned. Notice that the order total amount is the same for each row that has the same Order ID. That is correct because that field comes from the Orders table.

Exercise 7.5: Find Products That Have Not Been Ordered

In this exercise, you will create a query to find products that have not been ordered.

1. Create this query.

```
SELECT Products.ProductID, ProductName
FROM Products LEFT OUTER JOIN OrderDetails
  ON Products.ProductID = OrderDetails.ProductID
WHERE OrderDetails.ProductID IS NULL;
```

2. Save the query as `E7.5 Products that have not been ordered.`

   Figure 7-5 shows the result. 12 rows were returned.

	productid integer	productname character varyi
1	9000	Test Product
2	9001	Test Product
3	9002	Test Product
4	9003	Test Product

Figure 7-5 List of products that have not been ordered

Exercise 7.6: Use LEFT OUTER JOINS To Return Data From Multiple Tables

The query created in Exercise 7.4 achieved the expected result. However, the data would be more meaningful if the Customer, Sales Rep and Product Names were displayed. To accomplish this, LEFT OUTER JOINS will be added to the query in Exercise 7.4. These tables will be used to look up the names.

1. Create the query shown below. Typing the comments is optional. You can save or copy the E7.4 query and make the changes, if that is easier. The query is continued on the next page.

```
SELECT Orders.OrderID, OrderDate,
  Customers.FirstName || ' ' || Customers.LastName AS CustomerName,
  SalesReps.FirstName || ' ' || SalesReps.LastName AS SalesRep,
  OrderAmount, ProductName, Quantity

FROM Orders LEFT OUTER JOIN OrderDetails
  ON Orders.OrderID = OrderDetails.OrderID

-- The line below joins the Customers and Orders tables
-- This will let you add any field from the Customers table to the query
LEFT OUTER JOIN Customers ON Orders.CustomerID = Customers.CustomerID

-- The line below joins the Sales Reps and Orders tables
-- This will let you add any field from the Sales Reps table to the query
LEFT OUTER JOIN SalesReps ON Orders.SalesRepID = SalesReps.SalesRepID
```

```
-- The line below joins the Products and Order Details tables
-- This will let you add any field from the Products table to the query
LEFT OUTER JOIN Products ON OrderDetails.ProductID = Products.ProductID

WHERE OrderDetails.ProductID = Products.ProductID
  AND date_part('year', OrderDate) IN ('2017', '2018') AND Quantity >= 5;
```

2. Save the query as `E7.6 LEFT OUTER joins.`

   Figure 7-6 shows the result. The same 5,125 rows were returned. There are now three new columns, that were able to be added, because of the LEFT OUTER JOINS that were added to the query.

	orderid integer	orderdate date	customername text	salesrep text	orderamount numeric (18,2	productname character varying	quantity integer
1	2450	2017-01-03	Elizabeth Anderson	Margaret Peacock	6839.10	Vertigo Helmet	8
2	2450	2017-01-03	Elizabeth Anderson	Margaret Peacock	6839.10	XL U Lock	7
3	2451	2017-01-04	John Edwards	Steven Buchanan	9612.47	Vertigo Helmet	10
4	2452	2017-01-04	John Rodman	Michael Suyama	40.50	Chain Lock	10

Figure 7-6 Order information from 5 tables

In this exercise, INNER joins could have been used because I know that there is a match for the ID fields in the lookup tables. While that is the way that it is "suppose" to be in the real world, that is not always the case. In my opinion, you are safer using LEFT OUTER joins in many cases, so that you can be sure that you are retrieving all of the rows from the primary table in each join. This is what you will want and need most of the time.

In many cases, it is better to have all of the rows from the primary table returned and not have the value in the lookup field (from the table on the right side of the join) find matches in the table on the right, then to not have the row returned from the primary table. Otherwise, you or the person using the data to create a report, will not have all of the data that they should have.

If this query does not demonstrate the importance of understanding relationships, I don't know what query will. <smile>

Using Aggregate Functions With Joins

While aggregate functions are not formally introduced in this book until Chapter 10, I wanted to mention two of them in this chapter, because they are used frequently.

The COUNT function seems pretty basic, just count the rows. As you will see, counting rows is determined by the context of the query criteria. The COUNT examples below cover one of the most important concepts that you need to take away from this book, in my opinion.

The COUNT function has been used a few times already in this book. As you know, INNER and OUTER joins return different rows of data. The next three examples, illustrate the differences between the join types and how they dictate how records are counted. The goal is to provide a list of all customers and a count of their orders. The keyword in this criteria is "All", meaning all customers need to be returned, whether or not they have placed an order.

Example #2 Use An INNER JOIN To Count Customer Orders

The query below will count the number of orders each customer has placed. Figure 7-7 shows the result. Notice that there is no row for customers 13 or 15. That is a problem in this scenario.

```
SELECT Customers.CustomerID, COUNT(Orders.OrderID) AS NbrOfOrders
FROM Customers INNER JOIN Orders
  ON Customers.CustomerID = Orders.CustomerID
GROUP BY Customers.CustomerID
ORDER BY Customers.CustomerID;
```

	customerid integer	nbroforders bigint
11	11	68
12	12	83
13	14	91
14	16	101

Figure 7-7 Count of customer orders

Using The COUNT Function With An OUTER JOIN And GROUP BY Clause

As you know, there are two ways to use the COUNT function, with the * or with a column. The COUNT(*) function works like it does in any other query, but as you will see in Example #3, it does not always return the expected result.

Example #3 Use The COUNT(*) Function In An OUTER JOIN Query

When the COUNT(*) function is used with an OUTER JOIN query, that also has a GROUP BY clause, the function counts inner and outer rows. That is because this function just counts rows, regardless of the data. This is a problem because the outer rows should not be counted. The query below is suppose to count the number of orders for each customer.

```
SELECT Customers.CustomerID, COUNT(*) AS NbrOfOrders
FROM Customers LEFT OUTER JOIN Orders ON Customers.CustomerID = Orders.CustomerID
GROUP BY Customers.CustomerID
ORDER BY Customers.CustomerID;
```

Figure 7-8 shows the result. As you can see, customers 13 and 15 have an order count of 1. Where did these orders come from?

While it is possible that these customers only placed one order, creating another query to confirm whether or not this is true, is a good idea.

	customerid integer	nbroforders bigint
12	12	83
13	13	1
14	14	91
15	15	1
16	16	101

Figure 7-8 Result of the COUNT(*) function used with an OUTER JOIN

Figure 7-9 is the result of a query that displays two fields in the Orders table, sorted in ascending order by the Customer ID field. As shown, there are no orders for customers 13 or 15. Hmmm, what's going on?

	customerid integer	orderdate date
975	12	2018-07-07
976	14	2016-02-08
977	14	2014-09-07
	⋮	
1066	14	2014-09-27
1067	16	2016-08-11

Figure 7-9 Orders table sorted by the Customer ID field

Example #4 Use The COUNT(Column) Function In An OUTER JOIN Query

As you saw in the previous example, the COUNT(*) function counted the outer rows, which in the context of the criteria for the query should not happen. The solution to this problem is to use the COUNT function with a column. This works because when used with a column, the COUNT function ignores NULL values. The outer rows returned, are the rows that will have NULL in the Customer ID field.

The fact that I used the COUNT function with a different column in this query, then the query earlier in Example #2, has no bearing on the result. I used a different column on purpose, so that you could see that different columns can achieve the same result. When selecting a column to count on, the key is to select a column that you are sure has a value in every row. Otherwise, the result (the count) will not be accurate.

The way to ensure this is to select a field that is required and has unique values (aka does not accept NULL values). In a primary table, ID fields have a unique value in every row because the field is required and is usually automatically generated, when a new row of data is created in the table.

The query below fixes the NULL value issue in Example #3. The result is shown in Figure 7-10. Notice that customers 13 and 15 now have zero in the last column, which means that they do not have any orders. Compare the result from this query to the results shown earlier in Figures 7-7 and 7-8.

```
SELECT Customers.CustomerID,
  COUNT(Orders.CustomerID) AS NbrOfOrders
FROM Customers LEFT OUTER JOIN Orders
  ON Customers.CustomerID = Orders.CustomerID
GROUP BY Customers.CustomerID
ORDER BY Customers.CustomerID;
```

	customerid integer	nbroforders bigint
12	12	83
13	13	0
14	14	91
15	15	0

Figure 7-10 Result of using the COUNT(Column) function with an OUTER JOIN

Self Joins

Chapter 6 introduced self joins (also known as recursive joins). There may be times when you need to join a table to itself. Unlike the other join types that have been covered up to this point, this join type does not have it's own keyword operator.

If you look at the data in the Sales Reps table and look at the record for Tim Smith (row 11), you will see that his Supervisor's ID is 10, which is Albert Hellstern. You will also see that Albert Hellstern's supervisor's ID is 2, which is Andrew Fuller. If you understand this hierarchy, then you understand self joins.

Table Alias
When you create a self join (join a table it itself), both instances of the table must use an alias. The reason an alias has to be created for both instances of the table is because you need to **QUALIFY THE COLUMN NAMES.** Keep in mind that virtually, you are using the same table twice in the same query, so initially, the tables have the same column names.

Exercise 7.7: Create A Query Using A Self Join

In this exercise, you will create a query that will show who each employee (sales reps in this book) reports to. The table alias "Emp", is the Employee (sales reps) table. The table alias "Mgr", is the table that will be used to find who each employee reports to.

The query that you will create, says to return all of the records in the "Emp" table, whether or not there is a matching record in the "Mgr" table. Using the INNER JOIN, join type would not return all of the rows from the "Emp" table. The goal is to return a list of **ALL** employees, regardless of whether or not they report to someone.

1. Create the query shown below.

```
SELECT Emp.SalesRepID,
  Emp.FirstName || ' ' || Emp.LastName AS "This Employee ...",
  Mgr.FirstName || ' ' || Mgr.LastName AS "Reports To This Manager",
  Mgr.SalesRepID AS ManagerID
FROM SalesReps AS Emp LEFT OUTER JOIN SalesReps AS Mgr
  ON Emp.SupervisorID = Mgr.SalesRepID
ORDER BY Emp.SalesRepID;
```

It is not a requirement to put each calculated field on it's own line. I do it to make the query easier to read.

2. Save the query as
   `E7.7 Self join query.`

   Figure 7-11 shows the result. 15 rows were returned, which is how many rows are in the Employee (Sales Reps) table.

   The first two columns are from the "Emp" table, which is the Employee (Sales Reps) table.

   The last two columns are from the "Mgr" table. This table is used to return who each employee reports to.

   The reason that the manager information for Andrew fuller is NULL, is because he is the CEO.

	salesrepid integer	This Employee ... text	Reports To This Manager text	managerid integer
1	1	Nancy Davolio	Steven Buchanan	5
2	2	Andrew Fuller	[null]	[null]
3	3	Janet Leverling	Steven Buchanan	5
4	4	Margaret Peacock	Steven Buchanan	5
5	5	Steven Buchanan	Andrew Fuller	2
6	6	Michael Suyama	Steven Buchanan	5
7	7	Robert King	Steven Buchanan	5
8	8	Laura Callahan	Steven Buchanan	5
9	9	Anne Dodsworth	Steven Buchanan	5
10	10	Albert Hellstern	Andrew Fuller	2
11	11	Tim Smith	Albert Hellstern	10
12	12	Caroline Patterson	Albert Hellstern	10
13	13	Justin Brid	Andrew Fuller	2
14	14	Xavier Martin	Justin Brid	13
15	15	Laurent Pereira	Justin Brid	13

Figure 7-11 Self join query results

While a self join is the easiest option, it is not the only way to join a table to itself. You can create a recursive **COMMON TABLE EXPRESSION** (also known as a **CTE**). However, it is more difficult to create and is beyond the scope of this book.

Example #5 Who Is The CEO?

In the previous exercise, you saw who the CEO was. If you added the WHERE clause below, to the end of the query in Exercise 7.7, you will see the row shown in Figure 7-12.

WHERE Mgr.LastName IS NULL

If there were other people that did not report to anyone, they would also be displayed in the result of this query.

	salesrepid integer	This Employee ... text	Reports To This Manager text	managerid integer
1	2	Andrew Fuller	[null]	[null]

Figure 7-12 Result of query to just return the CEO record

Exercise 7.8: Group Orders By Region Name And Year

In this exercise, you will create a query that calculates the order total amount for each region. The data will be grouped and sorted on the region name and order year.

1. Create the query shown below.

```
SELECT RegionName, date_part('year', OrderDate) AS OrderYear,
  SUM(OrderAmount) AS OrderTotal
FROM Customers INNER JOIN Orders
  ON Customers.CustomerID = Orders.CustomerID
  INNER JOIN Regions ON Customers.RegionID = Regions.RegionID
GROUP BY RegionName, date_part('year', OrderDate)
ORDER BY RegionName, OrderYear;
```

2. Save the query as `E7.8 Orders grouped & sorted by region & year.`

   Figure 7-13 shows the result. 21 rows were returned.

   The only rows that will be created are those that have orders for the region and year.

   If the data was not sorted by the order year, it would be very easy to miss that there were no orders for the Northeast region in 2019, as shown in the figure.

	regionname character var	orderyear double prec	ordertotal numeric
4	Midwest	2017	630272.27
5	Midwest	2018	1089429.40
6	Midwest	2019	5545.42
7	Northeast	2014	366184.05
8	Northeast	2015	871596.98
9	Northeast	2016	720403.94
10	Northeast	2017	359357.78
11	Northeast	2018	517951.35
12	South	2014	324497.99

Figure 7-13 Data grouped and sorted by region and year

UNION Operator

This operator is used to join the result of two or more SELECT statements that are in the same query. Duplicate rows are removed, when this operator is used. The result from the SELECT statements are combined and the output from both queries is displayed together, when the UNION operator is used.

Use The UNION Operator To Combine Queries

So far in this book, the queries that were covered, used one SELECT statement that returned data from one or more tables. You can create multiple queries, using multiple SELECT statements and return the results as one result set. The main reasons that you would need to combine queries, are explained below.

☑ When you need to create more than one query for a table and return the results of each query as one query.

☑ When you need to return the result from two or more tables, that have a similar data structure, as one query.

Example #6 Queries To Combine Using The Union Operator

The two queries below will be combined, using the UNION operator, in the next exercise.

This query returns the products in three product categories. Figure 7-14 shows some of the 60 rows that were returned.

```
SELECT ProductID, QtyOnHand, ProductCategoryID
FROM Products
WHERE ProductCategoryID IN (1, 3, 5);
```

This query returns products that have a Qty On Hand >= 1,000. Figure 7-15 shows some of the 65 rows that were returned.

```
SELECT ProductID, QtyOnHand, ProductCategoryID
FROM Products
WHERE QtyOnHand >= 1000;
```

	productid integer	qtyonhand integer	productcategoryid integer
1	1101	456	5
2	1102	123	5
3	1103	789	5
4	1104	1200	5

Figure 7-14 Products that are in one of three product categories

	productid integer	qtyonhand integer	productcategoryid integer
1	1104	1200	5
2	2206	1106	6
3	2207	1107	6
4	2208	1108	6

Figure 7-15 Products that have at least 1,000 pieces on hand

Exercise 7.9: Combine Queries Using The UNION Operator

In this exercise, you will create a query that uses the UNION operator to combine the queries above, in Example #6.

1. Create the first query shown above in Example #6. Do not type a semi-colon at the end of this query.

2. On the next line, type the word `UNION`.

3. On the next line, type the second query in Example #6.

4. Sort the data by the Product ID field.

5. Save the query as `E7.9 UNION query`.

Figure 7-16 shows the result of the UNION query. 95 rows were returned.

Individually, the queries returned 125 rows (60 + 65).

When combined, the query returned fewer rows. This means that 30 rows met the criteria for both queries individually. Each record is only returned once, even if it meets the criteria for both queries, when the UNION operator is used.

	productid integer	qtyonhand integer	productcategoryid integer
1	1101	456	5
2	1102	123	5
3	1103	789	5
4	1104	1200	5

Figure 7-16 Result of using the UNION operator

More than two queries can be combined. Just add the UNION operator before each additional query that you need to add.

While the **UNION OPERATOR** example and exercise selected fields in the same order, that is not a requirement. If the fields are in a different order, they will be displayed in the order of the first query. Each query must have the same number of fields.

Example #7 The WHERE Clause Equivalent Of The UNION Operator

What you will see is that combining two or more queries using the UNION operator is the same as creating one query that has multiple filter conditions on the WHERE clause. This query is the equivalent of the UNION query that you created in Exercise 7.9.

```
SELECT ProductID, QtyOnHand, ProductCategoryID
FROM Products
WHERE ProductCategoryID IN (1, 3, 5) OR
  QtyOnHand >= 1000;
```

UNION ALL Operator

The UNION ALL operator returns all values. It does not eliminate duplicate rows from the rows that each query returns. If the first query returns five rows and the second query returns 10 rows, 15 rows will be returned in the result set. This is the opposite of the **UNION OPERATOR**, which only returns distinct values and eliminates duplicate rows.

Exercise 7.10: Learn The Difference Between The UNION And UNION ALL Operators

In this exercise, you will modify the Exercise 7.9 query, to use the UNION ALL operator.

1. Save the E7.9 query as `E7.10 UNION vs UNION ALL operators`.

2. Type the world `ALL` after the word UNION.

Figure 7-17 shows the result. 125 rows were returned.

As shown, duplicate rows are displayed.

	productid integer	qtyonhand integer	productcategoryid integer
2	1102	123	5
3	1103	789	5
4	1104	1200	5
5	1104	1200	5

Figure 7-17 Result of using the UNION ALL operator

Summary

The focus of this chapter is learning how to use the LEFT OUTER JOIN to join tables. If you thought that you read the same thing more than once in this chapter, you are correct. I did this on purpose for some topics, because they are worth repeating. In my opinion, they are that important. It is my way of trying to keep you from making some of the most common mistakes that many new to creating queries tend to make, when joining tables.

If you have used other SQL databases like SQL Server, you may notice that rows are returned in a different order, then they are in PostgreSQL. That is because queries are processed differently, by some SQL databases. When the rows are not returned in the order that you expect, use the ORDER BY clause.

What you will find whether you are creating inner or outer joins, is that sometimes you will have to create a join that includes a table that you do not need data from. Not understanding relationships and how the tables in a database are related, you may not realize that an extra join (known as an intermediate table join) is needed, to be able to use data in what seems like a table that cannot be joined. This is the **INTERMEDIATE TABLE JOIN** concept that was covered in Chapter 6.

In this chapter, you also were able to see how using a LEFT OUTER JOIN changed the data that the query returned, when compared to an inner join. While joining three or more tables with different join types is often necessary, make sure to test each join individually, to make sure that the join retrieves the expected rows of data.

FORMATTING TEXT AND NUMERIC DATA

After reading this chapter and completing the exercises, you will know what functions are used to format text and numeric data.

CHAPTER 8

Overview

You have learned how to create a variety of queries. One topic that has not been covered is formatting the data that the query retrieves. Examples include formatting numeric values to display commas and dollars signs. Another example is formatting dates to not display the time portion of the field. The only formatting that you have learned so far in this book, is how to combine the values in two or more fields, so that they can be displayed together as one field. From time to time, you will have the need to format the data that the query returns. Having said that, most formatting is done in the software that is used to present the data. Sadly, unlike other SQL databases, PostgreSQL does not support as many formatting related functions, as you would probably like it to.

As you have seen, data, in particular date and numeric data is not formatted as you would like it to be, when retrieved. That's fine because the purpose of creating queries is to retrieve data. The data that is retrieved, is often not displayed in a report, the way that it is displayed in the query editor.

When the need arises, PostgreSQL supports some functions that are designed to format string, numeric and date data type fields. The functions covered in this chapter and the next, are not all of the functions that are available. The ones covered are the ones that are used the most. Being able to use these functions in queries, expands the functionality that you can add to the queries that you create. These functions are used to transform and manipulate the data.

> The formatting that you create is only available in the query that it is created in. The functions covered in this book do not change the data in the database. They only change how the data that is retrieved, is displayed.

> While it is more efficient to format data at the database level in a query, then it is to do the formatting in client reporting software, like Crystal Reports™, you will probably need to do some formatting in the reporting software to compensate for what you cannot do in PostgreSQL.

What Is A Function?

Like the keywords that were covered earlier, functions are pre-written code that carries out an action. Some SQL functions will remind you of functions in Excel.

While the queries that you have created so far, that do not use functions, are very portable from one SQL database to another. The same is not true of queries that use functions. Almost every SQL database supports functions that other SQL databases do not support. For example, PostgreSQL uses the LIMIT function to find the TOP N rows and SQL Server uses the TOP function to find the TOP N rows. Queries like this are not portable. Having said that, for the most part, you will need to use at least some of the functions that are available in the version of SQL that you are using.

Built-In Functions

PostgreSQL has built-in functions. While you are free to create your own functions, you should check to see if there is a built-in function that will handle your needs. There is no point in trying to reinvent the wheel, as they say. <smile>

So far in this book, the queries focused on joining tables, selecting and filtering data. Sometimes, you will have the need to transform or modify the data, before it is used to create a report or chart. This is done to make the output (the data that the query retrieves) more meaningful, because it is easier to read. An example of transforming the data is learning how to combine data in multiple fields into one field, so that the data could be displayed as one field.

> While many of the queries in this chapter will seem basic, compared to the queries that you have created in previous chapters, it is done on purpose. The reason is because the focus of each example and exercise, in this chapter, is for a specific function.

String Formatting Functions

String functions perform operations (transformations) on string (char or varchar data types) fields and values. They return a string or numeric value. These functions are known as **SCALAR FUNCTIONS**.

The functions in this category are mostly used with columns that have a string data type, to manipulate the data. They can be used to search a field for specific characters, find the length of a field or extract part of the data in a field. Some functions can be used to replace characters in a field. Other functions convert the text to all uppercase or all lowercase. Some of the most used string formatting functions are explained in Table 8-1. The string_expression argument can be a field, constant or variable.

Function	This Function . . .
CONCAT	Creates a new string field by combining (joining or concatenating) two or more string fields into one field. This function automatically converts all values to strings before the data is combined. Fields with a NULL value are automatically converted to an empty string. **Syntax** CONCAT(string_value1, string_value2 [, string_valueN])
CONCAT_WS	Works like the CONCAT function. The "WS" stands for With Separator. The difference is that this function also has an argument that is used to include a separator that will be placed between each string field or value. This argument is required. **Syntax** CONCAT_WS(separator, argument1, argument2 [, argumentN]...)
INITCAP	Converts the string to title or proper case. The first letter of each word is converted to upper case and the remaining letters in each word are converted to lower case. **Syntax** INITCAP(string_expression)
LEFT	Returns the number of characters (including leading spaces) specified in the expression, starting from the beginning of the field. **Syntax** LEFT(string, n)
LENGTH	Counts the number of characters in the field. **Syntax** LENGTH(string)
LOWER	Converts all of the characters in the field, to lower case letters. This function works the same as the **LCASE FUNCTION**, in other languages, that you may be familiar with. **Syntax** LOWER(string_expression)
LPAD	Returns the string padded on the left, with the pad string used with the function. **Syntax** LPAD(string, length [, fill])
LTRIM	Removes spaces from the beginning of the field. **Syntax** LTRIM(string, [character])
POSITION	Returns the location of a substring in a string. **Syntax** POSITION(substring IN string)
REPEAT	Repeats the string for the number of times specified in the expression. **Syntax** REPEAT(string, n)
REPLACE	Replaces a character in the field with anther character. **Syntax** REPLACE(source, old text, new text)
RIGHT	Works the opposite of the LEFT function. This function returns the number of characters specified in the expression, starting from the end (the right) of the data in the field. **Syntax** RIGHT(string, n)
RPAD	Works the opposite of the LPAD function. The padding is added to the end (the right) of the string. **Syntax** RPAD(string, length [, fill])
RTRIM	Works the opposite of the LTRIM function. This function removes spaces from the end of the field. **Syntax** RTRIM (string, [character])
SUBSTRING	Retrieves characters from the starting position, for the number of characters specified in the expression. This function works the same as the **MID FUNCTION** in other languages, that you may be familiar with. **Syntax** SUBSTRING(string, start_position, length)
TRIM	Removes all spaces at the beginning or end of the field. Single spaces between words are not removed. **Syntax** TRIM(string)
UPPER	Converts all of the characters in the field, to uppercase case letters. This function works the same as the **UCASE FUNCTION** in other languages, that you may be familiar with. **Syntax** UPPER(string_expression)

Table 8-1 String formatting functions explained

Concatenation Expressions

The concatenation expressions that are covered in this chapter, build on the concatenation expressions that were covered in Chapter 3. Concatenation expressions, unlike math and date expressions, are used to make data easier to read or display. While literals can be used in concatenation expressions, keep in mind that the literal is added to every row that is returned. It is a good idea to keep the literal, as short as possible. Literals must be enclosed in double quotes.

Using The CONCAT Function vs Using ||
The queries in this chapter that use the CONCAT function, can also be created using the || operator, like you learned in Chapter 3. Unlike the || operator, the CONCAT function ignores null values.

Converting Data

As you will see, you will have the need to work with various data types. Often, you will need to convert data from one data type to another. While PostgreSQL can automatically convert a lot of data, it does not always convert the data the way that you need. That is why you need to understand how this automatic conversion works.

When PostgreSQL automatically converts a data type, it is known as an **IMPLICIT CONVERSION**. When you need to control the conversion, you can use the **CAST FUNCTION**. This is known as an **EXPLICIT CONVERSION**. This function is covered later in this chapter.

Conversion FYI
Some string functions are used with fields that have numeric data. When that is the case, the numeric data is automatically converted to string data. When a data type is converted, either automatically or by using a function, the data type **IS NOT** changed in the table. It is only changed when the query is running. This conversion takes place behind the scenes.

Example #1 Combine Two Text Fields And A Literal

The query below will combine the Company Name and Country fields, and will add parenthesis around the Country field. Figure 8-1 shows the result.

```
SELECT CONCAT(CompanyName, ', (',Country,')')
  AS "Company And Country"
FROM Customers;
```

	Company And Country text
1	City Cyclists, (USA)
2	Pathfinders, (USA)
3	Bike-A-Holics Anonymous, (USA)
4	Psycho-Cycle, (USA)

Figure 8-1 Company and Country fields combined

Using Single And Double Quotes
Most of the time, using single quotes to join strings, works as expected. The one time when you will run into a problem is when you need to use a single quote as an apostrophe, as part of the text that is being combined. When that is the case, use double quotes around the single quotes, as shown below.
CONCAT(CompanyName, " 's Contact Information ") AS "Company Contact".

While I used double quotes around the single quote that needed to be displayed, you can also use two single quotes instead of the double quotes. I just find seeing three single quotes together, difficult to recognize, if that makes sense.

Example #2 Use The CONCAT Function To Display A Dollar Sign

The Order Amount field, which has the DECIMAL data type, in this example, will automatically be converted to a string data type, because it needs to be combined with the $ literal.

I know. Is there no end to what the CONCAT function can do? <smile> The query below will display a dollar sign with the value. Figure 8-2 shows the result.

```
SELECT CONCAT('$', OrderAmount) AS OrderAmount
FROM Orders;
```

	orderamount text
1	$2645.87
2	$8908.05
3	$39.80
4	$43.80

Figure 8-2 Dollar sign combined with a numeric value

Example #3 Use The CONCAT Operator To Display A Dollar Sign

The previous example showed you how to display a dollar sign using the CONCAT function. This query uses the CONCAT operator, which you are already familiar with, to display a dollar sign. The result is the same as shown above in Figure 8-2.

```
SELECT '$' || OrderAmount AS OrderAmount
FROM Orders;
```

Exercise 8.1: Use The CONCAT Function To Combine Fields

In this exercise, you will use the CONCAT function to combine the city, state and zip code fields. A comma will be added after the City field.

1. Create this query.

```
SELECT CONCAT (City, ', '
   , State, ' '
   , ZipCode) AS "City, State Zip"
FROM Customers;
```

2. Save the query as `E8.1 Use CONCAT to combine the city state & zip code fields.`

   Figure 8-3 shows the result.
   Notice the comma in the column heading.

	City, State Zip text
1	Sterling Heights, MI 48358
2	DeKalb, IL 60148
3	Blacklick, OH 43005
4	Huntsville, AL 35818

Figure 8-3 City, State and Zip Code fields combined

Exercise 8.2: Use The CONCAT Function To Combine Data In String And Numeric Fields

While the CONCAT function is a string function, it can be used with numeric fields. That is because the function automatically converts fields with a numeric data type to a string data type. In this exercise, you will create a query that combines string and numeric fields.

1. Create this query.

```
SELECT CONCAT(SalesRepID, ' '
   , SalesRep) AS "RepID & SalesRep"
FROM SalesReps;
```

2. Save the query as `E8.2 Combine string & numeric fields using CONCAT function.`

   Figure 8-4 shows the result.

	RepID & SalesRep text
1	1 Nancy Davolio
2	2 Andrew Fuller
3	3 Janet Leverling
4	4 Margaret Peacock

Figure 8-4 String and numeric fields combined

Example #4 Use The CONCAT Function To Combine Text And Numeric Fields

The query below adds text (a literal) before and after a numeric value. Figure 8-5 shows the result.

```
SELECT CONCAT('Total order is: ', '$', OrderAmount,
  ', not including tax') AS OrderAmount
FROM Orders;
```

	orderamount text
1	Total order is: $2645.87, not including tax
2	Total order is: $8908.05, not including tax
3	Total order is: $39.80, not including tax
4	Total order is: $43.80, not including tax

Figure 8-5 Literal added before and after a numeric value

Exercise 8.3: Use The CONCAT_WS Function To Combine Three Fields

In Exercise 8.2, you used the CONCAT function to combine data in two fields. The result of that query could be easier to read, if there was a delimiter between the two fields of data. While the CONCAT function allows you to use delimiters, which you did in Exercise 8.1, you may find it easier to use the CONCAT_WS function when combining three or more fields and need to put the same separator between the fields. In this exercise, you will learn how to combine the data in three fields.

A space is also a separator.

1. Create this query.

```
SELECT CONCAT_WS(' - ', SalesRepID, SalesRep, Position)
  AS "Sales Rep Information"
FROM SalesReps;
```

2. Save the query as `E8.3 CONCAT_WS function.`

   Figure 8-6 shows the result. I don't know about you, but I think that this query is easier to create, then previous queries that needed a separator.

	Sales Rep Information text
1	1 - Nancy Davolio - Sales Representative
2	2 - Andrew Fuller - Vice President, Sales
3	3 - Janet Leverling - Sales Representative
4	4 - Margaret Peacock - Sales Representative

Figure 8-6 Result of using the CONCAT_WS function

Example #5 Use The CONCAT_WS Function To Create A CSV File

This function can also be used to create a comma delimited file, commonly known as a CSV file. This is helpful when you need to get data out of a database, to import into another application or software package like Excel.

The query below separates the fields with a comma, which is what is needed to create a csv file. The result is shown in Figure 8-7. While this example only uses fields from one table, you can join as many tables as needed, to create the CSV file.

```
SELECT
CONCAT_WS (', ', LastName, FirstName, JobTitle) AS CustomerInfo
FROM Customers
ORDER BY LastName, FirstName;
```

	customerinfo text
1	Abbibi,Elan,Engineer
2	Accorti,Paolo,Quality Control Specialist
3	Al Majid,Paja,Statistician
4	Alvarez,Alex,Owner

Figure 8-7 Data in csv file format

Example #6 LEFT Function

The query shown below retrieves the first 5 characters in the Region Name field, as shown in Figure 8-8. If the field has less than the number of characters specified in the expression, spaces will be added to the end of the field.

```
SELECT RegionName, LEFT(RegionName,5) AS RegionAbbr
FROM Regions;
```

	regionname character vary	regionabbr text
8	Northeast	North
9	Northeast	North
10	Midwest	Midwe
11	Midwest	Midwe

Figure 8-8 First 5 characters returned from the Region Name field

The **RIGHT FUNCTION** can also be used to filter data, the same way that the **LEFT FUNCTION** can.

Exercise 8.4: Use The LEFT Function

If you needed to modify an expression that combined the first and last name columns, to only display the first letter of the first name, you would use the LEFT function. ,3 in an expression that uses the LEFT function, means to select the first three characters in the field, starting from the left.

In this exercise, the query that you will create, will display the first letter of the Customers first name and the full last name.

1. Create this query.

```
SELECT CustomerID, CONCAT(LEFT(FirstName,1) , '. '
  , LastName) AS FirstInitialLastName
FROM Customers;
```

2. Save the query as `E8.4 First initial last name.`

   Figure 8-9 shows the result.

	customerid integer	firstinitiallastname text
1	1	C. Christianson
2	2	C. Manley
3	3	G. Jannis
4	4	A. Mast

Figure 8-9 First initial and last name

Example #7 LENGTH Function

The query below returns the number of characters in the Company Name field, as shown in Figure 8-10.

```
SELECT CompanyName,
  LENGTH(CompanyName) AS NbrOfCharacters
FROM Customers;
```

	companyname character varying (75)	nbrofcharacters integer
1	City Cyclists	13
2	Pathfinders	11
3	Bike-A-Holics Anonymous	23
4	Psycho-Cycle	12

Figure 8-10 Result of using the LENGTH function

Example #8 LOWER Function

The query below converts the value in the Company Name field to all lower case letters, as shown in Figure 8-11.

```
SELECT CompanyName,
  LOWER(CompanyName) AS LowerCase
FROM Customers;
```

	companyname character varying (75)	lowercase text
1	City Cyclists	city cyclists
2	Pathfinders	pathfinders
3	Bike-A-Holics Anonymous	bike-a-holics anonymous
4	Psycho-Cycle	psycho-cycle

Figure 8-11 Result of using the LOWER function

Example #9 REPLACE Function

The query below replaces every occurrence of the lower case letter i, with the capital letters ZZ, as shown in the Replace Characters column, in Figure 8-12.

```
SELECT CompanyName,
  REPLACE(CompanyName, 'i', 'ZZ') AS ReplaceCharacters
FROM Customers;
```

	companyname character varying (75)	replacecharacters text
1	City Cyclists	CZZty CyclZZsts
2	Pathfinders	PathfZZnders
3	Bike-A-Holics Anonymous	BZZke-A-HolZZcs Anonymous
4	Psycho-Cycle	Psycho-Cycle
5	Sporting Wheels Inc.	SportZZng Wheels Inc.

Figure 8-12 Result of using the REPLACE function

What If The Character That You Want To Replace Is Case Sensitive?
If you type in a lower case letter to replace, the upper case occurrence of the same letter will not be replaced. In the query above, I used the lower case i. If you look on the last line of the figure, the upper case letter "I" was not replaced, in the second column.

Exercise 8.5: Reformat The Phone Number Field

In this exercise, you will create a query that removes the parentheses in the Phone Number field.

1. Create this query.

```
SELECT LastName, FirstName, PhoneNumber,
  REPLACE (REPLACE (PhoneNumber, '(', ''), ')',''
    AS "Formatted Phone Number"
FROM Customers
ORDER BY LastName, FirstName;
```

2. Save the query as `E8.5 Phone number reformatted.`

   Figure 8-13 shows the result.

   If the Phone Number field is empty, the query will not generate an error, as indicated by the null values on the last row in the figure.

	lastname character va	firstname character v	phonenumber character varyin	Formatted Phone Number text
7	Anderson	Sandra	(702) 276-6213	702 276-6213
8	Anderson	Sandra	(975) 987-1224	975 987-1224
9	Andover	Jerry	(404) 456-7037	404 456-7037
10	Antoine	Claude	[null]	[null]

Figure 8-13 Phone number reformatted

Example #10 Use The RTRIM Function

You have learned how to combine data in different columns by using the concatenation operator ||. It worked as expected, because the fields had a variable length data type.

As covered in Chapter 3, Table 3-1, there are fixed length data types. When using fields with a fixed length data type, the initial result when combining data from string fields, may not be what you are expecting.

Fixed length means that a specific number of characters are allocated for the field, whether or not the data that is entered in the field needs all of the allocated space. Fields with this data type are padded with spaces at the end, to fill up the number of characters allocated for the field.

When you use a field with this data type, the query below may not display the data as you expect. Figure 8-14 shows the result.

```
SELECT FCompanyName || ' (' || FCountry || ')'
  AS "Company Name and Country"
FROM Customers;
```

	Company Name and Country text
63	Feel Great Bikes Inc. (USA)
64	SAB Mountain (Switzerland)
65	Platou Sport (Norway)
66	Piccolo (Austria)

Figure 8-14 Possible result of a query using fields that have a fixed length data type

There is nothing wrong with the data in the columns in the expression above or the data type. I just wanted to demonstrate how some data may be displayed, in case you run into it on your own. I don't want you to think that you had done anything wrong in creating the query. Trust, I remember the early SQL query learning days. <smile>

As covered earlier in Table 8-1, the **RTRIM FUNCTION** removes spaces from the end of the field. The query below uses the RTRIM function. The result is shown in Figure 8-15. Much better. <smile>

```
SELECT RTRIM(FCompanyName) || ' ('
  || RTRIM(FCountry) , ')'
    AS "Company Name and Country"
FROM Customers;
```

	Company Name and Country text
63	Feel Great Bikes Inc. (USA)
64	SAB Mountain (Switzerland)
65	Platou Sport (Norway)
66	Piccolo (Austria)

Figure 8-15 Result of adding the RTRIM function to the query

Example #11 SUBSTRING Function With A Range

The query shown below, returns 4 characters from the Company Name field, starting with the second character, as shown in Figure 8-16. The reason that the first row in the figure only has 3 characters is because the 4th character in the Company Name field for the record, is a space.

```
SELECT CompanyName, SUBSTRING(CompanyName, 2, 4)
  AS SubstringCharacters
FROM Customers;
```

	companyname character varying (75)	substringcharacters text
1	City Cyclists	ity
2	Pathfinders	athf
3	Bike-A-Holics Anonymous	ike-
4	Psycho-Cycle	sych

Figure 8-16 Result of using the SUBSTRING function

The SUBSTRING function needs three pieces of information to work, as explained below.

- ☑ The field that has the data that you want to extract from.
- ☑ The position starting from the left, that has the first character that you want to extract.
- ☑ The total number of characters that you want to extract.

Exercise 8.6: Use The SUBSTRING Function

If you needed to modify an expression that combined the first and last name columns, to only retrieve the first letter of the first name, you would use the SUBSTRING function. This function works the same as the **LEFT FUNCTION**. In this exercise, the query that you will create, will extract the first letter of the customers first name and the full last name.

1. Create this query.

```
SELECT CustomerID, SUBSTRING(FirstName,1 ,1) || '. '
    || LastName AS FirstInitialLastName
FROM Customers;
```

2. Save the query as `E8.6 First initial last name.`

   Figure 8-17 shows the result.

	customerid integer	firstinitiallastname text
1	1	C. Christianson
2	2	C. Manley
3	3	G. Jannis
4	4	A. Mast

Figure 8-17 First initial and last name

Exercise 8.7: Filter Data Using A Function

In this exercise, you will use the SUBSTRING function to extract the Region Code. The same logic can be used to filter the data in the table. This will let you create a filter by using part of the data in the field. In this exercise, you will create a query that selects rows that have one of the following region codes: N03, W33 or G10.

1. Create the query shown below.

```
SELECT InvoiceID,
  SUBSTRING(InvoiceNumber, 8, 3) AS RegionCode, InvoiceDate, InvoiceTotal
FROM Invoices
WHERE SUBSTRING(InvoiceNumber, 8, 3) IN ('N03', 'W33','G10');
```

2. Save the query as `E8.7 Filter data using the SUBSTR function.`

   Figure 8-18 shows the result. 59 rows were returned.

   All of the rows returned have one of the region codes listed on the WHERE clause.

	invoiceid integer	regioncode text	invoicedate date	invoicetotal numeric (18,
1	742	N03	2018-06-01	118.58
2	743	G10	2018-06-01	19.25
3	749	W33	2018-06-01	1251.90
4	754	N03	2018-06-02	1682.67

Figure 8-18 Result of data filtered by a function

Exercise 8.8: Use The UPPER Function

In this exercise, you will create a query that will convert the City field to all uppercase letters.

1. Create this query.

```
SELECT UPPER(City) || ', '
    || State || ' '
    || ZipCode AS "City, State Zip"
FROM Customers;
```

2. Save the query as `E8.8 Convert to upper case.`

   Figure 8-19 shows the result. The City field is now displayed in all upper case letters.

	City, State Zip text
1	STERLING HEIGHTS, MI 48358
2	DEKALB, IL 60148
3	BLACKLICK, OH 43005
4	HUNTSVILLE, AL 35818

Figure 8-19 City field converted to upper case letters

Exercise 8.9: Combine Text With A String Field

So far in this chapter, you have created queries that used a function to transform data. At some point, you may need to add the same text to each row of data that is returned, as covered earlier in Example #4. The text that you add, must be in single quotes. This is how SQL knows that you are adding text. In this exercise, you will modify a query to identify the sales reps name, as such.

1. Save the E6.3 query as `E8.9 Add text to a string field on each row.`

2. Modify the Sales Rep field, as shown below. Figure 8-20 shows the result.

```
'Sales Rep - ' || SalesReps.SalesRep AS "Sales Rep",
```

	salesrepid integer	Sales Rep text	orderyear double pre	nbroforders bigint	yearlytotal numeric
3	1	Sales Rep - Nancy Davolio	2016	390	619317.88
4	1	Sales Rep - Nancy Davolio	2017	178	339795.20
5	1	Sales Rep - Nancy Davolio	2018	302	537708.75
6	2	Sales Rep - Andrew Fuller	2014	2	3374.25

Figure 8-20 Result of text added to a string field

CAST Function

This function is used to convert a value in a column or a literal value to a different data type. Being able to convert values is very helpful when creating expressions. For example, this function can be used to convert a numeric column to a string column, as you will learn later in this chapter. The CAST function is often used on the WHERE, JOIN or HAVING clause to return a value that has a specific data type. This function can also be used to convert a column with the TIMESTAMP data type to the DATE data type. This is covered in the next chapter.

CAST Function Restrictions

While being able to convert a column from one data type to another, can be a real life saver, there are some restrictions that you need to be aware of, as explained below.

☑ When converting a column that has a numeric data type to another numeric data type, the data can be truncated, if the new data type is not large enough to hold the value.
☑ When converting a column that has a numeric decimal data type to a numeric data type that is not a numeric decimal data type, the value after the decimal point will be rounded or truncated as needed, to fit the new data type.
☑ When converting a string data type to another string data type, data can be truncated if the new string data type is not long enough to store the data.
☑ When converting a string data type to any other data type, you need to make sure that the new data type is compatible with the data that it will store.

Example #12 Use The CAST Function

This query converts a numeric value to an integer and converts a date to a string. Figure 8-21 shows the result. The converted column is next to the original column in the result.

```
SELECT OrderID, OrderAmount,
  CAST(OrderAmount AS integer) AS CAST_OrderAmount, OrderDate,
  CAST(OrderDate AS VARCHAR(10)) AS CAST_OrderDate
FROM Orders;
```

	orderid integer	orderamount numeric (18,2)	cast_orderamount integer	orderdate date	cast_orderdate character varyin
1	1	2645.87	2646	2016-01-01	2016-01-01
2	2	8908.05	8908	2016-01-01	2016-01-01
3	3	39.80	40	2016-01-02	2016-01-02
4	4	43.80	44	2016-01-02	2016-01-02

Figure 8-21 Result of using the CAST function to convert data types

Formatting Numbers And Dates
What may not be obvious is that when numbers are formatted, they are automatically converted to text. For the most part, this means that SQL cannot use the converted data in a calculation. Therefore, format the data when you are sure that the value does not need to be used in a calculation, in the query.

Math Expressions

You can create addition, subtraction, multiplication and division expressions, for numeric data. Chapter 4, covered the importance of the placement of parentheses. That also applies to math expressions, to ensure that the expressions are evaluated the way that you intended. In Chapter 4, you also learned about the order of precedence for operators. Math expressions (operations) have their own **ORDER OF PRECEDENCE**, as explained below.

- ☑ Multiplication and division are on the same level, and will be processed first.
- ☑ Addition and subtraction are on the same level, and are processed after multiplication and division.

Example #13 Math Expressions Using Literal Values

The expressions below use the same numbers and operators, but return different results. That is because the placement of the parentheses is different.

The expression (3*4) + 5 returns 17.
The expression 3* (4+5) returns 27.

While the expression examples above used literals, columns can be used to create math expressions. A key thing to keep in mind when creating math expressions is to make sure that the columns data types are compatible. If the columns that you need to use are not compatible, all is not lost. Use the **CAST FUNCTION** to convert the data type of a column. Depending on the data type that you are converting a column to, the value may be rounded automatically.

Example #14 Math Expressions Using Columns In A Table

The query below, calculates the sales reps projected income. The expression multiplies a literal ($100,000), the amount of expected sales, times the commission rate. That value is added to the salary. Figure 8-22 shows the result.

```
SELECT SalesRep,
  Salary + (100000 * CommissionRate)
    AS Income
FROM SalesReps;
```

	salesrep character varying(5	income numeric
1	Nancy Davolio	45000.00
2	Andrew Fuller	91000.00
3	Janet Leverling	38000.00
4	Margaret Peacock	40000.00

Figure 8-22 Result of a math expression that uses columns in a table

Exercise 8.10: Calculate The Inventory Value

In this exercise, you will create a query that uses numeric fields in the expression to calculate the value of the products.

1. Create this query.

```
SELECT ProductID, ProductName,
  RetailPrice * QtyOnHand AS InventoryAmount
FROM Products;
```

2. Save the query as `E8.10 Calculate the inventory amount.`

   Figure 8-23 shows the result. 127 rows were returned.

	productid integer	productname character varyin	inventoryamount numeric
2	1102	Crochet Glove	1783.50
3	1103	Crochet Glove	11440.50
4	1104	Crochet Glove	17400.00
5	1105	Crochet Glove	8250.50

Figure 8-23 Product inventory amount calculated

Mathematical Formatting Functions

In addition to creating math expressions, that were covered in the previous section, SQL also has math formatting functions. Mathematical functions perform calculations on numeric fields and values, and return numeric values. These functions are known as **SCALAR FUNCTIONS**. The functions in this category are for fields that have a numeric data type. I suspect by now that you have seen some numeric data that was returned by the queries that you have created, that you wished was formatted better, or formatted a different way. For example, a whole number greater than 999 should have a comma and currency values would look better if they had a dollar sign. Both of these formatting options can be done in the software that is used to create the report or visualization.

While the functions in this category are designed to work with fields that have a **NUMERIC DATA TYPE**, they do work with fields that store a money (aka currency) value. Table 8-2 explains the math formatting functions that are commonly used.

Function	This Function Returns . . .
ABS	The absolute value of a number.
CEILING or CEIL	The next whole number up from the value that is being evaluated. This function works similar to the **ROUND FUNCTION** because it rounds values up. **Syntax** CEILING(numeric_expression) (1)
FLOOR	The next whole number down from the value that is being evaluated. This function works the opposite of the CEILING function, because it rounds the value down to the nearest whole number. **Syntax** FLOOR(numeric_expression) (1)
ROUND	A rounded number. The optional precision argument is used to specify the number of places after the decimal point, that you want returned, after rounding. **Syntax** ROUND(value, precision)
TRUNC	The number truncated to a whole number or shortened to the number of decimal places specified. This function does not round. **Syntax** TRUNC(number [, [precision]). The number can be a literal, a field or numeric expression. Precision is the number of decimal places to shorten the value to.

Table 8-2 Mathematical formatting functions explained

(1) This function removes the decimal point and the number after the decimal point, if they exist.

Exercise 8.11: Use The CEILING And FLOOR Functions

In this exercise, you will create a query that applies these functions to the same numeric field. This will let you see the difference between these functions.

1. Create this query.

```
SELECT ProductID, ProductName, RetailPrice,
  CEILING(RetailPrice) AS "CEILING Retail Price",
  FLOOR(RetailPrice) AS "FLOOR Retail Price"
FROM Products;
```

2. Save the query as E8.13 CEILING & FLOOR functions.

   Figure 8-24 shows the result of both functions applied to the same field.

   Notice the values are different in the last two columns.

	productid integer	productname character varyinç	retailprice numeric (1ŧ	CEILING Retail Price numeric	FLOOR Retail Price numeric
26	2215	Vertigo Helmet	53.90	54	53
27	3301	Chain Lock	4.50	5	4
28	3302	U Lock	17.50	18	17
29	3303	XL U Lock	19.90	20	19

Figure 8-24 Result of using the CEILING and FLOOR functions

Exercise 8.12: Use The ROUND Function

The query in this exercise will round the Order Amount field to the nearest whole number, to one decimal place and two decimal places.

1. Create this query.

```
SELECT OrderAmount,
  ROUND(OrderAmount) AS "To Whole Number",
  ROUND(OrderAmount, 1) AS "1 Decimal Place",
  ROUND(OrderAmount, 2) AS "2 Decimal Places"
FROM Orders;
```

2. Save the query as
`E8.12 Use the ROUND function.`

Figure 8-25 shows the result.

	orderamount numeric (18,2)	To Whole Number numeric	1 Decimal Place numeric	2 Decimal Places numeric
1	2645.87	2646	2645.9	2645.87
2	8908.05	8908	8908.1	8908.05
3	39.80	40	39.8	39.80
4	43.80	44	43.8	43.80

Figure 8-25 Result of different variations of the ROUND function

Conditional Functions

There are two conditional functions that PostgreSQL supports: **CASE** and **COALESCE**. You have already created queries that use these functions. This section covers these functions in a way that you may not have thought of.

> PostgreSQL currently does not support the **IF FUNCTION**, the **IIF FUNCTION** or the **IFNULL FUNCTION**. You can create a CASE statement to accomplish the same result. Exercise 8.13 shows you how to create a CASE statement that emulates using IF function.

Exercise 8.13: How To Emulate The IF Function

This query uses the IF function (it was created in MySQL). It checks the Payment Type field to see if the value is "Check". If it is, display Yes in the Paid By Check column. If it isn't, display No in the column.

```
SELECT CompanyName,
  IF (PaymentType = 'Check', 'Yes', 'No') AS PaidByCheck
FROM Orders, Customers
WHERE Orders.CustomerID = Customers.CustomerID;
```

The query that you will create in this exercise, uses a CASE statement, which emulates the functionality of the query above, that uses the IF function.

1. Create this query.

```
SELECT CompanyName,
  CASE PaymentType
  WHEN 'Check' THEN 'Yes'
  ELSE 'No'
  END AS "PaidByCheck"
FROM Orders, Customers
WHERE Orders.CustomerID = Customers.CustomerID;
```

2. Save the query as
`E8.13 Emulate the IF function.`

Figure 8-26 shows the result, that both queries return.

	companyname character varying (75)	PaidByCheck text
4	Trail Blazer's Place	No
5	Piccolo	No
6	Paris Mountain Sports	Yes
7	Hercules Mountain Bikes	Yes

Figure 8-26 Result of using the CASE statement to emulate the IF function

COALESCE Function

This function is similar to the IFNULL function (that is not supported in PostgreSQL), because it allows you to display something in place of NULL values. The COALESCE function goes a step further. It lets you specify a list of values, similar to how the CASE function works. This means that as needed, the COALESCE function can use some or all of the data from a field to display, instead of null values.

Exercise 8.14: Emulate The IFNULL Function

The query that you will create in this exercise, checks to see if the Payment Type field has a value. If it doesn't, "Missing Payment Type" will be displayed. The difference between this query and the one in Exercise 8.13, is that this query only checks for null values. The query in the Exercise 8.13, checks for a specific value. Null values in that exercise displayed No, in the Paid By Check column. The COALESCE function will be used to emulate the IFNULL function. This query returns the same result that the IFNULL function would return.

1. Create this query.

```
SELECT CompanyName,
  COALESCE(PaymentType, 'Missing Payment Type') AS PaidBy
FROM Orders, Customers
WHERE Orders.CustomerID = Customers.CustomerID;
```

2. Save the query as `E8.14 Emulate the IFNULL function`.

As shown in Figure 8-27, Wheels Inc is missing the payment type and in Figure 8-26 above, all you know is that the order was not paid by check. These queries illustrate how the same data can be interpreted differently.

The option that you choose, depends on how you want to convey the data. By that I mean that in some instances, it is ok to not display anything, when the value is null and in other instances, something needs to be displayed, when the value is null.

	companyname character varying (75)	paidby character varying
1	Tandem Cycle	Check
2	Wheels Inc.	Missing Payment Type
	⋮	
7	Hercules Mountain Bikes	Check
8	Backpedal Cycle Shop	Missing Payment Type

Figure 8-27 Result of using the COALESCE function to display a value, when the field has a null value

Exercise 8.15: Use The COALESCE Function

The query that you will create in this exercise, will display the value in the Customer Type field if the Payment Type field is null.

1. Create this query.

```
SELECT CompanyName,
  COALESCE(PaymentType, CustomerType) AS PaidBy
FROM Orders, Customers
WHERE Orders.CustomerID = Customers.CustomerID;
```

2. Save the query as `E8.15 Use the COALESCE function`.

As shown in Figure 8-28, rows 2 and 8 display the value in the Customer Type field.

Notice that those are the same rows in Figure 8-27 above, that display 'Missing Payment Type'.

	companyname character varying (75)	paidby charact
1	Tandem Cycle	Check
2	Wheels Inc.	Retail
	⋮	
7	Hercules Mountain Bikes	Check
8	Backpedal Cycle Shop	Retail

Figure 8-28 Result of using the COALESCE function to display data from a field, when the field has a null value

Summary

This chapter formally introduced you to text and numeric functions. The next chapter covers date functions. While this chapter covered formatting techniques and options for text and numeric fields, more formatting is often done when reports are created. By formatting, I mean adding dollar signs and text. Most report writing software has this functionality. Using functions to extract part of a field and creating new columns of data, are the types of formatting transformations that should be done in the query, because it can be more difficult to do that at the report level.

Another important topic that was covered is handling NULL values. As you learned, if not handled correctly, they can alter the result that the query returns, by producing a result that is not accurate.

Using the CAST function in expressions to covert the data type of a column, to be compatible with another column that is being used in the expression, was also covered. This function can really be helpful when data is imported from a file, like Excel, opposed to data imported from another database.

FORMATTING AND USING DATE FIELDS

After reading this chapter and completing the exercises, you will know what functions can be used to format and transform date fields. You will also learn how to use date fields to select the rows to retrieve.

CHAPTER 9

Overview

This chapter formally introduces you to using date functions in queries. You will learn about using date fields in expressions and the functions that are used for time intelligence solutions. In addition to creating expressions with date fields to filter data, SQL has functions that are used to format date fields and manipulate or extract part of a date. Some of the queries up to this point have used the DATE_PART date function, but it was not explained. It is covered in more detail in this chapter.

What Is Time Intelligence?

As you will see, a lot of data analysis requirements include dates. That is because data often needs to be analyzed over a period of time. For example, the sales from the first quarter of this year needs to be compared to the sales from the first quarter of last year.

Dates are a very important component of analyzing data. Dates are used to quantify other data. Examples include last years sales, year to date sales and sales reps total order amounts this quarter, compared to the same time last year. The expressions that can be created with date fields can use addition and subtraction operators. A date or interval literal can also be used in an expression. The CAST function can be used to convert a date field, if needed.

Some time intelligence functions are used to jump ahead or back in time, to retrieve data. While in SQL, there is no official "Time Intelligence" function category, these functions are very helpful when you need to compare data between or across time periods. Other examples include being able to define a date range, year on year changes or compare current data to future or past data, from a date or date range that you specify in the query. A popular use of some date functions is creating running totals, like year to date (YTD) and month to date (MTD). The date values that these functions return are sometimes used by other functions to help calculate additional values.

What you will find is that many of these functions require a calculated column, plus a date column. Earlier in this book, I said that many reports are date driven. Many of the functions covered in this chapter are used to create queries that are date driven.

Some of the date functions will remind you of accounting functionality, because they allow you to compare today's sales to sales from a year ago, calculate the sales for the last 30 days, calculate sales for the previous quarter and more. These functions use a range of dates to get the aggregate and related values.

While these functions are often referred to as "time" intelligence functions, you will see that most of the queries that you need to create, use dates, opposed to times. Later in this chapter, I point out a problem when times (hours, minutes, etc.) are used in an expression.

What you will learn is that there are several ways to analyze data, using date fields. Some of the ways are listed below.

- ☑ Aggregate data over time.
- ☑ Group data by year or month.
- ☑ Filter data by a specific date or by a date range.

Date Functions

Date and time functions perform operations on fields that have date or time data type, and return a date, time, numeric or string value. As luck would have it, SQL has several date functions that can be used to analyze data over time. But, sadly, like the text and numeric functions, PostgreSQL only supports a few of the SQL date functions that are available. Having said that, PostgreSQL has what is called "identifiers" that can emulate some of the date functions that you may have used in other software, that are not supported in PostgreSQL. They may handle at least some of your needs. When that is not the case, in many instances, you will have to think outside of the box, to find a solution.

Readers of this book that have a T-SQL/SQL Server background will say otherwise. That is because SQL Server has built-in functions, that will display the month name and day name spelled out and allow dates to be displayed in several formats.

Dates are such an integral part of creating queries. In Chapter 4, you created queries that use dates. You learned how to create queries that used dates to filter the data. The rest of this chapter picks up where Chapter 4 left off, in terms of using date fields in queries. Table 9-1 explains the commonly used date functions that PostgreSQL supports.

Date Formatting Options
If you have used another SQL database, like MySQL or SQL Server, many of the formatting options and functions that you are use to, like YEAR, MONTH and QUARTER are not supported in PostgreSQL. Instead, you have to use the DATE_PART function and identifiers, which are somewhat similar to those functions. While there is a function specifically for time in PostgreSQL, it is not demonstrated in this book.

Function	This Function . . .
AGE	Calculates the age between two dates. The result is displayed in years, months and days, as appropriate.
CURRENT_DATE	Returns today's date.
DATE_PART	Selects a portion of the date, like the year or month. It is often used to compare part of the date to a specific value. The **EXTRACT FUNCTION** works the same as the DATE_PART function.
DATE_TRUNC	Selects a portion of the date, like the year or month. It automatically converts the date to a timestamp or interval data type. One use for this function is to calculate past and future dates.
INTERVAL	Is used to calculate a date.
NOW()	Returns the current date and time, on your computer. This function bases the date on your computers clock. Parentheses are required after this function.
TO_CHAR	Converts an integer, timestamp or interval data type value to a string value.
TO_DATE	Converts a string to a date.

Table 9-1 Date functions explained

DATE_PART Function Identifiers

The DATE_PART function uses what are called identifiers. They are codes that tell PostgreSQL which portion of the date to select. Table 9-2 explains some of the identifiers. Examples of what the identifiers return are in parentheses.

Identifier	This Identifier Displays . . .
day	The day of the month without a leading zero. (1, 2 . . . 9)
week	The week of the year (00-53), which includes leap year.
month	The month number without a leading zero. (1, 2 . . . 9)
quarter	The quarter that the date is in. (1, 2, 3, 4)
year	A 4 digit year. (2018, 2019)
dow	The day of the week. (0 = Sunday, 1 = Monday, 6= Saturday)
isodow	The day of the week. (1 = Monday, 7 = Sunday)
doy	The day of the year. (1-365)

Table 9-2 DATE_PART function identifiers explained

Example #1 Using The DATE_PART Identifiers

This query demonstrates how the identifiers in Table 9-2 can be used to format dates. Figure 9-1 shows the result.

```
SELECT OrderDate AS "OrderDate",
  date_part('month', OrderDate) AS "Month",
  date_part('year', OrderDate) AS "Year",
  date_part('day', OrderDate) AS "DayOfTheMonth",
  date_part('doy', OrderDate) AS "DayOfTheYear",
  date_part('dow', OrderDate) AS "DayOfTheWeek",
  date_part('week', OrderDate) AS "WeekOfTheYear"
FROM Orders;
```

	OrderDate date	Month double p	Year double	DayOfTheMonth double precision	DayOfTheYear double precisio	DayOfTheWeek double precision	WeekOfTheYear double precision
66	2016-01-19	1	2016	19	19	2	3
67	2016-01-20	1	2016	20	20	3	3
68	2016-01-21	1	2016	21	21	4	3
69	2016-01-21	1	2016	21	21	4	3

Figure 9-1 DATE_PART function identifier examples

Date Formatting Options

Table 9-3 explains some of the date formatting options, that can be used with the TO_CHAR function. As you will see in Example #2, more than one formatting option can be used to format a date.

Character	Displays The . . .
Day	Day of the week, spelled out in mixed case characters. (Monday, Tuesday)
DAY	Day of the week, spelled out in all upper case characters. (MONDAY, TUESDAY)
Dy	Three letter abbreviation for the day of the week, in mixed case characters. (Mon, Tue)
DDD	Day of the year. (001-366)
DD	Day of the month. (01-31)
Month	Name of the month spelled out in mixed case characters. (January, February)
MON	Name of the month spelled out in all upper case characters. (JANUARY, FEBRUARY)
Mon	Three letter abbreviation for the month, in mixed case characters. (Jan, Feb)
MM	Month number. (01-12)
YY	Last two digits of the year.
YYYY	Four digit year.

Table 9-3 Date formatting options explained

Example #2 Day Formatting Options

This query will display the day formatting options, shown in Figure 9-2. Notice the differences between how the day is displayed in the columns.

```
SELECT ShipDate AS "OriginalDate",
  TO_CHAR(ShipDate, 'Dy, Mon DD, YYYY') AS "Option1",
  TO_CHAR(ShipDate, 'Day Month DD, YYYY') AS "Option2",
  TO_CHAR(ShipDate, 'DAY MON DD, YYYY') AS "Option3"
FROM Orders;
```

	OriginalDate date	Option1 text	Option2 text	Option3 text
1	2016-01-03	Sun, Jan 03, 2016	Sunday January 03, 2016	SUNDAY JAN 03, 2016
2	2016-01-04	Mon, Jan 04, 2016	Monday January 04, 2016	MONDAY JAN 04, 2016
3	2016-01-14	Thu, Jan 14, 2016	Thursday January 14, 2016	THURSDAY JAN 14, 2016

Figure 9-2 Day formatting options

Example #3 Month Formatting Options

This query will display the month formatting options shown in Figure 9-3.

```
SELECT ShipDate AS "OriginalDate",
  TO_CHAR(ShipDate, 'MM/DD/YYYY') AS "Option1",
  TO_CHAR(ShipDate, 'Mon DD, YYYY') AS "Option2",
  TO_CHAR(ShipDate, 'MON DD, YYYY') AS "Option3",
  TO_CHAR(ShipDate, 'Month DD, YYYY') AS "Option4",
  TO_CHAR(ShipDate, 'MONTH DD, YYYY') AS "Option5"
FROM Orders
ORDER BY ShipDate;
```

	OriginalDate date	Option1 text	Option2 text	Option3 text	Option4 text	Option5 text
99	2014-01-31	01/31/2014	Jan 31, 2014	JAN 31, 2014	January 31, 2014	JANUARY 31, 2014
100	2014-01-31	01/31/2014	Jan 31, 2014	JAN 31, 2014	January 31, 2014	JANUARY 31, 2014
101	2014-02-01	02/01/2014	Feb 01, 2014	FEB 01, 2014	February 01, 2014	FEBRUARY 01, 2014

Figure 9-3 Month formatting options

Exercise 9.1: Format A Date Field Without The Time

As you have seen, the majority of date fields in the database, used in this book, do not have a time. Out in the real world, you will probably use date fields that have a time. If so, this may be one of your top 3 favorites exercises in this book. <smile> Did you really think that I would skip the most used date formatting option? Absolutely not. I wanted you to have the hands on experience of being able to just display the date.

1. Create this query.

```
SELECT SalesRep, HireDate,
  TO_CHAR(HireDate, 'MM/DD/YYYY') AS FormattedHireDate
FROM SalesReps;
```

2. Save the query as `E9.1 Format the Hire Date field.`

Figure 9-4 shows the result. The second column is how the date is stored in the Sales Reps table.

On your own, it may be helpful to create the code (like the second line in the query above) for the date format that you will use the most and save it. Then, when needed, you would only have to type in the name of the date field that you need to be formatted.

	salesrep character varying (5	hiredate timestamp without tim	formattedhiredate text
1	Nancy Davolio	1993-04-16 00:00:00	04/16/1993
2	Andrew Fuller	2011-08-30 00:00:00	08/30/2011
3	Janet Leverling	2005-09-19 00:00:00	09/19/2005
4	Margaret Peacock	2003-07-25 00:00:00	07/25/2003

Figure 9-4 Hire Date field formatted without the time

Exercise 9.2: Calculate Weekly Totals

The query that you will create in this exercise, will count the number of orders and calculate the total order amount by week, for orders in 2017.

1. Create this query.

```
SELECT date_part('week', OrderDate) AS Week_NBR,
  COUNT(*) AS Nbr_Of_Orders,
  '$'|| SUM(OrderAmount) AS Total_For_Week
FROM Orders
WHERE date_part('year', OrderDate) = '2017'
GROUP BY date_part('week', OrderDate);
```

2. Save the query as `E9.2 Count & sum orders by week.`

Figure 9-5 shows the result. 50 rows were returned. One row for each week that has orders.

	week_nbr double prec	nbr_of_orders bigint	total_for_week text
1	1	18	$52846.67
2	2	20	$33566.95
3	3	17	$32441.31
4	4	25	$53249.28

Figure 9-5 Order totals by week

Example #4 Use The DATE_PART Function

In Chapter 5, Exercise 5.25, you created a query that grouped orders by the order date. This query accomplishes the same task. The difference is that instead of displaying the order date, the order year is displayed.

```
SELECT date_part('year', OrderDate) AS "OrderYear",
  SUM(OrderAmount) AS "OrderAmount"
FROM Orders
GROUP BY OrderDate;
```

	OrderYear double prec	OrderAmount numeric
1	2015	1382.18
2	2017	14766.08
3	2014	12938.57
4	2018	1222.08
5	2017	2219.81
6	2018	15492.32
7	2018	16050.13

Figure 9-6 Result of using the year date_part

Exercise 9.3: Create Monthly Order Totals By Year

The query that you will create in this exercise, will display order total amounts by year and month number.

1. Create this query.

```
SELECT date_part('year', OrderDate) AS "OrderYear",
  date_part('month', OrderDate) AS "Month Number",
  SUM(OrderAmount) AS "OrderAmount"
FROM Orders
GROUP BY date_part('year', OrderDate),
  date_part('month', OrderDate)
ORDER BY date_part('year', OrderDate),
  date_part('month', OrderDate);
```

2. Save the query as `E9.3 Order totals by year & month number.`

   Figure 9-7 shows the result. 61 rows were returned.

   If you scroll to the end of the grid, you will see that in 2019, there are only orders for the month of May.

	OrderYear double preci	Month Number double precision	OrderAmount numeric
1	2014	1	253573.93
2	2014	2	317900.02
3	2014	3	173797.45
		⋮	
10	2014	10	123200.52
11	2014	11	233258.41
12	2014	12	11147.60
13	2015	1	437014.06
14	2015	2	417565.09

Figure 9-7 Order totals grouped by year and month number

Example #5 Alternate Way To Create The Query In Exercise 9.3

The query below is another way to calculate monthly order totals by year. The major change is the date format on the second line. Figure 9-8 shows the result.

```
SELECT date_part('year', OrderDate) AS OrderYear,
  TO_CHAR(OrderDate, 'MM-YYYY') AS "Month-Year",
  SUM(OrderAmount) AS OrderAmount
FROM Orders
GROUP BY date_part('year', OrderDate),
  date_part('month', OrderDate) , "Month-Year"
ORDER BY date_part('year', OrderDate),
  date_part('month', OrderDate);
```

	orderyear double prec	Month-Year text	orderamount numeric
1	2014	01-2014	253573.93
2	2014	02-2014	317900.02
3	2014	03-2014	173797.45
4	2014	04-2014	183837.69

Figure 9-8 Alternate way to display the month

Exercise 9.4: Group Orders By Month

In Exercise 9.3, you created a query that grouped all of the orders by year and month. The query that you will create in this exercise will group the orders by month for a specific year.

1. Create this query.

```
SELECT date_part('month', OrderDate) AS "2018OrderMonth",
  COUNT(*) AS "OrdersThisMonth",
  SUM(OrderAmount) AS "OrderAmount"
FROM Orders
WHERE date_part('year', OrderDate) = '2018'
GROUP BY date_part('month', OrderDate)
ORDER BY date_part('month', OrderDate);
```

2. Save the query as
   E9.4 Group orders by month.

   Figure 9-9 shows the result. 12 rows were returned. One for each month in 2018, that has orders.

   Each row displays the number of orders for the month and the order total amount for the month.

	2018OrderMonth double precision	OrdersThisMonth bigint	OrderAmount numeric
1	1	239	383434.81
2	2	163	313929.72
3	3	205	313386.42
4	4	224	327130.84
5	5	147	304173.17

Figure 9-9 Orders grouped by month for a specific year

Exercise 9.5: Filter Data For Specific Months

The query in Exercise 9.4 filtered on the year of the Order Date field. In this exercise, you will modify that query to only select orders for two months in the year.

1. Save the E9.4 query as `E9.5 Filter data for specific months.`

2. Change the WHERE clause, as shown below.

```
WHERE date_part('year', OrderDate) = '2018' AND
  date_part('month', OrderDate) IN ('06', '09')
```

   Figure 9-10 shows the result.

   Months 6 and 9 are June and September.

	2018OrderMonth double precision	OrdersThisMonth bigint	OrderAmount numeric
1	6	134	294646.27
2	9	118	181894.82

Figure 9-10 Data filtered for specific months

Example #6 Group Orders By Quarter

The query below will calculate the total order amount by quarter. Figure 9-11 shows the result. While this query creates totals for each quarter, the problem, from an analysis perspective, is that the totals are for all of the records in the table. More than likely, you only want to see quarterly totals for each year or a specific year.

```
SELECT date_part('quarter', OrderDate) AS "Quarter",
 SUM(OrderAmount) AS "OrderAmount"
FROM Orders
GROUP BY date_part('quarter', OrderDate)
ORDER BY date_part('quarter', OrderDate);
```

	Quarter double pı	OrderAmount numeric
1	1	4210117.04
2	2	3384858.55
3	3	6168823.53
4	4	3644979.81

Figure 9-11 Quarterly totals for all records

Exercise 9.6: Count And Sum Orders By Quarter

Exercise 9.2 counted orders by week in a specific year. The query that you will create in this exercise will count and sum orders by quarter, for one year. It is similar to the query in Example #6. There are other ways to create this query, but I think that this is the most straight forward and easiest way to understand the code. Figure 9-12 shows the result.

1. Create the query shown below.

```
SELECT date_part('quarter', OrderDate) AS "QuarterIn2017",
 COUNT(*) AS "Nbr_Of_Orders",
 '$' || SUM(OrderAmount) AS "Total_For_Quarter"
FROM Orders
WHERE date_part('year', OrderDate) = '2017'
GROUP BY "QuarterIn2017";
```

2. Save the query as
   `E9.6 2017 order totals by quarter.`

	QuarterIn2017 double precision	Nbr_Of_Orders bigint	Total_For_Quarter text
1	1	211	$460092.72
2	2	283	$543016.31
3	3	363	$680167.06
4	4	259	$357803.90

Figure 9-12 Orders counted and totaled by quarter, for 2017

Exercise 9.7: Create Quarterly Order Totals By Year

While the query in Exercise 9.6 works, it may be more helpful if the quarterly totals were grouped by year. In this exercise, you will modify the query in Exercise 9.6, to display quarterly totals for each year.

1. Create the query shown below.

```
SELECT date_part('year', OrderDate) AS "OrderYear",
  date_part('quarter', OrderDate) AS "Quarter",
  COUNT(*) AS "Nbr_Of_Orders",
  '$' || SUM(OrderAmount) AS "Total_For_Quarter"
FROM Orders
GROUP BY date_part('year', OrderDate), date_part('quarter', OrderDate)
ORDER BY date_part('year', OrderDate), date_part('quarter', OrderDate);
```

2. Save the query as
   `E9.7 Quarterly totals by year.`

   Figure 9-13 shows the result. 21 rows were returned. Compare the column headings to the ones shown above in Figure 9-12.

   Now you can see the quarterly totals for each year. In the real world, keep in mind that while it is possible that there are no orders for a specific quarter, that is not the norm and should be looked into, to make sure that there is no data for the quarter in question.

	OrderYear double precision	Quarter double precision	Nbr_Of_Orders bigint	Total_For_Quarter text
1	2014	1	327	$745271.40
2	2014	2	301	$420184.71
3	2014	3	409	$771208.94
4	2014	4	245	$367606.53
5	2015	1	619	$1248730.57
6	2015	2	627	$1069977.12

Figure 9-13 Orders grouped by year and quarter

Exercise 9.8: Filter, Group And Sort Data

The query that you create in this exercise will use the year and month identifiers to filter, group and sort the data. This query is based on the query that was created in Chapter 7, Exercise 7.8. The result will display order totals by region, order year and order month.

1. Create the query shown below.

```
SELECT RegionName, date_part('year', OrderDate) AS OrderYear,
   date_part('month', OrderDate) AS OrderMonth,
   SUM(OrderAmount) AS OrderTotal
FROM Customers INNER JOIN Orders ON Customers.CustomerID = Orders.CustomerID
  INNER JOIN Regions ON Customers.RegionID = Regions.RegionID
WHERE RegionName = 'South'
  AND date_part('year', OrderDate) IN ('2014', '2015', '2016')
  AND date_part('month', OrderDate) IN ('01', '02', '03')
GROUP BY RegionName, date_part('year', OrderDate),
  date_part('month', OrderDate)
ORDER BY RegionName, date_part('year', OrderDate),
  date_part('month', OrderDate);
```

2. Save the query as
   `E9.8 Filter group & sort data.`

   Figure 9-14 shows the result.

   The 9 rows that were returned, are for the first quarter of each year.

   When displayed in a bar chart, you would be able to easily compare the data for the same month, in each of the three years.

	regionname character var	orderyear double pre	ordermonth double preci	ordertotal numeric
1	South	2014	1	63441.78
2	South	2014	2	42700.86
3	South	2014	3	29347.39
4	South	2015	1	98481.54
5	South	2015	2	96127.25
6	South	2015	3	91140.40
7	South	2016	1	63917.73
8	South	2016	2	3306.72
9	South	2016	3	24014.58

Figure 9-14 Result of using the year and month identifiers

Exercise 9.9: Filter Data For A Specific Quarter

In this exercise, you will modify the query in Exercise 9.8, to select data in the second quarter of specific years.

1. Save the E9.8 query as `E9.9 Filter by quarter.`

2. Change the last row on the WHERE clause to
```
AND date_part('month', OrderDate)
  BETWEEN 4 AND 6
```

   Figure 9-15 shows the result. 8 rows were returned.

   As shown in 2014, there were no sales in the month of June.

	regionname character var	orderyear double prec	ordermonth double precis	ordertotal numeric
1	South	2014	4	33947.29
2	South	2014	5	15200.99
3	South	2015	4	45568.50
4	South	2015	5	60165.64
5	South	2015	6	122313.39
6	South	2016	4	52384.47
7	South	2016	5	15200.99
8	South	2016	6	23865.58

Figure 9-15 Result of data filtered by quarter

The INTERVAL Function

This function can be used to calculate a date or date range in the future or in the past, that will be used to retrieve data. The query in Example #7 demonstrates how this function can be used. The INTERVAL function has the three parameters explained below.

- ☑ The first parameter is the date (a hard coded date or the name of the date field) that the other two parameters will be applied to.
- ☑ The second parameter is used to select the interval that you want to add to or subtract from the date. To go forward in time, type a plus sign before the word interval. To go back in time, type a minus sign before the word interval.
- ☑ The third parameter is used to select the time period, like months or years, that you want to go forward or back in time.

Example #7 Calculate Days, Months And Years

This query demonstrates how to use the INTERVAL function to calculate periods of time. Figure 9-16 shows the result.

The numbers with the minus sign return a date in the past, based on the interval (day, year, etc), that is used.

```
SELECT OrderDate,
  OrderDate + interval '1' day AS "AddOneDay",
  OrderDate - interval '1' day AS "SubtractOneDay",
  OrderDate + interval '1' month AS "AddOneMonth",
  OrderDate - interval '1' month AS "SubtractOneMonth",
  OrderDate + interval '1' year AS "1YearForward",
  OrderDate - interval '1' year AS "1YearBack"
FROM Orders;
```

	orderdate date	AddOneDay timestamp wi	SubtractOneDay timestamp withou	AddOneMonth timestamp with	SubtractOneMonth timestamp without t	1YearForward timestamp with	1YearBack timestamp
1	2016-01-01	2016-01-02...	2015-12-31 00:...	2016-02-01 0...	2015-12-01 00:00...	2017-01-01 0...	2015-01-01
2	2016-01-01	2016-01-02...	2015-12-31 00:...	2016-02-01 0...	2015-12-01 00:00...	2017-01-01 0...	2015-01-01
3	2016-01-02	2016-01-03...	2016-01-01 00:...	2016-02-02 0...	2015-12-02 00:00...	2017-01-02 0...	2015-01-02
4	2016-01-02	2016-01-03...	2016-01-01 00:...	2016-02-02 0...	2015-12-02 00:00...	2017-01-02 0...	2015-01-02

Figure 9-16 Result of using the INTERVAL function

Example #8 Calculate Previous And Future Dates

This query calculates dates in the future and in the past. The dates that are calculated are based on the order date.

For example, the quarter expressions calculate a date, three quarters ahead and three quarters back from the Order Date. Figure 9-17 shows the result.

```
SELECT OrderDate,
  OrderDate + interval '90' day AS "Next90Days",
  OrderDate + interval '2' month AS "Next2Months",
  OrderDate - interval '2' month AS "2MonthsBack",
  OrderDate + interval '9' month AS "Next3Quarters",
  OrderDate - interval '9' month AS "Previous3Quarters"
FROM Orders;
```

I used the month identifier to calculate the quarters because the INTERVAL function does not have a quarter option.

	orderdate date	Next90Days timestamp witl	Next2Months timestamp wit	2MonthsBack timestamp witl	Next3Quarters timestamp withc	Previous3Quarters timestamp without
1	2016-01-01	2016-03-31 ...	2016-03-01 ...	2015-11-01 ...	2016-10-01 00...	2015-04-01 00:00:...
2	2016-01-01	2016-03-31 ...	2016-03-01 ...	2015-11-01 ...	2016-10-01 00...	2015-04-01 00:00:...
3	2016-01-02	2016-04-01 ...	2016-03-02 ...	2015-11-02 ...	2016-10-02 00...	2015-04-02 00:00:...
4	2016-01-02	2016-04-01 ...	2016-03-02 ...	2015-11-02 ...	2016-10-02 00...	2015-04-02 00:00:...

Figure 9-17 Result of a query that calculates previous and future dates

Exercise 9.10: Calculate The Expected Order Ship Date

Some companies say that they will ship orders within three days of when the order was placed. In this exercise, you will create a query that calculates the expected ship date based on this criteria.

1. Create this query.

```
SELECT OrderID, OrderDate,
 OrderDate + interval '3' day AS ExpectedShipDate
FROM Orders;
```

2. Save the query as `E9.10 Calculate the expected ship date.`

   Figure 9-18 shows the result.

   The dates in the Expected Ship Date column are three days greater than the Order Date. The date in this column is when the order should ship by.

	orderid integer	orderdate date	expectedshipdate timestamp without
1	1	2016-01-01	2016-01-04 00:00:0
2	2	2016-01-01	2016-01-04 00:00:0
3	3	2016-01-02	2016-01-05 00:00:0
4	4	2016-01-02	2016-01-05 00:00:0

Figure 9-18 Result of the Expected Ship Date calculation

Exercise 9.11: Use The INTERVAL Function To Create A Date Range

In previous chapters when you needed to create date range filter criteria, you typed in the start date and end date, with the BETWEEN operator.

In this exercise, you will use the INTERVAL function, in addition to the BETWEEN operator, to return orders that are at least 60 days before the date specified in the query. Another way to say it is, "Create a date range that is between the specified date (9/19/2016) and 60 days prior to that date".

1. Create this query.

```
SELECT OrderID, SalesRep, OrderDate, OrderAmount
FROM Orders INNER JOIN SalesReps
  ON Orders.SalesRepID = SalesReps.SalesRepID
WHERE OrderDate BETWEEN date '2016-09-19' - interval '60' day
  AND '2016-09-19'
ORDER BY OrderDate;
```

2. Save the query as `E9.11 Date range created with the INTERVAL function.`

Figure 9-19 shows orders that are between 9/19/2016 and up to 60 days prior.
758 rows were returned.

	orderid integer	salesrep character varying	orderdate date	orderamount numeric (18,2)
1	836	Michael Suyama	2016-07-21	2294.55
2	837	Robert King	2016-07-21	1619.40
3	838	Anne Dodsworth	2016-07-21	1205.24
4	839	Robert King	2016-07-21	11759.40

Figure 9-19 Result of using the INTERVAL function

> If you have used the **DATEDIFF FUNCTION** with a SQL Sever database, the **INTERVAL FUNCTION** in PostgreSQL, works in a similar way.

Exercise 9.12: Calculate The Order Processing Time

In this exercise, you will create an expression to find out how long it is between the day an order is placed and the day the order was shipped. This is known as the order processing time. The result of this expression will let you know if the expected number of days, that orders need to be shipped in, is met. For example, if all orders need to be shipped in three days, any order with a number greater than three, in the calculated column that you will create, indicates that the order was not shipped within the expected time frame.

1. Create this query.

```
SELECT OrderID, OrderDate, ShipDate,
  ShipDate - OrderDate AS "OrderProcessingTime"
FROM Orders;
```

2. Save the query as `E9.12 Calculate the order processing time.`

Figure 9-20 shows the result.

All of the rows in the Orders table were returned.

	orderid integer	orderdate date	shipdate date	OrderProcessingTime integer
6	6	2016-01-03	2016-01-23	20
7	7	2016-01-03	2016-01-04	1
8	8	2016-01-04	2016-01-05	1
9	9	2016-01-04	2016-01-04	0

Figure 9-20 Order processing times calculated

> A zero in the Order Processing Time column, shown above in Figure 9-20, means that the order was shipped within 24 hours of when it was placed. Depending on the time that an order was placed and shipped, the Ship Date could be the next day and still have a zero in the Order Processing Time column. That is because the order was shipped in 24 hours or less. Remember that in the real world, that both of these date fields would use the time portion of a date field. For the order processing time to really be accurate, the time portion of the date field needs to have data.

Exercise 9.13: Find Out If Orders Were Shipped On Time

In this exercise, you will create a query that will determine whether or not orders were shipped on time. The query will check to see if the Ship Date is greater than the Required Date. If it is, the order was shipped late.

1. Create this query.

```
SELECT OrderID AS OrderNbr, RequiredDate, ShipDate,
  CASE
   WHEN ShipDate - RequiredDate >0
   THEN 'Shipped Late'
   ELSE 'On Time'
   END Status
FROM Orders;
```

2. Save the query as
   `E9.13 Was the order shipped on time.`

   Figure 9-21 shows the result.

   The name of the last column, "Status" was created on the last line of the CASE statement, on the END clause.

	ordernbr integer	requireddate date	shipdate date	status text
1	1	2016-01-10	2016-01-03	On Time
2	2	2016-01-07	2016-01-04	On Time
3	3	2016-01-09	2016-01-14	Shipped Late
4	4	2016-01-09	2016-01-03	On Time

Figure 9-21 Order shipped status

Understanding The TIMESTAMP Data Type
As you know, the TIMESTAMP data type (which is the same as the DATETIME data type in other SQL databases) stores the date and time. In PostgreSQL, the following also applies to any field that stores a date and time. As shown in Figure 9-22, some of the time values are displayed as zeros. This means that when data is written to the table that stores the Order Date field, the time portion is not being used. On your own, you have to find out if the time portion of a date field that you need to use, actually writes the time to the field. If not, you are home free and can continue to use date fields, as you have been using them in this book. You are also home free if the date fields that you use have the DATE data type.

If you find out that the time is written to any date field that you need to use, you will have to take that into account when using a date field. The reason is because the time is included in the filter criteria, whether you type in the time or not. For example, the first query shown in Example #9 does not include any time in the filter criteria, but SQL will default the time to all zeros. In some expressions, like the one in Exercise 9.13, this means that if the date field has a time other then all zeros, the row will not be returned. This can drastically alter the rows that are returned, or should I say, the rows that are not returned, that should be returned. Yes, this is a big problem if you are not aware of it. I have often referred to this as the "dirty little date field secret".

Example #9 Using Dates To Filter Data

What you have probably figured out by now is that PostgreSQL does not use the same rules when it comes to dates, that other SQL databases follow and enforce. If you need to search a field that has the TIMESTAMP data type or a field that stores a date and time, you need to be aware of the following, as the query may not return the records that you are expecting.

Figure 9-22 shows a table where the Order Date field has the TIMESTAMP data type. As shown, some dates have a time and others do not.

If I run the query below, which looks for orders on June 24, 2018, I expect row 2 in Figure 9-22 to be returned. Instead, no rows are returned, as shown in Figure 9-23. What gives?

	DateID characte	OrderDate timestamp without ti
1	1	2018-03-01 00:00:00
2	2	2018-06-24 10:45:12
3	3	2018-06-25 09:02:25
4	4	2018-09-19 00:00:00

Figure 9-22 Field that stores a date and time

```
SELECT *
FROM practice_dates
WHERE OrderDate = '2018-06-24';
```

DateID characte	OrderDate timestamp

Figure 9-23 Result of the query

Because the query above did not include a time, a zero time of midnight ('00:00:00') is automatically added to the code behind the scenes. The 6/24/2018 order date has a time, but the query is searching for this date and time '2018-06-24 00:00:00' and that date and time is not in the table. (See Figure 9-22 above) There are a few ways to resolve this problem, as explained below.

Option 1 Create A Date Range

Create a date range that only includes the specific date that you want to retrieve records for. Figure 9-24 shows the result. The one row with the 6/24/2018 date was retrieved, when the query below is run. This concept can also be used if you want to find records in a date range, by changing the second date in the query below, to the date **AFTER** the last date that you want to retrieve data for.

You may be thinking that the last date in the query should be the same date as the first date. Using the same date with a field that has the TIMESTAMP (aka date/time) data type and not typing in a time, would not achieve the expected result.

```
SELECT *
FROM practice_dates
WHERE OrderDate >= '2018-06-24' AND OrderDate
  < '2018-06-25';
```

	DateID	OrderDate
1	2	2018-06-24 10:45:12

Figure 9-24 Result of creating a date range

Option 2 Split The Date Up

This option uses a function to select a specific portion of the date, as shown in this query. This query returns the row shown above in Figure 9-24.

```
SELECT *
FROM practice_dates
WHERE date_part('month', OrderDate) = '6'
  AND date_part('day', OrderDate) = '24'
  AND date_part('year', OrderDate) = '2018';
```

As the queries in this example demonstrate, there is often more than one way to solve a problem.

Calculating The Last Day Of The Month Dates

Being able to create an expression that finds the last day of the month is useful when you need to calculate a maturity date, like when a warranty expires. While some other SQL databases have functions that calculate at least one of these dates (a start or end of month date), PostgreSQL does not support any SQL function that can calculate a start or end of month date. This is one of those times, when you need to think outside the box to come up with a solution. In this case, the **DATE_TRUNC FUNCTION** will be used with the **INTERVAL FUNCTION** to calculate the last day of the month.

Exercise 9.14: Find Past, Current And Future End Of Month Dates

In this exercise, you will create a query that will display several end of month dates based on the value in the Order Date field.

1. Create the query shown below.

```
SELECT OrderDate,
date_trunc('month', OrderDate) + interval '1 month - 1 day' AS "ThisMonth",
date_trunc('month', OrderDate) + interval '2 month - 1 day' AS "NextMonth",
date_trunc('month', OrderDate) + interval '4 month - 1 day' AS
  "3MonthsForward",
date_trunc('month', OrderDate) - interval '1 day' AS "LastMonth",
date_trunc('month', OrderDate) - interval '2 month + 1 day' AS "3MonthsBack"
FROM Orders
WHERE OrderDate BETWEEN '2016-12-30' and '2017-01-04'
ORDER BY OrderDate;
```

2. Save the query as `E9.14 Calculate end of month dates.`
   Figure 9-25 shows the result, which is based on the date in the first column.

	orderdate date	ThisMonth timestamp wi	NextMonth timestamp wi	3MonthsForward timestamp with tim	LastMonth timestamp wi	3MonthsBack timestamp wit
12	2016-12-31	2016-12-31...	2017-01-31...	2017-03-31 00:0...	2016-11-30...	2016-09-30 0...
13	2017-01-01	2017-01-31...	2017-02-28...	2017-04-30 00:0...	2016-12-31...	2016-10-31 0...
14	2017-01-01	2017-01-31...	2017-02-28...	2017-04-30 00:0...	2016-12-31...	2016-10-31 0...

Figure 9-25 Result of using the DATE_TRUNC function

The "This Month" column stores the end of month date, for the order date.
The "Next Month" column stores the end of month date, for the month after the order date month.
The "3 Months Forward" column stores the end of month date, for the 3rd month after the order date month.
The "Last Month" column stores the end of month date, for the month before the order date month.
The "3 Months Back" column stores the end of month date, for the 3rd month prior to the order date month.

Exercise 9.15: Calculate Daily Sales Totals

The query that you will create in this exercise, will calculate the sales total for each day in September 2017.

1. Create this query.

```
SELECT date_part('day', OrderDate) AS "Sept",
  COUNT(*) AS "# Of Orders",
  SUM(OrderAmount) AS "Daily Total"
FROM Orders
WHERE OrderDate BETWEEN '2017-09-01' AND '2017-09-30'
GROUP BY date_part('day', OrderDate)
ORDER BY "Sept";
```

2. Save the query as `E9.15 Daily sales totals.`

   Figure 9-26 shows the result. 30 rows were returned. One row for each day that there are orders in September 2017.

	Sept doubl	# Of Orders bigint	Daily Total numeric
1	1	8	9140.06
2	2	1	542.86
3	3	5	4002.72
4	4	1	617.60

Figure 9-26 Daily sales totals

> An alternate way to create the WHERE clause portion of the query in Exercise 9.15, especially if you can't remember how many days are in the month used in a query is:
> WHERE date_part('year', OrderDate) = '2017' AND date_part('month', OrderDate) = '06'.
> This is probably a better solution to use, if the year used in the query is a leap year.

Example #10 Daily Shipping Totals

The logic needed to create this query is the same as the logic used to create the daily sales totals query, that you just created in Exercise 9.15. The difference is that this query will use the Ship Date field instead of the Order Date field. This means that orders placed before 9/1/2017 could be included in the shipping totals because the order date is not part of the equation. Think about orders that were placed in August, but were out of stock or orders placed on the last day of August. In either scenario, it is very possible that the order will not be shipped until some time in September.

The query below calculates how many orders were shipped in September 2017. Figure 9-27 shows the result. 27 rows were returned. That means that there are three days in September 2017 that no orders were shipped.

```
SELECT date_part('day', ShipDate) AS "Sept",
  COUNT(*) AS "# Of Orders Shipped",
  SUM(OrderAmount) AS
    "Shipped Total For The Day"
FROM Orders
WHERE ShipDate BETWEEN '2017-09-01'
   AND '2017-09-30'
GROUP BY date_part('day', ShipDate)
ORDER BY "Sept";
```

	Sept doub	# Of Orders Shipped bigint	Shipped Total For The Day numeric
1	1	6	680.27
2	2	4	5224.30
3	3	5	5040.72
4	4	6	7103.41

Figure 9-27 Orders shipped in September 2017

Example #11 Calculate Monthly Order Totals

The query below calculates the order totals by month in 2017. It is similar to the query that you created in Exercise 9.15.

Figure 9-28 shows the result. As you may have guessed, 12 rows were returned. One for each month of the year.

```
SELECT
  date_part('month',OrderDate) AS "Month",
  COUNT(*) AS "# Of Orders",
  SUM(OrderAmount) AS "Total For The Month"
FROM Orders
WHERE date_part('year', OrderDate) = '2017'
GROUP BY date_part('month', OrderDate)
ORDER BY "Month";
```

	Month double	# Of Orders bigint	Total For The Month numeric
1	1	89	214190.08
2	2	49	92130.36
3	3	73	153772.28
4	4	96	152757.72
5	5	67	123442.93
6	6	120	266815.66
7	7	116	287134.78
8	8	129	211137.46
9	9	118	181894.82
10	10	91	123200.52
11	11	36	67343.10
12	12	132	167260.28

Figure 9-28 Monthly sales totals

Exercise 9.16: Calculate A Persons Age

In this exercise, you will create an expression to calculate the sales reps current age. More than likely, you will see different ages (higher), then the ones shown in the figure. That is because you are creating this query after I did and some people in the database will have had another birthday.

1. Create this query.

```
SELECT SalesRep, BirthDate AS Birthday,
  AGE(CURRENT_DATE, BirthDate) AS "AGE"
FROM SalesReps;
```

2. Save the query as `E9.16 Calculate age.`

   Figure 9-29 shows the age of the sales reps.

	salesrep character varying (5	birthday date	AGE interval
1	Nancy Davolio	1972-12-08	47 years 7 days
2	Andrew Fuller	1969-02-19	50 years 9 mons 24 days
3	Janet Leverling	1971-08-30	48 years 3 mons 16 days
4	Margaret Peacock	1973-09-19	46 years 2 mons 26 days

Figure 9-29 Age calculated

Calculate The Retirement Year

In this part of the exercise, you will add a field to the query that calculates the earliest retirement year, based on being able to retire at age 67. The calculated field expression, adds 67 years to the birth date.

1. Save the E9.16 query as `E9.16 Calculate the retirement year.`

2. Add the expression on the third line shown below, to the query.

```
SELECT SalesRep, BirthDate AS Birthday,
  AGE(CURRENT_DATE, BirthDate) AS "AGE",
   date_part('year', BirthDate) + 67 AS "Earliest Retirement Year"
FROM SalesReps;
```

Figure 9-30 shows the earliest retirement date, in the last column.

	salesrep character varying (5(	birthday date	AGE interval	Earliest Retirement Year double precision
1	Nancy Davolio	1972-12-08	47 years 8 days	2039
2	Andrew Fuller	1969-02-19	50 years 9 mons 25 days	2036
3	Janet Leverling	1971-08-30	48 years 3 mons 17 days	2038
4	Margaret Peacock	1973-09-19	46 years 2 mons 27 days	2040

Figure 9-30 Earliest retirement date calculated

Displaying Month Names

You may need to display the month name or day of the week, instead of the corresponding number. Some of the date formatting options covered earlier in Table 9-3, allow you to do that.

Sorting on an expression that uses one of the date formatting options will display the result in alphabetical order. That may or may not be what you want. If you want to sort the data and want the results displayed in the order that they would appear in, if the numeric values were used to sort on, using one of these options will get the job done. In some instances, using one of the date formatting options on the GROUP BY clause, will sort the rows in the order that you need, without adding it to the ORDER BY clause.

Exercise 9.17: Format A Date Field To Display The Month Name

In this exercise, you will modify the query that you created in Exercise 9.4, to display the month name.

1. Save the E9.4 query as `E9.17 Display the month name.`

2. Change the second and seventh lines, as shown in Figure 9-31.

```
1 SELECT date_part('month', OrderDate) AS "2018OrderMonth",
2   TO_CHAR(OrderDate, 'Month') AS "MonthName",
3   COUNT(*) AS "OrdersThisMonth",
4   SUM(OrderAmount) AS "OrderAmount"
5 FROM Orders
6 WHERE date_part('year', OrderDate) = '2018'
7 GROUP BY date_part('month', OrderDate), TO_CHAR(OrderDate, 'Month')
8 ORDER BY date_part('month', OrderDate);
```

Figure 9-31 Modified query

Figure 9-32 shows the result.

The ORDER BY clause did not have to be modified, because it sorts on the month number of the Order Date field, which is what you want in this exercise.

	2018OrderMonth double precision	MonthName text	OrdersThisMonth bigint	OrderAmount numeric
1	1	January	239	383434.81
2	2	February	163	313929.72
3	3	March	205	313386.42
4	4	April	224	327130.84
5	5	May	147	304173.17
6	6	June	134	294646.27
7	7	July	123	313481.73
8	8	August	132	219437.06
9	9	September	118	181894.82
10	10	October	127	244805.39
11	11	November	139	241880.36
12	12	December	112	156269.27

Figure 9-32 Month name displayed

Example #12 Revise The Query In Exercise 9.3

In Exercise 9.3, you created a query that calculated monthly order totals. That query would be easier to understand if it displayed the month name, instead of the month number. The query below is a revised version of the query in that exercise. The changes are on the second, 5th and 6th lines. This query displays the month name, as shown in Figure 9-33. As you can see, the month names are not in calendar month order. You can work that out on your own.

```
SELECT date_part('year', OrderDate) AS "OrderYear",
  TO_CHAR(OrderDate, 'Month') AS "MonthName",
  SUM(OrderAmount) AS "OrderAmount"
FROM Orders
GROUP BY date_part('year', OrderDate),  TO_CHAR(OrderDate, 'Month')
ORDER BY date_part('year', OrderDate),  TO_CHAR(OrderDate, 'Month');
```

	OrderYear double prec	MonthName text	OrderAmount numeric
1	2014	April	183837.69
2	2014	August	211137.46
3	2014	December	11147.60
4	2014	February	317900.02
5	2014	January	253573.93

Figure 9-33 Result of revised query for Exercise 9.3

Exercise 9.18: Group Orders By The Week Day

In this exercise, you will create a query that groups the orders by the week day and provides a total order amount for each day. The day DATE_PART identifier allows you to see which day of the week has the most orders. The total column will let you see which day made the most money. The query will only use data for one month. On your own, you do not have to filter the data this way.

1. Create the query shown below.

```
SELECT TO_CHAR(OrderDate, 'Day') AS "WeekDay",
  COUNT(*) AS "NbrOfOrders",
  SUM(OrderAmount) AS "WeekDayTotal"
FROM Orders
WHERE OrderDate Between '2018-09-01' AND '2018-09-30'
GROUP BY date_part('dow', OrderDate), TO_CHAR(OrderDate, 'Day')
ORDER BY date_part('dow', OrderDate);
```

2. Save the query as `E9.18 Group orders by the week day.`

   Figure 9-34 shows the seven rows that were returned.

   Notice that the weekday names are in the order that you expected.

   The value in the Nbr Of Orders column is a count of orders for all occurrences of that day of the week, in the date range. Keep in mind that these totals are for a month.

	WeekDay text	NbrOfOrders bigint	WeekDayTotal numeric
1	Sunday	21	39669.35
2	Monday	8	4218.82
3	Tuesday	17	35097.77
4	Wednesday	14	23962.10
5	Thursday	8	19939.14
6	Friday	27	34677.40
7	Saturday	23	24330.24

Figure 9-34 Data grouped and totaled by the day

Summary

This chapter covered dates, dates and more dates functionality. You learned how to create expressions, format dates and use some of the most popular ways to use dates, to create queries that are date driven.

Unlike the majority of chapters in this book, this chapter only focused on one topic; using date fields in calculations. I did this on purpose, because on your own, you will probably find that a large percent of the queries that you will need to create, are date driven.

Some of the date concepts that were introduced are used to analyze data over time. These concepts can be used to compare current data with data in previous or future periods of time, return data for months, quarters or years and much more. This chapter also covered how to create totals by month and year, filter data for a range of dates, filter data for a specific date and more.

This chapter also covered a variety of options and techniques that you will be able to use to format dates. The options covered, should let you get the dates in a format that helps make the data easier to understand, when presented in a report.

While the list of queries that are date driven is probably longer then this chapter, hopefully this chapter has given you the foundation to create date driven queries using your own data. I tried to provide more than the basics of creating queries that will be used to analyze data over time.

Now, it's time to learn about aggregate functions.

USING AGGREGATE FUNCTIONS AND CREATING SUMMARY QUERIES

After reading this chapter and completing the exercises you will:

- ☑ Know what the aggregate functions are and how to use them
- ☑ Be able to create summary queries
- ☑ Know about the GROUP BY subclauses: ROLLUP, CUBE and GROUPING SETS

CHAPTER 10

Overview

The primary goal of this chapter is to provide an understanding of the aggregate functions. This understanding will allow you to explore the new techniques covered in this chapter, which may be the answer for some of the types of queries that you already know that you need to create on your own. In addition to the aggregate functions, summary queries are also covered in this chapter. As you will see, aggregate functions and summary queries go hand in hand. Some of the queries that you created in previous chapters, used the COUNT and SUM aggregate functions. Those queries are summary queries.

This chapter is where you will take a deeper dive into creating queries that will be used to analyze data. I say that because analyzing data is much more than selecting records in a table. Selecting the correct tables and columns is the starting point. Then comes filtering the data as needed. And when using more than one table, joining the tables correctly is a must.

Aggregating data creates what is known as a **SUMMARY QUERY**. A summary query does not display the detail rows that the majority of queries that this book has presented, up to this point. Instead, the aggregate functions are used to calculate a total, count or value for one or more columns and present a summary of the detail rows that have been selected.

This type of query rolls up the detail rows, if you will, and presents the data with averages, counts and totals. While this may sound complex or like there is a lot of math involved, the reality is that there are really only four types of aggregate calculations that you will use on a regular basis. The four types of aggregate calculations that you will use most often are:

① Group data using aggregated expressions. This is the equivalent of creating sub totals. (1)
② Creating grand totals. This type of calculation creates a total for the rows in a table, minus any rows that are filtered out. (1)
③ Calculate the average value of data in a column.
④ Find the minimum or maximum value in a column of data.

(1) This type of calculation primarily uses the SUM or COUNT aggregate function.

More than likely, 90 to 95% of the summary queries that you will create are the first two types of aggregate calculations listed above. It may seem that some of the queries in this chapter are duplicates. They are not. A goal is to help you understand the difference between what each query needs to accomplish. That way, when you are on your own, you will take your time to understand the requirements for the query and not rush to judgment and create a query that really does not answer the question.

While you have already created a few summary queries, earlier in this book, this chapter is the formal introduction to summary queries and starts from the beginning, so to speak. By that I mean that in addition to explaining the aggregate functions, the basics of creating summary queries is also explained. Some of the expressions and summary queries covered in this chapter are easier then some of the summary queries that you have already created in this book. And there are a few summary queries covered in this chapter that may make you want a spirited beverage. <smile>

Introduction To Aggregating Data

This section provides an overview of aggregate functions and how they are used. Understanding the power of aggregate functions will be very helpful when creating queries. This is especially true for anyone that has not created a lot of expressions (aka formulas) or queries before.

You have already learned about relationships and how they are used to join tables, to be able to use data from more than one table, at the same time. Hopefully, taking that knowledge and combining it with the knowledge that you will gain in this chapter about aggregate functions, will make it easier to understand the data that is needed to create aggregate expressions.

Aggregate expressions are used to group or summarize data. The way that data is displayed in a table makes it difficult to know column totals, see trends in the data, or answer "What-If" analysis type questions. For example, if you looked at the data in Figure 10-1, can you tell which sales rep had the most sales or what the top five selling products were? Probably not.

When added to a report, the result of a query that has at least one aggregate function (one column with aggregated data), will allow the data shown in Figure 10-1, to be grouped or summarized to answer these questions and much more.

	orderid integer	orderamount numeric (18,2)	customerid integer	salesrepid integer	orderdate date
1	1	2645.87	55	9	2016-01-01
2	2	8908.05	39	9	2016-01-01
3	3	39.80	61	7	2016-01-02
4	4	43.80	9	3	2016-01-02

Figure 10-1 Table of raw data

Aggregating data includes averaging, counting and totaling data. Aggregating data also includes finding the minimum or maximum value. You will also learn how to perform aggregations on a subset of data in tables, which allows you to create subtotals and grand totals. This is accomplished by using the GROUP BY clause to extend the functionality of the aggregate functions.

Being able to create these types of aggregate calculations allows the reports that are created from the data retrieved by a query, to be more precise and informative. That is because the reports can display the overall picture (a summary query) of the data to be visualized, in a way that looking at rows (possibly hundreds or thousands) of raw data cannot. Hopefully, you are starting to see how important aggregated data is to creating reports.

What Is A Summary Query?

A summary query is a SELECT statement that uses one or more aggregate functions. This type of query summarizes the detail rows of data that you have seen queries up to this point return. For example, you can create a summary query to provide a count of the number of products, in each category or a summary query that provides quarterly and yearly sales totals by state.

Aggregate Functions

Aggregate functions are used to calculate one value from the rows returned or from the values calculated in an expression. These functions can be applied to all values or rows. They can also be applied to a specific set of rows or values, based on the criteria on the WHERE clause. For example, you can use an aggregate function to count the number of rows retrieved or sum the values in a column, based on the WHERE clause criteria.

The previous sections explained what aggregated data is used for. Aggregate functions could be the most used category of functions, because many types of reports need sub totals or grand totals. The functions in Table 10-1 are the aggregate functions. Aggregate functions are most often used with the SELECT, GROUP BY and HAVING clauses.

Aggregate functions are used to create calculated fields. If you have used the options on the drop-down list of the Auto Sum button in Excel, you are already familiar with most of the aggregate functions covered in this chapter.

How Aggregate Functions Calculate Values
Aggregate functions only include records that have a value in the field used in the calculation. This means that records that do not have a value in the field, are not included in the calculation. The exception is the COUNT(*) function. Why is there always an exception? <smile>

Earlier in this book, you learned how to use **SCALAR FUNCTIONS**, which use a single value and return a single value. Aggregate functions work differently. They operate by using a series of values and return a single summarized value.

Aggregate functions return a single value from a calculation that uses a set of values (a column in most cases). This is what makes an aggregate function different from the other types of functions that have been covered in this book. The other functions that were covered, are applied to each row in a table. Aggregate functions do not work at this detail level and do not display details for each individual row. Instead, aggregate functions provide the result of grouping detail rows of data.

> **Aggregate Function Tips**
> ① While aggregate functions are used in an expression, the "expression", if you will, is usually just the column that you want to apply the aggregate function to.
> ② By default, aggregate functions do not create a column name. The aggregate function will be displayed as the column name, if a column alias is not provided, as shown in Figure 10-2. Therefore, a good programming technique is to include an alias when using aggregate functions.

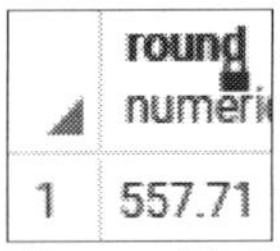

Figure 10-2 Result of not using a column alias

Function	This Function . . .
ARRAY_AGG	Accepts a set of values and returns an array from a set of values.
AVG	Calculates the average of the values in a column. (2)
COUNT(*)	Returns a single value. This value is the number of rows in the dataset. **THIS IS THE ONLY FUNCTION THAT DOES NOT IGNORE NULL VALUES.** This function counts rows. It does not count values.
COUNT()	Returns the number of rows that have a (non null) value in the column.
MAX	Finds the largest value in the column.
MIN	Finds the smallest value in the column.
STDDEV	(standard deviation) Calculates how far from the mean (the average) each value in the selected column deviates, based on the sample of the data population.
STRING_AGG	Concatenates string values and places a separators between them.
SUM	Adds the values in a column to get a total. (2)

Table 10-1 Aggregate functions explained

(2) This function only works with numeric values. Non numeric values and string data in the column is ignored.

Aggregate Function Syntax

The syntax for aggregate functions is: aggregate function name ([ALL | DISTINCT] expression). The options are explained below.

The **ALL KEYWORD** is used with the aggregate function. It tells the aggregate function to use all values. This is the default, which means that you do not have to type the ALL function in the query. The exception is NULL values, which are excluded from all of the aggregate functions, except the COUNT(*) function.

The **DISTINCT KEYWORD** returns unique values that are not NULL. Most of the time, this keyword will only be used with the COUNT function. It doesn't make sense to use it with the AVG and SUM functions. While you can use the DISTINCT keyword with the MIN or MAX function, it does not alter the value that is returned. That is because the MIN and MAX functions only return one value.

The **EXPRESSION** can use any data type except the **LARGE OBJECT BINARY (LOB)** data types. The expression cannot use an aggregate function or a **SUBQUERY**.

AVG, MIN And MAX Function Characteristics

These functions create a value, exactly as their names suggest. Each of these functions have characteristics that you should be aware of. The characteristics are covered when the function is covered in this chapter.

AVG Function

This function adds (sums) all of the values in the column and then divides that value by the number of rows in the context of the query.

AVG Function Characteristics

This function handles non numeric values in the column, in the following ways.

☑ Rows that have a zero are included in the calculation and are counted as a row in the expression.

☑ Empty cells, NULL or logical values are ignored and are not counted as a row in the expression.

☑ The expression created with this function must produce a numeric value.

☑ Columns used with this function must have values. If not, the expression will evaluate to NULL and the function does not process/include the row.

☑ If the column contains text, the query will return blanks.

Exercise 10.1: Calculate The Average Retail Price Of All Products

In this exercise, you will create a query that calculates the average retail price of all products.

1. Create this query.

```
SELECT AVG(RetailPrice) AS AvgRetailPrice
FROM Products;
```

2. Save the query as `E10.1 Average retail price.`

   Figure 10-3 shows the result.

	avgretailprice numeric
1	57.7124347826086957

Figure 10-3 Average retail price calculated

Example #1 Rounding Numeric Values

Sometimes, you will want numeric values to only display 2 decimal places. To accomplish this, the ROUND function is used.

The query below calculates the average shipping amount shown. As shown in Figure 10-4, the value has several decimal places.

```
SELECT AVG(ShippingAmount) AS AvgShippingAmount
FROM Orders;
```

	avgshippingamount numeric
1	18.1011451084731887

Figure 10-4 Average shipping amount

The query below includes the code to round the number to 2 decimal places, as shown in Figure 10-5.

```
SELECT ROUND(AVG(ShippingAmount), 2)
  AS AvgShippingAmountRounded
FROM Orders;
```

	avgshippingamountrounded numeric
1	18.10

Figure 10-5 Average shipping amount rounded

Exercise 10.2: Calculate The Average List Price For Each Product Category

The query that you will create in this exercise, will calculate the average retail price for the products in each product category. Like other functions that you have used with the GROUP BY clause, the AVG function returns a value for each group, instead of a single value for the entire table, like you saw in Exercise 10.1.

1. Create the query shown below.

```
SELECT CategoryName, ROUND(AVG(RetailPrice),2) AS AvgRetailPrice
FROM Products INNER JOIN ProductCategory
  ON Products.ProductCategoryID = ProductCategory.ProductCategoryID
GROUP BY CategoryName
ORDER BY CategoryName;
```

2. Save the query as `E10.2 Product category average price.`

   Figure 10-6 shows some of the eight rows that were returned.

	categoryname character varying (	avgretailprice numeric
1	Bicycle Locks	18.19
2	Children's Bicycle	278.10
3	Gloves	15.21
4	Helmets	43.81

Figure 10-6 Average retail price for each category

Example #2 Using The DISTINCT Keyword With The AVG Function

This query is almost the same as the one that you created in Exercise 10.2. The difference is one word. In the query below, the DISTINCT keyword has been added. Figure 10-7 shows the result. Notice that some of the values returned are less than shown above in Figure 10-6. That is because rows in the result set that have the same average retail price, are not included in the result of this query, more than once.

```
SELECT CategoryName,
  ROUND(AVG(DISTINCT(RetailPrice)), 2) AS AvgRetailPrice
FROM Products INNER JOIN ProductCategory
  ON Products.ProductCategoryID = ProductCategory.ProductCategoryID
GROUP BY CategoryName
ORDER BY CategoryName;
```

	categoryname character varying (	avgretailprice numeric
1	Bicycle Locks	17.65
2	Children's Bicycle	278.10
3	Gloves	15.00
4	Helmets	43.23
5	Mountain Bicycle	1859.85
6	Road Bicycle	524.85
7	Saddles	188.33
8	Touring Bicycle	686.10

Figure 10-7 Result of the DISTINCT keyword added to the query

More than likely, on your own, when presented with a query that uses an aggregate function, you need to determine exactly what is being requested. For example, in the query above, what you need to find out is if all rows with the same retail price should only be counted once or if all rows with the same retail price should be counted. When the result shown in Figure 10-7 is compared to Figure 10-6, you can see the difference (reduction) in the values, in the last column. As you will see later in Example #9, the same logic also holds true for the COUNT(Column) function, when the DISTINCT keyword is used.

Example #3 Calculate The Average Retail Price For Each Sub Category

If the query in Exercise 10.2 was modified as shown below, the average retail price would be calculated for the sub category, as shown in Figure 10-8.

```
SELECT SubCategory, ROUND(AVG(RetailPrice), 2)
  AS AvgRetailPrice
FROM Products INNER JOIN ProductCategory
  ON Products.ProductCategoryID =
    ProductCategory.ProductCategoryID
GROUP BY SubCategory
ORDER BY SubCategory;
```

	subcategory character varyi	avgretailprice numeric
1	Adult Helmet	43.81
2	ATB Lock	18.19
3	Chain Locks	18.19
4	Child Helmet	43.81

Figure 10-8 Subcategory average retail price

If you look at the average retail price for bicycle locks in Figure 10-6, you will see that the average retail price is the same as the average price for each sub category, in the category. For example, the average price for the ATB Lock and Chain Locks sub categories shown in Figure 10-8, is the same as the Bicycle Locks category in Figure 10-6. The reason that the values are the same in both figures is because all of the products in a sub category have the same category.

Tips For Using The GROUP BY Clause With Aggregated Data

① The fields that you add to the GROUP BY clause need to be listed in an order that makes sense. The rule of thumb is to put the highest level field first on the GROUP BY clause, then work your way down. For example, if you wanted a group for each of these three fields, city, state and country, the order that you would list them in, on the GROUP BY clause is country, state, city.

② When a query has two or more fields on the GROUP BY clause, they provide a hierarchical view of the data. One example is grouping on the Product Category and Sub Category columns. The hierarchy corresponds to the order that are in, on the GROUP BY clause.

Exercise 10.3: Filter The Product Categories Average Retail Price

In this exercise, you will modify the query created in Exercise 10.2 to select product categories that have an average retail price >= $250.

1. Save the E10.2 query as `E10.3 Average retail price 250 plus.`

2. Make the changes on the last two lines in this query.

```
SELECT CategoryName, ROUND(AVG(RetailPrice), 2) AS AvgRetailPrice
FROM Products INNER JOIN ProductCategory
  ON Products.ProductCategoryID = ProductCategory.ProductCategoryID
GROUP BY CategoryName
HAVING AVG(RetailPrice) >= 250
ORDER BY AvgRetailPrice;
```

Figure 10-9 shows the four categories that meet the criteria on the HAVING clause.

	categoryname character varying	avgretailprice numeric
1	Children's Bicycle	278.10
2	Road Bicycle	476.59
3	Touring Bicycle	686.10
4	Mountain Bicycle	2129.85

Figure 10-9 Filtered by product category average retail price

MAX Function

This function finds the largest value in the column and can process any type of data. The value returned, depends on the data type of the column used in the expression.

MAX Function Characteristics

Below is how this function processes data.

- ☑ Blanks, numbers and dates in the column are counted.
- ☑ Empty cells and NULL values in the column are ignored.
- ☑ The expression created for this function can result in a numeric, string or date value.
- ☑ When used with numbers, this function returns the largest number. (3)
- ☑ When used with string data, this function returns the largest value based on the collating sequence used by the database. (3)
- ☑ When used with a date field, the most recent date is returned. (3)

(3) The MIN function returns the smallest value or the oldest date, depending on the fields data type.

Example #4 Find The Highest Retail Price

The query below finds the highest retail price of all of the products. Figure 10-10 shows the result.

```
SELECT MAX(RetailPrice) AS HighestPrice
FROM Products;
```

	highestprice numeric
1	2939.85

Figure 10-10 Highest retail price of all products

Exercise 10.4: Find The Highest Retail Price In Each Product Category

In this exercise, you will create a query that finds the product with the highest retail price in each product category.

1. Create the query shown below.

```
SELECT CategoryName, MAX(RetailPrice) AS HighestRetailPrice
FROM Products INNER JOIN ProductCategory
  ON Products.ProductCategoryID = ProductCategory.ProductCategoryID
GROUP BY CategoryName
ORDER BY CategoryName;
```

2. Save the query as `E10.4 Highest priced product in each category.`

   Figure 10-11 shows the highest retail price in each category. 8 rows were returned.

   The GROUP BY clause groups the products by category. Then the MAX function finds the highest retail price of the products in each category.

	categoryname character varying (	highestretailprice numeric
1	Bicycle Locks	37.90
2	Children's Bicycle	281.85
3	Gloves	16.50
4	Helmets	53.90

Figure 10-11 Highest retail price in each category

Example #5 Find The Highest Retail Priced Product In Each Sub Category

The query shown below is suppose to return the highest priced product in each sub category. The Sub Category field was added to the first and fourth lines of the query created in Exercise 10.4. Figure 10-12 shows the result. 29 rows were returned, which is the total number of sub categories.

In this query, it probably is not necessary to display the category name. I did it to make it easier for you to compare the values in this example to the highest priced product in the category. As you can see, the highest price in the category (Figure 10-11) is also the highest price in the sub category (Figure 10-12).

```
SELECT CategoryName, SubCategory,
  MAX(RetailPrice) AS HighestRetailPrice
FROM Products INNER JOIN ProductCategory
  ON Products.ProductCategoryID =
    ProductCategory.ProductCategoryID
GROUP BY CategoryName, SubCategory
ORDER BY CategoryName;
```

This query does not produce the expected results. The first red flag should be that all sub categories for the same product category have the same highest retail price. The problem is that the query is grouping and calculating the highest retail price for the product category. The next example, shows the correct way to calculate the highest retail price for each sub category.

	categoryname character varying (	subcategory character varying (	highestretailprice numeric
1	Bicycle Locks	ATB Lock	37.90
2	Bicycle Locks	Chain Locks	37.90
3	Bicycle Locks	Mini Lock	37.90
4	Bicycle Locks	Mtn Lock	37.90
5	Bicycle Locks	Rhino Lock	37.90
6	Bicycle Locks	Titan Lock	37.90
7	Bicycle Locks	U Lock	37.90
8	Children's Bicycle	Children's Bicycles	281.85
9	Children's Bicycle	Nicos Child	281.85

Figure 10-12 Highest retail price in each sub category

Example #6 Joining Tables To Find The Highest Priced Product

Depending on the structure of the tables that are in the database, it may not be necessary to go through one table (in this example, the Product Category table), to get to another table (in this example, the Product Sub Category table), as you saw in Example #5 above. When that is the case, this query is used to join the Products table directly to the Product Sub Category table.

```
SELECT SubCategory, MAX(RetailPrice)
  AS HighestRetailPrice
FROM Products INNER JOIN ProductSubCategory
  ON Products.SubCategoryID =
    ProductSubCategory.SubCategoryID
GROUP BY SubCategory
ORDER BY SubCategory;
```

As shown in Figure 10-13, the highest retail price for each sub category is different then the values shown above in Figure 10-12. That is because the Category Name column is not grouping the data.

Hopefully, in the database that you use on your own, the Products table stores the key to the Product Sub Category table, as the values shown in Figure 10-13 are probably the values that someone needs to see.

	subcategory character varyi	highestretailprice numeric
1	Adult Helmet	33.90
2	ATB Lock	21.90
3	Chain Locks	4.50
4	Child Helmet	33.90
5	Child Saddle	129.00

Figure 10-13 Result of revised query to find the highest price in each sub category

As you learned in Example #5, the query did not produce the expected result. While the table structure can be an issue, that was not the case in Example #5. The problem was including the Category Name column on the GROUP BY clause.

Exercise 10.5: Categories With A Product That Has A Retail Price Over $300

In this exercise, you will modify the query created in Exercise 10.4, to only select product categories that have a product with a retail price over $300.

1. Save the E10.4 query as `E10.5 Retail price over 300.`

2. Add this HAVING clause to the query.

```
HAVING MAX(RetailPrice)
  > 300
```

Figure 10-14 shows the four categories that have a product with a retail price over $300.

	categoryname character varying (	highestretailprice numeric
1	Mountain Bicycle	2939.85
2	Road Bicycle	764.85
3	Saddles	336.00
4	Touring Bicycle	832.35

Figure 10-14 Categories that have a product with a retail price over $300

MIN Function

This function finds the smallest value in the column and can process any type of data. The value returned, depends on the data type of the column used in the expression.

MIN Function Characteristics

This function has the same characteristics as the MAX function, covered earlier in this chapter.

Example #7 Use The MIN And MAX Functions With String Data

Believe it or not, these functions can be used with string data, as shown in the query below. Both functions put the values in alphabetical order, when used with string data. The MIN function returns the first value from the alphabetical list. The MAX function returns the last value from the alphabetical list, as shown in Figure 10-15.

```
SELECT MIN(ProductName) AS MinProductName,
  MAX(ProductName) AS MaxProductName
FROM Products;
```

	minproductname text	maxproductname text
1	Adult Helmet	Youth Helmet

Figure 10-15 First and last values from an alphabetical list

Exercise 10.6: Use The AVG, MAX And MIN Functions

In this exercise, you will create a query that finds the average, maximum and minimum order amount.

1. Create this query.

```
SELECT ROUND(AVG(OrderAmount),2) AS AvgOrderAmount,
  MAX(OrderAmount) AS MaxOrderAmount,
  MIN(OrderAmount) AS MinOrderAmount
FROM Orders;
```

2. Save the query as `E10.6 AVG MAX & MIN order amount.`

Figure 10-16 shows the result.

	avgorderamount numeric	maxorderamount numeric	minorderamount numeric
1	1781.50	17658.81	4.05

Figure 10-16 Average, maximum and minimum order amounts

Exercise 10.7: Calculate The AVG, MIN And MAX Product Selling Price By Category

In this exercise, you will create a query that calculates product price, by category.

1. Create the query shown below, which is continued on the next page.

```
SELECT CategoryName,
  ROUND(AVG (UnitPrice * Quantity), 2) AS "AVG Product Price",
  MIN(UnitPrice * Quantity) AS "MIN Product Price",
  MAX(UnitPrice * Quantity) AS "MAX Product Price"
FROM OrderDetails INNER JOIN Products
  ON OrderDetails.ProductID = Products.ProductID
```

```
    INNER JOIN ProductCategory ON
      Products.ProductCategoryID = ProductCategory.ProductCategoryID
GROUP BY CategoryName
ORDER BY CategoryName;
```

2. Save the query as `E10.7 Calculate category values.`

Figure 10-17 shows the values for each category.

Based on the result, the Mountain Bicycle category has the highest average, minimum and maximum product prices.

These values are based on the quantity of each product.

	categoryname character varying	AVG Product Price numeric	MIN Product Price numeric	MAX Product Price numeric
1	Bicycle Locks	77.66	4.50	379.00
2	Children's Bicycle	1566.08	274.35	2818.50
3	Gloves	73.43	13.50	165.00
4	Helmets	220.36	33.90	539.00
5	Mountain Bicycle	10288.76	899.85	29398.50
6	Road Bicycle	2465.63	329.85	7648.50
7	Saddles	968.30	112.00	3360.00
8	Touring Bicycle	3143.79	539.85	8323.50

Figure 10-17 Category average, minimum and maximum product prices

MIN And MAX Function Tips
① The reason to use the MIN and MAX functions is because you do not know the value that you are looking for or because the value returned can change. If you know the value that you are looking for, you can use the WHERE clause.
② These functions are often used in the same query because together, they display a range or contrasting information. For example, as demonstrated earlier in Exercise 10.6, they show the range of order amounts.
③ In addition to finding the smallest or largest value in a column, the MIN and MAX functions can also calculate the smallest or largest value between the result of two expressions.

Exercise 10.8: Calculate The Standard Deviation

In this exercise, you will create a query that calculates the standard deviation of all order amounts.

1. Create this query.

```
SELECT ROUND(STDDEV(OrderAmount) ,2) AS OrderAmountSTDDEV
FROM Data.Orders;
```

2. Save the query as `E10.8 Standard deviation.`

   Figure 10-18 shows the result.

	orderamountstddev numeric
1	2499.59

Figure 10-18 Standard deviation of all order amounts

COUNT Function

As covered earlier, there are two ways that this function can be used. The options are explained below.

COUNT(*) Function

This version of the COUNT function was briefly explained in Chapter 5. An expression that uses this function, counts all of the rows in the table. COUNT(*) does not require an expression parameter, because it does not use data in any column. Just an FYI, the * is a parameter.

The COUNT(*) function does not support the DISTINCT keyword. That is because this function counts all rows, including rows that contain null or duplicate values.

COUNT(Column) Function

This version of the COUNT function is used with a specific field, like this: SELECT COUNT(ProductID) AS NbrOfProducts. When used like this, the COUNT function only counts rows that have a value in the field specified in the expression.

By default, this function counts duplicate rows. It ignores rows that have a null value in the field used in the expression.

As you will see, the DISTINCT keyword can be used with the COUNT(Column) function. When the two are used together, the COUNT(Column) function only counts rows that have a unique value in the field specified.

Example #8 COUNT(*) vs COUNT(Column)

The differences between these functions are:

① COUNT(*) counts NULL values. COUNT(Column) does not count rows that have a NULL value, in the column specified.
② COUNT(*) counts rows. COUNT(Column) counts rows, if the specified column has a value.

The query below produces the result shown in Figure 10-19.

```
SELECT COUNT(*) AS CountRows
FROM Products;
```

	countrows bigint
1	127

Figure 10-19 Result of the COUNT(*) query

The query below produces the result shown in Figure 10-20.

```
SELECT COUNT(ProductCategoryID) AS CountRows
FROM Products;
```

	countrows bigint
1	115

Figure 10-20 Result of the COUNT(ProductCategoryID) query

Notice that the same table is used in both queries. The first query counts all of the rows in the Products table. The second query did not count rows where the Product Category ID field is null.

Example #9 Using The DISTINCT Keyword With The COUNT Function

The query below adds the DISTINCT keyword to the second query in Example #8. This keyword will reduce the count because only rows with unique values will be counted. As shown in Figure 10-21, this query only returned eight rows and the second query in Example #8 returned 115 rows.

```
SELECT COUNT(DISTINCT ProductCategoryID)
  AS CountRows
FROM Products;
```

	countrows bigint
1	8

Figure 10-21 Result of COUNT function with the DISTINCT keyword

Example #10 Use The COUNT(*) Function With Another Aggregate Function

The query below counts the number of sales reps that have a sales quota that is greater than $20,000 and calculates their average bonus. The COUNT(*) function in the first query in Example #8 counted all of the rows in the table. The COUNT(*) function expression in this example only counts rows that meet the filter criteria on the WHERE clause. Figure 10-22 shows the result.

```
SELECT COUNT(*) AS NbrOfReps,
  AVG(Bonus) AS AvgBonus
FROM SalesRep
WHERE SalesQuota > 20000;
```

	nbrofreps bigint	avgbonus numeric
1	8	4078.1250000000000000

Figure 10-22 Count of sales reps and their average bonus

Exercise 10.9: Count The Number Of Orders With An Order Amount >= 5000

The query that you will create in this exercise, will create a count of orders that have an order amount >= $5,000.

1. Create this query.

```
SELECT COUNT(*) AS OrderCount
FROM Orders
WHERE OrderAmount >= 5000;
```

2. Save the query as `E10.9 Count of orders greater than or equal to 5000.`

Figure 10-23 shows the result.
1,234 orders out of 9,772 orders have an order amount >= 5,000. I could not have made up the 1,234 value if I tried.<smile>

	ordercount bigint
1	1234

Figure 10-23 Count of orders with an order amount >= $5,000

Exercise 10.10: Count The Number Of Customers With Each Job Title

In this exercise, the query that you create will display a count of customers by job title.

1. Create this query.

```
SELECT JobTitle, COUNT(*) AS CustomerCount
FROM Customers
GROUP BY JobTitle
ORDER BY JobTitle;
```

2. Save the query as `E10.10 Customer count by job title.`

Figure 10-24 shows the result. 14 rows were returned.

The result shows how many customers have the same job title.

	jobtitle character varying	customercount bigint
1	Accountant	48
2	Business Analyst	70
3	Consultant	50
4	Data Analyst	38

Figure 10-24 Customer count by job title

Exercise 10.11: Count The Number Of Products In Each Category

In this exercise, you will create a query that counts the number of products in each product category.

1. Create the query shown below.

```
SELECT CategoryName, COUNT(*) AS NbrOfProducts
FROM Products INNER JOIN ProductCategory
  ON Products.ProductCategoryID = ProductCategory.ProductCategoryID
GROUP BY CategoryName
ORDER BY CategoryName;
```

2. Save the query as `E10.11 Count of products in each category.`

Figure 10-25 shows some of the eight rows that were returned. One for each product category.

The result shows how many products are in each category.

	categoryname character varying	nbrofproducts bigint
1	Bicycle Locks	56
2	Children's Bicycle	8
3	Gloves	68
4	Helmets	92

Figure 10-25 Count of products in each category

Example #11 Use The COUNT(*) Function To Filter The Product Categories

The query below is based on the query created in Exercise 10.11. This query is modified to only select product categories that have more than 60 products. Figure 10-26 shows the three product categories that have more than 60 products.

```
SELECT CategoryName, COUNT(*) AS NbrOfProducts
FROM Products INNER JOIN ProductCategory
  ON Products.ProductCategoryID =
    ProductCategory.ProductCategoryID
GROUP BY CategoryName
HAVING COUNT(*) > 60
ORDER BY CategoryName;
```

	categoryname character varyir	nbrofproducts bigint
1	Gloves	68
2	Helmets	92
3	Road Bicycle	92

Figure 10-26 Categories with more than 60 products

Example #12 Using The STRING_AGG Function

This query will concatenate the zip codes for customers in the south region. Figure 10-27 shows some of the zip codes that were concatenated and automatically separated by a comma.

```
SELECT STRING_AGG(ZipCode, ', ') AS ListOfZipCodes
FROM Customers
WHERE RegionID BETWEEN 22 AND 38;
```

	listofzipcodes text
1	35818, 78770, 22618, 22616,

Figure 10-27 Result of using the STRING_AGG function

SUM Function

This function was briefly explained in Chapter 5. The SUM function requires numeric values to calculate a total. The expression created that uses this function must produce a numeric value. If this function is used with a text field, an error will be generated when the query is run.

Example #13 Creating A Grand Total

The query below, creates a total of all orders placed. Figure 10-28 shows the result. This type of query is sometimes called a **TOTALS TABLE** or **TOTALS QUERY**. This query uses the SUM function to add up all of the values in the Order Amount column. Aggregate functions keep the detail rows from being displayed and instead, returns a total of some type.

```
SELECT SUM(OrderAmount)
  AS "Grand Total Order Amount"
FROM Orders;
```

	Grand Total Order Amount numeric
1	17408778.93

Figure 10-28 Grand total of all orders in the table

Exercise 10.12: Calculate The Store Inventory

In this exercise, you will create a query that calculates the total inventory by product, for all of the stores.

1. Create this query.

```
SELECT StoreInventory.ProductID, ProductName,
  SUM(StoreInventory.QtyOnHand) AS QtyInStock
FROM StoreInventory INNER JOIN Products
  ON StoreInventory.ProductID = Products.ProductID
GROUP BY StoreInventory.ProductID, ProductName
ORDER BY StoreInventory.ProductID;
```

2. Save the query as `E10.12 Store inventory count by product.`

   Figure 10-29 shows the result. 32 rows were returned.

   The Qty In Stock is how many of each product, all of the stores have collectively.

	productid integer	productname character varyi	qtyinstock bigint
1	1102	Crochet Glove	2
2	1103	Crochet Glove	23
3	2201	Pro Helmet	4

Figure 10-29 Count of inventory in all stores

Exercise 10.13: Calculate The Gross Profit

In this exercise, the query that you create will calculate the gross profit. The standard formula to calculate the gross profit is sales minus cost. In the database used in this book, the sales field is the Line Item Total field and the Cost field is the Unit Cost field. This is an example of understanding and knowing the data that you are using. Sometimes, field names may not clearly represent the data that it stores.

1. Create this query.

```
SELECT SUM(LineItemTotal) AS TotalSales,
  SUM(UnitPrice) AS TotalCost,
  SUM(LineItemTotal) - SUM(UnitPrice) AS GrossProfit
FROM OrderDetails INNER JOIN Products
  ON OrderDetails.ProductID = Products.ProductID;
```

2. Save the query as `E10.13 Calculate the gross profit.`

   Figure 10-30 shows the result.

	totalsales numeric	totalcost numeric	grossprofit numeric
1	27150979.15	5363616.74	21787362.41

Figure 10-30 Result of the gross profit calculation

Exercise 10.14: Use The DISTINCT Keyword With The COUNT Function

Earlier in this chapter, you learned that the DISTINCT keyword is best suited to be used with the COUNT(Column) function. The query that you will create in this exercise will use the COUNT function with and without the DISTINCT keyword with the same field, so that you can see the difference. The query will count the number of unique sales rep id's in the Orders table. A count of rows will also be created using the sales rep id field. The average order amount total will be created.

1. Create this query.

```
SELECT COUNT(DISTINCT SalesRepID) AS NbrOfSalesReps,
  COUNT(SalesRepID) AS NbrOfOrders,
  ROUND(AVG(OrderAmount),2) AS AVGOrderAmount,
  SUM(OrderAmount) AS TotalOrderAmount
FROM Orders
WHERE OrderDate >= '2017-01-01';
```

2. Save the query as `E10.14 Use DISTINCT keyword with the COUNT function.`

   Figure 10-31 shows the result.

	nbrofsalesreps bigint	nbroforders bigint	avgorderamount numeric	totalorderamount numeric
1	14	2980	1792.31	5341095.27

Figure 10-31 COUNT function used with the DISTINCT keyword

In this query, the first COUNT expression uses the DISTINCT keyword to count the number of unique sales reps. The second COUNT expression counts every order. The data is filtered, based on the criteria. Yes, the COUNT(*) function could have been used in the second COUNT expression, but the goal of this exercise was to demonstrate the effect of using the DISTINCT keyword with the COUNT(Column) function. <smile>

Example #14 Understanding COUNT(*) vs COUNT(Column)

As covered earlier in Example #8, these functions can return different results. One problem that can easily be missed is when the COUNT(*) function is used, especially when other aggregate functions are used in the same query.

For example, this query uses almost all of the aggregate functions. The goal is to display a count of orders for each customer, a total dollar amount of each customers orders, the smallest, largest and average amount of each customer. Figure 10-32 shows the result.

```
SELECT Customers.CustomerID,
 FirstName || ' ' || LastName AS CustomerName,
 COUNT(*) AS NbrOfOrders,
 MIN(OrderAmount) AS SmallestOrder,
 MAX(OrderAmount) AS LargestOrder,
 ROUND(AVG(OrderAmount), 2) AS AverageOrder,
 SUM(OrderAmount) AS TotalOfAllOrders
FROM Customers
LEFT OUTER JOIN Orders
 ON Customers.CustomerID = Orders.CustomerID
GROUP BY Customers.CustomerID, FirstName, LastName;
```

While the query returned one row for each customer in the Customers table as expected, there is a problem with the data in one of the rows in the figure. Can you figure out which row has bad data and more importantly, why the data is bad?

	customerid integer	customername text	nbroforders bigint	smallestorder numeric	largestorder numeric	averageorder numeric	totalofallorders numeric
15	214	Drew Broadwin	2	539.85	539.85	539.85	1079.70
16	411	Gary Trent	21	29.00	8846.03	1915.91	40234.05
17	342	Jean-Paul Voltaire	1	[null]	[null]	[null]	[null]
18	456	Heather Dixon	4	16.50	8996.75	4507.20	18028.78

Figure 10-32 Customer data

The reason that you group on the Customer ID field in the Customers table, in this example, is because you want one row of data for each customer, whether or not the customer has any orders.

If you said that the problem is in the third row, you are correct. If you said that the problem is the NULL values in the last row, you are not correct. The problem is that there is a count of 1, in the Nbr Of Orders column. Remember that an OUTER JOIN returns all records in one table, regardless of whether there are matching rows in the linked table. In this example, all of the rows are returned from the Customers table, which is what you want. Also, remember that the COUNT(*) function counts all of the rows. That is why the Nbr Of Orders column has a 1 in the third row, which should not be. In this example, the NULL values indicate that the customer does not have any orders, which is not a problem, in this query.

I know that I have said a few times, that it is very important that you understand the data that you are using and that attention to detail (in this example, the "detail" is why there is a count of 1 and no order amount values) is key to making sure that the data returned is correct. This is why at the beginning of this example, I said that this is an easy mistake to make.

Hopefully, this example clearly demonstrates that just because the data "looks" correct, does not mean that the data is correct.

Exercise 10.15: Fix The Query In Example #14

Surely, you did not think that I was not going to show you how to fix the problem in Example #14. <smile>

1. Type the query shown above in Example #14.

2. Change COUNT(*) to `COUNT(Orders.CustomerID)`.

3. Save the query as `E10.15 Fix the query in Example 14.`

   Figure 10-33 shows the result. Notice that the third row, now has a Nbr Of Orders count of zero, which is correct.

	customerid integer	customername text	nbroforders bigint	smallestorder numeric	largestorder numeric	averageorder numeric	totalofallorders numeric
15	214	Drew Broadwin	2	539.85	539.85	539.85	1079.70
16	411	Gary Trent	21	29.00	8846.03	1915.91	40234.05
17	342	Jean-Paul Voltaire	0	[null]	[null]	[null]	[null]
18	456	Heather Dixon	4	16.50	8996.75	4507.20	18028.78

Figure 10-33 Result of the modified query

One way to test the change is as follows. The Orders table has 9,772 rows. If you added up all of the values in the Nbr Of Orders column, the value should be less than or equal to 9,772. In the real world, most of the time it will be equal to. The reason that it would not be equal to, is if referential integrity between the tables had not been set up or heaven forbid, it was set up wrong.

The total of the values in the Nbr Of Orders column in the query, in Example #14 is 9,781. That is 10 orders too many. That should be a "hint" that something is wrong, because the number of orders returned by the query cannot be more than the number of rows in the Orders table.

The total of the values in the Nbr of Orders column in the query, in this exercise, is 9,771. That is one less than the number of rows in the Orders table. In the real world you would have to find the row in the Orders table that either has a missing Customer ID or a Customer ID in the Orders table, that is not in the Customers table. In the database used in this book, it is the latter. I know because I created the data. <smile>

Test Your Query Results
On your own, it is imperative that you look at and test **EVERY** query that you create. If you don't, you could be handing off a query that does not return and/or calculate the correct values. This means that reports that are created based on the query will not report the data correctly. If the report is used to make a business decision, this becomes even more problematic. When the error is discovered, who do you think is responsible? So, yes, you will fair better if you test the query results before handing the query off (aka putting the query into production). When you are not sure how to test a query, please ask someone to help you.

Example #15 Use The COUNT Function And The DISTINCT Keyword

The query below demonstrates using the DISTINCT keyword with the COUNT function. The first COUNT function in the query, uses the DISTINCT keyword to count the number of unique sales reps that have a sale (an order), with an order date that is greater than or equal to 9/19/2018. The second COUNT function counts the number of sales reps that meet the WHERE clause criteria. This count is really the number of orders, on or after 9/19/2018. Figure 10-34 shows the result.

```
SELECT COUNT(DISTINCT SalesRepID) NbrOfSalesReps,
  COUNT(SalesRepID) AS NbrOfOrders,
  SUM(OrderAmount) AS TotalOrderAmt
FROM Orders
WHERE OrderDate >= '2018-09-19';
```

	nbrofsalesreps bigint	nbroforders bigint	totalorderamt numeric
1	6	430	726191.61

Figure 10-34 Result of using the DISTINCT keyword

As shown in the figure, the COUNT function returned different values, even though they both used the Sales Rep ID field. The first COUNT function counted 6 unique sales reps that met the filter criteria. There are 15 reps in the Sales Reps table. The second COUNT function returned the same value as using COUNT(*), meaning it counted the number of rows that met the filter criteria.

Exercise 10.16: Use An Aggregate Function On The HAVING Clause

In this exercise, you will create a query that calculates the average quantity sold of each product and the total amount of each product sold.

1. Create this query.

```
SELECT OrderDetails.ProductID, ProductName,
  ROUND(AVG(Quantity), 0) AS AverageQuantitySold,
  SUM(LineItemTotal) AS ProductTotalAmount
FROM OrderDetails INNER JOIN Products
  ON OrderDetails.ProductID = Products.ProductID
GROUP BY OrderDetails.ProductID, ProductName
HAVING AVG(Quantity) > 1
ORDER BY SUM(LineItemTotal) DESC;
```

2. Save the query as `E10.16 HAVING clause using a function.`

Figure 10-35 shows the result. 115 rows were returned.

In the real world, you would probably use a quantity greater than one. I used it for illustration purposes.

	productid integer	productname character varying (	averagequantitysold numeric	producttotalamount numeric
1	7006	Mountain Bicycle	6	987789.60
2	7009	Mountain Bicycle	5	823158.00
3	7008	Mountain Bicycle	6	808458.75
4	7007	Mountain Bicycle	6	767300.85

Figure 10-35 Result of using an aggregate function on the HAVING clause

Exercise 10.17: Group Orders By Region And Order Year

In this exercise, you will create a query that has an order count and a customer count. The data will be grouped by the region and order year.

1. Create the query shown below, which is continued on the next page.

```
SELECT Customers.RegionID, RegionName, DivisionName,
  date_part('year',OrderDate) AS OrderYear,
  COUNT(OrderID) AS OrderCount,
  COUNT(DISTINCT Orders.CustomerID) AS CustomerCount,
  SUM(OrderAmount) AS TotalSales
FROM Customers INNER JOIN Orders
  ON Customers.CustomerID = Orders.CustomerID
INNER JOIN Regions ON Customers.RegionID = Regions.RegionID
```

```
GROUP BY RegionName, DivisionName, date_part('year',OrderDate),
  Customers.RegionID
ORDER BY Customers.RegionID, RegionName, date_part('year',OrderDate);
```

2. Save the query as `E10.17 Orders grouped by region division & order year.` Figure 10-36 shows the result. 227 rows were returned.

	regionid integer	regionname character vary	divisionname character varyi	orderyear double prec	ordercount bigint	customercount bigint	totalsales numeric
26	6	Northeast	New England	2015	17	2	46003.08
27	6	Northeast	New England	2016	1	1	274.35
28	6	Northeast	New England	2017	1	1	8159.40
29	7	Northeast	Mid-Atlantic	2014	34	4	89203.57

Figure 10-36 Orders grouped by region, division and order year

Exercise 10.18: Create A Grouped Aggregation

In this exercise, you will create a query that calculates the total cost of each product that is in the Store Inventory table. The Quantity On Hand field in the Store Inventory table has to be multiplied by the Unit Cost field in the Products table. How cool is that? Being able to multiply fields in different tables. This is why you have to love joining tables. <smile>

1. Create this query.

```
SELECT StoreInventory.ProductID, ProductName,
 SUM(StoreInventory.QtyOnHand * Products.UnitCost)
   AS "Store Inventory Total Cost"
FROM Products INNER JOIN StoreInventory
  ON Products.ProductID = StoreInventory.ProductID
GROUP BY ProductName, StoreInventory.ProductID
ORDER BY StoreInventory.ProductID;
```

2. Save the query as `E10.18 Store inventory total cost.`

Figure 10-37 shows the result. 32 rows were returned.

The data shows the total cost of each product that collectively, all of the stores have in inventory.

	productid integer	productname character varyi	Store Inventory Total Cost numeric
1	1102	Crochet Glove	14.46
2	1103	Crochet Glove	167.21
3	2201	Pro Helmet	73.00
4	2202	Pro Helmet	821.25

Figure 10-37 Store inventory total cost

Exercise 10.19: Count The Quantity Of Products Sold

In this exercise, you will create a query to calculate the number of orders and the quantity sold for each product.

1. Create this query.

```
SELECT OrderDetails.ProductID, ProductName,
  COUNT(OrderDetails.ProductID) AS NumberOfOrders,
  SUM(Quantity) AS QuantitySold
FROM OrderDetails INNER JOIN Products
  ON OrderDetails.ProductID = Products.ProductID
GROUP BY OrderDetails.ProductID, ProductName
ORDER BY OrderDetails.ProductID;
```

2. Save the query as `E10.19 Count quantity of products sold.`

Figure 10-38 shows the result of the query. 115 rows were returned.

	productid integer	productname character varyi	numberoforders bigint	quantitysold bigint
1	1101	Crochet Glove	269	998
2	1102	Crochet Glove	262	1033
3	1103	Crochet Glove	507	2428

Figure 10-38 Count of orders and quantity sold

Exercise 10.20: Count Orders By Status

In this exercise, you will create a query that creates a count of orders and products, by status. The Order Details table has a row for each item, that was ordered by all customers. This means that the Number Of Products count is the number of rows that have a status, **NOT** the number of orders.

1. Create the query shown below.

```
SELECT OrderDetailsStatus.StatusID, OrderDetailsStatus.Status,
  COUNT(DISTINCT OrderID) AS LineItemCount,
  COUNT(*) AS NumberOfProducts
FROM OrderDetails INNER JOIN OrderDetailsStatus
  ON OrderDetails.StatusID = OrderDetailsStatus.StatusID
GROUP BY OrderDetailsStatus.StatusID, OrderDetailsStatus.Status
ORDER BY OrderDetailsStatus.StatusID;
```

2. Save the query as `E10.20 Count of orders & products by status.`

   Figure 10-39 shows how many orders have each status and how many products (rows) are in each status.

   In this database, the allocated status means that the product has been requested from inventory (the Qty On Hand field), but has not been shipped to the customer yet.

	statusid integer	status character v	lineitemcount bigint	numberofproducts bigint
1	0	None	4955	6196
2	1	Allocated	2091	2515
3	2	Invoiced	3776	5432
4	3	Shipped	2756	3084
5	4	On Order	3149	4224

Figure 10-39 Count of line items and products, by status

Example #16 Revised Join For Exercise 10.20

What is not obvious by the result shown in Figure 10-39 above, is that there are records in the Order Details table that have a Status ID of 9.

Those records are not returned because the Order Details Status table does not have a record that has that value. If the report that you are creating the query for, requires a count of all rows, in the Order Details tables, regardless of the Status ID, the query would have to be modified as shown. Figure 10-40 shows the result of the modified join.

```
SELECT OrderDetailsStatus.StatusID,
  OrderDetailsStatus.Status,
  COUNT(DISTINCT OrderID) AS LineItemCount,
  COUNT(*) AS NumberOfProducts
FROM OrderDetails LEFT OUTER JOIN OrderDetailsStatus
  ON OrderDetails.StatusID = OrderDetailsStatus.StatusID
GROUP BY OrderDetailsStatus.StatusID,
  OrderDetailsStatus.Status;
```

The last row in Figure 10-40 contains the totals for rows in the Order Details table that do not have a Status ID. In this example, this row is the totals for the rows that have a Status ID = 9. There are 24,776 rows in the Order Details table. If you add up the values in the last column, you will see that it is the same as the number of rows in the Order Details table, which is what it should be. This is how you know that the query has accounted for all of the rows in the Order Details table.

	statusid integer	status character v	lineitemcount bigint	numberofproducts bigint
1	0	None	4955	6196
2	1	Allocated	2091	2515
3	2	Invoiced	3776	5432
4	3	Shipped	2756	3084
5	4	On Order	3149	4224
6	[null]	[null]	2786	3325

Figure 10-40 Count of all rows in the Order Details table, by status

If you added up the values in the last column, in Figure 10-39 shown earlier, then looked in the Order Details table and looked at the total number of rows, you would have seen that the totals did not match, which in this scenario is a problem. On your own, you have to think about how you can test the result of a query. I will admit that it can be a little more difficult to test the result of a summary query, but it has to be done.

Exercise 10.21: Create Yearly Order Totals

In this exercise, you will create a query that groups the orders by the order year. Totals will be created for the number of orders, number of customers that placed an order in the year and order total for the year.

1. Create this query.

```
SELECT date_part('year', OrderDate) AS OrderYear,
  COUNT(*) AS "Number Of Orders",
  COUNT(DISTINCT CustomerID) AS "Number Of Customers",
  SUM(OrderAmount) AS "Order Total For The Year"
FROM Orders
GROUP BY date_part('year', OrderDate)
ORDER BY date_part('year', OrderDate);
```

2. Save the query as `E10.21 Yearly order totals.`

   Figure 10-41 shows the result.

   The DISTINCT keyword is needed to count the customers. Many customers may place multiple orders in a year, but each customer that places an order should only be counted once per year.

	orderyear double pre	Number Of Orders bigint	Number Of Customers bigint	Order Total For The Year numeric
1	2014	1282	296	2304271.58
2	2015	3064	242	5458331.83
3	2016	2446	235	4305080.25
4	2017	1116	181	2041079.99
5	2018	1863	375	3294469.86
6	2019	1	1	5545.42

Figure 10-41 Count of customers and order totals by year

Exercise 10.22: Count Customer Totals By Year

This query is similar to the query created in Exercise 10.21. The difference is that this query is driven by the Customer ID field. By that I mean, the same expressions are used, but the way that the data is grouped is different.

1. Save the E10.21 query as `E10.22 Customer totals per year.`

2. Modify the FROM clause as shown below, to join the tables.

```
FROM Orders LEFT OUTER JOIN Customers
  ON Customers.CustomerID = Orders.CustomerID
```

3. Add the Customer ID field from the Orders table to the beginning of the SELECT clause.

4. Delete the COUNT DISTINCT field from the SELECT clause.

5. Add the Customer ID field from the Orders table to the beginning of the GROUP BY and ORDER BY clauses.

   Your query should look like this one.

   Figure 10-42 shows the result. 1,330 rows were returned.

```
SELECT Orders.CustomerID,
  date_part('year', OrderDate) AS OrderYear,
  COUNT(*) AS "Number Of Orders",
  SUM(OrderAmount) AS "Order Total For The Year"
FROM Orders LEFT OUTER JOIN Customers
  ON Customers.CustomerID = Orders.CustomerID
GROUP BY Orders.CustomerID, date_part('year', OrderDate)
ORDER BY Orders.CustomerID, date_part('year', OrderDate);
```

   The query displays the number of orders and order total amount by year, for each customer. Keep in mind that all customers do not place an order every year.

   As shown in the figure, customer 2, did not place any orders in 2019.

   This query would make a good view, because the rows for the current year would be up to date, each time the query is run.

	customerid integer	orderyear double pre	Number Of Orders bigint	Order Total For The Year numeric
6	1	2019	1	5545.42
7	2	2014	9	14337.57
8	2	2015	11	16404.00
9	2	2016	31	43724.83
10	2	2017	12	14215.80
11	2	2018	22	42601.14

Figure 10-42 Customer order totals by year

Example #17 Alternate Customer Totals By Year Query

The query in this example is another way to create the summary table in Exercise 10.22.

Notice in Figure 10-43, that the second row does not display a Customer ID or Company Name. 1,330 rows were returned.

Perhaps your first thought is that a record in the Customers table does not have a Customer ID and Company Name. The query in Exercise 10.22 did not return any rows that had NULL values.

```
SELECT date_part('year',OrderDate) AS CalendarYear,
  Customers.CustomerID, CompanyName,
  COUNT(Customers.CustomerID) AS NbrOfOrders,
  SUM(OrderAmount) AS TotalForYear
FROM Orders LEFT OUTER JOIN  Customers
  ON Orders.CustomerID = Customers.CustomerID
GROUP BY date_part('year', OrderDate),
  Customers.CustomerID, CompanyName
ORDER BY date_part('year', OrderDate),
  Customers.CustomerID, CompanyName;
```

Now what?
Think about it for a few minutes.

What steps would you take to solve this?
I'll continue this discussion, later in the chapter.

	calendaryear double precisio	customerid integer	companyname character varying (7!	nbroforders bigint	totalforyear numeric
295	2014	299	C&C Sports People	10	26034.06
296	2014	[null]	[null]	0	5879.70
297	2015	1	City Cyclists	13	18120.49
298	2015	2	Pathfinders	11	16404.80

Figure 10-43 Customer yearly totals

Exercise 10.23: Find The Top 10 Selling Products

In this exercise, you will create a query that displays the top 10 products sold, based on the dollar amount of the product sold. To calculate the dollar amount sold, the expression has to calculate the Quantity * Unit Price for each row, then SUM that value. While the SUM function is used to calculate the total of the values in a specific column, it can also be used to create a total of calculated values.

1. Create this query.

```
SELECT OrderDetails.ProductID, Products.ProductName,
  SUM(Quantity) AS QuantitySold,
  SUM(Quantity * UnitPrice) AS ProductSoldAmount
FROM OrderDetails INNER JOIN Products
  ON OrderDetails.ProductID = Products.ProductID
GROUP BY OrderDetails.ProductID, Products.ProductName
ORDER BY SUM(Quantity * UnitPrice) DESC
LIMIT 10;
```

2. Save the query as `E10.23 Top 10 selling products.`

Figure 10-44 shows the result.

Notice that the rows are grouped by the Product ID field, but sorted on the Product Sold Amount calculation in descending order.

Keep in mind that the rows returned are the top 10 selling products, based on **ALL ORDERS** in the database.

	productid integer	productname character varying	quantitysold bigint	productsoldamount numeric
1	7006	Mountain Bicycle	336	987789.60
2	7009	Mountain Bicycle	280	823158.00
3	7008	Mountain Bicycle	275	808458.75
4	7007	Mountain Bicycle	261	767300.85

Figure 10-44 Top 10 selling products

More than likely, on your own, you would need to create filter criteria to select a time frame, like last month, to see the top 10 orders for.

Exercise 10.24: Group Customers By Region, State And Customer Type

In addition to grouping on three fields, the query that you will create in this exercise, will also provide a count of customers in each subgroup.

1. Create the query shown below.

```
SELECT RegionName, Customers.State, CustomerType,
  COUNT(*) AS NbrOfCustomers
FROM Customers INNER JOIN Regions
  ON Customers.RegionID = Regions.RegionID
GROUP BY RegionName, Customers.State, CustomerType
ORDER BY RegionName, Customers.State, CustomerType;
```

2. Save the query as `E10.24 Group customers on 3 fields.`

   Figure 10-45 shows the result. 68 rows were returned.

	regionname character var	state charac	customertype character varyir	nbrofcustomers bigint
13	Midwest	OH	Online	4
14	Midwest	OH	Retail	9
15	Midwest	SD	Retail	5
16	Midwest	WI	Online	10
17	Midwest	WI	Retail	8
18	Northeast	CT	Retail	3

Figure 10-45 Customers grouped on 3 fields

Observe the following about the query results.

- ☑ Notice that there are two rows for some states. That is because those states have online **AND** retail customers.
- ☑ What may not be obvious is that by joining the Customers and Regions tables, a filter was automatically created, because customers that do not have a region (in this database, that is customers that are not in the USA) are automatically excluded.
- ☑ While the result looks like detail rows of data, the data displayed is really summary data. (**HINT:** The GROUP BY clause creates summary data) In this query, each row in the result, is a subgroup and has a total.

GROUP BY Subclauses

The GROUP BY clause has the following three subclauses: ROLLUP, CUBE and GROUPING SETS. They extend the functionality of the GROUP BY clause and are used to create totals for the groups that are created. As you will see, each subclause returns different results.

ROLLUP Subclause

This subclause is used to define multiple grouping sets. It is often used to create sub totals and grand totals.
The ROLLUP subclause creates a group for each combination of column expressions.

ROLLUP works on the premise that there is a hierarchy between the (dimension) columns that are added to the GROUP BY clause in the query. This hierarchy structure is what is used to create the grouping sets. Unlike the CUBE subclause, the ROLLUP subclause does not create all of the possible grouping sets, based on the columns that are added to this clause. The ROLLUP subclause is often used to calculate aggregate values for hierarchical data like sales by year, quarter and month.

Exercise 10.25: Use The ROLLUP Subclause To Only Generate A Grand Total

When you need a data set that requires a grand total, using the ROLLUP subclause will give you what you need.

1. Create this query.

```
SELECT Category, SUM(Sales) AS TotalSales
FROM CategorySales
GROUP BY ROLLUP (Category)
ORDER BY Category;
```

2. Save the query as
   `E10.25 Create a grand total.`

   Figure 10-46 shows the nine rows that were returned. The subtotal for each category was calculated. The last row is the grand total of sales for all of the categories.

	category character varying	totalsales numeric
1	Bicycle Locks	1095707.50
2	Children's Bicycle	753639.90
3	Gloves	1147401.65
4	Helmets	711851.96
5	Mountain Bicycle	888508.35
6	Road Bicycle	676790.80
7	Saddles	550613.50
8	Touring Bicycle	468694.80
9	[null]	6293208.46

Figure 10-46 Grand total for all categories

Exercise 10.26: Use The ROLLUP Subclause To Calculate Grand Totals

In this exercise, you will create a query that uses the ROLLUP subclause to calculate the sales total by category and sub category. In this scenario, the ROLLUP subclause is creating a grand total for each category/subcategory combination. From some of the previous examples and exercises in this chapter, you know that the values in the Sales Total column are for the sub category.

1. Create this query.

```
SELECT Category, SubCategory,
 SUM(Sales) AS SalesTotal
FROM CategorySales
GROUP BY
 ROLLUP (Category, SubCategory)
ORDER BY Category, SubCategory;
```

2. Save the query as
   `E10.26 ROLLUP category & sub category.`

   Figure 10-47 shows the result. 38 rows were returned. There is a row for each category and sub category combination.

	category character varying(5	subcategory character varying(5	salestotal numeric
6	Bicycle Locks	Titan Lock	260107.90
7	Bicycle Locks	U Lock	84311.70
8	Bicycle Locks	[null]	1095707.50
9	Children's Bicycle	Children's Bicycles	131737.10

Figure 10-47 Sales totals for the sub categories

If the order of the fields on the ROLLUP subclause line in the query, in this exercise, were reversed, as shown in this query, the result would be different, as shown in Figure 10-48. 59 rows were returned.

```
SELECT SubCategory, Category,
 SUM(Sales) AS SalesTotal
FROM CategorySales
GROUP BY
 ROLLUP (SubCategory, Category)
ORDER BY SubCategory, Category;
```

The query to the right, would be considered a **PARTIAL ROLLUP QUERY**, compared to the query created in this exercise. That is because this query only uses one field with the ROLLUP subclause. This query produces the result shown in Figure 10-49. Notice that this query has the Category field on the GROUP BY clause.

```
SELECT Category, SubCategory,
 SUM(Sales) AS SalesTotal
FROM CategorySales
GROUP BY Category,
 ROLLUP (SubCategory);
```

	subcategory character varyi	category character varyi	salestotal numeric
1	Adult Helmet	Helmets	112980.86
2	Adult Helmet	[null]	112980.86
3	ATB Lock	Bicycle Locks	99570.50
4	ATB Lock	[null]	99570.50

Figure 10-48 Result of the fields on the ROLLUP line reversed

	category character varying (	subcategory character varying (50)	salestotal numeric
1	Children's Bicycle	Nicos Child	621902.80
2	Bicycle Locks	ATB Lock	99570.50
3	Bicycle Locks	Rhino Lock	140978.90
4	Road Bicycle	Road Bicycle (Slim Rock)	149591.40

Figure 10-49 Result of a partial ROLLUP query

Exercise 10.27: Use The ROLLUP Subclause To Calculate Subtotals And A Grand Total

As you have seen, when the GROUP BY clause is added to a query, the results are summarized for all of the combinations of values (fields) on the GROUP BY clause. [See Figure 10-45] If the ROLLUP subclause was added to the query in Exercise 10.24, new rows would be added. These new rows would be sub totals and a grand total. The sub totals are added from right to left. This means that the order that the columns are listed in, is important. In this exercise, you will modify the E10.24 query by adding the ROLLUP subclause to it.

1. Save the E10.24 query as `E10.27 ROLLUP subclause added`.

2. Type the word `ROLLUP` after GROUP BY.

3. Put parentheses around the columns on the GROUP BY line.

   Figure 10-50 shows the result. 123 rows were returned.

   Rows 23, 25 and 28 are the sub total rows for each state. The NULL value indicates that the column is being rolled up and a subtotal or grand total has been created.

   Row 29 is the grand total number of customers for the Midwest region. The last row in the result (not shown in the figure) is the total number of customers, in all of the groups.

	regionname character var	state charact	customertype character varyi	nbrofcustomers bigint
21	Midwest	OH	Online	4
22	Midwest	OH	Retail	9
23	Midwest	OH	[null]	13
24	Midwest	SD	Retail	5
25	Midwest	SD	[null]	5
26	Midwest	WI	Online	10
27	Midwest	WI	Retail	8
28	Midwest	WI	[null]	18
29	Midwest	[null]	[null]	125

Figure 10-50 Result of the ROLLUP subclause added to the query in Exercise 10.24

Replacing NULL Values In Queries That Use The ROLLUP Subclause

As you have seen in the previous three exercises, when the ROLLUP subclause is used, NULL values are displayed on the rows created by this subclause. Because you created the query, you know what the NULL values represent. For the people that will use the data retrieved from the query, it can and probably would be confusing to see so many NULL values. The solution is to replace the NULL values with text, as covered in the exercise below. Later in this chapter, you will learn another way to replace NULL values with text, in queries that use the ROLLUP subclause.

Exercise 10.28: Displaying Text Instead Of NULL Values

As you saw in the previous exercise, NULL was displayed in the result. You may find it more helpful if text was displayed instead of NULL, to help explain what the value represents.

Chapter 4 introduced the CASE function. The query in this exercise takes the CASE function to the next level. The **GROUPING FUNCTION** is explained later in this chapter.

In this exercise, you will modify the query created in the Exercise 10.27, by adding a CASE statement to each of the three columns that a sub total or grand total will be created for. When the CASE statement returns a zero, it means that the value is not summarized or rolled up. When the value is not zero, the column will be summarized.

1. Save the E10.27 query as `E10.28 Replace NULL values in a ROLLUP with text.`

2. Replace the current SELECT clause with the one shown below. I added an asterisk next to the text that will be displayed, instead of the null values, to make it easier to read.

```
SELECT
(CASE WHEN GROUPING (RegionName) = 0
  THEN RegionName
  ELSE '*Region Total' END) AS RegionName,
(CASE WHEN GROUPING (Customers.State) = 0
  THEN Customers.State
  ELSE '*State Total' END) AS State,
(CASE WHEN GROUPING (CustomerType) = 0
  THEN CustomerType
  ELSE '*Customer Type Total' END) AS CustomerType,
COUNT(*) AS NbrOfCustomers
FROM Customers, Regions
WHERE Customers.RegionID = Regions.RegionID
GROUP BY ROLLUP (RegionName, Customers.State, CustomerType)
ORDER BY RegionName, Customers.State, CustomerType;
```

Figure 10-51 shows the first row returned and the last rows for a region. The same 123 rows were returned.

The difference is that the NULL values were replaced with text, which helps make the value in the Nbr Of Customers column easier to understand.

The last row displays the total number of customers for the region.

	regionname character varyi	state character va	customertype character varying	nbrofcustomers bigint
1	*Region Total	*State Total	*Customer Type Total	377
2	Midwest	IA	*Customer Type Total	17
3	Midwest	IA	Online	8
4	Midwest	IA	Retail	9
			⋮	
29	Midwest	WI	Retail	8
30	Midwest	*State Total	*Customer Type Total	125

Figure 10-51 Result of replacing the NULL values with text

The first row displays the grand total. If you are like me, you were expecting to see the grand total as the last row displayed. Sorry, it doesn't work that way in PostgreSQL, by default. Yes, I know that the **NULLS LAST ARGUMENT** will display rows that have a null value in a field last, but remember that in this exercise, the null values were replaced with text, so the NULLS LAST argument would not work.

Exercise 10.29: Create A Grand Total For Each Group

Earlier in Exercise 10.25, you created a query that calculated a grand total for all categories. In this exercise, you will expand on that query by creating a total for each category and year combination.

1. Create this query.

```
SELECT Category, SalesYear, SUM(Sales) AS TotalSales
FROM CategorySales
GROUP BY ROLLUP (Category, SalesYear)
ORDER BY Category, SalesYear;
```

2. Save the query as
   `E10.29 Grand total for each group.`

   As shown in Figure 10-52, each category has a sub total for each year of sales. The grand total for each category is the row with the NULL value in the Sales Year column. The grand total for all categories is on the last row in the figure. 33 rows were returned.

	category character varying	salesyear numeric	totalsales numeric
25	Saddles	2016	247347.50
26	Saddles	2017	89322.00
27	Saddles	2018	213944.00
28	Saddles	[null]	550613.50
29	Touring Bicycle	2016	13224.00
30	Touring Bicycle	2017	167365.50
31	Touring Bicycle	2018	288105.30
32	Touring Bicycle	[null]	468694.80
33	[null]	[null]	6293208.46

Figure 10-52 Grand totals for each group

Example #18 Create Subtotals And Grand Totals By Year

The query in Exercise 10.29 created subtotals and grand totals for each category, by year. The query in this example flips the fields so to speak, and calculates subtotals for each year/category combination.

```
SELECT SalesYear, Category,
  SUM(Sales) AS TotalYearlySales
FROM CategorySales
GROUP BY ROLLUP (SalesYear, Category)
ORDER BY SalesYear, Category;
```

Figure 10-53 shows some of the 28 rows that were returned. As shown, a subtotal is created (by the ROLLUP subclause) each time the year changes.

	salesyear numeric	category character varying	totalyearlysales numeric
10	2017	Bicycle Locks	304558.20
11	2017	Children's Bicycle	302218.60
12	2017	Gloves	656032.80
13	2017	Helmets	554948.36
14	2017	Mountain Bicycle	226994.90
15	2017	Road Bicycle	323033.00
16	2017	Saddles	89322.00
17	2017	Touring Bicycle	167365.50
18	2017	[null]	2624473.36
19	2018	Bicycle Locks	327298.50
20	2018	Children's Bicycle	439392.80
21	2018	Gloves	454400.75
22	2018	Helmets	22027.50
23	2018	Mountain Bicycle	136158.15
24	2018	Road Bicycle	207588.00
25	2018	Saddles	213944.00
26	2018	Touring Bicycle	288105.30
27	2018	[null]	2088915.00
28	[null]	[null]	6293208.46

Figure 10-53 Grand totals for each year

CUBE Subclause

In the previous section, you learned how the ROLLUP subclause creates group sub totals and a grand total. The CUBE subclause will create the same group subtotals. In addition to those sub totals, subtotals will also be created for all combinations of the columns listed on the CUBE subclause. For example, if there are three columns listed on the CUBE subclause, 8 totals (7 sub totals and 1 grand total) will be created.

CUBE Subclause Syntax

The CUBE subclause is used to create multiple grouping sets. As shown in the syntax below, the CUBE subclause will create all possible grouping sets for Column 1, Column 2 and Column 3, that you specify on this clause. I used three columns and one aggregate column for illustration purposes. You can use as many or as few columns and aggregate columns, as needed.

```
SELECT
 Column1,
 Column2,
 Column3,
 aggregated column
FROM table name
GROUP BY
 CUBE (Column1, Column2, Column3)
```

Example #19 GROUPING SETS

To the right, is the (sample) syntax for the **GROUPING SETS** subclause. It creates the same result as the CUBE syntax above.

Clearly, one sub clause can require more typing, then the other. <smile>

The GROUPING SETS subclause is covered in more detail, later in this chapter.

```
SELECT
 Column1,
 Column2,
 Column3,
 aggregated column
FROM table name
GROUP BY
 GROUPING SETS (
  (Column1),
  (Column2),
  (Column3),
  (Column1, Column2, Column3),
  (Column1, Column2),
  (Column1, Column3),
  (Column2, Column3),
  () )
```

> **CUBE Subclause vs GROUPING SETS Subclause**
> As you can see, if you need to create all possible grouping sets, use the CUBE subclause. If you only need specific grouping sets, use the GROUPING SETS subclause. However, as you will learn later in Exercise 10.31, you can list specific sets with the CUBE subclause.

Exercise 10.30: Use The CUBE Subclause

The query that you will create, will create four grouping sets.

1. Create this query.

```
SELECT Category, SubCategory,
  SUM(Sales) AS SalesTotal
FROM CategorySales
GROUP BY
  CUBE (Category, SubCategory);
```

2. Save the query as `E10.30 CUBE subclause.`

   Figure 10-54 shows the result. 67 rows were returned.

   The first row is the grand total of all sales, for the rows that were returned.

	category character varying(	subcategory character varyi	salestotal numeric
1	[null]	[null]	6293208.46
2	Children's Bicycle	Nicos Child	621902.80
3	Bicycle Locks	ATB Lock	99570.50
4	Bicycle Locks	Rhino Lock	140978.90

Figure 10-54 Result of using the CUBE subclause

Example #20 Partial CUBE

A partial CUBE is similar to a partial ROLLUP, because it allows you to limit the number of subtotals/grouping sets that are created.

This query reduces the number of grouping sets from the query created in Exercise 10.29. The result is shown in Figure 10-55. 37 rows were returned.

```
SELECT Category, SubCategory,
  SUM(Sales) AS SalesTotal
FROM CategorySales
GROUP BY Category,
  CUBE (SubCategory)
ORDER BY Category, SubCategory;
```

	category character varying	subcategory character varying (5	salestotal numeric
7	Bicycle Locks	U Lock	84311.70
8	Bicycle Locks	[null]	1095707.50
9	Children's Bicycle	Children's Bicycles	131737.10
10	Children's Bicycle	Nicos Child	621902.80

Figure 10-55 Result of a partial CUBE

Exercise 10.31: Create Specific Grouping Sets With The CUBE Subclause

While the CUBE subclause can create all possible grouping sets, it can also be used to create specific grouping sets. That is the type of query that you will create in this exercise. It is similar to the query created in Exercise 10.30. If you want, you can save or copy that query, then make the changes.

1. Create this query.

```
SELECT SalesYear, Category, SubCategory,
  SUM(Sales) AS SalesTotal
FROM CategorySales
GROUP BY SalesYear,
  CUBE (Category, SubCategory)
ORDER BY SalesYear, Category, SubCategory;
```

2. Save the query as `E10.31 CUBE with specific sets.`

Figure 10-56 shows the result. 201 rows were returned.

The sales total is now grouped by year, in addition to being grouped by category and sub category.

	salesyear numeric	category character varying (5	subcategory character varying (50	salestotal numeric
6	2016	Bicycle Locks	Titan Lock	118633.90
7	2016	Bicycle Locks	U Lock	59667.30
8	2016	Bicycle Locks	[null]	463850.80
9	2016	Children's Bicycle	Children's Bicycles	8365.50

Figure 10-56 Specific grouping sets created using the CUBE subclause

Exercise 10.32: Replace The ROLLUP Subclause With The CUBE Subclause

In this exercise, you will replace the ROLLUP subclause with the CUBE subclause. This will let you see the difference between the data that these subclauses retrieve.

1. Save the E10.27 query as `E10.32 Replace ROLLUP with CUBE.`

2. Replace the word ROLLUP with `CUBE`.

Figure 10-57 shows the result. 251 rows were returned.

As you can see, there are a lot more sub totals, one for each region name, state and customer type combination.

Sometimes, changing the order that the columns appear in, in the result, will make the data easier to understand.

	regionname character vary	state charac	customertype character varyi	nbrofcustomers bigint
5	Midwest	IL	Retail	4
6	Midwest	IL	[null]	28
7	Midwest	KS	Online	3
8	Midwest	KS	[null]	3

Figure 10-57 Result of replacing the ROLLUP subclause with the CUBE subclause

In the next section, you will learn that the GROUPING SETS subclause is used to specify the grouping of data in one query. Later, in Exercise 10.34, you will create a query that defines a single grouping set for the Sub Category field.

GROUPING SETS Subclause

This is the third subclause that can be added to the GROUP BY clause. A grouping set, is a set of columns that you want to group by. As you saw, the CUBE subclause creates a lot of subtotals, most of which may not be of any value to the person reading the report. If you are using a dataset that has hundreds of thousands of rows, using a CUBE subclause will require a lot of processing.

If you do not need all of the subtotals that the CUBE subclause creates, but you need more totals than the ROLLUP subclause or GROUP BY clause can create, the GROUPING SETS subclause may create enough subtotals to handle your needs.

A grouping set is a group of columns that you group on. Technically, any query that aggregates data is a grouping set. What you will see is that the GROUPING SETS subclause creates similar results as combining multiple GROUP BY queries. It will remind you of applying the **UNION ALL OPERATOR** to specific groups. That is because when GROUPING SETS have two or more elements, the result is a union of the elements.

Example #21 GROUPING SETS Example

Both GROUP BY expressions below will return the same rows of data.

GROUP BY GROUPING SETS (ROLLUP (Country, RegionID))

GROUP BY ROLLUP (Country, Region)

The query below uses the UNION ALL operator to combine two GROUP BY statements. Figure 10-58 shows the result. Notice that the first GROUP BY clause uses the ROLLUP subclause and the second GROUP BY clause uses the CUBE subclause.

```
SELECT Country, RegionID,
  SUM(LastYearsTotalOrderAmount) AS TotalSales
FROM Customers
GROUP BY ROLLUP (Country, RegionID)
UNION ALL
SELECT Country, RegionID,
  SUM(LastYearsTotalOrderAmount)
FROM Customers
GROUP BY CUBE (Country, RegionID);
```

	country character v	regionid integer	totalsales numeric
1	[null]	[null]	18647316.90
2	USA	41	168487.24
3	Pakistan	[null]	5486.70
4	Mongolia	[null]	5223.50

Figure 10-58 Result of using two GROUP BY statements

Exercise 10.33: Use The GROUPING SETS, CUBE And ROLLUP Subclauses

If the query in Example #21 has you frowning and saying "What the bleep?", hopefully, after you complete this exercise, these subclauses will make more sense.

1. Create this query.

```
SELECT Country, RegionID,
  SUM(LastYearsTotalOrderAmount) AS TotalSales
FROM Customers
GROUP BY GROUPING SETS (ROLLUP (Country, RegionID),
  CUBE (Country, RegionID))
ORDER BY Country, RegionID;
```

2. Save the query as `E10.33 Use the grouping sets, cube & rollup subclauses.`

   This query returns the same data that the query in Example #21 returned. The difference is that the 435 rows in this query, are not returned in the same order as they were in Example #21. Figure 10-59 shows the result. Even with adding sort criteria, the rows are not returned in the same order.

	country character varying (75)	regionid integer	totalsales numeric
260	United Arab Emirates	[null]	95900.85
261	United Kingdom	[null]	578229.17
262	United Kingdom	[null]	578229.17
263	United Kingdom	[null]	578229.17
264	United Kingdom	[null]	578229.17
265	USA	1	12175.95

Figure 10-59 Result of using the GROUP BY subclauses

Example #22 Understanding Empty Sets

Using the GROUP BY() clause is how to specify an empty group. It creates the grand total, of the rows retrieved. The query below creates the last years total order amount for each country and then calculates the grand total for all countries, as shown at the bottom of Figure 10-60. Row 72 in the figure is the grand total.

```
SELECT Country,
  SUM(LastYearsTotalOrderAmount) AS TotalAmount
FROM Customers
GROUP BY GROUPING SETS ( Country, () )
ORDER BY COUNTRY;
```

	country character va	totalamount numeric
67	USA	11970239.56
68	Venezuela	36000.00
69	Vietnam	15492.32
70	Wales	72000.00
71	Zimbabwe	22600.23
72	[null]	18647316.90

Figure 10-60 Result of using the GROUP BY() empty set

Example #23 Category And Sub Category Grouping Set

The query below emulates a grouping set, because it uses an aggregate expression and groups on the category and sub category fields. It returns a sales total for each category and sub category group. Figure 10-61 shows the result. 29 rows were returned.

```
SELECT Category, SubCategory, SUM(Sales) AS SalesTotal
FROM CategorySales
GROUP BY Category, SubCategory
ORDER BY Category, SubCategory;
```

Another way to explain the result is that this query really only returns the sales totals for the sub categories. Remember that when more than one field is added to the GROUP BY clause, the results are for the last field on the GROUP BY clause.

	category character varying (	subcategory character varying (5	salestotal numeric
7	Bicycle Locks	U Lock	84311.70
8	Children's Bicycle	Children's Bicycles	131737.10
9	Children's Bicycle	Nicos Child	621902.80
10	Gloves	Crochet Gloves	205306.20

Figure 10-61 Grouping set

Example #24 Category Grouping Set

The query below returns the sales total by category. It defines the (category) grouping set, as shown in Figure 10-62.

```
SELECT Category,
 SUM(Sales) AS SalesTotal
FROM CategorySales
GROUP BY GROUPING SETS (Category);
```

	category character varying (	salestotal numeric
1	Bicycle Locks	1095707.50
2	Gloves	1147401.65
3	Children's Bicycle	753639.90
4	Road Bicycle	676790.80

Figure 10-62 Category grouping set

Exercise 10.34: Create The Sub Category Grouping Set

In this exercise, you will create a single grouping set for the sub category field.

1. Create this query.

```
SELECT SubCategory, SUM(Sales) AS SalesTotal
FROM CategorySales
GROUP BY GROUPING SETS (SubCategory)
ORDER BY SubCategory;
```

2. Save the query as `E10.34 Sub category grouping set.`

   Figure 10-63 shows the result. 29 rows were returned.

   The result displays the sales total for all products in each sub category.

   Notice that the Sales Total values are the same as the ones shown earlier in Figure 10-61.

	subcategory character varying (5	salestotal numeric
4	Child Helmet	245460.50
5	Child Saddle	80204.00
6	Children's Bicycles	131737.10
7	Crochet Gloves	205306.20

Figure 10-63 Sub category grouping set

Example #25 Empty Grouping Set

The query below creates an empty grouping set(). An empty grouping set returns a single value, which is a total for the table (aka a **TOTALS TABLE**, as discussed earlier in this chapter). This set returns the sales grand total for all categories and sub categories, as shown in Figure 10-64.

This query is different from the one in Example #22, because this query does not use the GROUP BY clause.

```
SELECT SUM(Sales) AS SalesTotal
FROM CategorySales;
```

	salestotal numeric
1	6293208.46

Figure 10-64 Result of an empty grouping set

Grouping Sets Recap

The four queries above (in the three examples and one exercise) returned result sets that emulated the four different grouping sets, listed to the right. These grouping sets can be combined into one query, as you will see in Example #26.

① Category, Sub Category
② Category
③ Sub Category
④ Empty Set

Example #26 UNION ALL Operator

To create a consolidated set with the aggregated data for the four grouping sets listed above, you could use the **UNION ALL OPERATOR**, shown in the query, to the right.

The UNION ALL operator requires each result set to have the same number of columns. That means that NULL has to be added to some of the queries, as shown in bold, in the query.

Figure 10-65 shows the result. 67 rows were returned.

The UNION ALL query worked as expected, because it created a single result set with the aggregate values for all of the grouping sets. While the query worked as expected, there are two problems, as explained below.

① With a large data set, the UNION ALL query will run slow, because it has to run four queries and combine the results from each query into one result set.
② It is a whole lot of typing! Aren't you happy that the query in this example wasn't an exercise? <smile>

```
-- Category, Subcategory group
SELECT Category, SubCategory,
  SUM(Sales) AS SalesTotal
FROM CategorySales
GROUP BY Category, SubCategory

UNION ALL

-- Category group
SELECT Category, NULL,
  SUM(Sales) AS SalesTotal
FROM CategorySales
GROUP BY Category

UNION ALL

-- Subcategory group
SELECT NULL, SubCategory,
 SUM(Sales) AS SalesTotal
FROM CategorySales
GROUP BY Subcategory

UNION ALL

-- Empty set group
SELECT NULL, NULL, SUM(Sales) AS SalesTotal
FROM CategorySales

ORDER BY Category, SubCategory
```

	category character	subcategory character vary	salestotal numeric
1	[null]	[null]	6293208.46
2	[null]	Adult Helmet	112980.86
3	[null]	ATB Lock	99570.50
4	[null]	Chain Locks	66877.30

Figure 10-65 Result of the UNION ALL query

The solution is to use the GROUP BY **GROUPING SETS** subclause.

The GROUPING SETS subclause is used to define many grouping sets in the same query. To the right, is the basic syntax for this subclause.

```
SELECT Column1, Column2, Column3,
   Aggregate function (Column4)
FROM table
GROUP BY
 GROUPING SETS (
 (Column1),
 (Column1, Column2),
 (Column2),
 (Column3) )
```

Exercise 10.35: Create A Query That Uses The GROUPING SETS Subclause

In this exercise, you will create a query that accomplishes the same result as the UNION ALL query, shown above in Example #26. The query will create four grouping sets. This is also another way to create the query in Exercise 10.30, that used the CUBE subclause.

1. Create this query.

   Each line of code below "GROUPING SETS", is one of the four grouping sets that is in the UNION ALL example above.

   They are also the same grouping sets listed right above Example #26.

```
SELECT Category, SubCategory,
  SUM(Sales) AS SalesTotal
FROM CategorySales
GROUP BY
  GROUPING SETS (
    (Category, SubCategory),
    (Category),
    (SubCategory),
    ()    )
ORDER BY Category, SubCategory;
```

2. Save the query as `E10.35 Grouping Sets`.

   The same 67 rows shown earlier in Figure 10-65 were returned, which is what is expected. This is way less typing then the UNION ALL query in Example #26.

GROUPING Function

This function is in the Aggregate function category, even though it is not listed in Table 10-1. This function is used to indicate whether or not a column or expression is aggregated. This is done by checking to see whether the NULL in the result is a subtotal or a grand total. The GROUPING function returns a 1 if the column is aggregated. A 0 (zero) is returned if the column is not aggregated. The GROUPING function can only be used on the SELECT, ORDER BY or HAVING clause, when the GROUP BY clause is used.

Example #27 Understanding The Grouping Function

The query in Example #18 was modified in this example to include using the GROUPING function. This query creates two columns in the result. One for each of the GROUPING columns in the query.

As discussed in the previous section, the GROUPING function returns a 1 or zero.

```
SELECT SalesYear, Category,
  SUM(Sales) AS TotalYearlySales,
  GROUPING(SalesYear) AS "Grouping(SalesYear)",
  GROUPING(Category) AS "Grouping(Category)"
FROM CategorySales
GROUP BY ROLLUP (SalesYear, Category)
ORDER BY SalesYear, Category;
```

As shown at the bottom of Figure 10-66, the GROUPING (Sales Year) column will display a 1, when the Sales Year column has a NULL value.

The GROUPING (Category) column displays a 1, when the Category column has a NULL value.

	salesyear numeric	category character varying (	totalyearlysales numeric	Grouping(SalesYear) integer	Grouping(Category) integer
18	2017	[null]	2624473.36	0	1
19	2018	Bicycle Locks	327298.50	0	0
20	2018	Children's Bicycle	439392.80	0	0
21	2018	Gloves	454400.75	0	0
22	2018	Helmets	22027.50	0	0
23	2018	Mountain Bicycle	136158.15	0	0
24	2018	Road Bicycle	207588.00	0	0
25	2018	Saddles	213944.00	0	0
26	2018	Touring Bicycle	288105.30	0	0
27	2018	[null]	2088915.00	0	1
28	[null]	[null]	6293208.46	1	1

Figure 10-66 GROUPING function example

Exercise 10.36: Use The GROUPING Function

In this exercise, you will modify the query created in Exercise 10.35 by adding criteria for the GROUPING function.

1. Save the E10.35 query as `E10.36 GROUPING function`.
2. Change the sort of the Category field to descending.
3. Add the two lines that start with the word GROUPING, as shown below.

```
SELECT
 GROUPING (Category) AS "Is Category Grouped?",
 GROUPING (SubCategory) AS "Is SubCategory Grouped?",
 Category, SubCategory, SUM(Sales) AS SalesTotal
FROM CategorySales
GROUP BY
 GROUPING SETS (
  (Category, SubCategory),
  (Category),
  (SubCategory),
  () )
ORDER BY Category DESC, SubCategory;
```

Figure 10-67 shows the result. The same 67 rows were returned.

This layout makes it easier to know which category the subtotal is for.

	Is Category Grouped? integer	Is SubCategory Grouped? integer	category character varying	subcategory character varying (50)	salestotal numeric
29	1	0	[null]	Vertigo Helmet	87803.20
30	1	1	[null]	[null]	6293208.46
31	0	0	Touring Bicycle	Touring Bicycle (Romeo)	194696.85
32	0	0	Touring Bicycle	Touring Bicycle (Wheeler)	273997.95
33	0	1	Touring Bicycle	[null]	468694.80

Figure 10-67 Result of using the GROUPING function to indicate how the sales total is aggregated

Sometimes, the GROUPING function is used as a substitute for creating labels for null values that the ROLLUP clause generates.

The number 1 in either of the first two columns, means that the sales total is aggregated for the row, by that field. For example, in row 29, the sales total is aggregated by the Category field, but not by the Sub Category field. In row 33, the opposite is true. The sales total is aggregated by the Sub Category field, but not by the Category field. In row 30, the sales total is aggregated by both fields.

Exercise 10.37: Group On Four Fields

The query that you will create in this exercise takes the query in the previous exercise up a level. By that I mean that this query will create groups based on the values in four fields.

1. Create this query.

```
SELECT SalesYear, Category, SubCategory,
  SUM(Sales) AS SalesTotal,
  GROUPING(SalesYear) AS "GroupOnYear",
  GROUPING(Category) AS "GroupOnCategory",
  GROUPING(SubCategory) AS "GroupOnSubCategory"
FROM CategorySales
GROUP BY ROLLUP (SalesYear, Category, SubCategory)
ORDER BY SalesYear, Category, SubCategory;
```

2. Save the query as `E10.37 Group on 4 fields`.

   As shown in Figure 10-68, adding the year as a field to group on, creates more subtotals. 115 rows were returned. The next to last row in the figure shows the totals for 2016.

Figure 10-69 shows the rows at the end of the result. The last row in the figure displays the grand total for all groups.

	salesyear numeric	category character varying	subcategory character varying (50)	salestotal numeric	GroupOnYear integer	GroupOnCategory integer	GroupOnSubCategory integer
34	2016	Saddles	[null]	247347.50	0	0	1
35	2016	Touring Bicycle	Touring Bicycle (Romeo)	1783.50	0	0	0
36	2016	Touring Bicycle	Touring Bicycle (Wheeler)	11440.50	0	0	0
37	2016	Touring Bicycle	[null]	13224.00	0	0	1
38	2016	[null]	[null]	1579820.10	0	1	1
39	2017	Bicycle Locks	ATB Lock	7293.00	0	0	0

Figure 10-68 Subtotals for categories and subcategories

	salesyear numeric	category character varying	subcategory character varying (50)	salestotal numeric	GroupOnYear integer	GroupOnCategory integer	GroupOnSubCategory integer
106	2018	Road Bicycle	[null]	207588.00	0	0	1
107	2018	Saddles	Child Saddle	63581.00	0	0	0
108	2018	Saddles	Ladies Saddles	55363.50	0	0	0
109	2018	Saddles	Mens Saddle	94999.50	0	0	0
110	2018	Saddles	[null]	213944.00	0	0	1
111	2018	Touring Bicycle	Touring Bicycle (Romeo)	120533.85	0	0	0
112	2018	Touring Bicycle	Touring Bicycle (Wheeler)	167571.45	0	0	0
113	2018	Touring Bicycle	[null]	288105.30	0	0	1
114	2018	[null]	[null]	2088915.00	0	1	1
115	[null]	[null]	[null]	6293208.46	1	1	1

Figure 10-69 Grand total for all groups

Exercise 10.38: Use The GROUPING SETS Subclause Instead Of The ROLLUP Subclause

In this exercise, you will modify the E10.27 query to use the GROUPING SETS subclause, instead of the ROLLUP subclause.

1. Save the E10.27 query as `E10.38 Replace ROLLUP with GROUPING SETS`.

2. Replace the word ROLLUP with `GROUPING SETS`.

   Figure 10-70 shows the result. 56 rows were returned.

   Rows 1-4 are the grand totals for each region that has customers.

   The last two rows are grand totals for customers in the USA that have a customer type. Notice that there is only one row per state. These rows provide the total number of customers for the state.

	regionname character var	state charac	customertype character varyi	nbrofcustomers bigint
1	Midwest	[null]	[null]	125
2	Northeast	[null]	[null]	71
3	South	[null]	[null]	90
4	West	[null]	[null]	91
5	[null]	AK	[null]	4
6	[null]	AL	[null]	12
			⋮	
53	[null]	WV	[null]	5
54	[null]	WY	[null]	4
55	[null]	[null]	Online	181
56	[null]	[null]	Retail	196

Figure 10-70 Result of replacing ROLLUP with GROUPING SETS

Summary

This chapter formally introduced the aggregate functions and demonstrated a variety of ways to use them, including calculating the average price of products by category, finding the highest retrial price and calculating the gross profit. More than likely, on your own, you will probably use the aggregate functions on a regular basis. Keep the following in mind when creating a summary query.

☑ The WHERE clause cannot have an expression that uses an aggregate function.

☑ The WHERE and HAVING clauses can use any column in the tables in the query.

The GROUP BY subclauses, ROLLUP, CUBE and GROUPING SETS, were covered. As you learned, they add more functionality to the GROUP BY clause by being able to create more complex groups, that have totals. This is accomplished by specifying more than one set of criteria to group on. This takes the grouping that you learned in Chapter 5, to the next level.

As you learned, there are two ways that the COUNT function can be used: COUNT(*), counts every row and COUNT(Column), only counts rows that have a value in the field used with the COUNT function. Unless you need a count of all rows in a table or all rows in a data set, use the COUNT(Column) option.

The query in Example #17, Customer totals by year, presented an issue. Have you come up with any ideas? The query created a summary table that had a row that did not display a Customer ID or name. If you filtered the Orders table to display all records in 2014 that have the order amount of $5,879.70, several records will be displayed. You will also see that all of these rows have a Customer ID. Now what?

If you compared the Customer ID's in the Orders table to the ones in the Customers table, you will see that the Customers table does not have a customer with the ID of 200. You may be saying, no big deal. There should not be an order for a non existent Customer ID in the Customers table. What if this order should be shipped?

Look at it this way. What if the Customers table was the Employee table and the Orders table was the file that will be used to print pay checks next week and your Employee ID is 200. Is this still no big deal? I am not trying to piss you off. I just want you to learn to pay more attention to the data, question and research why data is displayed the way that it is, especially when the data does not look quite right. Because I created the data used in this book, I created bad data on purpose, so that I could illustrate topics like this.

CREATING SUBQUERIES

After reading this chapter and completing the exercises, you will be able to create a variety of subqueries by using several different operators. This includes learning how to create correlated subqueries.

CHAPTER 11

What Is A SubQuery?

A subquery is a SELECT expression that is embedded inside of a SELECT statement. A query inside of another query, if you will. Technically, SQL supports the three types of subqueries explained below.

① A **ROW SUBQUERY** is an embedded SELECT expression that will return only one row and more than one column (value). While there are some uses for this type of subquery, some commercial databases do not currently support this type of subquery. This type of subquery returns multiple values.
② A **TABLE SUBQUERY** is an embedded SELECT expression on the FROM clause, that retrieves zero to many rows and one or more columns. In this chapter, you will learn how to create and use this type of subquery which will be used as the source for a list of values for the IN operator. This type of subquery returns a whole table of data and is also known as a **DERIVED TABLE**. **VIEWS**, which are covered in the next chapter, are one of the **TABLE EXPRESSIONS** that return a whole table of data.
③ A **SCALAR SUBQUERY** is an embedded SELECT expression that retrieves no more than one row and only one column of data. A calculated (column) expression can be returned, instead of a column from a table. Either column can be returned from a table on the FROM clause of the main (outer) query or from another table. The scalar (single column) value that the subquery retrieves, can be used in the list of columns requested on a SELECT clause or as a comparison value on a WHERE clause. This type of subquery is also known as a **SINGLE VALUE QUERY**, because it only returns one value.

So far in this book, all of the SELECT statements that have been created, are single statements that return data from one or more tables. Like the queries that you have already created, subqueries also use a SELECT statement. This means that a query that uses a subquery will have at least two SELECT statements. The primary focus of this chapter is learning how to create subqueries on the WHERE clause. While the SUM function is used to get a total of the values in a specific column, the function can also be used to get a total of calculated values.

Do you remember the UNION operator? Each query that was joined with the UNION operator had its own SELECT statement. Subqueries work the same way.

Some of the exercises in this chapter will sound familiar. That is because you created them using criteria on the WHERE clause in previous chapters. As you will see, other clauses like the GROUP BY, HAVING and ORDER BY can be used in queries that have subqueries.

The result of the inner query, known as a subquery, is used by the outer query. The inner/subquery performs like an expression and is based on the variables or constant values that you provide. The subquery is evaluated at run time. However, unlike expressions that use a constant value, the result of a subquery can change, as a result of data changes in the tables that are being queried.

Clauses That A Subquery Can Be Created On

In addition to being nested in a SELECT statement, a subquery can also be nested on other clauses. Below is a list of the clauses that a subquery can be added to and what functionality they provide.

① On the SELECT clause to replace using a column.
② On the FROM clause as a table subquery. The subquery can return any number of columns and rows.
③ On the WHERE clause as search criteria.
④ On the HAVING clause as search criteria.
⑤ On the INSERT, UPDATE and DELETE clauses. These options are beyond the scope of this book.

How Subqueries Process Data

There are basically two ways that subqueries process data, as explained below.

① **SUBQUERIES THAT CREATE AN OUTPUT COLUMN**. Subqueries can be used to create an output column (aka return a value from a related table) or to create a comparison on the WHERE clause. One of the best uses that I can think of for using a subquery is when the query needs some type of aggregated total.
② **SUBQUERIES THAT ARE USED AS A FILTER**. This type of subquery is used to create the criteria that will filter data returned from the outer query.

Subqueries are sometimes called an **INNER QUERY** or **NESTED QUERY**.

The statement that contains the subquery is also known as the **OUTER QUERY**. Figure 11-1 illustrates an outer query and a subquery.

```
SELECT OrderID, CustomerID, OrderDate
FROM Orders
WHERE CustomerID IN(
  SELECT CustomerID
  FROM Customers
  WHERE State = 'CA' )
ORDER BY OrderID;
```

outer query

subquery

Figure 11-1 Outer query and subquery illustrated

If a query has a subquery and the ORDER BY clause is used, as shown above in Figure 11-1, the ORDER BY clause only works with the outer query. The ORDER BY clause does not sort rows in a subquery.

Subqueries can be **SELF CONTAINED** or **CORRELATED**. A self contained subquery is one that is not dependent on tables from the outer query. A correlated subquery is dependent on tables from the outer query. Both of these types of subqueries can return a scalar value or multiple values.

How The Query In Figure 11-1 Processes Data

The steps below explain how the query shown above in Figure 11-1, processes the data.

☑ **Step 1** The subquery is processed first. It finds all customers in California.

Step 2 The Customer ID's of the customers in California are passed to the WHERE clause in the outer query. The values are passed in a comma delimited format, which is required by the **IN OPERATOR** (on the third line in Figure 11-1).

☑ **Step 3** The WHERE clause in the outer query changes to "WHERE customer IN (the Customer ID's from Step 2 above)". The outer query is run and returns the orders for customers in California, as shown later in Figure 11-14.

What may not be obvious is that the SELECT statement for a scalar subquery can only return data from one column. Trying to return data from multiple columns in this type of subquery will cause an error. An exception is when the subquery uses the **EXISTS KEYWORD**.

Queries that have subqueries can be hard to read, understand and debug. It is a good idea to type the query on several lines, add comments, add blank lines and indent lines, to make the query easier to read.

Subqueries have a lot of uses. Complex subqueries are used to create **DERIVED TABLES**. Because this is an introduction book, the focus of this chapter is using subqueries on a WHERE clause. The section "Where Subqueries Can Be Used", later in this chapter, has a list of additional places and conditions of valid subquery uses. Like many other SQL features, there are other ways to accomplish the same result that subqueries provide.

Subqueries are often used to create solutions for in-depth analysis. Being able to create subqueries is a skill that is needed when there is a need to dig deeper into the data. They are used to take raw data and turn the data into something meaningful.

Creating subqueries is just one way to tackle the queries created in this chapter. There are other ways of retrieving the result set that a subquery does. In many cases, joining tables or using PostgreSQL as a programming language and using variables or temporary tables, can be used instead of subqueries, to achieve the same result. Using PostgreSQL as a programming language is beyond the scope of this book.

SELF JOINS can be used instead of subqueries, when the outer query and subquery use the same table. The result of using a self join in this scenario, is the same.

Self Contained Scalar Subqueries

Every subquery is contained in an outer query. Self contained subqueries are independent of the tables used in the outer query. What you will like about subqueries is that you can test them independently of the rest of the query. This makes them easier to debug. As discussed earlier, a scalar subquery returns a single value. This type of subquery can be used anywhere in the outer query, that a single value expression can be used, like on the SELECT or WHERE clause.

Example #1 Scalar Subquery

This query finds the order with the earliest (lowest) Order ID. Figure 11-2 shows the order that has the earliest Order ID.

```
SELECT OrderID, CustomerID, OrderDate
FROM Orders
WHERE OrderID = (SELECT MIN(OrderID)
  FROM Orders);
```

	orderid integer	customerid integer	orderdate date
1	1	55	2016-01-01

Figure 11-2 Order with the earliest Order ID

Using Subqueries To Filter Data

A subquery will let you create complex filters that are not reliant on the tables on the FROM clause. Using a subquery on the WHERE clause is the only way that I am aware of to return the correct number of rows, when you want rows from a table based on the filtered rows from a related table.

Table Subquery Keywords

Not to be outdone, there are keywords that are only used with table subqueries. They are used to enhance the subqueries functionality. The keywords are explained in Table 11-1.

Keyword	This Keyword . . .
ALL	Returns TRUE if all of the comparison pairs in the subquery, evaluate to TRUE. Otherwise, FALSE is returned. Comparison pairs are **SCALAR EXPRESSIONS**. If the subquery does not return any rows, the comparison that is used with this keyword is true. (1) (2)
ANY	Compares a value to the values returned by a subquery. The comparison only needs to be true for one value in the list. (1) (2)
EXISTS	Is used to test and find out if there are any records that are returned from the subquery.
SOME	Compares a value to the values returned by a subquery. The comparison only needs to be true for one value in the list. (1) (2)

Table 11-1 Subquery keywords explained

(1) This keyword is used to find out whether the column or expression is greater than or less than any, all or some of the items (values) in the list. In this scenario, the SELECT expression has to be a table subquery that returns one column and zero or more rows. The values in the rows returned by the subquery are used to create the list.

(2) If you create search criteria without using one of these keywords, the subquery has to return a single value. If one of these keywords is used, the subquery can return a list of values.

Where Subqueries Can Be Used

As mentioned earlier, a subquery can be used in other places (in a query), in addition to the WHERE clause, as listed below.

① With the ALL keyword.
② With the EXISTS or NOT EXISTS keyword.
③ With the IN or NOT IN operator.
④ In place of an expression in the outer query.

Subquery Tips
① A subquery must always be enclosed in parentheses.
② Fields from a subquery can be displayed in the result. [See Exercise 11.1, below]
③ Subqueries are used to filter data in the outer query.

Exercise 11.1: Find Orders Shipped In September 2018

The query and subquery that you will create in this exercise, will find orders shipped in September 2018. The outer query returns orders in the date range. The subquery will return the customers company name for the orders returned from the outer query.

1. Create the query shown below.

```
SELECT OrderID, OrderDate, ShipDate,
  (SELECT CompanyName
  FROM Customers
  WHERE Customers.CustomerID = Orders.CustomerID) AS Customer
FROM Orders
WHERE ShipDate BETWEEN '2018-09-01' AND '2018-09-30';
```

2. Save the query as `E11.1 Subquery to find orders shipped in Sept 2018.`

Figure 11-3 shows the result.
113 rows were returned.

As I have said a few times, usually, there is more than one way to accomplish the same task in SQL. Creating subqueries is no exception.

	orderid integer	orderdate date	shipdate date	customer character varying (75)
1	4399	2018-08-26	2018-09-02	Piccolo
2	4402	2018-08-26	2018-09-01	Pedals Inc.
3	4404	2018-08-28	2018-09-03	Karma Bikes
4	4408	2018-08-28	2018-09-01	Rowdy Rims Company

Figure 11-3 Orders shipped in September 2018

Example #2 Another Way To Create The Query In Exercise 11.1

This query uses an **INNER JOIN** to accomplish the same result, shown above in Figure 11-3.

```
SELECT OrderID, OrderDate, ShipDate, CompanyName AS Customer
FROM Orders INNER JOIN Customers
  ON Customers.CustomerID = Orders.CustomerID
WHERE ShipDate BETWEEN '2018-09-01' AND '2018-09-30';
```

Using Aggregate Functions In A Subquery

You have learned how to create queries that used aggregate functions. As luck would have it, aggregate functions can be used in a subquery. The next three exercises show you how to use the MAX and COUNT(*) aggregate functions in a subquery.

Creating Subqueries On The SELECT Clause

When creating subqueries on the SELECT clause, the subquery is used in place of a column. This means that the subquery has to return a single value. The next three exercises show you how to create queries on the SELECT clause.

Exercise 11.2: Find The Most Recent Order Date For Each Customer

In this exercise, the subquery will use the MAX function to find the most recent order date for each customer.

1. Create the query shown below.

```
SELECT FirstName || ' ' || LastName AS Customer,
  (SELECT MAX(OrderDate) AS OrderDate
  FROM Orders
  WHERE Orders.CustomerID = Customers.CustomerID) AS LastOrderDate
FROM Customers;
```

2. Save the query as `E11.2 Subquery to find the most recent order date.`

Figure 11-4 shows the result. 555 rows were returned.

Rows that have NULL in the Last Order Date column, probably means that the customer has not placed an order. It could also be that the order that the customer placed, does not have a Customer ID. In the real world, there should not be any names in the Customers table or rows in the Orders table that do not have a Customer ID. However, I know that data entry errors like this can happen, so I wanted to let you see it in action, as they say.

	customer text	lastorderdate date
10	Anthony Shoemaker	2018-12-11
11	Bill Carter	2018-12-30
12	Gerry Wade	2018-12-07
13	Matthew Banks	[null]

Figure 11-4 Customers and their most recent order date

Exercise 11.3: Calculate The Number Of Orders Each Customer Has Placed

In this exercise, the subquery will use the COUNT(*) function to calculate the number of orders each customer has placed.

1. Create this query.

```
SELECT FirstName || ' ' || LastName AS Customer,
  (SELECT COUNT(*)
  FROM Orders
  WHERE Orders.CustomerID = Customers.CustomerID)
    AS NbrOfOrders
FROM Customers;
```

2. Save the query as `E11.3 Subquery counts the number of customer orders.`

   Figure 11-5 shows the result. 555 rows were returned.

   Rows that have a zero in the Nbr Of Orders column have the same issues as discussed above in Exercise 11.2.

	customer text	nbroforders bigint
12	Gerry Wade	83
13	Matthew Banks	0
14	Rick Pratt	91
15	Christopher Carmine	0

Figure 11-5 Count of customer orders

Exercise 11.4: Display All Customers And Their Largest Order Total

The query and subquery that you will create in this exercise, will return all customers and their largest order total.

1. Create this query.

```
SELECT FirstName || ' ' || LastName AS Customer,
  (SELECT (MAX(OrderAmount))
  FROM Orders
  WHERE Orders.CustomerID = Customers.CustomerID)
    AS LargestOrderTotal
FROM Customers;
```

2. Save the query as `E11.4 Subquery to find each customers largest order total.`

   Figure 11-6 shows the result. 555 rows were returned.

   Rows that have a NULL value means that the customer has not placed an order or there is one of the problems discussed earlier, in Exercise 11.2, with the data.

	customer text	largestordertotal numeric
11	Bill Carter	8819.55
12	Gerry Wade	11156.00
13	Matthew Banks	[null]
14	Rick Pratt	9290.30

Figure 11-6 Customers and their largest order total

Create Filters Using Aggregate Functions In Subqueries

The previous section introduced you to using aggregate functions in subqueries. This section goes a step further by showing you how to use aggregate functions in a subquery to create a filter.

As you have learned, an aggregate function returns one value. This means that the result of the aggregate function expression can be used as part of a comparison in a subquery. This in turn, lets the result of the aggregate function expression be compared to values in a column.

Exercise 11.5: Find Orders With An Order Amount >= The Average Order Amount

In this exercise, you will create a query that calculates the average order amount for all orders, then compares that value to the order amount for each row. The result will display the orders, that have an order amount >= the average of all orders.

1. Create this query.

```
SELECT OrderID, OrderAmount
FROM Orders
WHERE OrderAmount >=
  (SELECT AVG(OrderAmount)
  FROM Orders);
```

2. Save the query as `E11.5 Subquery to find orders greater than or equal to the avg order amount.`

   Figure 11-7 shows the result. 2,966 rows were returned.

	orderid integer	orderamount numeric (18,2)
1	1	2645.87
2	2	8908.05
3	7	6839.10
4	8	9612.47

Figure 11-7 Orders >= the average order amount

I used this query to calculate the average order amount for the table, to test the results shown above in Figure 11-7.

```
SELECT AVG(OrderAmount) AS AVGOrderAmount
FROM Orders;
```

This query calculated the average order amount to be $1,781.49. Every row returned in Exercise 11.5, has an order amount >= that value. This is an example of how to test a query.

The ANY Keyword

The ANY keyword returns TRUE if one of the comparison pairs in the list of values, that the subquery returns, evaluates to TRUE. Otherwise, the keyword returns FALSE. This means that if one of the pairs in the scalar expression returns FALSE, the ANY keyword returns FALSE.

> **ANY Keyword Syntax**
> The syntax to use a subquery with the ANY keyword is: scalar expression comparison operator ANY (subquery)
>
> A scalar expression is any valid expression.
> The comparison operators are =, <>, <, <=, > and >=.
> The subquery must be enclosed in parentheses. It is a SELECT statement that returns a single column of data, which must be the same data type as the scalar expression.

How Comparison Operators Work With The ANY And SOME Keywords

Table 11-2 explains how the ANY and SOME keywords test the values returned by the subquery. When you need to use the SOME keyword, use it in place of the ANY keyword in the first column.

Filter Criteria	The Criteria Translates To...	The Expression Evaluates To TRUE If...
Column = ANY(1,2)	Column IN(1,2)	The column is equal to any of the values returned by the subquery.
Column > ANY(1,2)	Column > 2	The value in the column is greater than the minimum value returned by the subquery.
Column < ANY(1,2)	Column < 2	The value in the column is less than the maximum value returned by the subquery.
Column <> ANY(1,2)	(Column <> 1) AND (Column <> 2)	The value in the column is not equal to at least one of the values returned by the subquery.

Table 11-2 How the ANY and SOME keywords process comparison operators explained

Exercise 11.6: Use The ANY Keyword In A Subquery

In this exercise, you will create a query and subquery that finds products that have a retail price greater than or equal to the average retail price in any category. In this query, the subquery results are grouped by the Product Category ID field.

1. Create this query.

```
SELECT ProductName, RetailPrice
FROM Products
WHERE RetailPrice >= ANY (
  SELECT AVG(RetailPrice)
  FROM Products
  GROUP BY ProductCategoryID);
```

2. Save the query as `E11.6 ANY keyword used in a subquery.`

Figure 11-8 shows the result. 104 rows were returned.

For each category, the subquery finds the average retail price. The outer query uses the average retail price to select the products with a retail price that is greater than or equal to **ANY** categories average retail price.

In other words, a product is returned when its retail price is greater than or equal to the lowest average retail price.

	productname character varyin	retailprice numeric (1
21	Vertigo Helmet	53.90
22	U Lock	17.50
23	XL U Lock	19.90
24	ATB Lock	21.90

Figure 11-8 Subquery used with the ANY operator

Exercise 11.7: Find Products With A Quantity Of Four Or More On One Order

In this exercise, you will create a query that finds orders that have products that have a quantity sold of four or more. As you will see, the outer query in this exercise has the ANY keyword on its WHERE clause.

1. Create this query.

```
SELECT ProductName, RetailPrice
FROM Products
WHERE ProductID = ANY (
  SELECT ProductID
  FROM OrderDetails
  WHERE Quantity >= 4);
```

2. Save the query as `E11.7 Qty 4 or more of a product sold.`

   Figure 11-9 shows the result.
   115 rows were returned.

	productname character varyin	retailprice numeric (1
26	Vertigo Helmet	53.90
27	Chain Lock	4.50
28	U Lock	17.50
29	XL U Lock	19.90

Figure 11-9 Products that sold 4 or more on an order

Exercise 11.8: Find Products With A Retail Price Greater Than The Average Retail Price

In this exercise, you will create a query that find products that have a retail price greater than any of the average retail prices that the subquery generates.

1. Create this query.

```
SELECT ProductName, RetailPrice
FROM Products
WHERE RetailPrice > ANY
  (SELECT AVG(RetailPrice)
  FROM Products
GROUP BY SubCategoryID)
ORDER BY RetailPrice ASC;
```

2. Save the query as `E11.8 Subquery calculates average retail price.`

   Figure 11-10 shows the result.

   The 114 rows returned, have a retail price greater than the average retail price, of all of the products in the table.

   This query does not display the average retail price.

	productname character varyi	retailprice numeric (1
1	Rhino Lock	9.98
2	Mtn Lock	11.90
3	Crochet Glove	13.50
4	Crochet Glove	13.50

Figure 11-10 Products with a retail price greater than any average retail price

The ALL Keyword

The syntax to use the ALL keyword with a subquery is the same as using the ANY keyword, covered earlier in this chapter. Just replace the word ANY with the word ALL.

While the syntax is the same as the ANY keyword, the keywords will return different results. For example, in Exercise 11.6, the query returned 104 rows of data. If you replaced the keyword AND with the keyword ALL in that query, the query will not return the same records, because the retail price would have to be greater than or equal to **ALL** categories average price.

How Comparison Operators Work With The ALL Keyword

Table 11-3 explains how the ALL keyword processes operators.

Filter Criteria	The Criteria Translates To...	The Expression Evaluates To TRUE If...
Column = ALL(1,2)	(Column = 1) AND (Column = 2)	The subquery returns a single value that is equal to the value in the column or if the subquery returns multiple values that are the same, and the values are all equal to the value in the column.
Column > ALL(1,2)	Column > 2	The value in the column is greater than the maximum value returned by the subquery.
Column < ALL(1,2)	Column < 2	The value in the column is less than the minimum value returned by the subquery.
Column <> ALL(1,2)	Column NOT IN(1,2)	The value in the column is not one of the values returned by the subquery.

Table 11-3 How the ALL keyword processes comparison operators explained

Exercise 11.9: Use The ALL Keyword In A Subquery

In this exercise, the query that you create is similar to the one created earlier in Exercise 11.6. The main difference is that you will change the ANY keyword to ALL. This query will find products with a Unit Cost that is greater than or equal to the average Unit Cost in any category.

1. Save the E11.6 query as `E11.9 ALL keyword used with subquery`.

2. Change the ANY keyword to `ALL`, on the third line.

3. Change every occurrence of the Retail Price field to `UnitCost`.

   Figure 11-11 shows the result. These are the products that have a Unit Cost that is greater than or equal to the average Unit Cost.

	productname character varyi	unitcost numeric
1	Test Product	9199.00
2	Test Product	8375.00

Figure 11-11 Result of using the ALL keyword

The IN And NOT IN Operators

The syntax for these operators is WHERE [NOT] IN (subquery).

When the IN operator is used in a subquery, it returns zero or more values. The outer query uses the values to return the rows.

A **TABLE SUBQUERY** can be used with the IN operator. When that is the case, the subquery will return one column and as many rows as necessary, to build the list of values for the IN operator.

> Subqueries that use the IN operator can be created using an **INNER JOIN**.
> Subqueries that use the NOT IN operator can be created using an **OUTER JOIN**.

Exercise 11.10: Use The IN Operator In A Subquery

The query that you will create in this exercise will find products that are in specific product categories (gloves or helmets). To accomplish this, the subquery will use a different table then the outer query uses.

1. Create this query.

```
SELECT ProductName, QtyOnHand, UnitCost
FROM Products
WHERE ProductCategoryID IN (
   SELECT ProductCategoryID FROM ProductCategory
   WHERE ProductCategoryID = 5 OR ProductCategoryID = 6);
```

2. Save the query as
   `E11.10 Use the IN operator with a subquery.`

   Figure 11-12 shows the result. 40 rows were returned.

   The products displayed are in the Gloves or Helmets categories.

	productname character varyi	qtyonhand integer	unitcost numeric
4	Crochet Glove	1200	7.27
5	Crochet Glove	569	7.27
6	Lycra Glove	111	4.29
7	Lycra Glove	507	4.29

Figure 11-12 Products in specific categories

When a subquery is used on the WHERE clause, the fields used or the result of the subquery cannot be displayed in the result. For example, in Exercise 11.10 above, the Product Category ID field will not be displayed. The reason is because the Product Category table is not on the FROM clause of the outer (main) query.

Example #3 Use The EXISTS Keyword Instead Of The IN Operator

This query uses the EXISTS keyword to produce the same 40 rows as the IN operator, in Exercise 11.10 above.

The EXISTS keyword is covered in more detail, later in this chapter.

```
SELECT ProductName, QtyOnHand, UnitCost
FROM Products
WHERE
EXISTS (
  SELECT ProductCategoryID
  FROM ProductCategory
  WHERE Products.ProductCategoryID =
    ProductCategory.ProductCategoryID
   AND (ProductCategoryID = 5 OR ProductCategoryID = 6));
```

Sometimes the EXISTS keyword processes records faster than the IN operator does.

Example #4 Use The NOT IN Operator In A Subquery

The query below will return all products that are not in the Gloves or Helmets categories. Figure 11-13 shows the result. 75 rows were returned.

```
SELECT ProductName, QtyOnHand, UnitCost
FROM Products
WHERE ProductCategoryID NOT IN (
  SELECT ProductCategoryID
  FROM ProductCategory
  WHERE ProductCategoryID = 5
    OR ProductCategoryID = 6);
```

	productname character varyi	qtyonhand integer	unitcost numeric
1	Chain Lock	2204	2.99
2	U Lock	2205	7.58
3	XL U Lock	7040	7.58
4	ATB Lock	2206	7.58

Figure 11-13 Products not in specific categories

Exercise 11.11: Use A Subquery To Find Customer Orders

In this exercise, you will create a query to retrieve all of the orders for customers in California. The subquery will return the customers in California.

1. Create this query.

```
SELECT OrderID, CustomerID, OrderDate
FROM Orders
WHERE CustomerID IN(
  SELECT CustomerID
  FROM Customers
  WHERE State = 'CA')
ORDER BY OrderID;
```

2. Save the query as
   E11.11 CA customer orders.

   Figure 11-14 shows the result. The 748 rows that were returned are for customers in California.

   If you ran the subquery on its own, you would see that there are 26 customers in California.

	orderid integer	customerid integer	orderdate date
1	19	5	2016-01-04
2	31	10	2016-01-11
3	44	10	2016-01-13
4	64	10	2016-01-18

Figure 11-14 Orders from customers in California

After the subquery retrieves the list of customers, that list is used to filter/find the orders that have one of the Customer ID's, that were returned from the subquery.

How To Run The Subquery By Itself

The steps below show you how to run a subquery. Running the subquery alone is helpful when you want to confirm that the subquery is returning the records that you expect it to. This is also helpful if an error is generated and you are having trouble figuring out what the problem is. Keep in mind that if the subquery fails, the entire query will fail.

1. Select (highlight) the code between the parentheses, as shown in Figure 11-15.

```
SELECT OrderID, CustomerID, OrderDate
FROM Orders
WHERE CustomerID IN(
  SELECT CustomerID
  FROM Customers
  WHERE State = 'CA')
ORDER BY OrderID;
```

Figure 11-15 Subquery code selected

2. Run the query. You will see the results shown in Figure 11-16.

   26 rows were returned. This is how many customers are in California.

   All of the 748 rows returned in the query, in Exercise 11.11, have one of these Customer ID's.

	customerid integer
1	5
2	10
3	19
4	34

Figure 11-16 Result of running the subquery alone

Creating A Calculated Field In A Subquery

This is another way to use a subquery. For example, you need a count of orders taken by each sales rep. The outer query would return a list of sales reps. The subquery will create a count of orders for each sales rep. You will create this query in Exercise 11.13.

When the subquery that you create returns a single value, it can be used wherever an expression (calculated field) is used in a query.

Exercise 11.12: Find The Largest Product Total In Each Order

In this exercise, you will use a subquery, instead of an expression (on the SELECT statement), to find the largest line item total (the product with the largest total) for each order.

On one computer that I tested the queries on, this query took over a minute to run.

1. Create the query shown below.

```
SELECT OrderDate, OrderID, SalesRepID,
  (SELECT MAX(LineItemTotal)
FROM OrderDetails
WHERE OrderDetails.OrderID = Orders.OrderID) AS LargestLineItemTotal
FROM Orders
ORDER BY OrderDate;
```

2. Save the query as `E11.12 Subquery used in place of an expression.`

Figure 11-17 shows the result.

The Largest Line Item Total value represents the product that has the largest total on that order.

	orderdate date	orderid integer	salesrepid integer	largestlineitemtotal numeric
1	2014-01-01	4920	9	124.00
2	2014-01-01	4919	9	1319.40
3	2014-01-02	4921	7	2699.55
4	2014-01-02	4922	3	8998.50

Figure 11-17 Largest product total for each order

Exercise 11.13: Count The Number Of Orders For Each Sales Rep

The query that you will create in this exercise will produce a count of orders taken by each sales rep.

1. Create the query shown below.

```
SELECT SalesRep,
  (SELECT COUNT(*)
  FROM Orders
  WHERE Orders.SalesRepID = SalesReps.SalesRepID) AS OrdersTaken
FROM SalesReps
ORDER BY LastName;
```

2. Save the query as `E11.13 Sales rep order count subquery.`

Figure 11-18 shows some of the 15 rows that were returned.

Notice that Laurent Pereira does not have any orders.

	salesrep character varying (5	orderstaken bigint
12	Margaret Peacock	1568
13	Laurent Pereira	0
14	Tim Smith	28
15	Michael Suyama	1578

Figure 11-18 Count of sales reps orders

Exercise 11.14: Calculate The Percent Of The Total

The query that you will create in this exercise, will calculate the total sales amount for each sales rep and their **PERCENT OF SALES.**

1. Create this query.

```
SELECT SalesRep, SUM(OrderAmount) AS SalesTotal,
  ROUND(SUM(OrderAmount) / (SELECT SUM(OrderAmount)
    FROM Orders) * 100 ,2) AS PercentOfSales
FROM SalesReps
  INNER JOIN Orders ON
    Orders.SalesRepID = SalesReps.SalesRepID
GROUP BY SalesRep;
```

The calculation that starts on the second line creates the ratio or percent. This code divides the sum of the order amount by the total amount of all orders. The grand total, if you will, for all orders is calculated in the sub query.

The Percent Of Sales calculation divides each aggregated total by the grand total to create the percent of the grand total, that each sales reps sales represents.

2. Save the query as `E11.14 Calculate the sales reps percent of the total sales.`

Figure 11-19 shows the result.
14 rows were returned.

	salesrep character varying	salestotal numeric	percentofsales numeric
1	Xavier Martin	44780.21	0.26
2	Michael Suyama	3034952.37	17.43
3	Andrew Fuller	29142.99	0.17
4	Robert King	3263593.66	18.75

Figure 11-19 Sales reps percent of total sales

Example #5 Another Way To Format A Value As A Percent

The code in this example will format the data in the Percent Of Sales column differently, then shown above in Figure 11-19. To use the code in this example, replace the second and third lines in the query created in Exercise 11.14, with the code in one of the options below.

This code will display the value with a percent sign and two places after the decimal point, as shown in Figure 11-20. What I find interesting is that really small numbers are not displayed with a value. They are displayed as zero percent, as shown on the last two rows of the figure.

```
ROUND(SUM(OrderAmount) /
 (SELECT SUM(OrderAmount)
FROM Orders), 2) || '%' AS PercentOfSales
```

When I changed the number of decimal places to 3, as shown in this code, the result shown in Figure 11-21 looks much better, in my opinion. I say that because the Sales Total column has a value, so the percent column should display a value that is greater than zero percent.

```
ROUND(SUM(OrderAmount) /
 (SELECT SUM(OrderAmount)
FROM Orders), 3) || '%' AS PercentOfSales
```

	salesrep character varying(5	salestotal numeric	percentofsales text
6	Margaret Peacock	2644886.34	0.15%
7	Anne Dodsworth	3120245.83	0.18%
8	Albert Hellstern	46098.32	0.00%
9	Justin Brid	26845.37	0.00%

Figure 11-20 Percent sign formatting applied with two decimal places

	salesrep character varying(5	salestotal numeric	percentofsales text
6	Margaret Peacock	2644886.34	0.152%
7	Anne Dodsworth	3120245.83	0.179%
8	Albert Hellstern	46098.32	0.003%
9	Justin Brid	26845.37	0.002%

Figure 11-21 Percent sign formatting applied with three decimal places

Exercise 11.15: Find The Top 5 Selling Products

In this exercise, you will create a query that finds the top 5 selling products based on the quantity sold. The total sales amount for the top 5 products will also be calculated.

1. Create the query shown below.

```
SELECT ProductName, COUNT(OrderDetails.ProductID) AS QtySold,
  SUM(LineItemTotal) AS TotalProductSales
FROM OrderDetails
  INNER JOIN Products ON
    OrderDetails.ProductID = Products.ProductID

WHERE ProductName IN (
  SELECT ProductName
  FROM Products
  INNER JOIN OrderDetails ON
    OrderDetails.ProductID = Products.ProductID

-- this group by clause is part of the subquery
GROUP BY ProductName)

-- this group by and order by clauses are part of the outer query
GROUP BY ProductName
ORDER BY QtySold DESC
LIMIT 5;
```

2. Save the query as `E11.15 Top 5 products based on quantity sold.`

   The query and subquery in this exercise are independent of each other. The way that you know this, is because both queries use the same tables.

   While the subquery counts the quantity per product, the value is not passed back to the outer query, which has been the case in other exercises.

Instead, the count of products sold is counted twice, once in the outer query to display the result and once in the subquery to filter the products to find the top 5, based on quantity sold.

These 5 products are used to filter the outer query. What is different about this query, is that the outer query and subquery aggregate data.

Figure 11-22 shows the result.

	productname character varyin	qtysold bigint	totalproductsales numeric
1	Vertigo Helmet	3766	954838.50
2	Lycra Glove	3663	289520.50
3	Crochet Glove	2900	192368.50
4	Pro Helmet	2146	442212.60
5	Road Bicycle	1708	3995143.50

Figure 11-22 Top 5 products sold, based on quantity

Nesting Subqueries

SQL supports several levels of nested subqueries. This means that one subquery is nested in another subquery. Each subquery has its own WHERE clause. The last subquery is processed first, then the next to last subquery is processed, and so on.

Exercise 11.16: Create A Query That Uses Two Subqueries

In this exercise, you will create a query that uses two subqueries. Collectively, they will find all products in category 3 or 5, that have a retail price that is greater than the average retail price of all products in category 3 or 5.

1. Create the query shown below.

```
SELECT ProductID, ProductName, Color, RetailPrice
FROM Products
WHERE RetailPrice > (
  SELECT AVG(RetailPrice)
  FROM Products
WHERE ProductCategoryID IN (
   SELECT ProductCategoryID
   FROM Products
   WHERE ProductCategoryID = '3' OR ProductCategoryID = '5' ))
ORDER BY RetailPrice;
```

2. Save the query as `E11.16 Nested subqueries`.

   Figure 11-23 shows the result. 55 rows were returned.

   The steps below explain how the query was processed.

   Step 1 The second subquery (the last WHERE clause) is processed first. It retrieves a list of products that are in category 3 or 5.

	productid integer	productname character varying (50)	color charact	retailprice numeric (1
1	7052	Mountain Bicycle Child	purple	281.85
2	7051	Mountain Bicycle Child	blue	281.85
3	7050	Road Bicycle	white	329.85
4	7049	Road Bicycle	steel	329.85
5	7048	Road Bicycle	purple	329.85

Figure 11-23 Result of nested queries

   Step 2 The first subquery calculates the average retail price of the products returned in step 1.

   Step 3 The outer query selects products that have a retail price greater than the average retail price of the selected products.

Correlated Subqueries

A correlated subquery is also known as a **REPEATING SUBQUERY** or a **SYNCHRONIZED SUBQUERY**. A correlated subquery is a subquery that depends on and uses the values from the outer query, meaning a correlated subquery depends on the outer query for its data. Most of the subqueries that you have created up to this point are **UNCORRELATED SUBQUERIES** and are only run once for the entire query.

A correlated subquery is executed (run) once for every row that is evaluated by the outer query. If you are familiar with Loops, or DO . . . WHILE statements, in other programming languages, you are familiar with the functionality of a correlated subquery.

> Earlier in this chapter, you learned how to test a subquery. Correlated subqueries cannot be tested like the subqueries that you have learned to create so far, because correlated subqueries depend on data from the outer query.

Exercise 11.17: Find Each Customers First Order

I think the name of this exercise clearly explains what the query will do. <smile>

1. Create this query.

```
SELECT CustomerID, OrderID, OrderDate, OrderAmount
FROM Orders AS Orders1
WHERE OrderDate =
  (SELECT MIN(Orders2.OrderDate)
  FROM Orders AS Orders2
  WHERE Orders2.CustomerID = Orders1.CustomerID)
ORDER BY Orders1.OrderDate;
```

2. Save the query as `E11.17 Find each customers first order.`

Figure 11-24 shows the result. 550 rows were returned.

The outer query filters the subquery, using the Customer ID field to find the first (MIN) order for each customer, based on the order date.

Customer ID's in the outer query (in the Orders1 table) that do not find a match in the Orders2 table are not returned.

	customerid integer	orderid integer	orderdate date	orderamount numeric (18,2)
1	272	4920	2014-01-01	8908.05
2	271	4919	2014-01-01	2645.87
3	273	4921	2014-01-02	39.80
4	274	4922	2014-01-02	43.80

Figure 11-24 Customers first order information

The rows are sorted on the Order Date column. If you scroll down the result, you will see that not all customers first order was in 2014.

Exercise 11.18: Use A Correlated Subquery To Find Products With A Maximum List Price

In this exercise, you will create a query that selects products that have a list (retail) price that is equal to the maximum list price of its category. "TProducts2" is the table alias name for another copy of the Products table.

1. Create the query shown below.

```
SELECT ProductCategoryID AS Category, ProductName, Color, RetailPrice
FROM Products
WHERE RetailPrice IN (
  SELECT MAX(TProducts2.RetailPrice)
  FROM Products AS TProducts2
  WHERE TProducts2.ProductCategoryID = Products.ProductCategoryID
  GROUP BY TProducts2.ProductCategoryID)
ORDER BY ProductCategoryID;
```

2. Save the query as `E11.18 Products with a maximum list price.`

Figure 11-25 shows the products in each category that have the highest price. 39 rows were returned.

In this query, each product is evaluated by the outer query. The subquery finds the highest retail price of all products in each category.

If the retail price of the current product is equal to the maximum retail price for the products category, the product is selected and displayed in the result.

	category integer	productname character varying (5	color character var	retailprice numeric (18
14	2	Touring Bicycle	red	832.35
15	3	Road Bicycle	yellow	764.85
16	3	Road Bicycle mens	champagne	764.85
17	3	Road Bicycle	white	764.85

Figure 11-25 Products that have the maximum list price in each category

This process is repeated for each product, which is what makes the subquery a correlated subquery.

While the subqueries in this chapter only used the equal to operator, other comparison operators can be used.

Exercise 11.19: Find Sales Reps That Sold A Specific Product

In this exercise, you will create two correlated subqueries to find the names of the sales reps that sold product 7054. Remember that the last subquery is processed first.

1. Create the query shown below.

```
SELECT DISTINCT SalesReps.SalesRepID, SalesRep
FROM SalesReps JOIN Orders ON SalesReps.SalesRepID = Orders.SalesRepID

-- find the sales reps id in the orders table & use that to get the
-- sales rep name from the Sales Reps table
WHERE SalesReps.SalesRepID IN
 (SELECT Orders.SalesRepID
FROM Orders

-- look in the order details table for the order id where the
-- product id is 7054
WHERE OrderID IN
 (SELECT OrderID
FROM OrderDetails

-- look in the products table for product 7054
WHERE ProductID IN
 (Select ProductID
FROM Products
WHERE ProductID = 7054)))

ORDER BY SalesReps.SalesRepID;
```

2. Save the query as `E11.19 Sales reps that sold product 7054`.

   Figure 11-26 shows the sales reps that have sold product 7054.

	salesrepid integer	salesrep character varying
1	1	Nancy Davolio
2	3	Janet Leverling
3	4	Margaret Peacock
4	5	Steven Buchanan
5	6	Michael Suyama
6	7	Robert King
7	9	Anne Dodsworth
8	11	Tim Smith

Figure 11-26 Sales reps that sold product 7054

The EXISTS Keyword

The EXISTS keyword checks to see whether or not a related row is in (exists) the result rows returned by the subquery. This keyword can be used in place of some complex INNER JOIN relationships.

Most of the time, the EXISTS keyword is used in a correlated subquery. While this keyword returns the same data as a subquery that uses the IN operator, the EXISTS keyword runs faster, probably at least in part because the subquery does not actually return a result.

When the EXISTS keyword is used on the WHERE clause, it does not look at a specific column of data. Instead, it looks at the result returned by the subquery. If the subquery returns rows, the EXISTS keyword returns True. If no rows are returned, the EXISTS keyword returns FALSE and there is no match on the WHERE clause. The subquery does not actually return a result set, when used with this keyword.

Another way to say it is, the EXISTS keyword checks to see if there are any records returned by the subquery. The EXISTS keyword accepts a subquery as input and returns TRUE if the subquery returns data. Otherwise, the keyword returns FALSE. If the subquery returns a NULL value, the EXISTS keyword evaluates to TRUE.

EXISTS Keyword Syntax
The syntax for this keyword is: WHERE [NOT] EXISTS (subquery)

JOIN Clause vs EXISTS Keyword

The JOIN clause extends the result set by returning rows from another table. The EXISTS keyword returns TRUE or FALSE, depending on whether or not the subquery returns rows.

Exercise 11.20: Use The EXISTS Keyword In A Subquery

In this exercise, you will create a query that retrieves all customers in the USA, that placed an order in 2018.

1. Create this query.

```
SELECT CustomerID, CompanyName, CustomerType
FROM Customers
WHERE EXISTS (
  SELECT CustomerID
  FROM Orders
  WHERE Customers.CustomerID = Orders.CustomerID
    AND date_part('year', OrderDate) = '2018'
    AND Country = 'USA')
ORDER BY CompanyName;
```

2. Save the query as `E11.20 Use the EXISTS keyword with a subquery`.

   Figure 11-27 shows the result.
   316 rows were returned.

	customerid integer	companyname character varying (75)	customertype character varyi
1	413	7 Bikes For 7 Brothers	Retail
2	425	Against The Wind Bikes	Retail
3	297	AIC Childrens	Online
4	482	AIC Childrens	Online

Figure 11-27 Customers in the USA that placed an order in 2018

Exercise 11.21: Find Customers That Placed An Order In June 2018

If this sounds familiar it is, because you created a query in Chapter 6, Exercise 6.5 that produced similar results. The difference in this query, is that each customer is only returned once, regardless of the number of orders that they placed in June 2018.

The query that you will create in this exercise uses the EXISTS keyword and a subquery to create the query.

1. Create the query shown below.

```
SELECT Customers.CustomerID, CONCAT(FirstName, ' ', LastName)
  AS CustomerName
FROM Customers
WHERE EXISTS (SELECT *
  FROM  Orders
  WHERE Customers.CustomerID = Orders.CustomerID
    AND date_part('year', OrderDate) = '2018'
    AND date_part('month', OrderDate) = '06');
```

2. Save the query as `E11.21 Customer orders in June 2018.`

   Figure 11-28 shows the result.

   The same 63 customers from Exercise 6.5, were returned.

	customerid integer	customername text
1	1	Chris Christianson
2	2	Christine Manley
3	4	Alexander Mast
4	5	Patrick Reyess

Figure 11-28 Customers that ordered in June 2018

Example #6 Use The EXISTS Keyword Instead Of The IN Keyword

Exercise 11.19 used the IN keyword in the subqueries to return information.

This query retrieves the same data as the query in Exercise 11.19.

The lines in Courier font are the ones that were modified.

```
SELECT DISTINCT SalesReps.SalesRepID, SalesRep
FROM SalesReps JOIN Orders
  ON SalesReps.SalesRepID = Orders.SalesRepID

WHERE SalesReps.SalesRepID IN (SELECT Orders.SalesRepID
FROM Orders

WHERE OrderID IN (SELECT OrderID
FROM OrderDetails

WHERE EXISTS(SELECT *
FROM Products
WHERE OrderDetails.ProductID = Products.ProductID
  AND ProductID = 7054)))
ORDER BY SalesReps.SalesRepID;
```

Using The HAVING Clause In A Subquery

In Chapter 5, you learned about the HAVING clause and how to use it with the GROUP BY clause to filter groups. It works the same way, when the query has a subquery. So far in this chapter, the queries that you have created, only filtered data using the WHERE clause. This section has exercises that filter the groups by using the HAVING clause.

Exercise 11.22: Find The Customers That Have Placed 10 Or More Orders

The query and subquery that you will create in this exercise, will return a list of customers that have placed 10 or more orders.

1. Create the query shown below.

```
SELECT CustomerID, FirstName || ' ' || LastName AS CustomerName
FROM Customers
WHERE EXISTS (
  SELECT COUNT(*)
  FROM Orders
  WHERE Customers.CustomerID = Orders.CustomerID
  GROUP BY Orders.CustomerID
  HAVING COUNT(*) > 9 );
```

2. Save the query as `E11.22 Customers with 10 or more orders.`

   There are 206 customers that have placed 10 or more orders, as shown in Figure 11-29.

	customerid integer	customername text
1	1	Chris Christianson
2	2	Christine Manley
3	3	Gary Jannis
4	4	Alexander Mast

Figure 11-29 Customers that have placed 10 or more orders

> When creating a subquery that uses a table that has a lot of records, you may find that using the (*) asterisk on the SELECT statement, as shown in the query above, instead of a column name, may cause the query to run faster.

Exercise 11.23: Find The Sales Reps That Have An Average Order Amount >= The Overall Average Order Amount

In this exercise, you will create a query to find each sales reps average order amount and the overall average order amount (the average of all orders). The query will return the sales reps whose sales average is >= the overall average order amount.

1. Create this query.

```
SELECT SalesRep
FROM SalesReps
INNER JOIN Orders ON SalesReps.SalesRepID = Orders.SalesRepID
GROUP BY SalesRep
HAVING AVG(OrderAmount) >= (SELECT AVG(OrderAmount)
  FROM Orders);
```

2. Save the query as
   `E11.23 Subquery to filter groups.`

   Figure 11-30 shows some of the 7 rows that were returned.

   These are the sales reps whose average order amount is >= the average of all orders.

	salesrep character varying
1	Xavier Martin
2	Michael Suyama
3	Andrew Fuller
4	Robert King

Figure 11-30 Sales reps with the largest average orders

Summary

This chapter covered creating subqueries, which are used to filter the data that the outer query uses. I think, at first creating a subquery can be somewhat confusing and a little intimidating. I get that. I think that the key to understanding what subqueries can do is to figure out what the outer query needs to do and what the subquery needs to do. It may help if you write out both queries on paper before sitting in front of the keyboard. The most popular uses for subqueries are on the WHERE clause with the EXISTS keyword and IN operator. Subqueries are also popular when used to create a calculated field.

Several keywords were introduced in this chapter, that are used in subqueries to be able to compare values. Many of the queries that you learned how to create in this chapter used aggregate functions, to get summary data from another table. I don't know about you, but I think that is a pretty cool feature. This chapter also covered nested and correlated subqueries. In addition to all of the subquery functionality covered in this chapter, there are other uses for subqueries, including derived tables.

Hopefully, you have an idea of how powerful subqueries are and how they can be used to create a solution for complex problems. On your own, if you find yourself creating the same subquery a few times, you should probably create a view (coming in the next chapter) for the subquery.

Subquery vs Join Advantages

Both options have advantages, as discussed below.

Subquery Advantages

① Complex or long queries are sometimes easier to create using a subquery.
② A subquery can pass an aggregate value to the outer (main) query.

Join Advantages

① A join may be easier to understand because the relationship between the tables is visible.
② The query can retrieve and display fields from multiple tables.

CREATING AND USING VIEWS

After reading this chapter and completing the exercises you will:

- ☑ Have a better understanding of views and their advantages
- ☑ Be able to create views
- ☑ Know how to create a view that checks for NULL values
- ☑ Know how to use a view in a query, as the data source
- ☑ Know how to modify a view

CHAPTER 12

Views

If you have completed the majority of exercises up to this point, you have probably realized that queries can be somewhat redundant, repetitive, complex or complicated, especially queries that have subqueries or multiple table joins. One solution to keep from having a create the same code in multiple queries is to create a view, that has the code that you need to use over and over. Views can save you time.

Views are often created by a Database Administrator (DBA), or someone that has administrator rights to the database, like you. <smile>. Views allow one to gather data from a variety of tables and combine the data into a "view". This makes it easier for end users to access just the data (the fields) that they need. Views are useful if you use the sorting and data selection (filter) options in the data model. Instead of having to recreate the joins for all of the tables that you need over and over again, to create different queries, select the view that has the fields that you need.

A view creates a **RECORDSET** (the result) of the data that a query retrieves. Views usually display a subset of the data in tables. Views are stored in the database and are like tables, but they do not have the physical characteristics of a table. For example, records cannot be added to or deleted from a view. Fields cannot be added to a view unless the view is modified to include more fields. The field length cannot be changed in a view, like it can in a table.

As business needs increase or change, often more sophisticated reports are needed. Guess what? At least some of the queries that you have created up to that point in this book, would need to be modified to support the new reporting needs. The battle begins when you need to keep the existing queries the way that they are and modify them for new reports.

Usually, this means that some of your queries will become more complex. Instead of having to create (type, save as or copy and paste) the same code over and over again, then add to it, you can save the existing query, in a different format. There are several ways of saving the SQL query, as explained below.

① **CREATE A VIEW** that has the SELECT statements. A view is a stored query. This is known as **ENCAPSULATION**. The view can be reused, over and over.
② **CREATE YOUR OWN USER-DEFINED FUNCTIONS**. This option is usually used to store calculations. This type of function uses table functions/expressions that can store SELECT statements. (1)
③ **CREATE STORED PROCEDURES**. A stored procedure can be used to store SELECT statements and calculations. (1)

(1) User defined functions and stored procedures allow you to do procedural programming, which views do not offer. These topics are beyond the scope of this book.

What Is A View?

A view is a **NAMED QUERY** that is stored in the database. The data returned from running a view looks and functions like a table, which means that it can be used to create queries. Views are created to select fields from one or more tables to create a data set. Often, views are created for sets of tables (like the Orders, Order Details, Sales Rep and Customers tables) to keep from having to create the same joins in multiple queries, over and over again. The views that are most helpful, are ones that have columns from two or more tables.

An example is creating a view that selects fields from the Orders and Order Details tables. What you will find is that like creating joins, creating a view uses ID fields. The code for creating views is just like the code for creating any query that returns data from tables.

Creating A View
Views are more flexible when they do not use filters. However, if you know that you need a view that only contains data for a specific year or years, or a view for customers in a certain country for example, by all means create it. The views that I am saying not to create are ones that have multiple filters, unless it is absolutely mandatory. The reason is because many reporting tools have functionality to create filters or parameters, that the person creating or running the report can use to select the filter values that they need. This allows a view to be more universal, and have the ability to be used as the data source for more than one report.

Advantages Of Creating Views

In addition to views being stored in the database, other reasons that views are created, are explained below.

① **TO MAKE IT EASIER TO CREATE COMPLEX QUERIES**. By this I mean, users may not understand table relationships (one-to-many, one-to-one, etc), which will make it difficult for them to create the appropriate table joins to get the data that they need.
② **FOR DATA SECURITY REASONS**. Users should not have direct access to the tables, which in the real world, is live data. Views are also used to protect sensitive data, as explained in the next item.
③ **TO CONTROL WHICH FIELDS USERS HAVE ACCESS TO**. For example, the Sales Reps table used in this book has date of birth and salary information. Uses should not have access to that data, so creating a sales rep view that does not have those columns is appropriate.
④ **TO REUSE SQL STATEMENTS** When a complex query is created, often there is a need to use it for more than one report.
⑤ **TO CHANGE THE FORMATTING OF SOME FIELDS** As you have seen, numeric data in particular, is not a format that is suitable for a report. It may be helpful to format some of the data for the person that uses the data to create a report.
⑥ **TO STORE CALCULATIONS THAT ARE USED ON A REGULAR BASIS**. For example, users may not know their companies formula to calculate the net profit. More realistically, the company may not want all users to know that information. The result of the net profit calculation is stored in a column named "Net Profit" in the view, and the user does not see the calculation, just the result of it. That is because they do not have access to see the code for the query or the view.

In a way, a view is a virtual table that has columns from one or more tables in the database. I say that because what is probably not obvious is that views **DO NOT** store data, like tables do. Views store a query that retrieves data from tables and sometimes, other views. The query that creates a view, is saved like any query that you have created so far. This allows the view to always use current (live) data.

View Requirements

Below are some of the requirements for creating views. Your company may have additional requirements.

☑ In the PostgreSQL environment used in this book, you have complete access to everything in the database. In the workplace, you will probably need to be given security access to the database, even in a test environment.
☑ A view must have a unique name in the database. If there is a table in the database with the name that you want to use for a view name, you cannot use the name.
☑ A view can be created using data that is returned from another view.

Restrictions And Limitations Of Views

While views have a lot of benefits, there are some features about views that you need to be aware of. These features are explained below.

☑ Views do not support the ORDER BY clause, when the clause is also used in a query that references the view.
☑ A subquery cannot be added to the FROM clause.
☑ The SELECT clause cannot reference variables or parameters.
☑ Triggers cannot be used in a view.

Creating Views

The **CREATE VIEW STATEMENT** is used to create a view. It must be the first line of code in the query, that will be used to create a view.

Syntax To Create A View
The syntax to create a view is:
CREATE [OR REPLACE] VIEW view name AS

[OR REPLACE] This argument is used to modify the existing view. This argument tells the database that if the view already exists, to replace it with this one. You can use this argument in every query that you create, to keep from having to remember to add it when you need to modify the view.

Unlike other SQL databases, PostgreSQL has a requirement when replacing a view. The requirement is that the revised query must have columns with the same names, in the same order, as the original view and the same data types. New columns can be added to the end of the list. If the revised query does not meet these requirements, right-click on the view that you want to replace ⇒ Select **DELETE/DROP**, to delete the view ⇒ Run the revised view.

Using A Wildcard Character

While the * wildcard character can be used to create a view, it is probably not a good idea. That is because new fields could be added to the underlying table(s) that should not be in the view.

As if that wasn't bad enough, the new field(s) could have sensitive data. A view that is created using this wildcard character would automatically add the new fields with the sensitive data to the view, if the correct security has not been applied to the fields that have sensitive data. This could be a huge problem, depending on the data that the new fields contain.

> Before creating views on your own, it would be a good idea to go back to Chapters 6 and 7 and re-read the information on join types, especially if you are new to joining tables. I say this because I know how incredibly easy it is to use the wrong join type and not even realize it. This is because most queries will return some data, even if the join type is incorrect.

> **Formatting Fields In A View**
> For the most part, when creating a view, it is best to not format numeric and date fields. Keep in mind that formatted numeric fields are converted to text. This means that when you create a query that uses the view as the data source, you will not be able to use the formatted numeric field as part of a calculation or filter and get the results that you expect. In a query that uses a view, you can format fields, as you have learned, throughout this book. Also remember that the two main reasons for creating views are:
> ① To make it easier for users to only have access to the fields that they need.
> ② To keep from having to join the same tables over and over in different queries.

> While I use the letter "v" as part of the view name in this book, that is not a requirement. I did it to help make it easier to know which data source is a view, versus a table data source, in a query.

Exercise 12.1: Create A Sales Reps View

As I said earlier, there can be fields in a table that most users should not have access to. In this exercise, you will create a view that does not include all of the fields in the Sales Reps table.

1. Create this query.

```
CREATE VIEW v_salesreps
AS
SELECT SalesRep, Position
FROM SalesReps;
```

> The order that the fields are listed in on the SELECT clause, is the order that they are added to the view.

2. Save the query as `E12.1 Sales Reps view` ⇒ Run the query, which will create the view.

> **How To Display Data Retrieved By A View, In A Query**
> When a view is run, it does not display data on the Data Output tab. Instead, you will see the CREATE VIEW message. Yes, it is strange not seeing data returned, when a query that creates a view is run. The data that the view selects can be viewed, just like data in a table can. If you do not see a view that you created in the Views folder, refresh the Views folder.

3. On the Browser panel, display the Views folder in the database. You will see the view that you just created, as shown in Figure 12-1.

Figure 12-1 Sales Reps view

> The columns in the view have the same data type as the column in the table that it came from. If you want the column to have a different name in the view, create an alias for the column in the query.

4. Right-click on the view name ⇒ View/Edit Data ⇒ All Rows.

   You will see the window shown in Figure 12-2.

   The Query Editor tab shows the view name and the query that was used to create the view.

   The Data Output tab displays the data that the view selected.

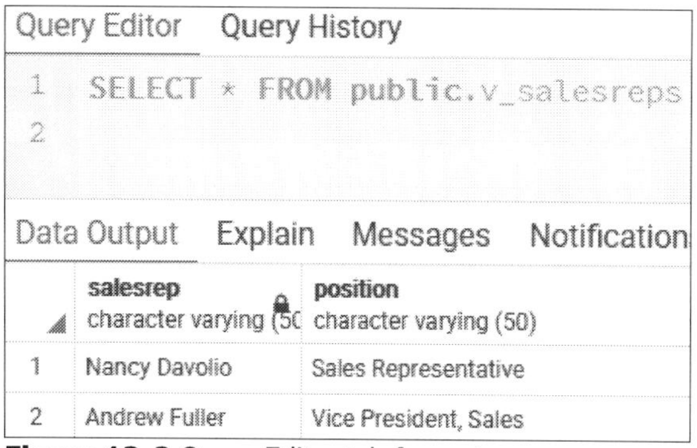

Figure 12-2 Query Editor tab for a view

If you make a mistake creating the view and did not include the OR REPLACE option, right-click on the view in the Views folder and select **DELETE/DROP**. Then run the query again. The other option is to include the OR REPLACE option in every view query that you create.

Exercise 12.2: Create A View Using Two Tables

In this exercise, you will create a view that uses fields from the Customers and Regions tables.

1. Create the query shown below.

```
CREATE VIEW v_CustomersWithRegion
AS
SELECT FirstName, LastName, LastYearsTotalOrderAmount AS LastYearsTotal,
  RegionName
FROM Customers INNER JOIN Regions ON
  Customers.RegionID = Regions.RegionID;
```

2. Save the query as `E12.2 Customers & Regions view`.

3. Run the query ⇒ Display the data that was retrieved.

   Figure 12-3 shows the columns in the view.

   This view only contains customers that have a region. The Customers table has 555 rows. You will see that the view has 377 rows.

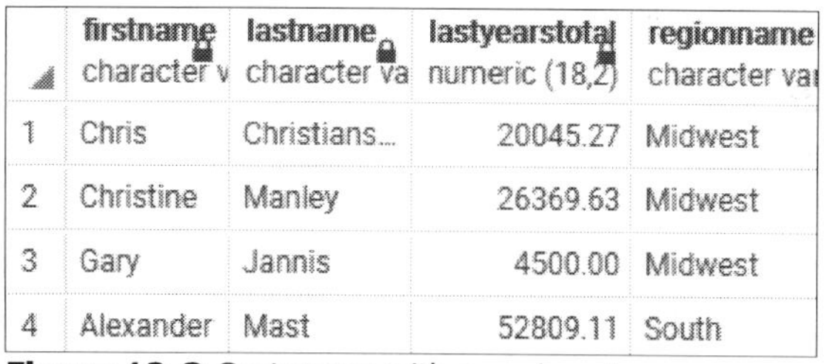

	firstname character v	lastname character va	lastyearstotal numeric (18,2)	regionname character va
1	Chris	Christians...	20045.27	Midwest
2	Christine	Manley	26369.63	Midwest
3	Gary	Jannis	4500.00	Midwest
4	Alexander	Mast	52809.11	South

Figure 12-3 Customers with a region view

Keep in mind that the number of rows in a view will change when the underlying tables have rows added or deleted.

Exercise 12.3: Use Multiple Tables To Create A View

In this exercise, you will create a view that uses fields from three tables. Yes, that is a lot of joins. But as luck would have it, the query created in Exercise 7.6 has the joins. Having this view means that the joins to get the Customer and Sales Reps names won't need to be recreated in queries that are created from this view. There are more fields that can be added to this view, but I don't want the query that will create the view, to be overwhelming. <smile>

1. Save the E7.6 query as `E12.3 Orders view`.

2. At the beginning of the query, type this code.

```
CREATE OR REPLACE VIEW v_Orders
AS
```

3. Delete the Product Name and Quantity fields.

4. Add the Payment Type, Shipping Amount and Region ID columns, to the end of the SELECT clause ⇒ Format the Shipping Amount field, with a dollar sign.

5. Replace the join for the Orders and Order Details tables with the join below. (Replace the first join in the query.)

```
FROM Orders LEFT OUTER JOIN Customers
  ON Orders.CustomerID = Customers.CustomerID
```

6. Delete the join for the Customers and Orders tables ⇒ Delete the last join at the end of the query.

7. Delete the WHERE clause. Your query should look like this one.

```
CREATE OR REPLACE VIEW v_Orders
AS
SELECT Orders.OrderID, OrderDate,
  Customers.FirstName || ' ' || Customers.LastName AS CustomerName,
  SalesReps.FirstName || ' ' || SalesReps.LastName AS SalesRep,
  OrderAmount, PaymentType, '$' || ShippingAmount AS ShippingAmount,
  RegionID

FROM Orders LEFT OUTER JOIN Customers
  ON Orders.CustomerID = Customers.CustomerID

LEFT OUTER JOIN SalesReps ON Orders.SalesRepID = SalesReps.SalesRepID;
```

Including Fields To Sort On In A View
This query combined the name fields, which is fine. However, if any queries are created using this view as the data source, it will not be possible to sort the data by the last name. If you think or know that there is a possibility that a query will need to sort on a field (like the last name field, in the query above) that is currently not in the view, include the last name field in the query that creates the view.

If you look at the data in the view, it should look like the data shown in Figure 12-4.

	orderid integer	orderdate date	customername text	salesrep text	orderamount numeric (18,2)	paymenttype character vary	shippingamount text	regionid integer
92	92	2016-01-27	Rick Pratt	Margaret Peacock	45.00	Check	$0.45	3
93	93	2016-01-27	Lori McIsaac	Nancy Davolio	83.80	Check	$0.84	10
94	94	2016-01-28	Dave Elkins	Anne Dodsworth	1121.40	Credit Card	$11.21	[null]
95	95	2016-01-28	Craig Jacobson	Margaret Peacock	107.80	Check	$1.08	17

Figure 12-4 Data from the Orders, Customers and Sales Reps tables combined in one view

On your own, what you may find helpful is to create the query without the CREATE VIEW statement to get the columns that you need. By that I mean, I include the CREATE VIEW . . . AS statement, but comment it out initially. Then test the query and when you have everything the way that you want it, remove the comment dashes.

I think that the most important task to get right, is the join type. For example, if the primary table has 10,000 rows and the other tables in the query, are lookup tables for the primary table, meaning you need a field or two from the lookup tables to complete the requirements for the query. After you have created the joins, you notice that only 9,500 rows are displayed. You need to figure out why, because in this scenario, the query should still return 10,000 rows, because adding columns to the original table, should not reduce or add rows to the result of the query.

Exercise 12.4: Create An Order Details View

The view that you will create in this exercise, will display all of the fields in the Order Details table and a field from the Products table.

1. Create the query shown below.

```
CREATE VIEW v_OrderDetails
AS
SELECT OrderID, OrderDetails.ProductID,
  ProductName, UnitPrice, Quantity, LineItemTotal,
  OrderDetails.StatusID, Status

FROM OrderDetails INNER JOIN Products ON
  OrderDetails.ProductID = Products.ProductID

LEFT OUTER JOIN OrderDetailsStatus ON
  OrderDetails.StatusID = OrderDetailsStatus.StatusID;
```

The Order Details table has a value in the Status ID field (the value is 9), that is not in the Order Details Status table. If these tables were joined using an INNER JOIN, all of the rows in the Order Details table that have 9 in the Status ID field, would not be returned. That is because the rows with a Status ID value of 9, would not find a match.

Remember that an INNER JOIN requires a match to return the row from the primary table, which in this exercise, is the Order Details table. This is an example of what I was referring to, in the tip before this exercise.

2. Save the query as `E12.4 Order Details view.`

Exercise 12.5: Filter The Orders Data

In this exercise, you will create a view that has order data. If you needed to create several reports that require order data for a specific year, you can filter the data, that the view retrieves.

1. Save the E12.3 query as `E12.5 2018 Orders view.`
2. Change the view name on the first line to `v_Orders2018`.
3. Add the following filter criteria. `WHERE date_part('year', OrderDate) = '2018'`

   This filter criteria means that the view will only return rows that have an order date in 2018. If you display the data in the view, 1,863 rows should be in the result set.

Exercise 12.6: Filter The Customers Table

In this exercise, you will create a view that only has customers in the USA.

1. Save the E12.2 query as `E12.6 Customers in the USA.`
2. Change the view name to `v_CustomersInTheUSA`.
3. Add the Country field to the end of the SELECT statement.
4. On a new line at the bottom of the query, type `AND Country = 'USA'`.
   If you look at the data in the view, there should be 377 customers.

Exercise 12.7: Check For NULL Values

There is often a need to know about data that is missing from a table. Having a view that retrieves rows that have missing values, will make it much easier for someone to update the data, as needed.

1. Save the E4.6 query as `E12.7 Missing Payment Type field view.`
2. Add the CREATE VIEW statement to the beginning of the query ⇒ Name the view, `v_MissingPaymentType`.
3. Add the Order ID field to the beginning of the SELECT clause.

4. Delete the filter criteria for the Sales Rep ID field. Your query should look like the one shown below.
   If you look at the data in the view, you should see the columns shown in Figure 12-5. 5,381 rows were retrieved.

```
CREATE VIEW v_MissingPaymentType
AS
SELECT OrderID, SalesRepID, OrderAmount,
  PaymentType
FROM Orders
WHERE PaymentType IS NULL;
```

	orderid integer	salesrepid integer	orderamount numeric (18,2)	paymenttype character vary
1	2	9	8908.05	[null]
2	8	3	9612.47	[null]
3	9	3	40.50	[null]
4	15	6	950.97	[null]

Figure 12-5 Orders that do not have a payment type

Exercise 12.8: Display The Top 10 Most Profitable Products Based On Production Costs

In this exercise, you will create a query that finds the top 10 most profitable products, based on how much it costs to make (produce) the product. This query **IS NOT** based on the quantity that has been sold, like the query that was created in Chapter 10, Exercise 10.23. This is a good query to save as a view because as new products are added, the top 10 products will change.

1. Create the query shown below.

```
CREATE OR REPLACE VIEW v_Top10ProfitableProducts
AS
SELECT ProductID, ProductName, RetailPrice,
  ROUND((RetailPrice - (UnitCost + ShippingCost))/RetailPrice , 2) || '%'
    AS PercentOfSales
FROM Products
WHERE RetailPrice IS NOT NULL
ORDER BY PercentOfSales DESC
LIMIT 10;
```

2. Save the query as `E12.8 Top 10 most profitable products view.`

   Figure 12-6 shows some of the 10 rows that were returned.

	productid integer	productname character varying (5	retailprice numeric (18	percentofsales text
1	5303	Titan Lock	37.90	0.88%
2	7040	Road Bicycle mens	479.85	0.73%
3	7033	Road Bicycle mens	479.85	0.73%
4	7037	Road Bicycle ladies	479.85	0.73%

Figure 12-6 Top 10 most profitable products

Exercise 12.9: Create A View That Displays The Top 10 Orders

In this exercise, you will modify a query that calculates the top 10 orders in 2018 and create a view for it.

1. Save the E3.7 Top 10 by order amount query as `E12.9 Top 10 Orders in 2018 view.`

2. Add the CREATE VIEW statement to the query ⇒ Name the view `v_Top10OrdersIn2018.`

3. Add the Sales Rep field, after the ORDER ID field, on the SELECT statement.

4. Delete the Payment Type field.

5. Replace the FROM clause and add the WHERE clause, as shown below.

```
CREATE VIEW v_Top10OrdersIn2018
AS
SELECT OrderID AS OrderNumber, SalesRep, OrderDate, OrderAmount
FROM Orders INNER JOIN SalesReps ON Orders.SalesRepID = SalesReps.SalesRepID
WHERE date_part('year', OrderDate) = '2018'
ORDER BY OrderAmount DESC
LIMIT 10;
```

The data from the view should look like the data shown in Figure 12-7.

10 rows were returned.

	ordernumber integer	salesrep character varying (5(	orderdate date	orderamount numeric (18,2
1	4202	Anne Dodsworth	2018-07-07	17658.81
2	4261	Michael Suyama	2018-07-24	17305.93
3	4087	Margaret Peacock	2018-06-15	15492.32
4	3760	Robert King	2018-03-02	14741.15
5	4021	Margaret Peacock	2018-05-26	14039.10

Figure 12-7 Data from the top 10 view

Exercise 12.10: Calculate The Sales Reps Total Sales By Year

In this exercise, you will create a view that will display the sales reps total sales, by year. In the next exercise, you will create a query to display the data from this view.

1. Create the query shown below.

```
CREATE OR REPLACE VIEW v_SalesRepYearlyTotals
AS
SELECT SalesRep, date_part('year', OrderDate) AS OrderYear,
   SUM(LineItemTotal) AS Total, FirstName, LastName
FROM OrderDetails
  INNER JOIN Orders ON OrderDetails.OrderID = Orders.OrderID
  INNER JOIN SalesReps ON SalesReps.SalesRepID = Orders.SalesRepID
GROUP BY LastName, date_part('year', OrderDate), SalesRep, FirstName;
```

2. Save the query as `E12.10 Sales Reps yearly totals.`

   62 rows were returned. One for each year that each sales rep has sales, as shown in Figure 12-8.

	salesrep character varying (!	orderyear double pre	total numeric
3	Justin Brid	2017	10111.10
4	Justin Brid	2018	1286.80
5	Steven Buchanan	2014	6150.55
6	Steven Buchanan	2015	22142.55

Figure 12-8 Data retrieved from a view

Exercise 12.11: Use A View In A Query

In this exercise, you will create a query using a view as the data source. When using a view as the only data source in a query, the fields in the view are the only ones available. That is why the First Name field was added to the SELECT clause and to the end of the GROUP BY clause, in Exercise 12.10, so that it could be used in other queries.

1. Create this query.

```
SELECT SalesRep, OrderYear, Total
FROM v_SalesRepYearlyTotals
ORDER BY LastName, FirstName, OrderYear;
```

2. Save the query as `E12.11 Retrieve data from a view.`

   You should see the data shown above in Figure 12-8. 62 rows were returned.

Exercise 12.12: Query The Data In A View

In this exercise, you will create a query that filters the data returned from a view, to find orders that have an order amount of at least $5,000.

1. Create the query shown below.

```
SELECT OrderDate, CustomerName, SalesRep, OrderAmount
FROM v_Orders
WHERE OrderAmount >= 5000
ORDER BY OrderDate;
```

2. Save the query as `E12.12 Retrieve & filter data from a view.`

   Figure 12-9 shows the result.
   1,234 rows were returned.
   Did you miss not having to join tables to use data from several tables? <smile>

	orderdate date	customername text	salesrep text	orderamount numeric (18,2)
1	2014-01-01	Christina Lee	Anne Dodsworth	8908.05
2	2014-01-03	Peter Kirschne	Michael Suyama	6839.10
3	2014-01-04	Roland Wacker	Janet Leverling	9612.47
4	2014-01-05	Warren Donovan	Robert King	6891.94

Figure 12-9 Result of querying the data returned from a view

Exercise 12.13: Join A View And A Table

In this exercise, you will create a query that uses a view. You will create a join between a table and a view, to return a column of data.

1. Create the query shown below.

```
SELECT OrderID, OrderDate, CustomerName, SalesRep, OrderAmount, RegionName
FROM v_Orders LEFT OUTER JOIN Regions ON
  v_Orders.RegionID = Regions.RegionID
WHERE OrderAmount >= 5000 AND date_part('year', OrderDate) IN
  ('2016','2017')
ORDER BY OrderDate;
```

2. Save the query as `E12.13 Join a view & table.`

   Figure 12-10 shows the result. 440 rows were returned.

   As you can see, there is no difference when using a view as a data source.

	orderid integer	orderdate date	customername text	salesrep text	orderamount numeric (18,2)	regionname character var
1	2	2016-01-01	Stacy Bodnar	Anne Dodsworth	8908.05	Midwest
2	7	2016-01-03	James Sergent	Michael Suyama	6839.10	Midwest
3	8	2016-01-04	Joe Lee	Janet Leverling	9612.47	Northeast
4	21	2016-01-05	Ian Kelly	Robert King	6891.94	Midwest

Figure 12-10 Result of joining a view and a table

Modifying Views

Over time, you may have a need to add or remove columns from a view or add or remove filter criteria. While you can make changes to a view, you need to keep in mind that there could be several reports that are based on the view. Some changes to a view can cause reports that use the view to no longer work, as expected. Usually, this happens when the change removes a column or an expression is changed.

At the beginning of this chapter, you learned that the CREATE VIEW statement has the REPLACE keyword. This keyword must be used when you want to modify an existing query that creates a view. Truth be told, on my own, all of the view queries that I create, I include the REPLACE keyword, so that when the query needs to be modified, I don't have to remember to add the keyword. Plus, if somehow the original view gets deleted from the server, using the REPLACE keyword will still work, without having to modify the query.

Exercise 12.14: Add A Field To An Existing View

In this exercise, you will modify a query that creates a view to include another field. This is the least harmful way to modify a view.

1. Save query 12.2 as `E12.14 Modified view.`

2. Add the word `Modified` to the end of the view name.

3. Add the Division Name field after the Region Name field.

4. Save the query, then run it.

   You will see the new column, as shown in Figure 12-11.

	firstname character va	lastname character vary	lastyearstotal numeric (18,2)	regionname character vai	divisionname character varying
1	Chris	Christianson	20045.27	Midwest	East North Central
2	Christine	Manley	26369.63	Midwest	East North Central
3	Gary	Jannis	4500.00	Midwest	East North Central
4	Alexander	Mast	52809.11	South	East South Central

Figure 12-11 View with a new column added

Summary

The primary goal of this chapter was to show you how to create views and to demonstrate how useful they are, especially because they can save you a ton of time by not having to repeatedly type all of the code the join tables. If for no other reason, creating views to join tables is worth it.

If you have completed the majority of exercises in this book, you have come a long way in learning how to create queries using data in a PostgreSQL database. Congratulations! You are well on your way to having a marketable skill set that is widely used.

Many of the examples and exercises in this book, illustrated that understanding the data that you are using, is a non negotiable. For example, if a field has a zero in it, you need to know that, that is different from a field that does not have any data. Without understanding the data, the result set that is returned may not have the correct data.

If you think that the data that is returned is incorrect, you may not have to rewrite the entire query. The first thing that you should do is to look at the data in the table(s). This should give you a better idea of why the data does not look right. The next thing to do while looking at the data in the table is to walk some of the data through the steps in the query and determine if the row should be included or excluded, based on the filter and group criteria.

You should also compare the number of rows in the table to the number of rows that were returned. If the query returned 1,500 rows and the primary table in the query, only has 800 rows, the filter criteria probably is not correct, unless the filter criteria is using two or more tables and the OR operator.

Another issue to look into is whether or not the query has the correct join type. If the wrong join type is used, the rows that are returned could also be wrong. If the expression has parentheses, you need to make sure that they are in the right place.

I've been there. It is very easy to not "see" the problem. If necessary, re-read the requirements for the query, then get a pen and piece of paper and write out the table joins, filter criteria and grouping requirements and compare that to the code in the query.

When you start out creating queries on your own, you may need to read the requirements more than once, to make sure that you understand the question that the query has to answer. Take your time and do not start typing until you are sure that you understand the requirements. I cannot think of an easy process or shortcut to tell you how to tackle creating queries. As I said in an earlier chapter, learning to create queries takes time, dedication, attention to detail and patience. Over time, it will get easier, if you put in the work.

You started off by learning how to create basic queries. Each chapter covered more options that are used to create more complex queries that return more specific data. Learning the techniques to join tables, opens up all of the possibilities of creating the queries to answer a variety of questions.

Another topic that was covered, was the order that filter criteria is listed in, in the query. While you did not encounter any performance issues with the queries that you created in this book (due to the small size of the tables), on your own, the tables that you will use, will have a lot more data, possible millions of rows of data, per table. This is when you can see performance issues, with your queries. Also keep in mind that the more tables that a query uses, the greater the chance that the query will run slower.

What I have learned is that often, the person requesting the query or report, does not always clearly explain what they are looking for. Without you questioning and providing sample data to the requestor, two wrongs don't make a right. I have lost count of how many queries and reports that were created by other people, that I have had to either fix or start from scratch, to actually provide the data that the requestor wanted. I've said it before in this book, attention to detail is key. In other words, you have to question the question.

Many of the mistakes that I have seen, have cost companies hundreds of thousands or millions or dollars. Please don't let the queries that you create, fall into that category. <smile>

My hope is that you have gained enough confidence to take a lot of what you have learned in this book, to start creating queries using your "real world data".

While this book covered a lot of SQL features and functions, there are more features and functions that can be used. When you are comfortable with the features covered in this book, I hope that you will learn about some of the advanced features that are not covered in this book.

Chapter 4 Query Solution

Hopefully, you were able to create a query for the question that I posed in the overview section in Chapter 4. If not, either of the queries below will produce the results shown in Chapter 6, Figure 6-35. The first query below is the preferred solution.

```
SELECT RegionID, OrderID, Customers.CustomerID, FirstName, LastName, OrderDate, OrderAmount
FROM Orders LEFT OUTER JOIN Customers
  ON Orders.CustomerID = Customers.CustomerID
WHERE RegionID = 3 AND (OrderDate BETWEEN '2018-04-01' AND '2018-06-30');
```

```
SELECT RegionID, OrderID, Customers.CustomerID, FirstName, LastName, OrderDate, OrderAmount
FROM Orders, Customers
WHERE Customers.CustomerID = Orders.CustomerID
  AND RegionID = 3 AND (OrderDate BETWEEN '2018-04-01' AND '2018-06-30');
```

Adding And Updating Data In A Table

In addition to using a view to retrieve data, views can also be used to add and update data in a table. While beyond the scope of this book, I wanted to let you know that the **INSERT** and **UPDATE FUNCTIONS** are available. Either is used in place of the SELECT clause. The **WITH LOCAL CHECK OPTION** is used to restrict inserts of updates to a table. This clause will reject any insert or update that does not meet the filter criteria on the WHERE clause.

An example is a view that is updating data in the Products table and you only want to update products that are in the Gloves category. The WHERE clause would have this criteria: WHERE Product Category ID = '5'. At the end of the query, you would type the WITH LOCAL CHECK clause. Any product that is not in the Gloves category would not be updated.

Common Beginner Query Mistakes

This list is in no particular order. My hope is that after reading this list a few times, it will help reduce the number of errors that you have.

1. Not testing each query that you create or modify.
2. Not accounting for NULL values in the query, as needed.
3. Using columns in an expression that do not have compatible data types.
4. Not understanding the difference between inner and outer joins.
5. Not adding comments to a query.
6. Not listening to what the person or department is requesting the query to do. Also keep in mind that they may not be clearly expressing their needs. You may find it helpful to create two or three queries with slightly different interpretations of the request and show them the result of each query and as clear as you can, explain the difference.
7. Missing commas or quotes. If you forget commas on the SELECT statement frequently, try putting the commas **BEFORE** the column name or expression.
8. Not understanding the data, primary keys and relationships of the tables being used to create the query.
9. Not using parentheses in expressions or using the parentheses incorrectly.
10. Not remembering that subqueries can only return one record.
11. Using a SELECT * statement without taking into consideration that the table may have fields added or deleted, in the future.

12. Not understanding what data the query should return.
13. Not asking for help.

Test Your Skills

This section contains queries to create on your own. They will let you know how much of the material covered in this book, that you are able to duplicate on your own. Try to create the queries without looking through this book for help. Format the fields as needed.

1. Create a query that returns a list of countries, in alphabetical order, that are in the Customers table.

   Save the query as `Skills1`.

   Figure 12-12 shows the rows at the top of the list. 71 rows were returned.

	country character
1	Argentina
2	Aruba
3	Australia
4	Austria

Figure 12-12 List of countries in the Customers table

2. Create a query to return the following fields, from the Products table: Product Name, Qty On Hand, Unit Cost.

   Display the Qty On Hand field as Quantity In Stock.

   Save the query as `Skills2`.

   Figure 12-13 shows the result. 127 rows were returned.

	productname character varyin	Quantity In Stock integer	unitcost numeric (1
4	Crochet Glove	1200	7.27
5	Crochet Glove	569	7.27
6	Lycra Glove	111	4.29
7	Lycra Glove	507	4.29

Figure 12-13 List of products and their available quantity

3. Create a query that combines the Category Name and Sub Category Name fields in the Product Category table, as shown in Figure 12-14.

   Save the query as `Skills3`.

   Figure 12-14 shows the result. 29 rows were returned.

	Category - Sub Category Combined text
1	Mountain Bicycle - Mountain Bicycle (Decent)
2	Mountain Bicycle - Mountain Bicycle (Mozzie)
3	Mountain Bicycle - Mountain Bicycle (Endorphin)
4	Touring Bicycle - Touring Bicycle (Romeo)

Figure 12-14 Result of combining the data in two fields

4. Group customers by their last years total order amount. Use the following criteria.

   Use the CASE function to create a query that groups the customers Last Years Order Total Amount as follows: Less than $10,000 is Low, <= $50,000 is Medium and any value over $50,000 is High.
   In the CASE statement, create the Category field to display which group the customer is in.

   Display the fields shown in the figure.
   Save the query as `Skills4`. Figure 12-15 shows the result. 555 rows were returned.

	customerid integer	firstname character vary	lastname character v	lastyearstotalorderamount numeric (18,2)	category text
2	2	Christine	Manley	26369.63	Medium
3	3	Gary	Jannis	4500.00	Low
4	4	Alexander	Mast	52809.11	High
5	5	Patrick	Reyess	85642.56	High

Figure 12-15 Customers grouped by their last years order total amount

5. Create a SUM of each product sold, in the Order Details table. Group and sort the data on the Product ID field.

   Save the query as `Skills5`.

   Figure 12-16 shows the result. 115 rows were returned.

	productid integer	quantitysold bigint
1	1101	998
2	1102	1033
3	1103	2428
4	1104	2487

Figure 12-16 Quantity sold for each product

6. Create a query that displays the Sales Rep name and Order Year.

   Create a count of orders and a total order amount for the year. Format the total field, as shown in the figure. Group and sort the data on the Sales Rep ID and Order Year fields.

   Save the query as `Skills6`.
   Figure 12-17 shows the result.
   62 rows were returned.

	salesrep character varyir	orderyear double pre	ordercount bigint	totalorderamountforyear text
1	Nancy Davolio	2014	201	$327116.52
2	Nancy Davolio	2015	479	$805092.88
3	Nancy Davolio	2016	390	$619317.88
4	Nancy Davolio	2017	178	$339795.20
5	Nancy Davolio	2018	302	$537708.75
6	Andrew Fuller	2014	2	$3374.25
7	Andrew Fuller	2015	6	$6669.64

Figure 12-17 Orders grouped by sales rep and year

7. Combine the customers first and last name fields and display them as "CustomerName".

   Calculate the number of orders and order total for each year, for each customer.

   Display a $ in the Order Total Column.

   Save the query as `Skills7`.
   Figure 12-18 shows the result.
   1,329 rows are returned.

	customername text	orderyear double pre	Number Of Orders bigint	Order Total For The Year text
1	Chris Christianson	2014	10	$7949.13
2	Chris Christianson	2015	13	$18120.49
3	Chris Christianson	2016	27	$26520.48
4	Chris Christianson	2017	13	$12844.58
5	Chris Christianson	2018	13	$15347.81
6	Chris Christianson	2019	1	$5545.42
7	Christine Manley	2014	9	$14337.57

Figure 12-18 Customer totals by year

INDEX

Symbols

- - comment (single line), 3-20
!= (not equal to operator), 4-3, 4-6, 4-13
$ (display), 8-4
* (asterisk) argument, 3-7
.csv file, 2-5, 2-9
.sql query file extension, 2-17
.txt (text file), 2-5
/* */ comment (multiple lines), 3-20
|| double pipe, 3-16, 8-3
< (less than operator), 4-3, 4-8
<= (less than or equal to operator), 4-3, 4-8
<> (not equal to operator), 4-3, 4-6, 4-13
<select_list> argument, 3-7, 5-3
= (equal to operator), 4-3, 4-5
> (greater than operator), 4-3, 4-6
>= (greater than or equal to operator), 4-3, 4-6, 4-8

A

ABS function, 8-12
add comments to a query, 3-20
Adding outer rows phase, 6-3, 7-2
AGE function, 9-3, 9-15
aggregate functions, 10-3, 10-4, 11-5
aggregate functions explained, 5-13
alias name (column), 3-12
alias name (table), 6-13, 6-14, 7-9
ALL keyword (SELECT clause), 3-7
ALL keyword (used with a subquery), 11-4, 11-8
ALL keyword (used with an aggregate function), 10-4
AND operator, 4-3, 4-10, 4-11, 4-13, 4-14
ANY keyword, 11-4, 11-7
arguments (SELECT clause), 3-7
ARRAY_AGG function, 10-4
AS keyword, 3-12
ASC keyword (sort order), 5-2, 5-3
ASCII collating sequence, 5-2
attributes, 3-4
auto commit option, 2-13
auto completion, 2-19
auto completion option, 2-11
auto rollback option, 2-13
AVG function, 10-4, 10-5, 10-9, 11-6

B

backup option, 2-5
BETWEEN operator, 4-3, 4-6, 4-17, 4-19
BETWEEN operator with dates, 4-19
BETWEEN operator with text values, 4-19
bigint data type, 3-4
binary file, 2-5
boolean data type, 3-4, 4-26
boolean field, 3-4, 4-26
bottom n functionality, 5-7
brackets wildcard character, 4-24
browser nodes options, 2-11
browser panel, 2-2
browser tree control, 2-2
built-in functions, 8-2

C

calculate age, 9-15
calculate daily totals, 9-14
calculate days, months & years, 9-9
calculate end of month dates, 9-13
calculate grand total, 10-13
calculate previous & future dates, 9-10
calculate yearly totals, 10-19
calculated field, 3-14, 3-15
cancel query button, 2-9
cartesian join, 6-5, 6-12
Cartesian Product, 6-3, 6-5, 6-9
CASE function, 4-31, 4-32, 4-34, 8-13, 9-12
CASE statement (searched), 4-31, 4-32, 4-33, 4-34, 10-24
CASE statement (simple), 4-31, 4-32, 4-33, 4-34
CAST function, 8-4, 8-10, 8-11
CEIL function, 8-12
CEILING function, 8-12
char data type, 3-3
character data type, 3-2
child table, 1-18, 6-6
clear button, 2-9
client-server model, 2-2
clustered index, 5-2
COALESCE function, 3-17, 8-13, 8-14
code folding option, 2-12
collating sequence, 4-5, 5-2
column alias, 3-12
columns folder, 2-3
combine columns of data, 3-16
combine data in two or more columns, 3-16
combine text with a string field, 8-9
command line tool, 1-9
commit button, 2-9
common table expression (CTE), 7-10
compare date values, 4-30
comparison operator, 4-3, 4-5
CONCAT function, 3-16, 8-3, 8-5
CONCAT operator, 8-4
CONCAT_WS function, 8-3, 8-5, 8-6
concatenating fields, 3-16
concatenation expressions, 8-3
conditional functions, 8-13
connect to a PostgreSQL server, 2-2
constellation schema, 6-6
converting data, 8-3
copy button, 2-9
COPY function, 2-5
copy to query editor button, 2-7
correlated subquery, 11-3, 11-14, 11-15
COUNT function, 5-16, 10-10
COUNT(*) function, 5-16, 7-8, 10-4, 10-10, 10-14, 11-6
COUNT(Column) function, 7-7, 7-8, 10-4, 10-10, 10-14, 10-16
create - database dialog box, 2-14

create a database, 2-14
create group filters, 5-17
CREATE VIEW statement, 12-3
cross-join, 6-3, 6-5, 6-6, 6-12
csv output options, 2-12
CTE (common table expression), 7-10
cube operator, 3-19
CUBE subclause, 10-25, 10-26, 10-27, 10-28
CUBE subclause (partial), 10-26
currency values, 3-3
CURRENT_DATE function, 9-3, 9-15
customizing pgAdmin, 2-10

D

daily totals (calculate), 9-14
data output panel, 2-6, 2-7
data output tab, 2-7
data types, 3-2
database concepts, 1-14
database shortcut menu, 2-6
databases object, 2-4
date data type, 3-4
date format without the time, 9-4
date functions, 9-2
date range filters, 4-28
DATE_PART function, 4-30, 9-3, 9-5, 9-7, 9-17
DATE_PART function identifiers, 9-3
DATE_TRUNC function, 9-3, 9-13
day formatting options, 9-4
day identifier, 9-3, 9-14, 9-15
debugger display option, 2-11
decimal data type, 3-4
default PostgreSQL database, 2-3
delete button, 2-9
delete/drop a view, 12-3, 12-5
denormalization, 6-7
derived tables, 11-2, 11-3
DESC keyword (sort order), 5-2, 5-3
display a dollar sign, 8-4
display month names, 9-16
display options, 2-12
display text instead of a null value, 10-23
DISTINCT keyword, 3-7, 3-13, 3-14, 10-4, 10-6, 10-11
distinct values, 3-13
dollar sign (display), 8-4
double pipe ||, 3-16, 8-3
double precision data type, 3-4
dow identifier, 9-3, 9-17
download as csv button, 2-9
doy identifier, 9-3
duplicate records (suppress), 3-14

E

edit button, 2-9
editor options, 2-12
ELSE clause, 4-32, 10-24
empty grouping set, 10-29, 10-30
end of month dates (calculate), 9-13
equal to operator, 4-3, 4-5
EXCEPT keyword, 5-3
exclude data using a wildcard, 4-25
execute/refresh button, 2-9, 2-10
EXISTS keyword, 11-3, 11-4, 11-10, 11-16, 11-18
explain analyze button, 2-9
explain button, 2-9
explain tab, 2-7
explicit conversion, 8-4
exponentiation operator, 3-19
expression defined, 3-7, 3-14
extensions object, 2-4
EXTRACT function, 9-3

F

fact table, 6-6, 6-7
factorial operator, 3-19
file menu, 2-4
filter boolean fields, 4-26
filter button, 2-9
filter criteria for null values, 4-9, 4-10, 12-7
filter data, 4-2
filter data in a subquery, 11-4, 11-6
filter data using joins, 6-21
filter data using the underscore wildcard character, 4-24
filter date fields, 4-27
filter groups, 5-21
filter top 10 rows, 5-9
find button, 2-9
fixed length data type, 3-3
fixed point data type, 3-3
floating point data type, 3-3
FLOOR function, 8-12
font size option, 2-12
foreign key, 1-18
format a date without the time, 9-4
formatting functions (mathematical), 8-11
formatting functions (string), 8-2
formatting options for days of the week, 9-4
formatting options for months, 9-4
FROM clause, 3-8, 5-2, 6-9
full lock option, 2-4
full outer join, 6-3
functions (aggregate), 10-3, 10-4, 11-5
functions (built-in), 8-2
functions (date), 9-2
functions (math), 8-11
functions (string), 8-2
functions defined, 3-7, 8-2

G

grand total (calculate), 10-13
grand totals (rollup), 10-22, 10-23, 10-25
greater than operator, 4-3, 4-6
greater than or equal to operator, 4-3, 4-6, 4-8
GROUP BY clause, 5-2, 5-13, 6-20
GROUP BY subclauses, 10-21
group data by month, 9-6
group data by quarter, 9-7
grouping data, 5-13
grouping data (alternate option), 5-22
GROUPING function, 10-23, 10-24, 10-31, 10-32
grouping set (empty), 10-29, 10-30
GROUPING SETS, 10-26, 10-28, 10-30, 10-31, 10-33
grouping vs sorting data, 5-13, 5-22

H

HAVING clause, 5-2, 5-17, 5-18, 11-18
help menu, 2-5
hierarchical report, 6-5

I

identifiers (DATE_PART function), 9-3
IF function, 4-31, 8-13
IF...THEN...ELSE statement, 3-17
IFNULL function, 3-17, 4-9, 8-13
IIF function, 4-31, 8-13
ILIKE operator, 4-3, 4-23
implicit conversion, 8-4
import/export option, 2-5
IN operator, 4-3, 4-19, 4-20, 11-3
IN operator in a subquery, 11-3, 11-9
IN operator used with a numeric field, 4-20
IN operator used with a string field, 4-21
INITCAP function, 8-3
inner joins, 6-3, 6-4, 6-8, 6-9, 6-10, 6-11, 7-3, 11-5, 11-9
inner joins vs outer joins, 7-3
inner query (subquery), 11-3
insert bracket pairs option, 2-12
integer data type, 3-4
integer data types, 3-3
intermediate table, 1-19
intermediate table join, 6-18
INTERSECT keyword, 5-3
interval data type, 3-4
INTERVAL function, 9-3, 9-9, 9-10, 9-11, 9-13
is not equal to operator, 4-3, 4-6, 4-13
IS NULL operator, 4-3, 4-9, 4-10
ISNULL function, 3-17
isodow identifier, 9-3

J

join on multiple fields, 6-20
join three tables, 6-17
join types, 6-2
joining tables, 6-2

K

keyboard shortcuts, 2-13
keywords defined, 3-7

L

LCASE function, 8-3
LEFT function, 4-19, 8-3, 8-6, 8-8
left outer join, 6-3, 6-4, 7-3, 7-6
LENGTH function, 8-3, 8-7
less than operator, 4-3, 4-8
less than or equal to operator, 4-3, 4-8
LIKE operator, 4-3, 4-23, 4-24
LIKE operator wildcard search criteria, 4-23
limit button, 2-9
LIMIT clause, 3-18, 5-6, 5-7, 5-8, 10-20, 11-13
localhost, 2-3
lock layout option, 2-4
logical operator, 4-3
lookup table, 1-18, 6-7
LOWER function, 8-3, 8-7
LPAD function, 8-3
LTRIM function, 8-3

M

many-to-many relationship, 1-19, 6-18
math expressions, 8-11
mathematical formatting functions, 8-11
mathematical operators, 3-19
MAX function, 10-4, 10-7, 10-9, 11-6
menu bar, 2-4
messages tab, 2-8
MID function, 8-3
MIN function, 10-4, 10-9, 10-9
MOD function, 3-19
modifying views, 12-10
modulo operator, 3-19
month formatting options, 9-4
month identifier, 9-3, 9-6, 9-7, 9-8, 9-15
month names (display), 9-16
monthly totals by year, 9-6
MySQL, 1-2, 1-8, 2-8, 4-9

N

named query, 12-2
NATURAL keyword, 7-5
nested query (subquery), 11-3, 11-14
nested sort, 5-4
normalization, 6-7
NOT IN operator in a subquery, 11-9
NOT operator, 4-3, 4-21
notifications tab, 2-8
NOW function, 9-3
null value filter criteria, 4-9, 4-10, 12-7
null values, 2-19, 3-15, 3-17, 4-10, 4-25, 5-11, 5-12, 7-4, 10-23, 10-30
null values (replace), 10-23
null values in a join, 7-4
null values in a view, 12-7
nulls first option, 5-12, 5-15, 5-17
nulls last option, 5-12
numeric data type, 3-4
numeric data types, 3-3, 8-12
NVL function, 3-17

O

object menu, 2-5
offset argument (limit clause), 5-8
ON clause, 6-8, 7-2, 7-4
one-to-many relationship, 1-19
one-to-one relationship, 1-19
operators defined, 3-7
OR operator, 4-3, 4-12, 4-13, 4-14, 4-19, 4-20
Oracle, 1-8, 2-4, 3-17
Oracle packages, 2-4
ORDER BY clause, 5-2, 6-11
ORDER BY clause with a column alias, 5-11
order clauses are processed in, 3-9
order of evaluation (operators), 4-14
order of precedence (math expressions), 8-11
order of precedence (operators), 4-14, 5-2
outer joins, 6-3, 7-2, 7-3, 7-8, 11-9

outer query (subquery), 11-3

P

package, 2-4
parent-child relationship, 1-18, 1-19
parentheses placement in a query, 4-15, 5-27
partial CUBE, 10-26
partial rollup query, 10-22
paste button, 2-9
percent formatting, 11-13
percent of sales calculation, 11-12
percent sign wildcard character, 4-23, 4-24, 4-26
pgAdmin, 1-9, 2-2
pgAdmin customization options, 2-10
pgAdmin workspace, 2-6
plain text mode option, 2-12
POSITION function, 8-3
postgres database, 2-3
PostgreSQL command line tool, 1-9
PostgreSQL mailing lists, 1-10
preferences dialog box, 2-11
preferences option, 2-4
primary key, 1-17
psql command line tool, 1-9
public schema, 2-4

Q

qualify the column name, 3-7, 6-8, 7-9
quarter identifier, 9-3, 9-7, 9-8
quarterly totals by year, 9-8
queries explained, 3-2
query editor, 2-6
query editor panel, 2-6
query editor tab, 2-6
query editor toolbar, 2-9
query file extension, 2-17
query history tab, 2-7, 3-10
query info notifier timeout option, 2-12
query tool button, 2-6
query tool option, 2-5
query tool preferences, 2-11

R

real data type, 3-4
recursive join, 6-4
REGEXP operator, 4-26
regular expressions, 4-26
relational database management system, 1-17
relational databases, 1-17
relationships, 1-16, 1-18
remove panel option, 2-16
REPEAT function, 8-3
repeating subquery, 11-14
REPLACE argument, 12-3, 12-5, 12-10
REPLACE function, 8-3, 8-7
replace null values, 10-23
replace null values with option, 2-12
reset layout option, 2-4
restore a database, 2-14
restore dialog box, 2-15
restore options tab, 2-15
results grid options, 2-14
RIGHT function, 8-3, 8-6
right outer join, 6-3, 7-3, 7-4
rollback button, 2-9
rollup grand totals, 10-22, 10-23, 10-25
rollup query (partial), 10-22
ROLLUP subclause, 10-21, 10-23, 10-27, 10-28
ROUND function, 8-12, 10-5
row subquery, 11-2
RPAD function, 8-3
RTRIM function, 8-3, 8-8
run a subquery, 11-11

S

sales to cost ratio, 5-28
save data changes button, 2-9
save file dialog box, 2-10
scalar expression, 3-8, 4-31, 11-4
scalar functions, 8-2, 8-11, 10-3
scalar subquery, 11-2, 11-3, 11-4
schema (constellation), 6-6
schema (database), 1-16
schema (snowflake), 6-6
schema (star), 6-6
schemas object, 2-4
scratch pad, 2-8
script file, 2-6, 2-21, 3-21
searched CASE statement, 4-31, 4-32, 4-33, 4-34, 10-24
SELECT clause arguments, 3-7
select distinct values, 3-13
select file dialog box, 2-10
SELECT statement, 3-6
self contained subqueries, 11-3
self join, 6-3, 6-4, 7-9, 11-3
signed attribute, 3-4
simple CASE statement, 4-31, 4-32, 4-33, 4-34
single table queries, 3-2, 5-2
single value query, 11-2
smallint data type, 3-4
snowflake schema, 6-6
SOME keyword, 11-4, 11-7
sort data in a range, 5-10
sort on multiple columns, 5-4
sort on numeric data, 5-5
sort on string data, 5-5
sort using an expression, 5-11
sort using the limit clause, 5-6
sorting data, 5-2, 5-22
sorting vs grouping data, 5-13, 5-22
SQL (structured query language), 1-8
SQL Editor, 2-6
SQL query syntax, 3-7
SQL statement clauses, 3-6, 5-2
SQL statements, 3-5
SQL-89 syntax, 6-8, 6-10
SQL-92 syntax, 6-8, 6-10, 7-2
SQRT(N) function, 3-19
square root operator, 3-19
star schema, 6-6
STDDEV function, 10-4, 10-10
string data type, 3-2
string formatting functions, 8-2
STRING_AGG function, 10-4, 10-13

structured query language (SQL), 1-8
subquery, 3-11, 4-31, 10-4, 11-2
subquery (correlated), 11-3, 11-14, 11-15
subquery (table), 11-2, 11-9
subquery (uncorrelated), 11-14
SUBSTRING function, 4-19, 8-3, 8-8, 8-9
SUM function, 10-4, 10-13
summary query, 10-2, 10-3
suppress duplicate records, 3-14
syntax errors, 2-17

T

tab size option, 2-12
tabbed browser, 2-4
table alias, 6-13, 6-14, 7-9
table expressions, 11-2
table join (intermediate), 6-18
table subquery, 11-2, 11-9
table subquery keywords, 11-4
tables folder, 2-3
text (.txt) file, 2-5
text data type, 3-2, 3-3
themes, 2-11
THEN clause, 4-31, 4-32, 4-33, 10-24
time data type, 3-4
time intelligence, 9-2
timestamp data type, 3-4, 9-12
TO_CHAR function, 9-3, 9-4, 9-17
TO_DATE function, 9-3
tools menu, 2-5
top 10 view, 12-8
TOP N functionality, 3-18
TOP N queries, 3-18, 5-7, 5-8, 5-9, 5-10, 5-24, 5-25, 5-26, 10-20, 11-13, 12-8
totals query, 10-13
totals table, 10-13, 10-30
TRIM function, 8-3
TRUNC function, 8-12

U

UCASE function, 8-3
underscore wildcard character, 4-23, 4-24, 4-25
UNION ALL operator, 3-11, 7-12, 10-28, 10-30
union join type, 6-3
UNION operator, 3-11, 6-3, 7-11, 7-12
unsigned attribute, 3-4
UPPER function, 8-3, 8-9
use a view in a query, 12-9
USING clause, 7-5

V

values defined, 3-7
varchar data type, 3-3
variable length data type, 3-3
verbose messages option, 2-15
view (add a field), 12-10
view (create), 12-2, 12-3
view joined with a table, 12-10
view to check for NULL values, 12-7
view to display top 10, 12-8
view used in a query, 12-9
view using filtered data, 12-7
view using multiple tables, 12-5
viewing data in a database, 2-18
views, 12-2
views object, 2-4
virtual table, 1-18

W

week identifier, 9-3, 9-5, 9-6
weekly totals, 9-5
WHEN clause, 4-31, 4-32, 4-34, 10-24
WHERE clause, 4-2, 4-4, 4-8, 4-22, 5-18, 6-5, 6-11, 6-14
WHERE clause operators, 4-3
WHERE clause to join tables, 6-14
WHERE clause vs HAVING clause, 5-18
wildcard characters, 3-8, 4-23, 12-4

Y

year identifier, 9-3, 9-5, 9-8, 9-16
yearly totals (calculate), 10-19

Made in United States
Orlando, FL
10 November 2026

90506338R00157